Reading Emily Dickinson's Letters

Reading
Emily Dickinson's
Letters

CRITICAL ESSAYS

Edited by

Jane Donahue Eberwein
and
Cindy MacKenzie

University of Massachusetts Press   AMHERST AND BOSTON

LC 2009039769
ISBN 978-1-55849-741-2

Designed by Dennis Anderson
Set in Adobe Jenson by House of Equations, Inc.
Printed and bound by Thomson-Shore, Inc.

Library of Congress Cataloging-in-Publication Data

Reading Emily Dickinson's letters : critical essays / edited by Jane Donahue Eberwein and Cindy MacKenzie.
    p. cm.
  Includes bibliographical references and index.
  ISBN 978-1-55849-741-2 (cloth : alk. paper)
  1. Dickinson, Emily, 1830–1886—Criticism and interpretation. 2. Poets, American—19th century—Correspondence. 3. American letters—History and criticism. 4. Poetics—History—19th century. I. Eberwein, Jane Donahue, 1943– II. MacKenzie, Cindy.
  PS1541.Z5R425 2009
  811′.4—dc22

                                                                    2009039769

British Library Cataloguing in Publication data are available.

Contents

Foreword

MARIETTA MESSMER

When the first edition of Emily Dickinson's *Poems* was published in 1890, their enigmatic quality immediately stirred her readers' interest in this hitherto completely unknown author whom reviewers depicted as a somber recluse. Intrigued by various rumors about the "myth of Amherst," readers hoped, in particular, that Dickinson's voluminous correspondence would shed some bio-graphical light on the poet behind the poems. As a note in the February 1892 edition of the *Concord [N.H.] People and Patriot* states: "the world will not rest satisfied till every scrap of her writings, letters as well as literature, has been published" (Buckingham 295, item 343). For this reason, Mabel Loomis Todd soon began to prepare an edition of Dickinson's letters in order to satisfy her audience's curiosity. But when the first two volumes of 345 letters were pub-lished in November 1894, most readers were intensely disappointed. Rather than offering a key to Dickinson's life and an explicatory "companion to her poetry" (Buckingham 362, item 429), these letters, if anything, only increased the enigma. As Caroline Healey Dall commented with frustration in the *Boston Evening Transcript*, "Four years we have waited for these 'Letters,' hoping to find in their pages a clue to the whole life, and now we are as much at a loss as ever" (Buckingham 391, item 464).

Even though Dickinson's letters left many of her first readers' questions unanswered, they did provide some crucial insights into her family life (the first edition contained, among many others, letters to her siblings Austin and Lavinia and her beloved Norcross cousins, as well as her family's maid-of-all-work for thirty years, Maggie Maher). In addition, they illustrated Dickinson's practice of exchanging gifts, accompanied by warm and engaging notes, with many friends (including her schoolmate Abiah Root as well as Elizabeth and

Josiah Holland, and Mary and Samuel Bowles), and they offered first impressions of the poet's epistolary exchanges with prominent men of letters (Thomas Wentworth Higginson and Thomas Niles). Yet while this first edition of Dickinson's letters necessarily had to remain highly selective (it did not contain any of Dickinson's exchanges with Susan Huntington Gilbert Dickinson, for example), all of Dickinson's more than one thousand extant letters were finally made available in various print and electronic formats throughout the twentieth century, and many of her epistolary exchanges continue to engage biographical and cultural critics to this day. Next to some of the most important persons in Dickinson's life (Susan Huntington Gilbert Dickinson, Thomas Wentworth Higginson, the Holland family, and the Bowles family), current scholarship also brings to light crucial insights about some of the lesser-known correspondents. Moreover, Dickinson's letters are currently very productively placed in their larger sociohistorical contexts, thus revealing rare glimpses into nineteenth-century genteel women's culture.

Yet Mabel Loomis Todd had, from the start, also identified another aspect in Dickinson's letters that went unnoticed by many of her first readers: their literary quality. In her introduction, Todd had already emphasized the extent to which Dickinson's letters, rather than simply revealing personal or biographical information, exhibit a high degree of audience-consciousness and artistry (Buckingham 341, item 418). It took, however, largely until the second half of the twentieth century before Dickinson's letters were recognized as literary works of art in their own right—rather than as mere biographical or cultural background materials for her poems. This turn in reception emerged from the premise that Dickinson's correspondence constitutes her only "published" form of writing, her "letter to the world" that she was willing to share with an audience. While Dickinson left her poems (individual poems as well as those collected in fascicles) in various states of (in)completion, often featuring multiple variants and unresolved alternative readings, it was her correspondence that she finalized and specifically prepared for circulation among friends and family members. For this reason, Dickinson's correspondence can, as I have argued elsewhere, be regarded as her central form of public artistic expression. Some of the first critics to pioneer this approach include Judith Farr, Martha Nell Smith, and Agnieszka Salska, who related Dickinson's letters to specific literary traditions (Smith) or pre-Raphaelite paintings (Farr), and considered them as sites that "crystallize the principles of her poetics" (Salska 168). Most recently, this analysis of Dickinson's letters as genuine works of art has enjoyed some very fruitful extensions, resulting in animated discussions of similarities between Dickinson's "epistolary poetics" and her poems, as well as their indebtedness to contemporaneous musical principles.

One of the reasons why it has taken so long to appreciate Dickinson's poems and letters as two manifestations of the same artistic project is their editorial history. Starting with Mabel Loomis Todd and Thomas Wentworth Higginson, and including Ralph W. Franklin's most recent 1998–99 edition of *Poems*, almost all editors of Dickinson's manuscripts to date have chosen to reinforce a strict generic distinction between "poems" and "letters." This editorially foregrounded dichotomy not only encouraged a poetocentric reception of Dickinson's oeuvre, relegating her letters to the status of background materials, but—combined with the notion of letters as quasi-confessional discourse prevalent throughout the nineteenth and the first half of the twentieth century—it also prevented their appreciation as genuine works of *literary art*. Recent analyses of Dickinson's manuscripts, however, have revealed that this editorial subdivision of Dickinson's texts was shaped by then-current genre conceptions (such as a New Critical privileging of isolated lyrics as objects of inquiry, for example), yet never accurately reflected the state of Dickinson's manuscripts, in which prose and poetry passages are often hard to distinguish. Frequently, as Ellen Louise Hart and Martha Nell Smith were the first to document, poems were not only included in letters as separate texts that then entered into an intergeneric dialogic exchange with their prose context, but many poems consistently merged with their prose context, thus forming letter-poems or poem-letters that resist easy generic classification. Currently, these issues continue to be hotly debated in one of the most burgeoning fields within Dickinson studies and have had a decisive impact on some of the most recent electronic and print editing projects, notably Martha Nell Smith and Ellen Louise Hart's edition of *Open Me Carefully: Emily Dickinson's Intimate Letters to Susan Huntington Dickinson* (1998) as well as Hart and Lara Vetter's forthcoming electronic edition of the same correspondence; Marta Werner's edition of the Otis Phillips Lord letters; and Stephanie Tingley's ongoing digital edition of Dickinson's correspondence with Elizabeth Holland in the context of the online *Dickinson Electronic Archives* project (www.emilydickinson.org).

At this point in history, Dickinson's letters are overwhelmingly recognized as both culturally and artistically important; they have conquered a firm place in Dickinson scholarship, and more and more textbook anthologies include them as an integral part of Dickinson's literary oeuvre. Yet this development has also created a demand for more critical tools to facilitate the study of Dickinson's correspondence. While many such tools are readily available for students of Dickinson's poetry (including collections of critical essays, a *Cambridge* and a *Blackwell's Companion* to the author as well as the widely popular *Emily Dickinson Handbook*), which provide a comprehensive, state-of-the-art survey of criticism, very few critical publications are, at present, dedicated to Dickinson's correspondence—the most notable exception being Cynthia MacKenzie's *Concordance to the Letters of Emily Dickinson* (2000). Yet the burgeoning critical and editorial interest in Dickinson's correspondence also calls for an in-depth introduction to her letters from different methodological and theoretical angles that showcases a wide range of current approaches, themes, and interests. The present volume strives to provide such an introduction.

This is the first collection of essays exclusively devoted to Dickinson's correspondence and brings together many of the most renowned Dickinson scholars to highlight the current vigor and principal trends, as well as the most contentious issues, in contemporary Dickinson scholarship. Some of the approaches taken include biographical frameworks (focusing, in particular, on new insights into individual friendships with Susan Huntington Gilbert Dickinson, Helen Hunt Jackson, Thomas Wentworth Higginson, Otis Phillips Lord, and Catherine Dickinson Sweetser ["Aunt Kate"]); historico-cultural contextualizations (situating Dickinson's letters within nineteenth-century women's letter-writing conventions and gift-based circulation practices as well as the tradition of mourning); critical readings (analyzing literary and rhetorical strategies and identifying the striking similarities between Dickinson's epistolary and poetic discourses); and editorial concerns (framed by current theories of manuscript and genre studies).

This volume comprises some of the most animated debates that currently take place in the context of Dickinson's correspondence, and it vividly illustrates the important place that Dickinson's letters have gained in the canon of her artistic oeuvre. Yet even this collection cannot be the last word; it constitutes an invaluable starting point for future research, whose main goal, however, can only be to send readers back to Dickinson's correspondence with new insights and a heightened appreciation for this master of verbal artistry.

Acknowledgments

One of the pleasures of reading Emily Dickinson's correspondence is discovering her gift for expressing gratitude. Not only did she write numerous thank-you notes on behalf of family members as well as herself, but she scattered appreciative comments throughout her letters and often signed off with the salutation "Gratefully." Writing to her cousins Louise and Frances Norcross, for example, she promised to repay some kindness of theirs "in gratitude, which, though not canned like quinces, is fragrantest of all we know" (L734). In the process of co-editing this book, we too have incurred debts of gratitude that we are happy to acknowledge here.

Most of all, we are grateful to the Emily Dickinson International Society for its more than twenty years of fostering communication and fellowship among admirers of this poet. We have benefited from opportunities EDIS provides to share research interests both formally in conference settings and informally at research circles that are a welcome part of each annual meeting, and we appreciate what the *Emily Dickinson Journal* and *Emily Dickinson International Society Bulletin* have accomplished through articles they publish. In particular, we wish to thank the friends who have contributed essays to this collection, Georgiana Strickland, who prepared the subject index, and Connie Ann Kirk, whose vision helped conceive this project and whose energetic commitment got it well started. We are also grateful to Barton Levi St. Armand, who provided encouragement along the way.

We extend thanks also to our colleagues at Oakland University and the University of Regina for their interest and good will. Jane Eberwein expresses particular gratitude toward Susan Hawkins, Cynthia Ferrera, and Rebecca Fernandez of Oakland University's Department of English, along with Dean Julie Voelck, Associate Dean Frank Lepkowski, and Mildred Merz of the Kresge Library. She

also appreciates her charter faculty friend, the late Gertrude White, for exempli-
fying the rewards of stocking the mind with poetry, and her former students—
especially Alisa Clapp-Itnyre, Linda Johnson, Linda McCloskey, Denise Pilato,
Rebecca Roberts, Mary Ann Samyn, and Warren Keith Wright—for the inspiration they provide through their passion for language, literature, writing,
and research. Most of all, she thanks Robert Eberwein for interrupting his own
writing and editing tasks to provide advice or computer rescue and for being,
as ever, the model collegial spouse. Cindy MacKenzie thanks colleagues Garry
Sherbert and Nils Clausson for fruitful discussions about epistolarity. She acknowledges with gratitude the conscientious efforts and enthusiasm of student
assistant Liza Gilblom for her indexing of letters and poems. She is also profoundly grateful to the Dean of Arts, University of Regina, for course release
and to the Humanities Research Institute for its support through funding. She
thanks, especially, those loyal, patient, and supportive friends and family who
have watched the seeds of her ideas and efforts slowly mature into various forms.
With those accidental students of Dickinson—Jim and Vida MacKenzie, Sandy
Howell, Larry Beasley, Paulette Anderson, Sandy Logan, Gray Mitchem, Tim
Baker, and Maria Kurylo—she shares this latest flowering.

   We are grateful for the commitment of the University of Massachusetts
Press to this book focused on Emily Dickinson's letters, especially as it published Marietta Messmer's *A Vice for Voices: Reading Emily Dickinson's Correspondence* and *An Emily Dickinson Handbook* edited by Gudrun Grabher,
Roland Hagenbüchle, and Cristanne Miller; the *Handbook* contains Agnieszka
Salska's ground-breaking essay "Dickinson's Letters." We extend special thanks
to Cristanne Miller and Gary Lee Stonum for careful readings of our manuscript. Among those who have been especially helpful to us in preparing this
book for publication, we wish to thank Mary Bellino, Carol Betsch, Carla Potts,
Katherine Scheuer, and Bruce Wilcox. Other Amherst friends at the Emily
Dickinson Museum, Jones Library, and Amherst College have been helpful in
many ways to us and to authors of the essays included here, and we owe a special
debt of gratitude to Margaret Dakin of the Amherst College Library Special
Collections for guiding us toward the cover images for this book.

   We are happy to acknowledge permission from the following presses and
institutions to reproduce materials indicated below.

   Emily Dickinson's letters are reprinted by permission of the publishers from
The Letters of Emily Dickinson, Thomas H. Johnson, ed. Cambridge, Mass.:

The Belknap Press of Harvard University Press, Copyright © 1958, 1986, The President and Fellows of Harvard College; 1914, 1924, 1932, 1942 by Martha Dickinson Bianchi; 1952 by Alfred Leete Hampson; 1960 by Mary L. Hampson.

Her poems are reprinted by permission of the publishers and the Trustees of Amherst College from *The Poems of Emily Dickinson*, Ralph W. Franklin, ed., Cambridge, Mass.: The Belknap Press of Harvard University Press, Copyright © 1998, 1999 by the President and Fellows of Harvard College. Copyright © 1951, 1955, 1979, 1983 by the President and Fellows of Harvard College.

Excerpts from *Open Me Carefully: Emily Dickinson's Intimate Letters to Susan Huntington Dickinson* (Ashfield, MA: Paris Press, 1998), are reprinted by permission of the editors, Ellen Louise Hart and Martha Nell Smith.

Manuscript materials transcribed in Martha Nell Smith's essay come from the Amherst College Archives and Special Collections by permission of the Trustees of Amherst College and from the Boston Public Library, courtesy of the Trustees of the Boston Public Library, Rare Books and Manuscripts Department.

A portion of Paul Crumbley's essay originally appeared as "'As if for you to choose –': Conflicting Textual Economies in Dickinson's Correspondence with Helen Hunt Jackson" in *Women's Studies: An Interdisciplinary Journal* 31 (2002): 743–57.

Reading Emily Dickinson's Letters

Editors' Introduction

Emily Dickinson, preeminent American poet, distinguished herself also as a writer of letters. It has been estimated that the three volumes of her printed letters in the edition compiled by Thomas H. Johnson and Theodora Ward and the letters to Joseph Lyman later edited by Richard Sewall represent only about one-tenth of the letters Dickinson actually wrote. Others have yet to be recovered or were probably destroyed, according to the custom of her time, upon their recipients' deaths. Of the more than a thousand letters now available to the poet's admirers, some exist only in draft form and (as is the case with the three widely studied documents addressed to an unknown "Master") may or may not have been mailed. None of the letters Dickinson is known to have sent to such friends as Benjamin Newton and Charles Wadsworth has been found, and those to Louisa and Frances Norcross exist now only in those cousins' admittedly abbreviated transcriptions. Nonetheless, we have an extensive and profoundly revealing record of Emily Dickinson's correspondence with about a hundred friends and family members from 1842, when she was eleven years old, until the final note she sent to the Norcrosses, "Little Cousins, / Called back," just before her death in 1886 (L1046).

It was not until Lavinia Dickinson discovered her sister's poem manuscripts shortly after Emily died that she initiated the process that led to their publication. All those enlisted for this first stage of introducing a remarkable poet—her sister-in-law Susan Huntington Gilbert Dickinson, neighbor Mabel Loomis Todd, and literary "preceptor" Thomas Wentworth Higginson—quickly identified the letters as too closely connected with the poems to be disregarded. Susan's plan for the introductory volume she never had the chance to develop envisaged interspersing poems with "many bits of her prose—passages from early letters . . . quaint bits to my children" (Bingham, *Ancestors'*, 86). When

Thomas Wentworth Higginson published articles in *The Christian Century* and *Atlantic Monthly* to interest readers in *Poems by Emily Dickinson* (1890) and *Poems by Emily Dickinson: Second Series* (1891) that he co-edited with Mabel Loomis Todd, he included passages from letters Dickinson had sent to him over the many years of their chiefly epistolary friendship. Todd herself soon discovered, when lecturing on Dickinson to promote those books, that reader interest in Emily Dickinson as a person justified interrupting the process of editing and publishing more poems in order to compile *Letters of Emily Dickinson* in two volumes (1894). Later, Susan and Austin Dickinson's daughter, Martha Dickinson Bianchi, published *The Life and Letters of Emily Dickinson* (1924) and *Emily Dickinson Face to Face: Unpublished Letters with Notes and Reminiscences by Her Niece* (1932); while Todd's daughter, Millicent Todd Bingham, edited both *Emily Dickinson: A Revelation* (1954), which featured Dickinson's letters to Judge Otis Phillips Lord, and *Emily Dickinson's Home: Letters of Edward Dickinson and His Family* (1955). In 1951, Theodora Van Wagenen Ward, granddaughter of the Dickinsons' close friends, made available *Emily Dickinson's Letters to Dr. and Mrs. Josiah Gilbert Holland*. Ward then collaborated with Thomas Johnson on the magisterial three-volume set of *The Letters of Emily Dickinson* (1958). Subsequent additions to this body of work include Richard Sewall's edition of *The Lyman Letters: New Light on Emily Dickinson and Her Family* (1965) and R. W. Franklin's facsimile edition of *The Master Letters of Emily Dickinson* (1986).

Yet commentaries on Dickinson's letters have been far less extensive than criticism devoted to her poetry. For the most part, they have been used to clarify biographical perspectives and to serve as complements to poems. Responses to them over a span of more than a century tend to reflect familiar questions in Dickinson scholarship. From early curiosity about what sort of person created those poems, interest shifted to answering questions about her relationships with important men in her life. Feminist critics then turned attention to socially transgressive aspects of her letters and paid increased attention to female correspondents such as Susan Dickinson and Elizabeth Holland. Study of poem fascicles elicited interest in letter manuscripts and in groupings of letters by individual correspondents in addition to chronology.

Today's critical climate opens new possibilities for appreciating Emily Dickinson's letters and thinking of them in fresh ways. Among the forces influencing current scholarship on the letters are manuscript study, genre theory, rhetorical and reader-response theories, and new approaches to historical contextualization. New resources available to Dickinson's readers include editorial developments such as the *Dickinson Electronic Archives,* Ellen Louise Hart and Martha Nell Smith's *Open Me Carefully: Emily Dickinson's Intimate Letters to Susan Huntington Dickinson* (1998), and Marta L. Werner's *Emily Dickinson's Open Folios: Scenes of Reading, Surfaces of Writing* (1995). The *Concordance to the Letters of Emily Dickinson* (2000), edited by Cynthia J. MacKenzie, facilitates ready reference to words and phrases throughout the Johnson edition. Scholars have long been pursuing various approaches to breaking down genre distinctions between Dickinson's poetry and prose, with a particularly controversial example of that impulse being *New Poems of Emily Dickinson,* which William H. Shurr co-edited in 1993 with Anna Dunlap and Emily Grey Shurr, printing metered passages in Dickinson's letters as additional poems. Marietta Messmer's *A Vice for Voices: Reading Emily Dickinson's Correspondence* (2001), the groundbreaking first book devoted entirely to the letters, argues for recognizing those, rather than poems, as Dickinson's "central form of public artistic expression" (3). Now this book, the first collection of critical essays devoted to her epistolary achievement, builds upon those foundations.

Readers today turn to Emily Dickinson's letters for many of the same reasons that her admirers since the 1890s have sought them out. One of the main incentives to their initial publication was to establish a context for the poet's life. Lest this reclusive woman seem too remote from events of her time and even from personal relationships, editors and readers turned to her correspondence for evidence of her family life and attachments to friends. Even though, as Marietta Messmer notes in her Foreword, readers of the 1894 edition seem to have been disappointed not to learn as much as they had hoped about Dickinson's life and loves, these letters have become essential sources of insight into her personality, habits of life, and emotional ties. Because they can often be more directly connected than her poems to specific recipients and occasions, they help readers situate the author in a particular sociocultural context and provide clues for unriddling her mysteries. The letters also contribute to thematic understanding; these writings still provide invaluable perspective on Emily Dickinson's views on love, death, faith, literature, and other topics central to her poetry. Another reason for paying close attention to her letters is that they afford rich perspective for admirers of Dickinson's verbal gifts and for those wishing to trace her development as a conscious literary artist. Because we have letters from her childhood, adolescence, and young adulthood before the amazing burst of poetic energy most evident from 1858 to 1865, scholars look to her early prose for evidence of emerging stylistic and tonal powers. They demonstrate Dickinson's acquaintance with literary and rhetorical models and her ways of circumventing their restraints. One can look to the letters to see how the sprawling amplitude of Dickinson's youthful writing gradually matured into the distilled, often startling power of her adult prose as well as her poems. Figurative language that puzzles a reader of a poem often finds its explanatory complement in one or more letters.

Contributors to this volume join in a scholarly conversation that began more than a century ago and has taken on fresh energy in recent years. Their essays grapple with biographical, thematic, and artistic questions of current interest; and they do so with appreciation for the complex interrelationships within these categories. Making sense of a comment about art often entails grounding that discussion with reference to the circumstances of Dickinson's relationship with the person to whom she addressed that comment. Sometimes the best evidence for exploring a thematic issue can be a pattern of imagery. To grasp the implications of an idea or image, one may refer to the cultural contexts in which she wrote; and scholars increasingly take into account the circumstances by which her writings have been mediated to readers when discussing the impact of Dickinson's art. The same observation holds true for appreciation of Emily Dickinson's letters as for her poems: everything connects. Consequently, the scholars whose critical essays we offer here engage in a mutually enlightening conversation with each other and with all those who have treasured the experience of reading her poetry and prose.

Reading, in fact, becomes a central issue of these essays, whether by their calling attention to Dickinson's own habits as a reader or the ways they identify the strategies by which she steered some of her correspondents toward fresher, subtler ways of reading her prose as well as her poems. Readers of these pages will see how this exceptional writer mastered and transcended epistolary conventions of her time, especially those for women, and will be encouraged to listen for sound effects as well as visual cues. These new approaches to her writing guide twenty-first-century readers to a fuller and more discerning experience than her letters have yet conveyed.

A volume devoted to new thought about reading Emily Dickinson's correspondence appropriately directs attention to the idea of "correspondence" itself—to the concept of co-respondence or responsive reading. Although, with a few exceptions the letters that Dickinson received from her friends have been lost, these essays intensify our awareness of her sense of audience—her different expectations for responses from Susan Dickinson, Thomas Wentworth

Higginson, Aunt Kate, Elizabeth Holland, Helen Hunt Jackson, and Otis Lord and her changing levels of engagement with school friends and Amherst neighbors. They also heighten awareness of our own role as co-respondents, more or less looking over the shoulders of those lucky enough to have received letters from her, imagining their reactions, and reconsidering our own responses in light of those initial readings and the many responses to her letters that have emerged since 1894. The question with which Judith Farr introduces her chapter, "What would it be like to receive a letter from Emily Dickinson?" lies at the heart of this project. So does awareness of our roles as literary scholars, approaching these texts with eyes and ears open to new possibilities and eager to learn from each other's findings.

Our first two essays direct attention to ways in which Dickinson herself provided subtle guidance to her original readers as to how her writing, both prose and poetry, might be approached. In "'This is my letter to the World': Emily Dickinson's Epistolary Poetics," Cindy MacKenzie focuses on the correspondence Dickinson initiated in 1862 with Thomas Wentworth Higginson to demonstrate how the riddling and haunted aspects of her letters reveal parallels between fundamental properties of epistolarity and her poetic. Recognizing the inherent quality of "immortality" in a letter as "the mind alone without corporeal friend," the poet strives to inscribe its qualities into her own art. MacKenzie demonstrates that through a performative exchange with the convention-bound Higginson, she offers him clues emphasizing the contiguity of letter and poem that would assist him in the understanding of her work. MacKenzie concludes that the emphatic self-reflexivity of Dickinson's poetry emerges from this exchange so that she herself takes on the role of reader. Paul Crumbley, in "Dickinson's Correspondence and the Politics of Gift-Based Circulation," also foregrounds the Higginson correspondence, while placing it in comparative context with Dickinson's letters to Helen Hunt Jackson and Susan Gilbert Dickinson. Of these three friends, it was Susan who fully shared in Emily's adherence to the habits and values associated with traditional nineteenth-century gift culture by which writings (letters and poems) were regarded as gifts for the recipient to adapt, circulate, and enjoy at will. Jackson and Higginson, by contrast, pursued literary careers in the emerging print marketplace and misunderstood Dickinson's expectations. Crumbley sees political implications to Emily's and Sue's assertions of individualism affirmed through mutual acceptance and reciprocity and finds in Dickinson's manner of circulating her writing and guiding her readers evidence of "an intransigent self."

Gift-based literary circulation relates Emily Dickinson's writing to genteel nineteenth-century women's culture, a topic of interest to many of our contributors. Stephanie A. Tingley addresses the close connection between letter-writing and aspects of feminine domestic culture in "'Blossom[s] of the Brain': Women's Culture and the Poetics of Emily Dickinson's Correspondence," where she represents Dickinson's letters as gifts to friends and neighbors, works of her hands and spirit comparable to cooking, sewing, and paying visits. They (along with the poems she often enclosed) were shared with friends like the flowers from the Dickinsons' garden beds and, again like flowers, spoke a symbolic language appropriate to the time; they served to comfort and nurture others. Tingley argues, therefore, that Dickinson regarded the reading and writing of letters as distinctively private, affectionate acts. One such correspondence that illustrates Tingley's points about epistolarity as a domestic art expressive of affection is the subject of Karen Dandurand's chapter, "'Saying nothing . . . sometimes says the Most': Dickinson's Letters to Catherine Dickinson Sweetser." In this first study directly focused on Emily Dickinson's relationship with her Aunt Kate, Dandurand opens perspective on family background and the poet's changing relationship with the aunt who had been her fellow occupant of the Homestead when Emily was a small child and Kate nearly adult and who re-entered her life to become a friend of her mature years. It was a correspondence that evoked shared love of flowers as well as people, shared pleasure in language, and mutual concern in times of trouble such as when Joseph Sweetser, Kate's husband, disappeared suddenly and forever.

The words Dickinson found to express love for her aunt in that strange bereavement reflected her long practice in using letters as instruments of consolation. That is the topic of Jane Donahue Eberwein's essay, "Messages of Condolence: 'more Peace than Pang,'" which shows how Emily Dickinson gradually learned what to say and how to write to friends caught up in grief. Drawing on nineteenth-century guides to polite behavior as well as letter-writing manuals, Eberwein demonstrates Dickinson's adherence to social conventions of her culture as well as literary imagery of journey, wilderness, and flight. Dickinson's exceptional sensitivity to each friend's needs and her transcendent gift for distilling and celebrating the essence of a life are highlighted—most memorably in the letter she wrote to Susan when her eight-year-old son died.

Although letters of condolence tend to be intensely private communications even when they reflect carefully cultivated social graces, Eleanor Heginbotham calls attention to a more outgoing, sociable aspect of Dickinson's writing in

"'What are you reading now?' Emily Dickinson's Epistolary Book Club." Likening Dickinson's lifelong tendency to share responses to books with her friends to behaviors typical of today's book discussion groups, Heginbotham shows how the letters reflect the poet's growing literary discernment as well as her eagerness to learn the reactions of her friends. Her study demonstrates how valuable the letters are as a resource for those seeking Dickinson's thoughts on a wide range of authors: classics like Shakespeare and Milton; great names of her own century like Dickens and Keats; emerging talents like Howells and James; and the women writers—Elizabeth Barrett Browning, George Eliot, and the Brontës—she especially admired. In the process she also notes differences in the degree of openness Dickinson showed in communications to correspondents like her Norcross cousins, who were integral to her epistolary "book club," and Helen Hunt Jackson, who was not.

Two essays relate in distinctive ways to Emily Dickinson's thoughts on love and marriage. Judith Farr focuses on an especially timely archaeological-artistic pattern of imagery in "Emily Dickinson and Marriage: 'The Etruscan Experiment.'" Paying close attention to a charmingly elliptical congratulatory note to a young bride, Farr explores Dickinson's allusions to the "Etruscan Experiment" and "a smile which will last a Life," associating them with recently discovered Etruscan sculptures that memorialized loving, complementary marriages. At the close of her life, according to Farr, Emily Dickinson's observations of friends' marriages and that of her parents led her to choose a diction that reflects a warmer, more hopeful view of marriage itself than many of her early letters reflect. James Guthrie also turns his attention to a late Dickinson correspondence, that with Judge Otis Phillips Lord, in "Heritable Heaven: Erotic Properties in the Dickinson-Lord Correspondence." In this case, the salient pattern of imagery in letters from this daughter and sister of lawyers to her jurist-lover employs legal language of wills, estates, inheritance, and even joint co-habitation. The "playful eroticism" typical of her writing to Lord bespeaks a cheerful attitude of trustful expectation but also an awareness of constraining forces, and Guthrie attends closely to evidence of shared doubt about the heavenly estate promised by Jesus on the Cross. Like Heginbotham, Guthrie considers Dickinson's debt to Shakespeare—in this case by highlighting references to *Antony and Cleopatra* that express both the bawdiness and the sadness in this late-life romance.

Ellen Louise Hart's essay, "Alliteration, Emphasis, and Spatial Prosody in Dickinson's Manuscript Letters," focuses on another intimate attachment, that of Emily and Susan Huntington Dickinson—not, in this case, chiefly for biographical revelations but for enhanced awareness of poetic features that are most evident when readers see the letters with texts represented as they appear in manuscript form. Hart argues that Dickinson's prose, like her poems, should be lineated according to the line breaks in her manuscripts so that aural as well as visual qualities become more noticeable to the reader. According to Hart, diplomatic transcription of letter texts (especially that of an 1870 letter to Susan) calls the reader's attention to prosodic qualities that Dickinson cultivated in her prose. Paying close attention to alliteration, consonance, and rhythmic effects, Hart demonstrates conscious aural artistry in the letters, grounding that analysis in the long tradition of English versification and the specific rhetorical and elocutionary practices of Dickinson's era. She finds much promise in new technologies for textual representation that will empower readers to hear as well as see the poetics of Dickinson's prose. These technologies, especially *Emily Dickinson's Correspondences: A Born-Digital Textual Inquiry*, also interest Martha Nell Smith in "A Hazard of a Letter's Fortunes: Epistolarity and the Technology of Audience in Emily Dickinson's Correspondences." Smith's concern is with restoring a meaningful sense of the "containers in which Dickinson placed her letters to respective audiences," arguing that taking account of these "containers" is as important as reflecting on their content, and she finds that those "containers" defy the generic labeling characteristic of efforts to translate Dickinson's manuscripts into print as poems and letters. Her essay pays especially close attention to Dickinson's writer-audience interchange with Thomas Wentworth Higginson as contrasted with that with Susan Huntington Dickinson, and she argues that even Dickinson's choices of writing paper for these two correspondences reflect distinctive relationships.

Obviously, it is not to be expected that today's informed readers will all take the same approaches to these engaging topics or arrive at the same conclusions. Like Dickinson's own friends and relations who were the original recipients of these communications, each contributor to this book brings something distinctive to the reading experience. Some make more use than others of manuscript scholarship, literary theory, or nineteenth-century cultural contexts. Not everyone approaches any one given epistolary friendship with the same expectations. Thomas Wentworth Higginson, for instance, probably gets more attention in these pages than any other Dickinson correspondent, though judgments differ on the astuteness of his responses to the writings she sent him and the value to her of his attempts at friendship. In any event, Higginson emerges as the best friend of later readers since he—like us—came to know Emily Dickinson initially through writings rather than personal acquaintance and because he left us a relatively detailed account of his responses to her epistolary and poetic overtures.

We offer these essays to highlight exciting new directions in the study of Emily Dickinson's letters and to encourage further exploration of this rich lode of witty, compassionate, and endlessly imaginative writing. As always, Dickinson herself said it best:

And what *is* Ecstasy but Affection and what is Affection but the Germ of the little Note?

A Letter is a joy of Earth –
It is denied the Gods –
(L960)

CINDY MACKENZIE

"This is my letter to the World"

Emily Dickinson's Epistolary Poetics

When Thomas Wentworth Higginson recalled retrieving his mail at the Worcester Post Office on the morning of April 16, 1862, he noted his bewilderment at finding an unusual letter containing four poems from an unknown poet written in a peculiar handwriting, what he described as "fossil bird-tracks" (Higginson, *Magnificent* 544). Mystified, he commented further that the "most curious thing about the letter was the total absence of a signature" explaining that the signature of the unknown poet was "written . . . on a card, and put . . . under the shelter of a smaller envelope inclosed in the larger; and even this name was written—as if the shy writer wished to recede as far as possible from view—in pencil, not in ink. The name was Emily Dickinson" (544). As the correspondence between the two continued, these mysteries could only be surpassed by Higginson's curiosity regarding the enigmatic poet herself. Years after their first exchange, Dickinson continued to pursue him as her "Preceptor," even seeking his advice while he was on the battlefield. However, he openly admitted his inability to comprehend the meaning of her poems and letters even though he recognized the "strange power" in them, later writing that it was clear to him that Emily Dickinson was "a wholly new and original poetic genius" (545). In one of the few extant responses to Dickinson's letters, he wrote of his wish to meet her in person:

> Sometimes I take out your letters & verses, dear friend, and when I feel their strange power, it is not strange that I find it hard to write & that long months

pass. I have the greatest desire to see you, always feeling that perhaps if I could once take you by the hand I might be something to you; but till then you only enshroud yourself in this fiery mist & I cannot reach you, but only rejoice in the rare sparkles of light.

It is hard [for me] to understand how you can live s[o alo]ne, with thoughts of such a [quali]ty coming up in you and even the companionship of your dog withdrawn. Yet it isolates one anywhere to think beyond a certain point or have such luminous flashes as come to you – so perhaps the place does not make much difference. (L330a)

For all his bewilderment, Higginson's impressions of Dickinson's letters and verses can be construed as going directly to the heart of her poetic style: the speaker "enshrouded" in a "fiery mist"; the reader enjoying brief moments of epiphanic lucidity; the "rare sparkles of light" and "luminous flashes" revealing "thoughts of such a [quali]ty"; each insight emphasizing the riddling and haunted quality that characterizes the poet's expression. Yet it seems that Higginson, a highly regarded nineteenth-century literary and public figure very much grounded in the conventions of his own time, needed information of a similarly conventional nature from his correspondent: first, a photograph that would confirm the physicality of the voice, the "fiery mist," he sensed within the writing; second, a traditional poetic form within which her "uncontrolled" and "spasmodic" expression could be restrained; and finally, a face-to-face meeting that might lend physical determinacy to the poetic spirit with whom he was corresponding.

While Higginson noted that Emily Dickinson artfully evaded each of these requests "with a naïve skill such as the most experienced and worldly coquette might envy" (545), it was not simply, as he had speculated, due to shyness and a penchant for reclusiveness, but because of her concept of the riddle as an integral element of her poetics. Moreover, Dickinson's gnomic tactics were not "naïve" at all, but deliberate in rendering far more deeply significant the metaphorical implications of her famous statement "This is my letter to the World" (Fr519). For if scholars continue to turn to Dickinson's letters to Higginson to find a rationale for her poetics, is it not reasonable to consider that they operated in the same way: that is, as an elaborate riddle, a performative act, which, if understood, would provide clues that would help him to unlock the meaning of her idiosyncratic expression?[1] In particular, was Dickinson, in her characteristically oblique fashion, writing to Higginson in a manner that purposefully emphasized the parallels between the properties of her poetics and those of epistolarity?

The question of the generic fluidity between Dickinson's poetry and letters has been regarded as negligible ever since Thomas H. Johnson published the entire canon in 1958, stating in his introduction to the collection: "the letters both in style and rhythm begin to take on qualities that are so nearly the quality of her poems as on occasion to leave the reader in doubt where the letter leaves off and the poem begins" (*Letters* xv). Struck by the highly poetic quality of Dickinson's prose and by her frequent habit of enclosing or embedding poems within the letters, scholars of the correspondence have concluded that Dickinson was experimenting with her poetic techniques within the form of the familiar letter, even as she consistently transgressed its conventions. Agnieszka Salska asserts that Dickinson's letters "became the territory where she could work out her own style, create her poetic voice, and crystallize the principles of her poetics" (*Handbook* 168). In *A Vice for Voices: Reading Emily Dickinson's Correspondence*, Marietta Messmer summarizes Salska when she says that, in her correspondence, Dickinson "best highlights the dialectical dynamic between 'life' and 'art'" so that "letters and poems become two manifestations of one artistic project" (17). Messmer's own study provocatively places the letters, rather than the "poetry" as the central form of Dickinson's expression. While these critics have argued that she incorporates her singular poetic techniques into letter-writing, thus using the personal letter as a place to experiment with her avant-garde style, my line of inquiry looks at the question from the opposite side to determine the extent to which fundamental elements of Dickinson's poetics emerge from and are inflected by the properties of epistolarity.

Despite the sincerity of her intentions in writing to Higginson, Dickinson's witty caprice began when she first wrote to him in response to his lead article in the *Atlantic Monthly*, "Letter to a Young Contributor," treating it as a personal letter, even alluding to and echoing his words with the characteristic etiquette of epistolary exchange.[2] Following from her habitual practices of witty repartee in early correspondence with her young friends and anticipating the riddle-games she would later play with her niece and nephews in her letters to them, this gesture, as well as the cryptic Russian-doll packaging of her letter, four poems, and a small envelope containing her signature, deliberately heightens the riddling quality that is a component of any correspondence. In her analysis of Dickinson's highly cryptic Master Letters, Elizabeth Hewitt points out that, while "they do not name the identity of the recipient, they reveal precisely the ways in which *not knowing* another is an essential aspect of any correspondence" and moreover, that, like the process of solving a riddle, the "Master Letters detail the ways in which guessing is an essential aspect of corresponding" (146). The fact that Dickinson did not know Higginson and that she was a stranger to him greatly increases the "guessing" that was an inherent part of their correspondence. Throughout her letters, and particularly the early ones such as that written in response to Higginson's very specific questions about her life, the content is famously "sparse in vital statistics and evasive in details" (Sewall, *Life* 543) in a way that shows the development of a style that could already be part of the poetics that places mystery, the riddle, at the forefront of her artistic aims.

To extend the point, letters produce, by their very nature, riddling properties, and Dickinson works to augment this characteristic for her own aesthetic purposes. The idea is theoretically supported by Jacques Derrida, who posits that "A letter does *not always* arrive at its destination, and from the moment that this possibility belongs to its structure one can say that it never truly arrives, that when it does arrive its capacity not to arrive torments it with an internal drifting" (194). To put it more simply, since a letter is always *vouloir-dire* (what you mean to say—rather than just what you say), the meaning differs from itself and is always deferred, requiring more letters to clarify its meaning. Consequently, the letter's meaning never really arrives. In this way, the structural lack of meaning in every letter makes every letter a riddle or an enigma that requires further deciphering. In this first letter to Higginson, Dickinson's self-introduction complicates rather than elucidates with its lack of the customary preliminaries. Offering almost no frame of reference except her allusion to his own words in "Letter to a Young Contributor," she addresses him with an abrupt salutation, "Mr Higginson," followed by an equally direct and disarming question, "Are you too deeply occupied to say if my Verse is alive?" (L260), a question that, while compelling in its startling tone, is nonetheless bewildering. Generic boundaries are also put into play by the very fact that Dickinson answers a journal article with a letter, inferring that Higginson himself had begun this witty repartee by suggesting the metaphor in the first place. Furthermore, within the letter, she conscientiously exaggerates the letter's inherent properties, in what we might call a "meta-letter," but at the same time, she expresses herself by means of the structures and principles of a poem. By enclosing poems within the letters, she further suggests their aesthetic contingency by obliquely offering a well-aimed directive that seeks to provide the recipient with a key to understanding her modus operandi. At the same time, Dickinson's performative act posits the riddle as a principal element of her poetics because she believes the success of a poem-riddle's "life" rests on the arduousness of its unraveling. She opens her October 1870 letter to Higginson with a simple poem that ironically states the complexity of her theory (L353):

> The Riddle we can guess
> We speedily despise –
> Not anything is stale so long
> As Yesterday's Surprise –
>
> (L353; Fr1180)

The aim of the riddle works paradoxically both to conceal and to reveal; that is, it creates deceptive descriptions even while it provides clues that would lead to its solution. Through this approach, the element of surprise necessary to the successful riddle marks the moment of recognition of its solution. The epiphanic moment removes the concealing veil in an instant even as "it illustrates the essential tension inherent to differentiated unity, in which a number of properties, each of which has an existence that is autonomous and exclusive of all others, are nevertheless drawn together as a unity" (Brown 154).

The inflection of ambiguity and mystery throughout her poetics is even more intricately pervasive, illustrating the extent to which Dickinson had internalized the letter form and how she saw in it a means of achieving immortality for her art. Writing to Higginson in June 1869, she theorizes that "a Letter always feels to me like immortality because it is the mind alone without corporeal friend" (L330). Providing ways to "imagine" her appearance demands the weaving of a textual construct that provides details of description that point to an *absence presente*, an image—riddling and haunted as it is—that she wishes to inspire in the recipient. The faint pencil marks of her signature in the small envelope enclosed within the larger, the impressionistic and coquettish self-description, each of these gestures seems deliberate in its effort to cause the physical self to recede from the foreground. Practicing a style of concision and ellipsis that foregrounds the density of significant words and images, Dickinson develops this image, lyrically expressed in her famously riddling self-description to Higginson, where she provides, with some irony, a photograph by way of "word[s] made Flesh" (Fr1715):

> Could you believe me – without? I had no portrait, now, but am small, like the Wren, and my Hair is bold, like the Chestnut Bur – and my eyes, like the Sherry in the Glass, that the Guest leaves – Would this do just as well? (L268)

Dickinson's autobiographic self-construct evolves under the self-conscious hand of the letter-writer, creating both a portrait of and a veil over the writer as a person, a kind of riddle-image that would defy the deadening effects of photography as "the Quick wore off those things, in a few days" (L268). Built into the writing of letters is a riddling element created by both a deliberate and an unconscious textual self-construction that never fully discloses the self, an element that Dickinson utilizes in an emphatic way. In this response to Higginson's request for a photograph, Dickinson, it would seem, utilizes this epistolary convention in a highly ironic way, the ironic stance creating a veil that would evade the determinacy of the corporeal. Through this strategy, along with her various poses, Dickinson attempts to leave no possible source of legitimate biography, an attempt suggested in her famous retort to Higginson's speculation that the "I" of the poems refers to the poet herself: "When I state myself, as the Representative of the Verse – it does not mean – me – but a supposed person." Her gnomic strategies work toward the effect Sara Polak identifies in "Emily Dickinson's Epistolary Immortality" as Dickinson's deliberate confusion of "the writing's physicality with that of her body as if she herself were in fact a letter or a poem" (4). "Thank you for the surgery" (L261) she wrote after having received Higginson's comments on the first four poems she sent to him, then again, after his response to the next two, "Perhaps the Balm, seemed better, because you bled me, first" (L265).

Distinguished by gaps, ellipses, dashes, and disjunction, her poems and letters became increasingly integrated with her life as she increasingly resembled her poems and letters and they resembled her. Epistolary representations of the self clearly make their way into Dickinson's poetry as her numerous personae express one facet of the poet's complex and often contradictory self. Moreover, she encourages the metaphor, as is evident in her witty remark to Higginson: "I thought being a Poem one's self precluded the writing Poems, but perceive the Mistake" (L413). The strategy coincides with real life as is evidenced when she finally meets Higginson on August 16, 1870. His published recollection of that event emphasizes her "quaint and aphoristic" narrative, and he concludes that "she was much too enigmatical a being for me to solve in an hour's interview" (*Magnificent* 558). Suitably, the form of the letter lends itself to the shaping of that complex spirit with all its contradictions, as Suzanne Juhasz observes: "We can indeed read Dickinson's letters as autobiography when we recognize that the mode and manner of self-representation is itself an essential self-revelation. Especially when we see how the mode is complex enough to accommodate contradiction and tension, so that it can release and reveal more than one version of Dickinson's 'self,' aspects of personality often in conflict with one another, kept in some kind of equilibrium by the very structure of the letter itself" ("Reading" 170).

The success of her strategy is particularly relevant since Higginson was a stranger to Dickinson as well as a writer with a good reputation, a fact that emphatically based their initial connection on the writing of poetry. That is, with friends and family, she could expect content and context of letters to overwhelm poetics, but with Higginson, more than any other correspondent, she presumably thought deeply about how he was reading her and about what the impact of his reading might have on her poetry. Salska suggests the poet's purpose in doing so:

> . . . in her letters to Higginson, Emily Dickinson for the first time clearly separates aesthetic concerns from emotional ones choosing a personally unknown correspondent with whom to raise professional questions. Such separation may be read as proof that she had arrived at artistic maturity. Her work in poetry until that time strongly supports such interpretation. By 1862 she had written enough poems to feel professional about what she was doing and possibly expected from Higginson not only criticism but help with publication, too. ("Poetics" 15)

The tone of Dickinson's replies to Higginson's initially instructive letters implies that, while she was apprehensive about hearing his remarks, she was certainly not discouraged by them and in fact, as has been much analyzed, she stood up to them with a remarkable confidence despite the veil of coy and sometimes defensive posturing. The "tenacity she showed Higginson in adhering to her poetic methods" (Farr, *Gardens* 76) underlines the degree to which she believed in herself as a poet and, by the time of her queries, in her singular poetic method.

If Higginson was distracted by his need for answers to questions about the poet's physical appearance and her life, Dickinson made every effort to keep the poetry in the foreground; in fact, she, her *self*, deliberately recedes into the background. Evidently, this epistolary effect is pleasing to her in its emphasis on "thought" over "talk" wherein we are "indebted . . . to attitude and accent" as "there seems a spectral power in thought that walks alone" (L330). When Higginson wrote to her after their meeting, he confirmed their epistolary friendship saying, "Each time we seem to come together as old & tried friends; and I certainly feel that I have known you long & well, through the beautiful thoughts and words you have sent me" (405a). For her part, however, Dickinson "knew" Higginson by this time through his writings, his "letters" having constructed a textual image of her correspondent. To Dickinson, this was a far more important mode of knowing as she sees beyond form and his conventional practice of it, to the spirit of his work. According to Tilden Edelstein's 1968 biography, *Strange Enthusiasm: A Life of Thomas Wentworth Higginson*, Dickinson read everything that the man she would call "Preceptor" had written, including more than sixty published articles, thirteen books, and numerous book reviews. Their shared interests, particularly in language and nature, would have drawn her to his work, and there is no doubt that her admiration of him was profound. Brenda Wineapple's recent literary biography, *White Heat*, also suggests that Dickinson admired Higginson's passionate stance in all his endeavors, literary and political, recognizing "a sensibility she could trust—that of a brave iconoclast conversant with botany, butterflies, and books and willing to risk everything for what he believed" (4). Despite the conventionality of his work, direct quotations are frequently inscribed in Dickinson's poetry and letters, as Richard Sewall assiduously points out in his biography of the poet. That she played a witty game, as Anna Mary Wells suggests, is evidenced in her habit of "picking up his metaphors, condensing them, and tossing the result back at him," which Wells regards as a form of "subtle flattery" ("Soul's" 224). But was it, indeed, "subtle flattery" or was it an "aesthetic lesson" through which she could illustrate how to improve his writing by adopting some of her own techniques? Or more pertinently to this discussion, does it serve to illustrate her own original style vis-à-vis his conventionality? Judith Farr comments about this aspect of Dickinson's reading of Higginson's work:

> Immensely generous in her comments about Higginson's published poems, meek in receiving (if not following) his advice on her poetic technique, she nevertheless did, on one occasion, send him a strong, terse quatrain that summed up his genteel, leisurely, and torpid six-stanza lyric, "Decoration." It showed how great a gulf was fixed between his schooled poetic fancy and the originality of Emily Dickinson's imagination, although the affectionate letter in which the poet includes her poem gives no tonal indication that on *this* occasion his "Scholar" was teaching her teacher. Was she merely rendering his theme in her own characteristic accents? Or was she giving him an aesthetic lesson, illustrating (among other principles) that less is more? (*Gardens* 64–65)

While a letter attempts to "compensate for corporeal absence" (Hewitt 155), metonymically, the letter is a representation of the self, the trace of the writer and recipient inscribed, as Franz Kafka suggests, as "spectres": "The great feasibility of letter writing must have produced—from a purely theoretical point of view—a terrible dislocation of souls in the world. It is truly a communication of spectres, not only with the spectre of the addressee but also with one's own phantom which evolves underneath one's own hand in the very letter one is writing or even in a series of letters, where one letter reinforces the other and can refer to it as witness" (Altman 2). Dickinson's letters foreground this haunting effect and are inscribed in her aesthetic as her famously enigmatic doctrine stated in a letter to Higginson signals: "Nature is a Haunted House – but Art – a House that tries to be haunted" (L459A). That the trace of the writer lies metonymically in her letter, in her "hand(writing)," inscribes a haunted quality in the letter itself. In her third letter to Higginson, responding perhaps to his wish to confirm her physicality ("if I could once take you by the hand"), Dickinson extends a different kind of hand to him, saying: "The 'hand you stretch me in the Dark,' I put mine in" (L265). This hand is bodiless, a metonymic image reminiscent of the "living hand, warm and capable" reaching out from Keats's poem, in its representation of the haunting and haunted space of her own interiority, the source of her poems and letters, and subsequently, of the "hand" of the poet herself. Just as the body dies to return to eternal spirit, so, too, the poet dies to his poem, the letter-writer to his letter. Disappearing into the word, Dickinson herself haunts her own House of Language, her art.

Her aversion to daguerrotypes and biographical details paralleled her concern for the enduring vitality of her verse, indeed, for its immortality. In that first letter to Higginson, she emphasized her concern for her poetry's vitality, asking him to tell her if her "Verse is alive," adding that should he "think it breathed" she "should feel quick gratitude" (L260). For Dickinson, vitality is preserved if the spirit is represented in impressionistic terms as is played out by her ironic pose as a private, reclusive woman in a white dress: a woman who took one of five exits in the back hallway of her house, what she called her "Northwest passage," her secret escape route, if a visitor came to call, leading to the private sanctuary of her bedroom. She made the point in a letter to Higginson written in 1885: "Biography first convinces us of the fleeing of the Biographied" (L972); and so she remains the embodiment of evanescence, as haunting and mysterious as the fleeting vision of the hemline of her white dress as she retreats to her room. Dickinson's flight keeps us in the "fiery mist" of those mystical spheres that Higginson described and in the eerie pallor of the ghostly white Indian pipes that adorn the cover of the Todd/Higginson editions: her physical presence is palpable, but only as signs of movement, of being.

Thus, as Sara Polak notes, "Dickinson uses the opaque and yet transient quality of letters in a very deliberate fashion" since "letters are flighty and ghostlike things" and prone to interpretations that the writer cannot foresee (4). Dickinson lamented the fact to her friend Abiah Root, "Shall it *always* be so Abiah – is there no *longer* day given for our communion with the spirits of our love? – writing is brief and fleeting" (L50). But eventually she not only accepted the indeterminacy of such evanescence but integrated it into her poetics, saying "To see the Summer Sky / Is Poetry though never in a Book it lie – / True Poems flee" (Fr1491). In a reading that brings the relationship between letter, poem, and nature together through this characteristic, Christopher Benfey makes some insightful points about Dickinson's "hummingbird" lyric as one poem in her oeuvre that particularly warrants our attention.

> A Route of Evanescence
> With a revolving Wheel –
> A Resonance of Emerald,
> A Rush of Cochineal,
>
> And every Blossom on the Bush
> Adjusts it's tumbled Head.
> The Mail from Tunis, probably –
> An easy Morning's Ride –
>   (Fr1489E)

As a riddle poem, it demonstrates the way in which Dickinson's riddles "render concrete things intangible" (210) imbuing the subject of the riddle with the very evanescent qualities she came to favor. Pointing out that she sent the poem to seven of her correspondents (including Higginson), more times than any other poem, that she used it "as her calling card . . . and sometimes signed it, 'Humming-Bird,' as though she herself were its evanescent subject," Benfey queries the poet's attachment to the poem (208–9).

> Why did the poem mean so much to Dickinson? It is unusually abstract, a poem of elusive aftermath rather than concrete description. The whirring bird is all rush and resonance, its presence felt only by its lingering effect on flower and bush. And what should one make of those mysterious closing lines about the mail from Tunis? She means that the bird moves at incredible speed, of course, but she is also saying something about the miracle of mail for her. Dickinson loved letters; they were her major way of "publishing" her poetry to her intimate circle of readers. Letters themselves were like migratory birds, humming with words. (209)

This reading brings into focus the way in which Dickinson's aesthetic principles in both letters and poems converge. In coming to terms with the failure of words and of the insufficiency of the size of the page to express herself to her recipient, she finds significance in the aftermath. As Denis Donaghue points out, experiences are more intensely apprehended just after their loss, an idea in poem Fr1749: "By a departing light / We see acuter, quite, / Than by a wick that stays" (26). Like her individual letters, so too her majestic oeuvre swells with meaning that emerges in the departing light, her "letter to the World" (Fr519).

Dickinson's riddling and haunted poems evoke the much larger riddle of immortality, a subject on which the very meaning of life hinges, as she writes to Higginson:

> You mention Immortality.
> That is the Flood subject.
>
> (L319)

Like the moment of death, the solving of a riddle, or finding meaning in a poem or letter, an epiphanic moment brings us to a brief but profound moment of revelation. However, the momentary "solution" inevitably gives way to renewed mystery and disequilibrium: "These sudden intimacies with Immortality, are expanse – not Peace – as Lightning at our feet, instills a foreign Landscape" (L641). Once a letter is received and read, a gap between the two correspondents opens, a gap "that can only be settled by the appearance of another letter" (Hewitt 150). Eventually, the poet Dickinson came to see this relationship as particularly relevant to her poetic project, as Elizabeth Hewitt aptly points out: "The formal requirements of the familiar letter interested Dickinson precisely because they emphasize the distance between writer and recipient that increasingly becomes a central topic of Dickinson's poetics" (149). In a poem that expresses this element of her poetics, Dickinson acknowledges the inability of language to "solder the Abyss" of those gaps:

> To fill a Gap
> Insert the Thing that caused it –
> Block it up
> With Other – and 'twill yawn the more –
> You cannot solder an Abyss
> With Air –
>
> (Fr 647)

But Dickinson's gaps, represented by ellipsis and riddle, are invitations, opportunities for possibility that, as Elise Davinroy describes, "prompt us to look to her densely metaphorical, syntactically compressed, stylized language animated by blanks, ruptures, and white spaces. Into the absence, we as readers are invited or required to construct ourselves as presence, but she always challenges the logic of our substitutions by affording us a set of equivalent possibilities, an eruption of meanings" (12). It follows that the idea of a hummingbird as the "mail from Tunis" is one such possibility. When Higginson described the voice of the poet as coming from some fiery mist, from another sphere, like the haunting voice of the speaker/spirit in the poems "Because I could not stop for Death" (Fr479) and "I Heard a Fly Buzz – when I died" (Fr591), his description evokes the image of the poet speaking to us from the realms of immortality through her poems. This effect, like "Bulletins all Day / From Immortality" (Fr820), is precisely what Dickinson imagined and was attempting to achieve.

When she wrote to Higginson, then, she respectfully alluded to the contents of his "letter," both to remind the writer of the specifics of its content and to demonstrate how carefully she had read it and implemented some of its advice. It is in this way that the language of a writer of letters is closely intertwined with the language of the recipient; that is, Dickinson takes into her own expression, not only the advice, but many of the words and images of Higginson himself. As part of epistolary form, the process is "unique in making the reader ... almost as important an agent in the narrative as the writer ... the epistolary experience, as distinguished from the autobiographical, is a reciprocal one" (Altman 88). In the end, it is highly ironic that Higginson was slow to understand her method since his own words and images were so frequently written into the text of her own letters and poems. Moreover, her intentions in doing so were probably not meant simply to outwit the correspondent or to establish herself as a superior writer, but to illustrate how poems, as letters, are co-creations of sender and recipient. So, while she may well have been disappointed in his inability to engage in a similar game of wits, nevertheless, she continued to send poems to him for more "surgery" over a period of twenty-four years even though it was clear to both of them that any instruction he offered was not likely to be followed by his "student."[3] If she felt at first that his advice would help her to gain the "discipline" and "control" she could not command in her work, by the end of this series of letters, she may well have recognized this would-be "flaw" in her poetry as exactly what contributes to its power.

Along with reciprocality, the seriality of letter-writing underpins the organizing principle in Dickinson's oeuvre. Organic in nature, the process demands ongoing correspondence; like the garden she fills with perennials, Dickinson foregrounds the way in which meaning and texture accumulate as each individual poem can stand on its own but also speaks to others in a way that stimulates endless possibilities. Dickinson's method of sequencing poetry, both in her fascicles and in the choices of poems she included in her correspondence with Higginson and others, directs us toward an understanding of the "orderless order" of the canon itself. Understanding the way in which an "intended recipient would not simply read a letter once and set it aside, but would continue to peruse and puzzle over it, to appreciate its artistic language and understand its ambiguity and epigrammatic allusiveness" (Davinroy 1), Dickinson takes especial pains to shape her texts, both epistolary and poetic. In addition, the internal allusions that emerge from this shaping create the intimacy, the shared language and "secrets" between writer and recipient that compel a profound engagement with the difficulties of the text, potentially leading toward its source.

Realizing that her oblique directives to Higginson on how to "read" a poem fell on the somewhat deaf ears of a man steeped in nineteenth-century literary sensibilities, she relied on herself as reader, a maneuver suggesting that his responses confirmed her poetic practices as inflected in the highly self-reflexive, autoaffective quality that characterizes the canon. Ironically, when she writes to Higginson seeking advice because, as she laments, "I could not weigh myself – Myself" (L261), in the end that is exactly what she must do as she, herself, becomes "the one to dwell delicious on" the art of her own poetry and to determine for herself whether or not she has the art "to stun [her]self / With Bolts – of Melody" (Fr348). Consequently, searching for the ideal reader, the "rare Ear / Not too dull" (Fr945), Dickinson implements a significant shift in her poetic practices in a way that inflects a key process in letter-writing; that is, reading and constructing the letter carefully before sending it, anticipating the response of the recipient, yet remaining well aware of the inevitability of misunderstood intentions and gaps in meaning.

As an inherent paradox in the letter itself, the reader who "permits a comfortable intimacy and yet lets the innermost Me remain behind its veil" is Dickinson's ideal reader (Salska, "Poetics" 8). Implementing this quality in her poetics, Dickinson negotiates the construction of a reader for a poetics that has not yet found an audience. Moreover, the process of self-discovery for Dickinson, encoded and safeguarded in the autoaffective expression of a female writer, enacts Luce Irigaray's theoretical claims for the re-discovery of woman: "(Re)-discovering herself, for a woman, thus could only signify the possibility of sacrificing no one of the pleasures to another, of identifying herself with none of them in particular, of *never being simply one*" (30–31). Moreover, despite the diversity of her libidinal economy, she is able to maintain her identity: "Woman always remains several, but she is kept from dispersion because the Other is already within her and is autoerotically familiar to her" (31). The absence of a sympathetic reader forces the only alternative: she "imagines" the presence of an Other (reader) but reads the poem herself, thus constructing an other-in-the-self, interiorizing what would be exteriorized, and making present what is absent. In this way, Dickinson experiments on herself, by reading as if she were the intended external reader, the "lover" of her poems, as she imagines that reader to be. In a paper presented to the American Literature Association in Boston in 2007, Jeffrey Steele explores the process by means of which Margaret Fuller achieved the self-reliance that affirmed women would no longer "learn their rule from without [but] unfold it from within." According to Steele, Fuller's insight was that the recipients of her letters could not "completely 'minister' to her emergent self" so that "the dialogue that she refined through writing to others eventually became a conversation that Fuller learned how to conduct with herself." Similarly, both Dickinson's discovery of her need to become reader as well as poet and Fuller's discovery "that her subjectivity was ultimately founded on her ability to address and witness herself" initiated the "dialectical structure of [the] imagination" where both learned to "internalize Self-Other dialogues and then test them in profound moments of intra-personal encounter."

It is possible then to look at Dickinson's "strategies" as the expression of her own insights, self-generated and self-contained, into both the power and limitation of language and, at the same time, the power and limitation of the self. While Higginson may not have been her ideal reader, he helped confirm for Dickinson the necessity of moving beyond the need for external affirmation toward self-reliance, self-affirmation, so that she learned to trust her own instincts in responding to and evaluating her own art. The relationship between poet/reader is intimately self-enclosed within the poem so that we become what I call the extrinsic (external) reader, watching from outside, drawn like a voyeur to "feel" the affective impact or the performance in the text. In this way, Higginson's "failure" to read with a "rare Ear" may have contributed to the development of a way of reading that is as radically innovative and daring as Dickinson's ways of writing, ways that we have only recently begun to understand.

Moreover, as a result of the intimate self-reflexivity of Dickinson's position as writer/reader, the text can be seen as not only or necessarily an Other that situates itself outside herself but, instead, as a manifestation of what is both inside and outside. The process is masturbatory, in that the text is Other, a virtual reality, wherein the poet plays out her desires; but it is also Self, the creation of the poet. This position of the Other problematizes the reader's response in that the poet writes and sends the poem, like a letter, to an imagined reader (Other), but because there is, in fact, no recipient, no "presence," the poem, like undelivered mail, returns to her. Because the letter never arrives, the process of transmission is frustrated and creates a site of failure in the text where the sender (Dickinson) is wounded by its return. In this way, Dickinson comes to learn that the power of her art is founded on the pain of renunciation, as she states in the second stanza of "I can wade Grief":

> Power is only Pain –
> Stranded – thro' Discipline,
> Till Weights – will hang –
> Give Balm – to Giants –
> And they'll wilt, like Men –
> Give Himmaleh –
> They'll carry – Him!
>
> (Fr312)

In "Emily Dickinson and Her American Women Poet Peers," Paula Bennett comes to the conclusion that because of Dickinson's determination "to purge her poetry of the specifically historical and social," she "wrote, finally, for only one reader. That reader was God, the God with whom she identified both poetic immortality and herself" (232). Dickinson's image of the letter as a symbol of "immortality" suggests that the principles of epistolary writing as she inscribed them into her poems contribute to the eternal life of her art. As "Bulletins from Immortality," her later letters and the poems that she folded into them exhibit a riddling quality, working to provoke the imagination in a way that echoes Keats's homage to the inscrutability of the Grecian Urn as they "detach from time and space, to render the subject as much a part of 'Forever' as of the 'Now'" (Bennett 229). The Keatsian notion of negative capability underpins Dickinson's poetics: the objet d'art—the Grecian urn and her poetry—must resist closure, must remain "forever warm and still to be enjoyed," forever desiring and desired as the figures on the urn enact the mechanism of desire in Keats's poem. The significance of the unknown, as she states in a letter to her Norcross cousins, is as essential to the vitality of art as it is to the vitality of life itself, though we are often ungrateful for it: "the unknown is the largest need of the intellect, though for it, no one thinks to thank God" (L471). The riddle must be no less significant than that stated in I Corinthians, its meanings no less significant in the exchange of letters between correspondents, or between poet and reader:

"For now we see through a glass, darkly; but then face to face: now I know in part; but then shall I know even as also I am known" (13:13).

For Dickinson, poetry must surely arise from the properties of letter-writing for "letters were as close as humans could come to divinity; with the winged words of letters, we become almost angelic messengers" (Benfey 243). Although her poetic practices appeared haunted and riddling to her lifelong correspondent, Wentworth Higginson, her correspondence with him tells us a great deal about what she expected the reader to do yet how much she enjoyed withholding a clear explanation of her method. Moreover, when Higginson began the editing of the first volume of Dickinson's poems with a conventional system of placing them in piles according to subjects ("Life," "Love," Nature," "Time and Eternity"), he soon became aware that these editing practices that he and Mabel Loomis Todd were imposing on the poet's work may well have provided a necessary transition for the poet's first public audience to become accustomed to this dynamic new voice but were, in fact, probably erroneous. By the time the Second Series was being prepared, Higginson wrote to Todd saying, "'let us alter as little as possible, now that the public ear is opened' including his own ear" (Frye, *Fables* 200). Having recognized that "the poet's liberties were not those of carelessness or incompetence," Higginson encouraged his co-editor to cease "improving on" Dickinson's idiosyncratic expression. However, the process of editing was apparently too far along; Todd was beginning to believe in the editorial changes she was making to Dickinson's manuscripts and, thus, continued to make them. The tendency for many scholars to dismiss Higginson's influence on Dickinson based on his decision not to promote publication of her work seems to me, then, to miss the mark seriously. Instead, we can make a much more positive assessment of his interaction with Dickinson and her work by the way in which their lifelong correspondence not only affirms their friendship but also serves to illustrate Higginson's direct influence on the evolution of Dickinson's poetic process and her faith that readers' "Judgment" would "Break, / Excellent, and Fair" over time (Fr804). His intuitive sense of her work's meaning exceeds his critical response to it but points toward an eventual deeper and fuller understanding. In her second-to-last letter to Higginson (L1043), Dickinson's words can be seen as evidence that she trusted him, her "safest friend," to become the kind of reader she calls on us to be—and that she appreciated his efforts:

> There is no Trumpet like the Tomb –
>   Of Glory not a Beam is left

But her Eternal House –
The Asterisk is for the Dead,
The Living, for the Stars –

The haunting words of Dickinson's "letter to the World," received by those of us who "never wrote to [her]," draw us into a private correspondence that ensures her immortality.

NOTES

1. Richard Sewall suggests that Dickinson may also have responded to an "enthusiastic notice" in the *Republican* dated March 29, 1862, stating that "The *Atlantic Monthly* for April is one of the best numbers ever issued. . . . Its leading article, T. W. Higginson's "Letter to a Young Contributor," ought to be read by all the would-be authors of the land . . . it is a text of latent power. Whoever rises from its thorough perusal strengthened and encouraged, may be reasonably certain of ultimate success" (*Life* 541). Christopher Benfey notes that her interest was in all likelihood piqued by Higginson's call for the originality of a "fresh voice" (23).

2. After all, this is the poet's characteristic approach, as Gary Stonum points out when he says that she was "programmatically unwilling to dictate how her work was to be taken," but was "content to create the poetic stimuli in the hopes that appropriate respondents might appear" (*Sublime* 106).

3. Higginson wrote later that he was under no illusion as far as his guidance was concerned: "These were my earliest letters from Emily Dickinson, in their order. From this time and up to her death (May 15, 1886) we corresponded at varying intervals, she always persistently keeping up this attitude of "Scholar," and assuming on my part a preceptorship which it is almost needless to say did not exist. Always glad to hear her 'recite,' as she called it, I soon abandoned all attempt to guide in the slightest degree this extraordinary nature, and simply accepted her confidences, giving as much as I could of what might interest her in return" (*Magnificent* 554).

PAUL CRUMBLEY

Dickinson's Correspondence and the Politics of Gift-Based Circulation

In a February 24, 2003 commentary on a cancelled White House literary symposium that was to have focused on Walt Whitman, Langston Hughes, and Emily Dickinson, Katha Pollitt noted that though Dickinson may at first "seem the least political" (2) and therefore the least likely of the three poets to appear in a literary event deemed too politically volatile to stage, she may in the final analysis be the most political. Pollitt concludes, "every line [Dickinson] wrote is an attack on complacency and conformity of manners, mores, religion, language, gender, thought." I want to provide historical reinforcement for this understanding by analyzing Dickinson's circulation of poetry through correspondence as an extension of nineteenth-century gift culture.[1] My aim is not to present Dickinson as advocating a particular political agenda, but rather to show how Dickinson incorporates the independent subjectivity central to gift exchange in her own efforts to promote the democratic exercise of individual sovereignty. My own position may be seen as an extension of Geoffrey Sanborn's suggestion that Dickinson's politics are grounded in an "emphasis on the subversiveness of intransitive existence"; noting that "Dickinson does not participate in Marxian or postcolonial discourses," Sanborn proposes that the poet "does model a practice that is a precondition of those discourses: the maintenance and enjoyment of one's distance from the properly social" (1340, 1345). In what follows, I examine Dickinson's correspondence with Helen Hunt Jackson,

Susan Huntington Gilbert Dickinson, and Thomas Wentworth Higginson to demonstrate that gift culture protocol enables Dickinson to activate the intransigence crucial to the exercise of personal sovereignty, thus making political action possible without necessarily determining what form the outward expression of that action might take.[2]

Dickinson establishes a politically significant epistolary practice in the context of a nineteenth-century gift culture that has been thoroughly described by literary scholars and anthropologists. Mary Louise Kete provides the underlying cultural logic in *Sentimental Collaborations*, where she argues that "the inalienable possession of self fundamental to liberalism is produced through a free circulation of gifts of the self" (53). A core property of the gift is its power to invest the writer's self with a distinct presence by means of recipients who affirm that self through acts of reciprocity. Kete sums up the essential paradox: "The way to keep the self is to give it away." When this occurs, and the self is affirmed through reception of the gift, "the isolated, dysfunctional 'one' or 'I'" is translated "into a 'we' able to act on and promote communal interests among the competing interests of other 'we's'" (54). The resultant "'little societies'" collectively contribute to a larger "national and authoritative 'We,'" as in "We the people," that ultimately shapes civic culture. Kete's association of gift exchange with the "We" of founding documents is echoed by Elizabeth Hewitt, who similarly understands that selfhood is achieved by giving the self away, though for Hewitt this is most clearly revealed through epistolary communication. In *Correspondence and American Literature, 1770–1865*, Hewitt argues that the Declaration of Independence is best understood as an epistolary document; it appears in numerous late eighteenth-century and early nineteenth-century letter-writing manuals as an example of epistolary form precisely because it "offers a consolidation of signers to send word (in this case to a mother nation) of disobedience, and it testifies to its sincerity by signatory power" (12). By means of the signers, whose united interests are harnessed by the pronoun "We" (as in "We hold these truths to be self evident"), the Declaration straddles the gulf between speech and print precisely in the manner that letters do, successfully demonstrating the capacity of the letter to confer both independence and unity.[3] Elizabeth Barnes makes a similar point about the unifying power of the Declaration of Independence when she describes its function within sentimental culture as bringing about "a surprising conflation of the personal and the political body" (1).[4] Read in this cultural context, Dickinson's gift-based distribution of poems through her correspondence surfaces as a particular expression of sentimental culture and epistolary politics.

As do other participants in gift circulation, Dickinson proclaims her individuality through collaborative acts in which she discloses personal values that recipients can choose to affirm through acceptance and reciprocity.[5]

Dickinson may well have seen gift culture as a particularly appropriate venue for her aim of both expressing an intransigent self and inviting the collaboration of her recipients. Studies of gift exchange consistently acknowledge that gift donation proceeds by means of a distinct and often resistant subjectivity that unites giver with receiver through mutual collaboration. Cultural anthropologist Jacques T. Godbout helpfully describes this process as operating "according to rules that are not those of the public institution and differ from it essentially in not making a distinction between 'them' and 'us,' in not creating that radical split that always exists between . . . a producer and a consumer" (166). The consequent merging of producer and consumer is one of the most important distinguishing features of a gift economy, a feature that Dickinson trades upon in her own efforts to engage correspondents as collaborators, as when she sends Higginson four poems in 1880 and urges him to "Reprove them as your own" (L675).[6] These collaborations reflect the participants' joint decision to resist institutionalized norms through their mutual affirmation of values perceived to be unique and unconventional. In this particular instance, Dickinson was inviting Higginson to suspend the conventional authorial claim to exclusive ownership and instead view her poems as shared property over which he exercised the same rights as she did.

The representation of gift culture in "Miss Grief" and "Collected by a Valetudinarian," short stories by Dickinson contemporaries Constance Fenimore Woolson and Elizabeth Stoddard, can further establish the lineaments of the system that Dickinson so effectively deploys and manipulates in her own correspondence. Both these works vividly portray the way gift recipients must prove themselves capable of resisting the demands of social and cultural convention as evidence that they have attained the intransigent subjectivity essential to participation in gift circulation. Woolson's short story "Miss Grief" describes a male author who receives an unsolicited manuscript from an unknown female writer and, as Higginson did with Dickinson, concludes that the author desires print publication. The female writer, however, replies that his opinion would be of little value "in a business way" though she would be grateful for a response that "might be – an assistance personally" (253).[7] The challenge attached to the gift surfaces when the male writer recognizes both that the obscure woman's talent is superior to his own and that her originality will not yield to conventional print standards: "her perversities," he concludes, "were as essential a part of her work as her inspirations" (265). Rather than questioning editorial orthodoxy and experimenting with modes of circulation more appropriate to the unruly manuscript, he insists on making the work conform to public expectations. "'I like it,'" he claims; "'To me originality and force are everything . . . but the world at large will not overlook as I do your absolutely barbarous shortcomings on account of them'" (259). Unable to imagine literary success in accordance with the artistic taste he shares with the author he calls "Miss Grief," he proves incapable of entering the gift economy. Frustrated in his efforts to "alter and improve" the work "himself," he grudgingly admits, "I could not succeed in completing anything that satisfied me, or that approached, in truth, Miss Grief's own work just as it stood" (264). At last admitting that he has "utterly failed," he abandons the effort. This brief cycle of earnest interest and failed effort effectively establishes the male author's inability to imagine how the nonconventional taste he shares with Miss Grief could become the basis for a viable alternative to conventional print norms, thereby demonstrating that he lacks the intransigence essential to forming a "little society."

Stoddard's 1870 story, like Woolson's of 1880, also concentrates on the way superior literature is withheld from circulation when the recipients of the literary gift prove incapable of thinking outside the parameters of social convention. In "Collected by a Valetudinarian," two unassuming women, Eliza Sinclair and Helen Hobson, contemplate the circulation of a literary estate that opens their eyes to what Helen refers to as a "world of beauty and truth" (290). But the challenge they face is quickly expressed when Eliza asks, "'Dear Helen, how shall we idlers be taught this ideal happiness?'"(290). Helen's response illuminates the demand for an intransigent self that departs from the conventional values that have guided their lives up to this point: "'As soon as we can be made to believe that what is called material or positive happiness is no more truthful or exact than that named visionary or romantic happiness'" (290). This challenge to rethink the material terms of their lives proves too much for them. Eliza concludes, "We were a couple of faded, middle-aged women. . . . Why should such indulge in aspirations for happiness, or the expectation of doing any farther [sic] work in this gay world?" Here, as in the Woolson story, circulation terminates when collaboration collides with social identity.

Read with these essential features of the Stoddard and Woolson stories in mind, Dickinson's correspondence with Helen Hunt Jackson stands out as perhaps her most striking failure to win a collaborator.[8] The available letters clearly show that Jackson was impressed by the power of Dickinson's literary gift but failed to contribute in any significant way to the circulation of the poems because she refused to accept gift exchange as a viable means to achieve literary fame. Despite her determination to win lasting recognition for Dickinson, she refused to view the poems that first reached her as gifts in any terms but those codified within the economy of print publication. Jackson's own successful experience in the print marketplace may have convinced her that Dickinson would also be successful, if she would only try. The fact that both women were born in Amherst, within two months of each other, knew each other in school, and in later life enjoyed friendships with Higginson may have contributed to Jackson's conviction that Dickinson would discover a similar if not greater success through commercial publication. For whatever reason, the letters indicate that Jackson was not finally willing to accept Dickinson's preferred mode of publication as a suitable route to fame. The correspondence falls roughly into three stages that effectively embody the cycle of initial enthusiasm and ultimate inaction that characterized gift reception in the Woolson and Stoddard stories. In the first stage, Jackson strives to educate Dickinson in the protocols of the printed page. Like the male author in "Miss Grief," she assumes Dickinson wants to appear in print and exhausts herself in the attempt to achieve that end.

Upon receiving her first literary gift from Dickinson in October 1875, on the occasion of her second marriage, Jackson immediately signifies her distance from the sensibility of gift culture by sending back Dickinson's letter, requesting clarification of the line "To Dooms of Balm" that concludes the gift poem and demanding that Dickinson view the letter as her (Jackson's) property and return it to her as the proper owner (L444). On the blank last page of Dickinson's letter, Jackson writes, "This is *mine*, remember, You must send it back to me, or else you will be a robber," leaving little doubt about her claim of ownership. Rather than reciprocating in kind, as would be appropriate in gift exchange, Jackson requests that Dickinson redefine the gift as a conventional literary commodity. That Dickinson never did return the letter suggests her refusal of Jackson's terms. Perhaps because of Dickinson's refusal, Jackson begins her next letter by emphatically reiterating the conventional literary values she has imposed on the correspondence: "But you did not send it back, though you wrote that you would. // Was this an accident, or a late withdrawal of your consent? // Remember that it is mine – not yours – and be honest." Jackson's language here makes evident the conflicting values that will characterize the entire correspondence: she questions Dickinson's honesty, presumes the logic of consent hinged to ownership, and may even be rejecting the terms of gift exchange.

A central feature of gift culture is the collaboration of giver and receiver that takes the place of ownership and recasts honesty as a factor of sincere response rather than action governed by consistency with prior statements. As Emerson has noted in "Gifts," "The gift, to be true, must be a flowing of the giver unto me, correspondent to my flowing unto him" (156–57). The "correspondence" part of gift-based epistolary correspondence is connected to resonance of character and the acceptance of departures from convention rather than adherence to widely held codes of conduct. Writing specifically of gift exchange, Pierre Bourdieu gives particular attention to the way participants must avoid overt declarations of duty or the obligation to reciprocate: "To betray one's haste to be free of an obligation one has incurred, and thus to reveal too overtly one's desire to pay off services rendered or gifts received, so as to be quits, is to denounce the initial gift retrospectively as motivated by the intention of obliging one. It is all a question of style" (*Outline* 6). With gift-based correspondence, especially, expressions of gratitude and even the implicit or indirect acknowledgment of obligation must be carefully avoided or managed with stylistic flourish that makes the discourse of gratitude or obligation itself a gift. When perceived in this context, Jackson appears to be either unaware that Dickinson is seeking to establish an alternative basis for their communication (concentrating instead on her own efforts to bring Dickinson into the fold of literary orthodoxy) or foreclosing the possibility of discourse founded on gift exchange. She concludes her March 1876 letter by affirming that Dickinson is a "great poet" while also accusing her of being "wrong to the day you live in" because she "will not sing aloud" (L444a).

The next letters in this first sequence show the two writers increasingly at cross-purposes: Jackson pushes more aggressively for the simplification and publication of poems while Dickinson seeks to change the subject. When Jackson next writes Dickinson in August, she opens her letter with the assurance that Dickinson has not offended her and asks that Dickinson submit poems to the upcoming Roberts Brothers "No Name" poetry volume. Whether or not Dickinson feared giving offense through her refusal to return the "Dooms of Balm" letter is not clear. Jackson appears to have concluded that Dickinson's hesitation has to do with fear of public exposure, not a preference for gift-based circulation. On the contrary, Jackson assures Dickinson of "*double*" anonymity and ends the letter proper with the following two sentences: "Thank you for writing in such plain letters! Will you not send me some verses?" (L476a). These last lines give the impression that Jackson is attempting to mentor Dickinson, an impression reinforced by her final letter of 1876, which contains the admission that upon rereading "the last verses" Dickinson sent her, "I find them more clear than I thought they were. Part of the dimness must have been in me" (L476c). Such qualified praise of poems that are "more clear" but not crystal clear, plus the admission of a partial "dimness" in her own reading may be designed to soften Dickinson up for the advice that follows. Jackson's declaration, "I like your simplest and [most direct] lines best," here functions as the verdict of the published poet who kindly guides the efforts of her fainthearted friend.

The next three letters from Jackson demonstrate that far from being deterred in her efforts to see Dickinson in print, Jackson has probably already submitted "Success is counted sweetest" (Fr 112) to Roberts Brothers. In her October 25, 1878 letter, Jackson takes a decidedly more aggressive approach, but one that appears to consider Dickinson's demand that the poems be circulated as gifts rather than marketable commodities: "Now – will you send me the poem? No – will you let me send the 'Success' – which I know by heart – to Roberts Bros for the Masque of Poets? If you will, it will give me a great pleasure. I ask it as a personal favor to myself – Can you refuse the only thing I perhaps shall ever ask at your hands?" (L573b). Tempting as it is to see Jackson's focused personal appeal as a recognition of Dickinson's insistence that the poems be treated as gifts, the possibility remains that Jackson is simply using all the tricks at her disposal to secure authorial approval. As Betsy Erkkila has noted, "The seeming desperation of Jackson's request is owing to the fact that in an act of rashness she had already submitted . . . 'Success' . . . and the poem was about to appear in print whether or not Dickinson gave her consent" (*Sisters* 91). The final letter in this initial phase of the correspondence conveys Jackson's doubt that the end result was worth the effort she invested in having her friend published. After expressing her hope that Dickinson has "not regretted giving me that choice bit of verse," she admits, "on the whole, the volume is a disappointment to me" (L573c).

The first phase of the Jackson correspondence, then, set the terms of the two writers' debate over literary ownership and circulation. In the second phase, that of 1879, Dickinson sent Jackson a number of poems that clarify her own position on these issues, perhaps feeling that Jackson would be open to an alternative approach following her disappointment with *A Masque of Poets*. The poem "Before you thought of Spring" (Fr1484C) can represent the general tenor of these poems and letters. In this work, Dickinson metaphorically equates the blue bird with the poet in an exploration of the relationship between poem, reader, and author that delineates a gift-based system of circulation. The poet, like the gift, makes a sudden, unexpected appearance—"God bless his suddenness"—and offers the reader choices—"Specimens of Song"—passing on to other locations after discrete but disinterested "gay delays," finally shouting for joy out of dedication to self-expression. Here the principles of gift circulation are clearly represented: the delight in both giving and receiving, the absence of reference to reciprocity, the freedom on the part of the recipient to engage collaboratively by selecting from among multiple "Specimens of Song." Perhaps it was Jackson's reading of the line, "As if for you to choose," that prompted her to choose a specific specimen in her May 1879 letter where she asked Dickinson to try her "hand on the oriole" (L601a).

The third and last letter in this second phase of the correspondence shows Dickinson responding with alacrity to Jackson's request, providing not only an oriole poem but an additional hummingbird poem as well. This response may demonstrate Dickinson's sense that Jackson's resistance is weakening, as well as her determination to offer Jackson choices among multiple poems, or specimens, as well as within poems themselves. The oriole poem, "One of the ones that Midas touched" (Fr1488), again describes the way poets and readers interact, this time giving special attention both to the multifarious guises assumed by the poet, and the reader's role in selecting among them. Dickinson begins by drawing attention to the unreliability of the poet's self-representations through lines that describe the oriole/poet as "So drunk he disavows it," "A Pleader – a Dissembler – / An Epicure – a Thief –" and "He cheats as he enchants." At last, the poet leaves the recipient not with a resolved sense of identity but, in Dickinson's words, he departs "like a Pageant / Of Ballads and of Bards."[9] The poem carries on for two more stanzas in which Dickinson shifts to the subjunctive mood in postulating that the oriole is in fact the golden fleece sought by the Jason of Greek mythology, but the explicit association of bird and poet ends with the reference to "Ballads and . . . Bards."

Following this offering of poems that included Dickinson's famous hummingbird, the correspondence ceases from May 1879 to April 1883, at which time Dickinson clarifies for Jackson and Thomas Niles, the Roberts Brothers editor who oversaw the "No Name" series, her belief that poetic achievement was not dependent on widespread public recognition. As if commenting on her detachment from the fashion of the moment, Dickinson sent the poem "How happy is the little Stone" (Fr1570E) to Niles in April 1882 (L749) after having received a letter from him in which he joined Jackson in wishing that she "could be induced to publish a volume of poems" (L749b). Though the copy sent to Jackson is lost, variorum editors Thomas H. Johnson and Ralph W. Franklin agree that one was sent. In light of Niles's letter and her awareness of Niles through his involvement with *A Masque of Poets*, Dickinson appears to be using the poem to inform both Niles and Jackson of her indifference to literary trends, thereby reducing Jackson's concerns about the quality of the volume and informing Niles that print publication was not essential to her poetic identity.[10] The opening three lines, "How happy is the little Stone / That rambles in the Road alone / And does'nt [*sic*] care about Careers," introduce the independence of the undistinguished stone that later in the poem "Associates or glows alone" whether or not "A passing Universe put on" its "Coat of elemental Brown." Here Dickinson adopts the poetic equivalent of Benjamin Franklin's snuff brown coat to emphasize the poet's willingness to accept a kind of intrinsic invisibility in the eyes of the world so long as doing so contributes to the larger poetic objective that the poem describes as "Fulfilling absolute Decree / In casual simplicity." With these lines, the poem tells Jackson and Niles that Dickinson is pursuing her poetic vocation unhindered by any present lack of public recognition.

In the third stage of the official correspondence between Dickinson and Jackson that follows this 1882 letter, Jackson returns to her earlier, more insistent commitment to commercial publication, while Dickinson continues to promote the value of gift-based circulation. Perhaps because of Jackson's forced confrontation with her own mortality, compelled by a serious leg fracture, when Jackson writes Dickinson in September 1884 she speaks about the management of Dickinson's literary estate. After imagining "[w]hat portfolios" Dickinson must by this time possess, she writes, "I wish you would make me your literary legatee & executor" (L937a). She then states that Dickinson perpetrates a "cruel wrong to your 'day & generation' that you will not give them light." Dickinson's September response to Jackson concludes with a prose sentence and the first three lines of a poem that together clarify the extent that her poetic vocation is an alternative to Jackson's: "Pursuing you in your transitions, / In other Motes – / Of other Myths / Your requisition be" (L937; Fr 1664). Here the word "requisition" performs a pivotal function in proclaiming that Jackson's efforts to enlist Dickinson's poems in her very different project have failed.[11] Dickinson represents herself as dedicated to her friend's "transitions," but at the same time acknowledges that Jackson has engaged "other Myths." No doubt in part because of the clarity with which she declares her poetic independence from Jackson, Dickinson closes by signing herself "Loyally, / E. Dickinson," indicating that she is loyally attached to Jackson despite their differences regarding publication.[12]

The two drafts of Dickinson's March 1885 final letter to Jackson include an extraordinary concluding observation on her preference for manuscript distribution over print publication. Read in the light of previous exchanges concerning publication, the most provocative portion of this letter is Dickinson's comment on having recently finished Jackson's novel *Ramona*. "Pity me," she writes, "I have finished Ramona," enigmatically adding, "Would that like Shakespeare, it were just published!" (L976). Deliberately inverting historical fact by presenting Shakespeare as "just published" when in reality *Ramona* had just appeared may underscore Dickinson's belief that *Ramona* is already part of the past, whereas for her Shakespeare is eternally reborn in the eyes of readers.[13] More important, the lines may also be stating that it would have been better if *Ramona* had been published *like* or in a manner similar to Shakespeare. Given Dickinson's awareness of editorial disputes surrounding multiple scholarly editions of Shakespeare, she may well have considered his mode of publication a significant factor in securing public interest.[14] Charles Knight, editor of the Dickinson family edition of Shakespeare (Leyda I, 352), provided further precedent, if such were needed, when he described his own editorial position: "I have found it necessary," he writes in the "Advertisement" to volume eight, "to combat some opinions of former editors which are addressed to an age nearly without poetry" (B).[15] Knight further explains the way editorial policy reflects transient reader taste: "These essays, therefore, are not to be received as the opinions of an individual, but as the embodiment of the genial spirit of the new school of Shakespearean criticism, as far as a humble disciple may interpret that spirit."

With this sort of editorial debate as background, the two meanings conveyed in Dickinson's comment on *Ramona* can be seen to work in tandem, collectively stating that an important source of Shakespeare's vitality comes from his having composed at a time when writers did not automatically seek print publication and thereby surrender authority to transient editorial norms. According to such logic, Shakespeare could in fact remain "just published" indefinitely, as publishers would never have access to a definitive, author-approved print text against which to measure the authority of their editions. In this sense, then, Shakespeare performs as a model for the sort of writing that Dickinson thinks most alive; that is, writing that continuously acquires new life through the collaborative engagement of readers.[16] The irony that has pervaded this correspondence and becomes most pronounced in this last letter is that Jackson discovered Dickinson's poems when Higginson showed her unedited manuscript poems he had received through his correspondence with Dickinson, thus validating the potential circulation available through a gift economy that Jackson never entered, despite Dickinson's efforts.

The correspondent who provides the sharpest contrast with Jackson and whose intentions most consistently meet the challenge posed by a gift-based system of circulation is Dickinson's sister-in-law, Susan. The letters that passed between the two women over the course of nearly thirty-six years repeatedly affirm the shared values so central to the notion of a mutually affirmed moral sensibility and the corollary understatement of reciprocity that went along with the gift recipient's freedom to dispense, dispose, or distribute the gift without consulting the giver. Not only is this Dickinson's most extensive correspondence, containing some 254 letters and letter-poems (OMC263), it is also the correspondence that most clearly expresses the collaborative spirit that she fosters in her poetry. These letters routinely communicate the shared understanding that both women were engaged in a joint enterprise that they viewed from the beginning as an effort to inject into their own little society—and by extension American culture as a whole—a habit of independent thought metaphorically associated with the liberating power of poetry, a power that they contrasted with the more pedestrian, rule-bound character of prose.

Through the collaborative production of poetry within the context of gift culture, Susan received drafts of Dickinson poems as well as fair copies that she treated in various ways, sometimes commenting on them, sometimes reading them to friends, sometimes submitting them for publication. The correspondence does not at any point indicate that Dickinson ever objected to any of these decisions, at least in part because the terms of gift exchange meant that the giver trusted the recipient to act in a manner consistent with the expansion of their little community of "we" that Kete has positioned at the heart of gift culture. Even though Dickinson did not herself seek print publication, she did not dispute Sue's freedom to do so as long as her motives reflected their shared sense of purpose. Unlike Jackson, who sought to convince Dickinson that she should accept her approach to circulation, Susan merely proceeded as she thought best and left Dickinson to continue with her preferred method of circulating poems through letters, a method that Susan also employed, though not so exclusively as her sister-in-law.

Even the earliest letters in this correspondence show that Susan and Emily Dickinson were aware that their joint undertaking challenged prevailing cultural norms. In an 1851 letter to Susan, Dickinson imagines the two of them creating what she describes as "a little destiny to have for our own" (OMC2; L56)[17] and declares, "we are the only poets – every one else is prose." Despite the apparent separation of self and other here designated by the metaphorical division of humanity into poetry and prose, Dickinson significantly stipulates that their overriding goal is that of drawing others into their destiny: "let us hope," she asserts, "they will yet be willing to share our humble world and feed upon such aliment as we consent to do!" Ever aware of the challenge their invitation to collaboration poses for readers, Dickinson makes it clear that in their hands words can perform a kind of martial service, as if enlisted in a patriotic enterprise that must penetrate the defenses of conformity before collaboration can become a realistic possibility. In a letter-poem to Susan written in the "late 1850s" (33), she describes a "word / Which bears a sword" and "Can pierce an armed man" for which act the word will be remembered "on patriotic day" (Fr42). Susan extends this martial theme in March 1862 when she describes the publication of Dickinson's "Safe in their Alabaster Chambers" (Fr124) and possibly a poem of her own titled "The Shadow of Thy Wing" as a "Fleet" that she compares to General Burnside's "siege and capture of Roanoke Island in February 1862" (OMC58).[18] As early as February 1852, when Susan was teaching in Baltimore, Dickinson described her as "the precious patriot at war in other lands" (OMC3; L73), suggesting that they associated their artistic aims with both conflict and national interest from early in their correspondence.[19]

At least as important as Susan's shared sense that the poetry of their particular little society could effect change in the larger world is the fact that Susan took significant steps to extend the circulation of Dickinson's poems. Most significant, perhaps, was Susan's introduction of Dickinson's poems to Mabel Loomis Todd in 1882 (Leyda II, 361), yet there is reason to believe Susan's efforts at circulation began much earlier. Thomas H. Johnson proposes that Susan was behind the 1866 publication of "A narrow Fellow in the Grass" (Fr1096, J713), and Martha Nell Smith has argued that Susan published both "Blazing in gold, and quenching in Purple" (Fr321) and "Success is counted sweetest" (Fr112) in 1864 (*Rowing* 156), fourteen years before Jackson's publication of the latter poem. Here it must be noted that seeking publication on her own initiative was not without risks for Susan. As Hart and Smith explain in *Open Me Carefully*,

Susan's publication of "There came a day at summer's full" (Fr325) in the August 1890 issue of *Scribner's Monthly* did not sit well with Dickinson's sister, Lavinia. "After the publication," Hart and Smith point out, "Lavinia, who had a fascicle of the poem, objected to Susan's presumption. However, Susan maintained that she had the right to publish any poems that Emily had sent to her" (116). Such an assertion of rights is perfectly in keeping with the practice of gift circulation, if not the legal system, as through collaboration the poem becomes a joint production, not the exclusive property of a single author. Dickinson's astonishing 1864 letter stating of Susan, "When my Hands / are Cut, Her / fingers will be / found inside" (OMC102; L288), metaphorically affirms a shared authority consistent with gift collaboration while also hinting at joint authorship through the synecdochic allusion to the authorial "Hand."

The shared sensibility crucial to gift culture and pointedly captured in the graphic image of Sue's hands inside of Emily's is one of the most pronounced features of this correspondence. In a letter written in February 1852, Dickinson observes to Sue, "How vain it seems to write, when one knows how to feel" (OMC3; L73). Further on in the same letter Dickinson again communicates the redundancy of writing when one has certain knowledge of the other's interior experience: "Never mind the letter Susie, I wont be angry with you if you dont give me any at all. . . . Only want to write me . . . and that will do." The idea conveyed here is that writing is important primarily as a gift that expresses depth of feeling and confirms shared values rather than as a means of communicating news. In a letter written around February 1852, Dickinson repeatedly affirms the redundancy of attempting to inform Sue about matters Sue already knows. "Oh Susie," she writes, "I often think that I will try to tell you how very dear you are . . . yet darling, you know it all – then why do I seek to tell you" (5). As if redundantly asserting her own redundancy, Dickinson cuts herself off a few lines later, stating, "I shall not tell you, because you know!" (16). Through language like this, Dickinson not only affirms her confidence in the community of "we" that she and Sue inhabit, but she also reiterates the logic of nonreciprocation that is a cornerstone of gift culture. As her own writing in these letters makes clear, the giving and receiving of the gift are ends in themselves; to register an obligation to respond would be to admit that the circuit of the gift was incomplete and that the gift had failed.

A sampling of letter-poems Dickinson sent Susan at different stages of their correspondence presents what can be read almost as a catechism on the logic of gift exchange. Writing to Sue in the mid-1860s (OMC115; L273), Dickinson spells out the circuit of exchange that begins and ends when the gift is both given and received: "Gratitude – is not / the mention / Of a Tenderness, / But its' [*sic*] still / appreciation / Out of Plumb of / Speech" (Fr1120B). Dickinson's disavowal of speech, or in the case of letters, writing, is a textbook instance of the completion achieved when giver and receiver merge. Dickinson makes this point in an even more explicit manner in a late 1870s letter-poem: "The sweetest / acts both exact / and defy, gratitude, / so silence is all / the honor there is" (OMC204; L586). Even into the 1880s, Dickinson reiterates the needlessness of saying thanks or acting in any way that does not affirm mutual understanding. The following letter-poem from the early 1880s (OMC221; L661) shows Dickinson's delight in pointing out the redundancy of gratitude in a friendship that has repeatedly affirmed its enduring strength through gifts each has given to the other: "'Thank you' / ebbs – between us, / but the Basis / of thank you, / is sterling and / fond." One of the most interesting features of these particular letter-poems is the way they function simultaneously as the redundant thanks that Dickinson decries and as new gifts themselves that affirm the shared sensibility that is itself the reason thanks are not required. In this sense, letters and letter-poems that celebrate the absence of thanks but give it anyway may be understood as a distinctive gift culture trope that endlessly loops the affirmation and erasure of reciprocity, thus compounding redundancy and magnifying the message that what is being given is free from obligation.

The confidence, trust, and affection so vividly conveyed in these letter-poems about redundant reciprocity help establish and maintain the crucial foundation that enabled Emily and Susan to launch their fleet of poems as a collaborative venture. The most well-known example of their working together on a poem appears in the correspondence that surrounds the March 1, 1862 publication of "Safe in their alabaster chambers" (Fr124A) in the *Springfield Republican*. As Martha Nell Smith has made clear, "at least in the case of 'Safe in their Alabaster Chambers,'" Susan "critiqued the text while Dickinson was in the process of writing and in that way participated in the creation of the poem" (*Rowing* 182). Smith has in mind Sue's letter to Dickinson, written about 1861 (OMC61; L238), in which Sue comments on a revision of the second stanza. She opens by stating, "I am not suited / dear Emily with the second / verse," then notes that "it does not go with the / ghostly shimmer of the first verse" and closes her critique by proposing that "the first verse / is complete in itself" and "needs / no other." At this point in her letter, Sue expresses her admiration for the first stanza in words that Dickinson will very nearly replicate nine years later when describing the physical sensations she associates with poetry. Sue writes, "You never made a peer / for that verse, and I guess you[r] / kingdom does'nt hold one – I / always go to the fire and get warm / after thinking of it, but I never / can again." Higginson reports that Dickinson's words to him during his August 1870 visit were, "'If I read a book [and] it makes my whole body so cold no fire ever can warm me I know that is poetry'" (L342a). Such striking similarity further magnifies the artistic interdependence that Dickinson expressed in her 1864 letter to Sue in which she wrote, "When my Hands / are Cut, [Sue's] / fingers will be / found inside" (OMC102; L288). Dickinson's response to Sue's criticism is to send yet another stanza, further expressing her serious appreciation of Sue's aesthetic judgment. "Your praise is good," Dickinson writes, "because I know / it knows" (OMC62).

To appreciate fully the representative nature of this particular correspondence, it must be seen in the context of a history of collaboration that runs through the letters that passed between Dickinson and Susan. As early as the late 1850s, Dickinson sent Sue a letter-poem containing a draft version of "Frequently the woods are pink" (OMC32; Fr24), a poem that she revised further and placed at the end of her first fascicle (Franklin, *Poems* 81–82). While there is no record of Susan's response to this draft, we do get a vivid sense of one of the varied forms such a response might have taken in a mid-1860s letter-poem from Dickinson that contains verse responses in Susan's hand (OMC122). After reading Dickinson's letter-poem that describes cricket song and the coming of night ("The Crickets sang" [Fr1104]), Sue writes the following in pencil on the reverse of the sheet: "I was all ear / And took in strains that / might create a seal / Under the lids of death." This, and another four-line response on the same page, also in pencil, do not offer a critique of the sort provoked by "Safe in their Alabaster Chambers," but do suggest an ongoing conversation that could take many forms: in this case, a highly appreciative poetic rejoinder from Susan. A letter-poem later that decade that Franklin has published as "The Face we choose to miss" (Fr1293) also contains a penciled note from Sue on the back, but this time she revises Dickinson's poem (OMC142). Susan's version of the poem makes it more conventional by eliminating unorthodox capitalization, indenting to show continued lines (or turnovers), moving the single dash to the end of the poem, and attaching Dickinson's name. These modifications may indicate that she was considering sending it out for publication, in which case the inclusion of Dickinson's name may have served as a reminder that the poem originated with Dickinson, even though Susan has copied it in her own hand. These and many additional examples of collaboration can be found in *Open Me Carefully*, where Hart and Smith usefully describe the usually penciled comments Susan makes. One of the most intriguing of these is a letter-poem dating from 1870 or later (148) that contains a draft version of "Who were 'the Father and the Son'" (Fr1280). Hart and Smith note that the "ink draft has many penciled changes and is further documentation of Emily and Susan working over poems." What these many examples of collaboration finally show is that Susan and Dickinson's community of "we" was part of a collective identity that at times nearly eclipsed the individual identities of the women as they dedicated themselves to the patriotic transformation of their world from prose to poetry.

By far the biggest challenge Susan faced as a collaborator came after Dickinson's death, when Lavinia requested that she edit a volume of Emily's poems for publication. Quite unlike the selective placement of isolated poems that she had pursued on a small scale in the past, Susan now faced the prospect of launching an entire collection that would conceivably advance the patriotic project she shared with Dickinson while also unveiling before the public an unruly poetic body, much of which may have been new to her. Key considerations would certainly have included both the creation of an appropriate print format and managing the potential social fallout she imagined in 1891 when she described herself as "dreading publicity for us all'" (qtd. in Smith, *Rowing* 213). Her circumstance in this sense mirrored the tribulations not only of the male writer in "Miss Grief" who confronted manuscript resistance to print demands but also that of the two women in "Collected by a Valetudinarian" who faced the hardship of imagining the new social role they would have to create for themselves. Understandably, Susan hesitated. The little we now know of her efforts to meet this challenge is conveyed in an 1890 letter to Higginson explaining that she envisioned a book of Dickinson's writing "'rather more full, and varied'" (Bingham, *Ancestors'* 86) than the one he had undertaken with Mabel Loomis Todd. In their analysis of Susan's efforts, Hart and Smith conclude that "Susan wanted to showcase the entire range of Emily's writings: letters, humorous writings, illustrations—in short, everything left out of the Loomis Todd and Higginson edition" (OMCxvi). This would have been a daunting undertaking indeed, one almost certainly guaranteed to bring Susan into the public spotlight and not only associate her with Dickinson's own innovations but, if her book appeared after the Higginson and Todd volumes, also identify her as an editor willing to exceed the limits of taste adhered to by Higginson, a nationally known writer and political activist.

Sue's inability to complete the ambitious project she envisioned for Dickinson's poems may be best explained by Emily Dickinson's absence. What the preceding overview of the Susan/Emily correspondence shows is that they gathered strength through mutual devotion to a shared undertaking. Their little community of "we" was in this sense stronger than either woman could be when acting independently. While it is impossible to know for certain why Sue did not progress further with her "more full, and varied" book of Emily's writings, gift culture does provide a logical explanation. The primary assumption behind the concept of a mutually affirmed sensibility is that it expresses a communal value system that acquires its unique power precisely because it is not limited to a single, isolated "I." The reception of the gift in this sense affirms values the giver expresses in the face of doubt and uncertainty. With Dickinson's passing, Susan had rich memories, certainly, plus a fabulous body of literary work, but she had lost forever the one person who could grant her the communal strength to confront the world. When the "we" of Susan and Emily became the "I" of Susan, their jointly imagined poetic fleet lost its way.

Though Higginson ultimately did more than any other correspondent to promote the circulation of Dickinson's literary gifts, his method was decidedly less ambitious than the multi-genre project Sue may have had in mind; he balked at the prospect of publicly aligning himself with poetry that he viewed as highly unruly and politically charged. As Dickinson's 1862 "I have no Tribunal" letter indicates (L265), he knew from the beginning that Dickinson exercised a sovereignty antagonistic to conventional editorial expectations. In that letter, her words, "you suggest that I delay 'to publish,'" make clear his reluctance to see her enter print. That reluctance is reiterated almost thirty years later in the opening sentence of his preface to the 1890 first edition: "The verses," he writes, "belong emphatically to what Emerson long since called 'the Poetry of the Portfolio'—something produced absolutely without the thought of publication" and, notably, without "whatever advantage lies in the discipline of public criticism and the enforced conformity to accepted ways" ("Preface [1890]" 13). Higginson's reference to Emerson here, as many scholars have observed, places Dickinson's poetry in a distinct democratic tradition by drawing on Emerson's identification of portfolio poems with what he termed a democratic "revolution" that gave "importance to the portfolio over the book" ("New Poetry" 220). Higginson recalls his reluctance to seek print publication in his essay on Dickinson that appeared in the October 1891 issue of the *Atlantic Monthly*, where he writes that her poems "were launched quietly and without any expectation of a wide audience" ("Emily Dickinson," *Magnificent* 543). Clearly, to be associated with a literary revolution gave him pause, just as the male writer in "Miss Grief" paused when confronted with a parallel prospect. That Higginson was willing to proceed where that writer was not may be the primary indication that Dickinson succeeded over time in winning some degree of unconscious collaboration from him through her gift of 103 poems (Franklin 1552). After all, we do know that he never received any compensation for his labors (Horan 89).

Perhaps the most remarkable aspect of the Higginson correspondence is the evidence that he did in fact act in accordance with the dictates of a gift economy, even though there is scant overt evidence that he knew he was doing so. His 1891 *Atlantic Monthly* account of the correspondence supports this notion in several instances, most strikingly through the distribution of individual authority evident in Dickinson's persistent reference to herself as "Scholar" and, in Higginson's words, "assuming on my part a preceptorship which it is almost needless to say did not exist" ("Emily Dickinson," *Magnificent* 554). Of particular interest here is the unstated agreement to maintain a hierarchical vocabulary of "scholar" and "preceptor" while in fact introducing a set of private meanings. This mutual creation of a private linguistic code is fully consistent with Higginson's restructuring of the terms of their relationship, so that a shared sensibility consistent with a distinct community of "we" replaces the initial hierarchical imbalance. "I soon abandoned all attempt to guide in the slightest degree this extraordinary nature," he writes, "and simply accepted her confidences, giving as much as I could of what might interest her in return." Surely his many references to books and authors, mutual friends, and personal reflections of the sort expressed in his New Year's note of 1874 (that he describes as "a New Year's gift") constitute that most essential of all gifts: the mutual affirmation of equality possible when customary cultural barriers are first resisted and then transgressed by shared assertions of individual authority (L405a). How could this experience not have had some influence on Higginson's decision to exercise his own sovereignty by doing what neither the male writer in "Miss Grief" nor the two women in "Collected by a Valetudinarian" could: risk censure by expanding the circuit of literary distribution?

In keeping with the inverted linguistic code that configured Dickinson as "scholar" and Higginson as "preceptor," when in fact authority was far more balanced than such terms would suggest, is the manner in which Dickinson consistently used Higginson to avoid publication. The first evidence of this appears in Dickinson's famous third letter to Higginson, in which she "smile[s]" at his suggestion that she "delay 'to publish'" and dismisses his early charges that her verse is "'spasmodic'" and "'uncontrolled'" (L265). Instead, she holds to the possibility that fame may be hers by alternative means: "If fame belonged to me, I could not escape her," concluding that her unruly "Barefoot-Rank is better" than conformity to Higginson's advice. Curiously, neither the offering of criticism nor the rejection of it leads to a schism in their relationship, though Higginson may have been confused at times by the ground rules governing the conduct of his new correspondent. While Dickinson aggressively dismisses Higginson's critical advice in her June 7, 1862, "no Tribunal" letter, she also pleads with him to give her more instruction: "But, will you be my Preceptor, Mr Higginson?" That her wish to correspond with him is not connected to print publication becomes stunningly clear in Dickinson's early 1866 letter where she informs Higginson that "A narrow Fellow in the Grass" (Fr1096) appeared in the February 14 issue of the *Springfield Daily Republican* purely because "it was robbed of me" (L316). Dickinson is emphatic here about removing any false impression that she set out to "deceive" him after having previously announced her refusal to print: "I had told you I did not print." In light of this adamant stand and her determination to appear consistent in her opposition to print publication, it is not surprising that she accepts Higginson's opposition to print publication without treating it as a blow to their burgeoning friendship. Neither is it a surprise that Dickinson appeals to Higginson in 1876 to "give me a note saying you disapproved" of Helen Hunt Jackson's efforts to print Dickinson's poems (L476).[20] What Dickinson's responses show is that her interest in sustaining a correspondence with Higginson did not grow out of a wish for his assistance in getting her poems into print. Her decision to open a correspondence with Higginson when she did, but not for the purpose of achieving print publication, is but the first of many instances of Dickinson's inviting Higginson to search beyond normative expectations in his efforts to understand their relationship.

What Dickinson *did* want from Higginson was for him to save her life. Twice Dickinson writes to Higginson that he has indeed saved her life though he may not have known that he had done so. In a letter written in June 1869, she observes, "You were not aware that you saved my Life" (L330). A decade or so later, she repeats this observation while asking why she has not received any recent letters: "Must I lose the Friend that saved my Life, without inquiring why?" (L621). Precisely what Dickinson had in mind when she writes about having her life saved is no doubt beyond recovery, but the logic of gift culture does provide a possible, if only partial, explanation. In the same letter in which she first declares that Higginson saved her life, Dickinson's opening paragraphs convey her concern with shared moral purpose and expressions of gratitude that so characterize her letters to Susan:

> A Letter always feels to me like immortality because it is the mind alone without corporeal friend. Indebted in our talk to attitude and accent, there seems a spectral power in thought that walks alone – I would like to thank you for your great kindness but never try to lift the words which I cannot hold.
>
> Should you come to Amherst, I might then succeed, though Gratitude is the timid wealth of those who have nothing. I am sure that you speak the truth, because the noble do, but your letters always surprise me. My life has been too simple and stern to embarrass any. (L330)

Dickinson's initial description of "immortality . . . without corporeal friend" celebrates the achievement of a shared sensibility not encumbered by gender codes grounded in cultural constructions of their male and female bodies. Her succeeding reference to "spectral power" reiterates this appreciation for a relationship not bounded by bodies while addressing the imaginative independence such boundlessness makes possible as "thought that walks alone." When she then goes on to tell Higginson that "your letters always surprise me," she affirms her reception of the gift that is his uniquely independent thought. Her surprise here is crucial, as it confirms her communion with another outside the boundaries of predictable intellectual or imaginative processes. The language of gratitude that accompanies these expressions of delight is entirely appropriate to gift exchange because it sets in motion the redundant cycle of offering the thanks it claims it is incapable of giving, thereby provoking a vision of expanded future gratitude while simultaneously offering an understated version of thanks in the present.

Higginson's gift of friendship might have been especially welcomed by Dickinson in 1862 due to her own re-evaluation of the domestic publication she had been engaged with since at least 1858 (Franklin, *Poems* 20). According to Ralph W. Franklin, Dickinson's approach to fascicle construction went through a period of "disorder that came into her workshop from late 1860 until early 1862" (22). Following the particularly stressful months of "early 1862," when "the fascicle idea had itself come apart," and after Dickinson has probably composed in the neighborhood of 300 poems and eleven fascicles, she writes to Higginson for the first time. After opening this correspondence with Higginson, Dickinson enters what Franklin estimates to be her most productive years, completing 227 poems in 1862 and 295 in 1863 (1533). This upsurge in the creation of manuscript poems suggests an additional explanation for the "life" Higginson saved: that his open expression of both interest and awe restored Dickinson's confidence in herself as a writer and gave her the courage to move forward with the daring experiments she was contemplating in her manuscript books. Franklin draws a clear picture of Higginson's probable influence: "In the summer of 1862, perhaps under the innocent influence of Higginson, whom she later called her 'safest' friend, one who had 'saved' her life, a new sense of order took hold in Dickinson's workshop, lasting until 1864" (24).[21] What Dickinson sought from Higginson, then, was indeed assistance with publication, but not the print publication he had in mind; her aim instead was the development of a friendship that would motivate her to eclipse even further the limits of conventional poetic form in the pages of her manuscript books. Higginson provided Dickinson precisely the impetus she needed through his repeated expressions of surprise and delight at his reception of her literary gifts.

Of the many examples of gift exchange that surface in the letters between Dickinson and Higginson, none are more revealing than those containing the epistolary dialogue surrounding Higginson's poem "Decoration." From the beginning of their correspondence, Dickinson sent Higginson poems along with letters and letter-poems, while she made note of and commented on published works of his that she discovered in the world of print. She eventually became so adept at identifying his style that she could even spot his anonymous publications.[22] The ensuing joint discussion of the other's writing became itself a form of gift exchange as the aim was not analysis or critique but rather the expression of personal appreciation. In this way each affirmed the values they saw conveyed through the writing of the other, often delighting in the surprising turns each discovered. After having first encountered "Decoration" around Memorial Day 1874 in *Scribner's Monthly* (L413), Dickinson provides Higginson with a single quatrain distillation of his poem in June 1877. Higginson in turn copies Dickinson's revision of his poem and sends it to Mabel Loomis Todd in May 1891 with the following declaration: "She wrote it after re-reading my 'Decoration.' It is the condensed essence of that & so far finer" (Bingham, *Ancestors'* 130). With this gesture, Higginson extends the circulation of Dickinson's gift to him, effectively acting on his prerogative as the recipient. This inclusion of Todd (and eventually the public who would read the second volume of Dickinson's poems that he and Todd were then collaboratively editing) exemplifies the way that gift exchange can transgress the boundaries of what Mary Loeffelholz has described as the often restrictive unilateral relationship scholars too often treat as the determining structure of familiar correspondence ("'Decoration'" 664). As Loeffelholz has noted in her careful analysis of Dickinson's 1877 letter that contains her revision of Higginson's poem, "Dickinson's letter . . . everywhere foregrounds the scene of writing and of writing's circulation" (680). Viewing all four of the Dickinson-Higginson letters that deal with "Decoration" as expressions of gift culture lends further strength to Loeffelholz's conclusion while also illuminating the pugilistic stance Dickinson often struck in her efforts to jolt Higginson's perceptions. Dickinson is almost certainly conflating herself with the biblical Jacob when she closes the last of these four letters by describing Jacob as "Pugilist and Poet" and then declares that "Jacob was correct" in blessing the angel with whom he wrestled (L1042). With these words, Dickinson notably revises the famous passage from Genesis to tell Higginson that her unanticipated moves and abrupt surprises constitute a form of linguistic wrestling predicated on the power of each to bless the other.

Higginson's final response to Dickinson, his last and most enduring gift, was to overcome his own trepidation and use his literary authority to advance her fame. In her account of Lavinia's early efforts to draw Higginson into the project, Millicent Todd Bingham describes Higginson's initial resistance to print publication: "He wrote that he was extremely busy, and that the confused manuscripts presented nearly insuperable obstacles to reading and judging such quantities of poems. Though he admired the singular talent of Emily Dickinson, he hardly thought enough could be found to make an even semi-conventional volume" (18). Concern with the unconventional nature of Dickinson's poems and his fear that they might not be made sufficiently palatable for the reading public inform Higginson's 1890 preface where he writes, "Such verse must inevitably forfeit whatever advantage lies in the discipline of public criticism and the enforced conformity to accepted ways" ("Preface," *Magnificent* 13). Fortunately, the public reception of Dickinson's work exceeded all expectation, and Higginson's joy as well as relief registers forcefully in his December 15, 1890 letter to Todd. "Pardon me if I bore you," he writes, "but I often wish for your sympathy, because you are the only person who can feel as I do about this extraordinary thing we have done in revealing this rare genius. I feel as if we had climbed to a cloud, pulled it away, and revealed a new star behind it" (Bingham 81). Higginson's obvious delight, together with his rhetoric of cosmic revelation, mark this final and greatest surprise that comes to him as Dickinson's last gift.[23]

The opening paragraph of his 1891 *Atlantic* essay shows that by this date Higginson has begun to understand that he has participated in a major literary event of historic proportions. He begins by acknowledging the unanticipated nature of Dickinson's success: "Few events in American literary history have been more curious than the sudden rise of Emily Dickinson into posthumous fame" ("Emily Dickinson" 543). Then he confirms the extent to which the magnitude of her success overwhelmed all expectations, including his own: "But for her only sister it is very doubtful if her poems would ever have been published at all; and when published, they were launched quietly and without expectation of a large audience; yet the outcome of it is that six editions of the volume have been sold within six months, a suddenness of success almost without a parallel in American literature." Perhaps Higginson appreciated the irony that Dickinson should at last achieve the fame she claimed she could not escape if it were hers and he should by contrast be the dumbfounded collaborator who reluctantly changed the landscape of American poetry.

No matter how misguided we now judge Higginson's editorial efforts to be, what we know of his correspondence with Dickinson and his decision to co-edit the first and second editions tells us that he went forward with a pronounced sense of dread, lending his name to a publication he fully expected to create an altogether different kind of sensation. Even though the form that Dickinson's texts take today differs markedly from the versions Higginson and Todd produced in 1890 and 1891, the presence of a sovereign self has remained consistent. When Katha Pollitt states that Dickinson is more political than Walt Whitman and Langston Hughes, her words reflect the history of Dickinson's initial gift-based method of circulation, according to which she intransigently resisted the tribunal of print convention, insisting instead on the power to unite distinct sovereign selves. Higginson's willingness to risk censure through his role in bringing Dickinson to the larger public reflects the responsiveness to Dickinson's insistent defiance of cultural codes that typifies the long correspondence he shared with her.

NOTES

1. References to gifts abound in Dickinson's letters, and much scholarship remains to be done on the function of flowers, baked goods, and other items that formed an important part of her correspondence. My concern more narrowly focuses on the specific function of poems, letter-poems, and letters in Dickinson's correspondence with Helen Hunt Jackson, Susan Huntington Gilbert Dickinson, and Thomas Wentworth Higginson. In these epistolary exchanges, I see Dickinson expressing the political resistance Pollitt alludes to in relationship to print publication and the circulation of her poems. Martha Nell Smith has described Dickinson's circulation of poetry in her cor-

respondence as "a consciously designed alternative mode of textual reproduction and distribution" (*Rowing* 1–2). This essay builds on her observation that "Dickinson found the printed transformations of her work dissatisfying" and chose "not to distribute her work in the mass-produced ways to which most unknown authors aspire." I also build on the observations of Marietta Messmer, who acknowledges Smith's foundational work and extends it to the world of politics and society: "an additional reason for Dickinson's choice to 'publish' her poems in epistolary format may also lie in the sociocultural and political connotations of these two genres in a nineteenth-century context" (47). I make the case that gift culture provides one of the most significant means Dickinson employs not only to distribute her poetry but to expand a politically subversive community of readers. What I have to say may also be understood as a response to Domhnall Mitchell's wish for "the historical context that can help us better appreciate" how with Dickinson "even refusal can be thought of as a form of relation, a social stance" (*Monarch* 2). As Mary Loeffelholz has noted in her response to Mitchell in *From School to Salon*, Dickinson's poetry fits into a "place of tension" between "'bourgeois art' and 'social art'" that emerges "in the second half of the nineteenth century by a double refusal: of the official honors, fame, and financial success attached to bourgeois art, on the one hand, and of social art's 'demand that literature fulfil a social or political function,' on the other" (135). See Loeffelholz's chapter "'Plied from Nought to Nought': Helen Hunt Jackson and the Field of Emily Dickinson's Refusals" in *From School to Salon* for a complete discussion of her response to Mitchell's treatment of refusal in Dickinson and her analysis of the Dickinson-Jackson correspondence.

2. This essay is part of a longstanding discussion of Dickinson's politics that has been informed by many scholars. Betsy Erkkila's important 1992 book, *The Wicked Sisters: Women Poets, Literary History, and Discord*, argues that Dickinson "never conceived of taking her struggle into the public sphere" (49) and that her "rhetoric" is most accurately "translated not into a dream of democracy but into a royalist dream of rule by hereditary and divine right" (51). Domhnall Mitchell departs from this position in his 2000 book *Emily Dickinson: Monarch of Perception* when he writes that Dickinson's poems "have more to do with . . . democratic politics than first appears" (111). He significantly notes the difficulty of anchoring her writing in a stable political position: "The weight of historical evidence does not necessarily enable us to fit Dickinson into a political or social scheme; she (or her speakers) may voice conservative, even reactionary, opinions, but she also demonstrates opposite tendencies" (109). My own position is that the presence of opposing political stances is evidence of the intransigence central to democratic sovereignty. For this reason I agree with Sanborn's recommendation that Dickinson *not* be viewed "as someone whose self-gratifying isolation is essentially at odds with democratic sociality" (1345). My argument also draws on Shira Wolosky's 2002 essay, "Emily Dickinson: being in the body," in which she argues that "Dickinson's texts are scenes of cultural crossroads, situated within the many and profound transitions taking place around her" (138).

3. "Epistolary writing," Hewitt explains, "paradoxically emphasizes the individual sovereignty of the letter-writer, even as it harnesses the atomism or anarchy that might

come from this model by ultimately connecting the individual to a matrix of other letter-writers" (12).

4. Barnes further describes this conflation as "a vision of 'the people' as a single and independent entity, asserting its liberal privilege in a body at once collective and individual" (1).

5. In anthropologist David Cheal's words, the gift economy is a *"system of redundant transactions within a moral economy, which makes possible the extended reproduction of social relations"* (19). These newly vitalized moral values then guide individual political acts, invigorating the civic self.

6. Marietta Messmer acknowledges Dickinson's epistolary fusion of public and private writing in *A Vice for Voices*: "Not quite public published documents ('literature') in the conventional sense, the mailed-out letters and letter-poems (especially in the form of double mailings) nonetheless challenge the boundaries of exclusively private missives and become—quite literally—a private form of publication" (48). Karen Dandurand makes clear in "Dickinson and the Public" that "sharing Dickinson's letters and poems" would not have been "an uncommon practice in the nineteenth century, and [was] one that Dickinson followed herself" (260). Dandurand provides a representative list of recipients who may have shared Dickinson's poems and letters with others, concluding, "The chain of transmission was potentially endless" (262).

7. The wishes of the woman writer, Aarona Moncrief, are never unambiguously stated. What I treat as the strongest support for the notion that she sought the collaboration of gift-based circulation rather than the fame of print publication is her decision to destroy all her manuscripts after the male writer lies to her about having successfully published the dramatic work she gave him. These she refers to as her "'poor dear children'" that she prefers to have "'depart with me—unread, as I have been'" (268).

8. Elizabeth A. Petrino usefully explains the obstacles Dickinson faced in her correspondence with Jackson in *Dickinson and Her Contemporaries*. Commenting specifically on Dickinson's failure to return the 1875 literary gift that Jackson returned for clarification (the significance of which I explore shortly), Petrino suggests the following: "Dickinson withheld it, perhaps because she lacked confidence that Jackson was her best audience" (164). The view Petrino expresses, and that I for the most part share with her, is not, however, the only way to interpret Dickinson's correspondence with Jackson. In "Emily Dickinson's Perfect Audience: Helen Hunt Jackson," Richard B. Sewall characterizes the relationship as "redemptive" for both parties in large part because each valued the other's writing and each stimulated the other in productive ways (202). Jackson provided Dickinson an appreciative audience and Dickinson provoked in Jackson a greater "concern for truth than for the marketplace and a heightened sense of style" (209). Sewall suggests that Jackson's later political works, *A Century of Dishonor* and *Ramona*, may have been influenced by Dickinson's insistence on truth (210). This would accord well with the argument I propose, in that Dickinson's intransigence would have communicated to Jackson a determination to oppose the status quo. Vivian Pollak's careful reading of the Dickinson-Jackson correspondence in "American Women

Poets Reading Dickinson: The Example of Helen Hunt Jackson" is more sensitive to the tensions between the two women. In my analysis, I draw on Pollak's argument that Jackson was "intent on using Dickinson to lend cultural authority to her own self-representation" (324).

9. Here it is worth mentioning that Dickinson engaged in gift-oriented selections of her own, choosing to send the oriole poem to her Norcross cousins, as well as Jackson, and sending the hummingbird poem to five other correspondents, including Higginson (Johnson, *Poems* 1011–12). It is in the letter to Higginson that accompanied that poem and three others, that Dickinson requested he "Reprove them as your own" (L675), giving special emphasis to the recipient's role as participant in a collaborative venture.

10. Dickinson's interest in extending her gift-based system to Niles is made even clearer in 1883 when she sent him what she described as "a chill Gift – My Cricket and the Snow" in response to his having sent her Mathilde Blind's *The Life of George Eliot* (L813). As part of their previous correspondence, Dickinson had sent him an edition of the Brontë sisters' poems. The cricket and snow references apply to the poems "Further in Summer than the Birds" (Fr895E) and "It sifts from Leaden Sieves" (Fr291E). Franklin indicates in his notes that both of these poems were written about thirteen years previously and were sent to numerous other correspondents. Virginia Jackson has identified Dickinson's departure from Niles's business model of exchange when she sent him the Brontë sisters' poems in the spring of 1883: "In the context of the exchange with Niles, Dickinson seems to have transgressed his sense of the decorum that separated gift and business exchange when she sent him her own copy of the Brontë sisters' poems" (254n.27). See Dickinson's *Letters* 813–813b.

11. The following is the 1843 Webster's definition of "requisition": "Demand; application made as a right." Dickinson's use of the term clearly reflects her sense of having been pressured by Jackson.

12. This is the only time this phrase appears in Dickinson's letters (MacKenzie, *Concordance* 448).

13. Eberwein and Capps both note that Dickinson consistently viewed Shakespeare as a contemporary (Eberwein, *Encyclopedia* 264; Capps 24). Sewall describes Dickinson as discovering "re-creative power, joy, and refreshment" in Shakespeare (*Life* 700).

14. Dickinson would have been aware of scholarly and popular debate about editing Shakespeare through the Shakespeare Club and the editorial commentary that appeared in the family edition of Shakespeare that her father purchased with great deliberation (Leyda I, 277, 352). Jay Leyda's presentation of Emily Fowler's letter describing the Shakespeare Club pays particular attention to Dickinson's insistence that the girls have access to unexpurgated Shakespeare texts, thus providing one instance of her awareness that the public willingly edited these texts (II, 478). In this case, her disapproval of editorial choices urged by male tutors in effect affirmed her own alternative editorial position.

15. "B" appears in the "Advertisement" section of the Knight volume where letters take the place of page numbers.

16. Páraic Finnerty makes a similar point about reader collaboration in *Emily Dickinson's Shakespeare*, where he describes the manner in which women writers of Dickinson's day "transformed Shakespeare" by discovering in his texts "an outlet for their creativity and critical ingenuity": "Despite acknowledgments of Shakespeare's 'firm' and fixed genius, he remained 'just published' because readers redeployed him, his plays becoming displaced by that which had more contemporary or personal relevance" (116).

17. I will follow Hart and Smith in representing Dickinson's line breaks in letters written after the mid-1850s (*OMC* 67–end). Johnson numbers are provided for the convenience of readers using his edition of the letters, as are Franklin numbers for poems that appear in Hart and Smith as letter-poems.

18. When Susan happily proclaims the publication of poems in this instance, she may expect Dickinson's approval for taking her own initiative, even though Susan has done what Dickinson herself would not do. Similarly, in the obituary Susan wrote in memory of her friend, she writes that Dickinson "never published a line" and that "now and then some enthusiastic friend would turn love to larceny, and cause a few verses surreptitiously obtained to be printed" (*OMC* 267). Susan might quite logically include herself in the category of larcenous friends, as her purpose is to focus on *Dickinson's* attitude toward publication, not her own. It is worth noting that at no point does Dickinson criticize Sue or anyone else for publishing one of her poems. In the case of her letter to Higginson where she objects to the print version of "A narrow Fellow in the Grass" (L450; Fr1096), Dickinson may be understood as expressing her exasperation at appearing to have desired print publication when in fact the print poem represents the efforts of another person.

19. The word "patriot" also appears in a letter Dickinson wrote to Elizabeth Holland during the autumn election season of 1884:

Before I write to you again, we shall have had a new Czar - Is the Sister a Patriot?
"George Washington was the Father of his Country" – "George Who?"
That sums all Politics to me – but then I love the Drums, and they are busy
now – (L950)

Here Dickinson's use of the term can be read as a light-hearted reminder that in a democracy all citizens are equal and none should be elevated above the rest, especially at election time. For Dickinson, the sum of "all Politics" may be the requirement that citizens refuse to view politicians—even those as iconic as Washington—as superior. In which case, her use of the term "patriot" can be read as her bantering challenge that Elizabeth follow her lead and accord Washington no greater status than the many unknown Americans who have not registered in official history. Dickinson's reference to drums invests her challenge with a martial air appropriate to her earlier reference to the President as "Czar," implying that Americans have begun to view their leaders as monarchs and that the struggle for democratic sovereignty is far from over. When this challenge is coupled with the fact that during election seasons women are reminded that they lack the right to vote, Dickinson's use of the term "Patriot" can be understood as calling for a resistance to cultural conventions that have distinct political implications for Americans in general and women in particular.

20. Dickinson also writes to Higginson in November 1880, requesting that he advise her regarding publication of three poems that she has promised to the Mission Circle (L674). Referring specifically to this letter, Higginson writes the following in "Emily Dickinson": "Sometimes . . . her verses found too much favor for her comfort, and she was urged to publish. In such cases I was sometimes put forward as a defense; and the following letter was the fruit of some such occasion" ("Emily Dickinson," *Magnificent* 555). Higginson quite clearly understands that Dickinson had used him as a means to avoid fulfilling her promise. In the letter Dickinson writes Higginson to thank him for his advice, she states, "I shall implicitly follow it" and then explains that when her poems were first requested the person appealing to her said that her donation "might 'aid unfortunate Children'" (L676). Dickinson then describes the use of "the name of 'Child'" as "a snare to me," implying that she felt trapped and is grateful to Higginson for releasing her. Her words, plus his, suggest that she did not send the poems and once again avoided this form of publication. Johnson and Ward conclude that "Higginson advised her to offer one or more," but no clear evidence of this exists.

21. The "terror – since September" (L261) that Dickinson alludes to in her April 25, 1862 second letter to Higginson could well refer to the struggle with fascicle construction that Franklin describes.

22. Writing Higginson in the spring of 1876, Dickinson describes her discovery of two of his unsigned reviews: "I inferred your touch in the Papers on Lowell and Emerson – It is delicate that each Mind is itself, like a distinct Bird" (L457).

23. Loeffelholz argues that the public response to poetry changed significantly in the second half of the nineteenth century and that this change accounts for the positive reception of Dickinson's poetry. She describes Dickinson as "enter[ing] . . . literary history . . . rather as Sarah Bernhardt was said to have descended a spiral staircase: 'she stood still and *it* revolved about her'" (*School* 131). Higginson's surprise suggests that he was not aware such a change had taken place.

STEPHANIE A. TINGLEY

"Blossom[s] of the Brain"

Women's Culture and the Poetics of Emily Dickinson's Correspondence

In her obituary for Emily Dickinson published three days after the poet's death in the May 18, 1886, edition of the *Springfield Republican*, Susan Gilbert Dickinson praises her sister-in-law's steadfast attention to her domestic duties and her generous lifelong ministry to others: "[T]here are many houses among all classes into which her treasures of fruit and flowers and ambrosial dishes for the sick and well were constantly sent, that will forever miss those evidences of her unselfish consideration" (Leyda II, 472–73). Susan writes, in part, then, to reassure readers that, despite her sister-in-law's well-known eccentricities and reclusion, Emily Dickinson unselfishly fulfilled duties expected of her as a female member of her upper-middle-class New England household. Such domestic chores and genteel hobbies, which included cooking, paying social calls, collecting and cherishing keepsakes from loved ones, and cultivating flowers, were not only essential to a well-run household, but also considered evidence of a refined feminine sensibility and a proper upbringing. Dickinson herself reminds us of how firmly grounded in her domestic context she was in a passage from a letter to Louise Norcross composed early in 1865, in which she describes how she gradually resumed her domestic pursuits after returning from a lengthy series of treatments for her eye troubles in Boston. She writes:

For the first few weeks I did nothing but comfort my plants, till now their small green cheeks are covered with smiles. I chop the chicken centres when we have roast fowl, frequent now, for the hens contend and the Cain is slain.... Then I make the yellow to the pies, and bang the spice for cake, and knit the soles to the stockings I knit the bodies to last June. (L302)

Although the invalid complains to her cousin that "[t]he snow-light" still "offends" her eyes, her catalog of domestic duties highlights her compulsion to win her family's approval by being "a help" (L302). Dickinson describes and participates in a world in which women did much of the work to establish and sustain networks of kin, neighbors, and friends and defined themselves, in large part, in terms of both the quantity and quality of the work they cheerfully (or at least without complaint) did for others.

Situating Emily Dickinson's work in such an extended network of family and friends challenges the stereotypical picture of the poet's isolation. In *Strategies of Reticence*, Joanne Dobson reminds us that "Dickinson's life and poetry . . . reveal significant indication of her attraction to domestic identification and accomplishment. It would be a mistake to undervalue the influence of women's culture on her" (142). Elizabeth Phillips concurs, noting that Dickinson "does not separate herself from what she writes any more than she can entirely separate herself from the act of making a garment or a loaf of bread" (7). And as Deborah A. Cadman observes in her dissertation, "Material Things and Expressive Signs," "Gift exchanges among family members, friends, and neighbors involved Dickinson in a social network as well as an expressive community of women who spoke by means of physical products and words which indicated their shared adult experiences" (9). Far from cutting herself off from others, the poet actively participates all her life in gift exchanges designed to strengthen social and family networks. Dickinson's is a poetics of exchange and kinship that is firmly grounded in the women's culture of her time and place.

Participation in nineteenth-century Amherst's women's culture of gift-giving (particularly cooking, paying social calls, treasuring keepsakes and mementoes from loved ones, and gardening) becomes a rich sources of metaphor for the poet. In addition, ideas about gift-giving and social exchange become a way for Dickinson to tell perceptive readers something about her poetic processes and aims. Since the poet left no manifesto or clear, sustained description of her aesthetics, we must rely, instead, on observing her practice as poet and correspondent as she shows us the intricate and complex ways these writerly roles are interdependent and connected to women's culture. Dickinson incorporates

materials and contexts drawn from her daily life, particularly the details of domestic routine, to transform some of the gift-giving activities common to her
mid-nineteenth-century women's world.

This argument builds on and blends ideas from several types of Dickinson
scholarship. First, it depends on the long and strong tradition of feminist scholarship about the poet, especially work by Jean McClure Mudge and Joanne
Dobson, which emphasizes Dickinson's place as a mid-nineteenth-century
American woman and ties her to her domestic and familial contexts. In addition, cultural anthropologists' work informs this analysis, most particularly
Lewis Hyde's work on kinship and gift culture and Joan N. Radner and Susan
Lanser's article "Strategies of Coding in Women's Cultures," where they point
out that most societies contain "a realm of practice that is primarily or exclusively women's domain, through which women may develop a [distinct] set of
common signifying practices (beliefs, understandings, behaviors, rituals)" (2).
Finally, the recent scholarly attention to the material world of the Dickinsons
at the Homestead by Jane Wald and others contributes to ideas here about how
Dickinson transformed her domestic situation into art. Wald argues persua-
sively that "without taking into account . . . Dickinson's material existence—the
texture, clamor, tang, fragrance of everyday life, the physical boundedness of
sensation and action—her life and experience remain two-dimensional, without
full context" (84). Important recent work on the Homestead gardens and Emily
Dickinson as gardener, including books by Judith Farr and Marta McDowell,
as well the 2006 publication of a facsimile edition of Emily Dickinson's herbarium, also ground the discussion of Dickinson's poetics here.

Despite Susan Gilbert Dickinson's emphasis in her obituary on Emily Dickinson's domestic contexts, service to others, and gift-giving, she does not comment explicitly on how often Emily Dickinson used her words, both poems and
letters, as well as her deeds, to help her fulfill her duty to serve and nurture
others. Emily Dickinson made the giving of gifts of her words central to her
own work as both woman and creative artist, making clear, both by what she
said and what she did, that she considered her poems and letters to be gifts to
those to whom she sent them. In what might be called a poetics of exchange,
Dickinson's words often served as the equivalent of sending cookies to a shut-in
or paying a social call, as physical tokens of her affection.

As an adolescent and young woman Dickinson experimented with a variety
of personae and writing styles in an effort to find ways to harness the power of
language—to find satisfying ways to use words to connect with people at a

distance and strengthen bonds between writer and reader. Cadman theorizes that "As Dickinson demonstrated her facility for letter writing at an early age, her mother may have ceded that task of kin work to her daughter, empowering her with the role of maintaining kin contact through language. . . . Her early correspondence . . . shows her establishing a network of kin and quasi-kin relations" (38). Since Mrs. Dickinson was often too busy to write and sister Vinnie often occupied with other things, Emily Dickinson handled most of the correspondence for the women in her family. She wrote thank-you notes and letters of congratulation on births, marriages, and graduations; she cheered the sick and offered solace to the bereaved. Witty notes often accompanied gifts to neighbors and friends. Fruit or flowers from her yard, desserts or wine from her kitchen, poems from her pencil—all were sent as tokens of her affection. Thus letters and the poems sent in and with them, together with other tangible keepsakes like pressed flowers and gifts from her kitchen, link writer to reader, for they become substitutes for the physical presence of the person who sent them.

Intended as tokens of the giver's esteem that worked to nurture and strengthen bonds between the gift-giver and recipient, such gifts served as signs of Dickinson's feelings. As Lewis Hyde notes in *The Gift: Imagination and the Erotic Life of Property*, "a gift makes a connection" (56). Gift-giving can strengthen both psychological and spiritual bonds between giver and recipient, he adds, for "[i]t is when someone's gifts stir us that we are brought close, and what moves us, beyond the gift itself, is the promise (or the fact) of transformation, friendship, and love" (68). Like many others in her culture, Emily Dickinson sought to build and sustain relationships by sending her writings as physical tokens of her affection to those about whom she cared.

The poet relies on the knowledge that her small circle of readers, as members of the same culture, will be able to understand at least something about her intentions and will work to decipher her meaning. Thus, in contrast to her more conventional schoolgirl epistles, Dickinson's mature letters and poems heavily depend upon indirection and allusion for their meaning. If the encoding is successful, the intended recipient, the one who possesses the key and knows the context, will be able to crack the code. Once possession of her written words has been transferred from writer to reader, it becomes the reader's job to work at interpreting them. In order to understand the enigmatic, encoded messages, to "pick the lock" of a letter or a poem, readers must become the writer's collaborators. They must be prepared to contribute to the meaning, provide omitted information, and reconstruct missing syntax and context. Readers of Dickinson's letters must participate in the process of the creation of meaning, must get in-volved, as Elizabeth Oakes notes: "Refusing to regard us as inferior 'others', she imagines an equality which enables and encourages the play of our imagination in the recreation of a poem-as-process" (201). Contemporary readers are invited to undertake similar work when confronted with one of the more cryptic of the poet's letters.

Crucial and central to these gift exchanges was the sending and receiving of letters, since Dickinson not only crafted letters designed as gifts for her intended recipients, but also used her letters as a vehicle by means of which she could transmit other gifts of words—namely, the 500 or so poems she included with letters or incorporated into letters. Dickinson's explicit comments in her extant correspondence (often the only traces that remain, as the enclosed objects them-selves often no longer exist) demonstrate that she received and sent hundreds of gifts over her lifetime, including food, flowers, stitched items, photographs, books, locks of hair, letters, and poetry.

Dickinson's domestic metaphors, grounded as they are in the social and cul-tural dynamics of letter-writing and poetry writing as two kinds of gift ex-change, illuminate her poetic practice. David Sprague Herreshoff, in his book *Labor into Art: The Theme of Work in Nineteenth-Century American Literature*, provides one example of how Dickinson transforms "Drudgery to Poetry" (69). Herreshoff notes that the Homestead's farmhouse and working farm would have afforded Dickinson opportunities to observe and perhaps participate in a broad range of tasks, some of which became sources of poetic imagery for her. In this context, the poem that begins:

> The Products of my Farm are these
> Sufficient for my Own
> And here and there a Benefit
> Unto a Neighbor's Bin
>
> (Fr1036)

is clearly a metaphor for Dickinson's career as a writer. She gathers her farm's "Products," concrete ideas and imagery, for her own uses, but also makes sure to share the bounty of her language with her friends and neighbors through her gift-giving.

Since Emily Dickinson considered words, as well as food and flowers, to be sources of sustenance, she frequently drew both physical and rhetorical connec-tions between her writing and other domestic arts, focusing particularly on the activities of cooking, visiting, treasuring keepsakes, and gardening. Jean McClure Mudge perceptively notes how Dickinson is able to make use of the day-to-day duties of housewife and housekeeper as metaphors and symbols for her creative life, for "the humble article of daily use, though its upkeep annoyed and postponed the ecstatic life, still pressed on her consciousness with its symbolic potential: bones, cobwebs, cups, brooms, aprons, balls of yarn, seams, baskets, but above all, windows and doors, pantries, chambers, and rooms" (84).

Among a number of early poems that center on gift-giving, one highlights how crucial language became to Dickinson in her attempts to establish and maintain an intimate connection between giver and recipient:

> It's all I have to bring today –
> This, and my heart beside –
> This, and my heart, and all the fields –
> And all the meadows wide –
> Be sure you count – sh'd I forget
> Some one the sum could tell –
> This, and my heart, and all the Bees
> Which in the Clover dwell.
>
> (Fr17)

Emotional intimacy and communication with readers at a distance, connections between "I" and "you," are closely linked here. In addition, these links become core ideas in Dickinson's poetics.

Feminist critics and scholars have written quite a bit about how domestic activities provided metaphors for Dickinson's poetry, but more needs to be said about how domestic metaphors illuminate her own poetic processes and purposes. In addition, much more attention needs to be paid to how crucial four other social rituals—cooking, paying social calls, the careful treasuring of keepsakes and talismans, and cultivating and sharing flowers—are to Dickinson's poetics. These sources of domestic and poetic imagery connect in crucial ways to Dickinson's lifelong and central letter-writing project. For her, domestic art is transformed into fine art. Now that we have examined the general dynamics and processes of Emily Dickinson's poetics of exchange, let us look closely at the code behaviors in four social contexts that provide essential vocabulary and imagery for Dickinson's poetics.

In an anecdote she includes in an article about Emily Dickinson, her husband Willie's cousin, written for the *Brooklyn Eagle* on April 28, 1892, Ellen E. Dickinson reminds us of the essential link Dickinson made in letters and poetry between culinary art and literary art as parallel creative endeavors. She reports:

> Emily Dickinson was a past mistress in the art of cookery and housekeeping. She made the des[s]erts for the household dinners; delicious confections and bread, and when engaged in these duties had her table and pastry board under a window that faced the lawn, whereon she ever had pencil and paper to jot down any pretty thought that came to her, and from which she evolved verses, later. (Leyda II, 482)

Ellen Dickinson's is not the only anecdote that reports that Dickinson often connected composition with kitchen duties. In "A Glimpse of Dickinson at Work," Gary Scharnhorst includes the following sketch of the poet at work taken from an early 1904 letter that Louise Norcross, Dickinson's cousin, wrote to the editors of the *Boston Women's Journal*. Norcross describes Dickinson's habit of blurring the boundaries between writing and housekeeping this way:

> I know that Emily Dickinson wrote most emphatic things in the pantry, so cool and quiet, while she skimmed the milk; because I sat on the footstool behind the door, in delight, as she read them to me. The blinds were closed, but through the green slats she saw all those fascinating ups and downs going on outside that she wrote about. (484–85)

Norcross highlights what Scharnhorst calls Dickinson's "improvisational method of composition" (485). Just as some of the best cooks improvise and amend recipes as they work until it "tastes right," we know from the worksheets and rough drafts that remain that Dickinson regularly jotted ideas and images for poems on pieces of scrap paper—the edges of used envelopes, the backs of chocolate wrappers—and left alternative word choices as part of her creative batter. Similarly, feminist critic and poet Sandra Gilbert celebrates the link between Dickinson's bread-baking and poem-crafting in "Emily's Bread," the title poem in her 1984 volume.

When Dickinson reports on her own activity as bread baker in a letter, the poet describes the event in witty, metaphoric language: "Twin loaves of bread have just been born into the world under my auspices – fine children – the image of their *mother*" (L36). Using a maternal metaphor here highlights the link the poet is making between domestic and artistic creativity. Other documents confirm her skill at baking bread. Higginson tells his wife in the letter that describes his first face-to-face meeting with Emily Dickinson that "[s]he makes all the bread for her father only likes hers" (L342a), while Leyda includes a note from the local paper that Dickinson's bread had won a prize at the 1856 county cattle show (I, 345).

Like other products of hearth and home she sent to others, Dickinson intended her gifts of language to be refreshments for a reader's body and soul; her words were designed to comfort, console and sustain those who received them, as they did the one who wrote them. To reinforce this connection, Dickinson often borrows the language of the kitchen to describe the nourishment that reading and writing letters afforded both her and her readers. In a letter to Mrs. Jonathan L. Jenkins, for example, she writes, "Austin brought the note and waited like a hungry Boy for his crumb of words" (L501). Similarly, in a note to Elizabeth Holland, she sends her friend nourishment for both the body and the soul, a gift of food as well as a gift of words: "I shall make Wine Jelly Tonight and send you a Tumbler in the Letter, if the Letter consents, a Fabric sometimes obdurate" (L888). On another occasion, she sends imaginary doughnuts to Austin, who was away in law school at the time, in a postscript to an 1851 letter: "Mother is frying Doughnuts – I will give you a little platefull [*sic*] to have warm for your tea! *Imaginary* ones – how I'd love to send you *real* ones" (L65). The poem "Deprived of other Banquet" (Fr872) further develops the metaphor, for here the speaker argues that words alone are ample nourishment. Like strong drink, words can even have the power to intoxicate. Sometimes words in poems and letters are equated with the Christian sacrament of Holy Communion, for the poet's words, like the blood and body of Christ, may connect and sustain her readers.

The social ritual of paying calls on neighbors and friends offers Dickinson a second way to describe her aims as poet and correspondent. Unmarried, middle-class young women in antebellum America were expected to pay social calls on relatives, friends, and acquaintances. As Lee Virginia Chambers-Schiller explains in *Liberty a Better Husband*, her study of unmarried women in nineteenth-century America, it was the custom that "unmarried women spend part of every day engaged in social visiting. The task of maintaining a family's social connections continued to be the responsibility of adult spinsters" (112). Such activity could take up a good share of a day and involved elaborate rituals, including the habit of visitors' leaving their calling cards in the foyer of a home, often on a specially designated silver dish, if a person they went to visit was not at home or declined to see visitors at that particular time. In *Rudeness and Civility: Manners in Nineteenth Century Urban America*, John F. Kasson describes a few of the complex, unwritten rules for visiting and the ways in which calling cards functioned as a kind of nonverbal social code:

> If the desired member of the house was "not at home" (either absent or simply not wishing to receive the caller), the genteel visitor left an engraved calling card. Leaving cards embroiled visitors in one of the most intricate social codes of late-nineteenth-century etiquette. Consider only one aspect, folding the corners. Each corner of the card assumed a distinct meaning when turned down: the upper right-hand corner signified a personal visit; the upper left, congratulations; the lower right, a formal leave-taking when departing the community for some time; the lower left, condolence. Bending the entire left-side of the card denoted a call upon the family at large. (173)

Emily Dickinson certainly understood the subtleties of the practice of paying social calls and leaving calling cards, as two occasions in her extant correspondence make clear. In an 1861 letter to Edward S. Dwight, she imagines the very moment of her letter's delivery as if she were arriving in person and reminds Dwight that he can turn the caller (in this case the letter that substitutes for Dickinson's physical presence) away if he chooses not to receive guests at the moment: "I knock tonight – on that far study door – that used to open kindly – but if you'd rather see no one – you need not say 'Come in'" (L243). Similarly, in response to his 1862 "Letter to a Young Contributor," and as a way of introducing herself to Thomas Wentworth Higginson and asking him if her verse was "alive," Dickinson enclosed a calling card with her signature on it, as well as four sample poems for his critique (L260).

By the late 1850s, it becomes clear that Emily Dickinson chose not to accompany her mother and sister on these kinds of social calls any longer, but she continued to "call" on others by sending letters, poems, and other gifts. Her written words, as well as the other tokens she sent relatives and friends, gradually take on more and more significance because they more and more often substitute for her physical presence. At first Emily Dickinson only grudgingly substitutes letters, poems, and other tokens of her esteem for face-to-face visits, often expressing her frustration that she and a cherished friend have to settle for knowing "each other only by symbols traced upon a paper" when meeting "'face to face'" to "'commune as a man communeth with his friend' one with another" would be so much better (L15). Such laments about the inadequacies of letters as substitutes for intimate face-to-face conversations, a commonplace in Victorian correspondence, appears in one of her first letters to Abiah Root. Dickinson writes: "I long to see you, dear Abiah, and speak with you face to face; but so long as a bodily interview is denied us, we must make letters answer, though it is hard for friends to be separated" (L8). On another occasion she complains that she has too much to tell; it would be easier to tell her news in person, for the "pen is not swift enough to answer my purpose at all" (L9). Being physically separated from those she loves is a temporary torment that must be endured, and she often writes about how eagerly she looks forward to the day when she can visit face-to-face once more. She vividly imagines one such day in a letter to her brother: "You will be here soon dear Austin, and then away with my pen" (L55).

Emily Dickinson departs from Victorian convention, however, when she gradually begins to make it clear that she actually *prefers* "the converse of the pen" to face-to-face encounters. By 1862 letter-writing has replaced face-to-face encounters almost entirely, no matter whether the person addressed lives abroad or next door. Anecdotes abound that describe Dickinson's habit of sending glasses of wine and sometimes poems to visitors to the Dickinson parlor, while she remained upstairs just out of sight. As Dickinson explains in one of her briefest lyrics, this kind of distance has nothing to do with physical geography:

> That Distance was between Us
> That is not of Mile or Main –
> The Will it is that situates –
> Equator – never can –
>
> (Fr906)

Through sheer force of will Emily Dickinson is able to keep careful control over both the physical and psychological terms of her epistolary relationships and gift exchanges, a strategy she makes explicit in an exultant comment to Elizabeth Holland, "How near, and yet how far we are!" (L204). As an adult woman she regularly exchanges letters with a number of individuals whom she has never met face-to-face, a fact to which she slyly alludes in a letter written to Mabel Loomis Todd: "I am glad you cherish the Sea. We correspond, though I never met him" (L1004). Her letters come to substitute for her physical presence almost all the time, rather than just when distance or circumstances require it.

For Dickinson distance thus becomes a necessary condition, absence the main impetus, for her art. The built-in limitations and frustrations of epistolary relationships are a source of inspiration for her rather than a source of limitation; clearly they stimulate this writer's creative imagination. For example, her physical and psychological isolation inspires this lyrical lament, composed in the winter of 1859:

> My garden is a little knoll with faces under it, and only the pines sing tunes, now the birds are absent. I cannot walk to the distant friends on nights

piercing as these, so I put both hands on the window-pane, and try to think how birds fly, and imitate, and fail, like Mr "Rasselas." (L212)

Language that defines relationships with readers in terms of absence and distance begins to dominate her letters. Since the physical transmittal of her written words from her hands to those of her reader is her sole means of maintaining connection, the actual moment when her reader receives her message often becomes a prominent part of the texts themselves, as in an 1861 letter to Mary Bowles: "I say I will go myself – I cross the river – and climb the fence – now I am at the gate – Mary – now I am in the hall – now I am looking your heart in the Eye!" (L235). Similarly, she begins a late letter to Elizabeth Holland with the words "I tell my Pencil to make no noise, and we will go to the House of a Friend" (L888). Often, such a strategy collapses the distance between the writer and what she has written, as in an 1884 letter to Forrest F. Emerson that begins: "I step from my pillow to your hand" (L922). Here, writer and written message have become one, their voices eerily indistinguishable.

As a result, the written words of a letter, its physical transmittal from writer's hand to reader's hand, becomes essential to maintaining a friendship through the mail. Emily Dickinson recognizes how crucial, and yet how fragile, such a link can be, and understands that both parties must share the desire to keep in contact and prove it by keeping up with the demands of the correspondence. In another letter she explains this to school friend Jane Humphrey: "I have written you a great many letters since you left me – not the kind of letters that go in post-offices – and ride in mail-bags – but queer – little silent ones – very full of affection – and full of confidence – but wanting in proof to you – therefore not valid – somehow you will not answer them – and you *would* paper and ink letters – I will try one of those – tho' not half so precious as the other kind" (L30). Hers becomes almost exclusively a textual art, an aesthetic that privileges the written word, autonomous and powerful, over the spoken word. As she writes in a letter to Higginson, "A Letter always feels to me like immortality because it is the mind alone without corporeal friend. Indebted in our talk to attitude and accent, there seems a spectral power in thought that walks alone" (L330).

Following another convention of Victorian women's culture, Dickinson cherished letters and gifts from others as keepsakes and talismans, and hoped her friends would do the same with gifts from her. Evidence in her early letters suggests that Emily Dickinson followed Victorian conventions and systematically saved personal letters that she received from her relatives and friends, together with other mementoes writers commonly enclosed such as dried and pressed flowers, locks of hair, jewelry, or photographs; and we know that some of the people Dickinson corresponded with saved her letters to them. In her February 23, 1845 letter sent to Abiah Root, for example, Dickinson comments explicitly on how physical tokens of affection exchanged between close friends mediate between presence and absence and strengthen kinship bonds: "I keep your lock of hair as precious as gold and a great deal more so. I often look at it when I go to my little lot of treasures, and wish the owner of that glossy lock were here" (L5). Letters transmit messages that are neither wholly private nor completely public. They are designed to cross boundaries—to move from one realm (the writer's or gift-giver's) to another (the reader's or recipient's). Unlike more perishable presents of food and fresh flowers, Dickinson's gifts of words could endure and be cherished as keepsakes, as lasting tokens of the writer's esteem and affection.

Years later, such long-cherished treasures could jog the memory and evoke long-dormant emotions, as Emily Dickinson explains in one early poem:

> In Ebon Box, when years have flown
> To reverently peer –
> Wiping away the velvet dust
> Summers have sprinkled there!
>
> To hold a letter to the light –
> Grown Tawny – now – with time –
> To con the faded syllables
> That quickened us like Wine!
>
> Perhaps a Flower's shrivelled cheek
> Among it's stores to find –
> Plucked far away, some morning –
> By gallant – mouldering hand!
>
> A curl, perhaps, from foreheads
> Our constancy forgot –
> Perhaps, an antique trinket –
> In vanished fashions set!
>
> And then to lay them quiet back –
> And go about it's care –
> As if the little Ebon Box
> Were none of our affair!
>
> (Fr180)

Similarly, in a letter Dickinson sent to Sue early in 1852, she takes time out from sharing the news to assure her friend that her letters are kept safe, describing both their physical location and their condition:"[D]ont think I forget them – Oh no – they are safe in the little chest which tells no secrets – nor the moth, nor the rust can reach them" (L77; OMC5). In another letter to her future sister-in-law, composed that same winter, she writes,"The precious billet, Susie, I am wearing the paper out, reading it over and o'er, but the dear *thoughts* cant wear out if they try" (L74; OMC4). Since it was very likely that a letter's recipient would keep it as a token of the writer's esteem and affection, epistolary guidebooks encouraged letter-writers to think carefully about appropriate subject matter, style, and format for their letters. As the female author of the advice manual *The Young Lady's Own Book* (1836) warns:

> It is wrong to imagine, that in a familiar or playful correspondence, or letters of intelligence, the slip-shod muse is to be paramount. False grammar, in good society, is not tolerated, even *en famille*, neither can it be in a letter. In the most familiar epistle, we should recollect what we owe to our language, to our correspondent, and to ourselves. We ought not to write any thing of which we may hereafter feel ashamed. Well-written letters are as often burnt, or destroyed, as slovenly epistles are, by accident or design, preserved to rise up in judgment against us hereafter." (119)

These precious keepsakes, which often "outlived" the person who sent them, enjoyed a kind of immortality available to neither writer nor recipient. The Victorians believed that years later, especially after the person who had sent them was deceased, these beribboned bundles of personal letters and other carefully preserved mementos took on added significance as emblems of new-made saints and provided ways to connect generations of family and friends. Contemporary feminist poet Adrienne Rich, in a poem titled "Natural Resources," celebrates small physical tokens of relationships long past such as china saucers, picture frames, ribboned letters and snapshots, scrapbooks and scraps, turned into patchwork, that can link past, present and future generations of women (*Dream* 216–63). Although these small remnants of women's lives may seem insignificant, Emily Dickinson, like Rich, recognizes their sacred and cosmic significance.

Such cultural and spiritual contexts certainly enrich our reading of a poem like "Essential Oils are wrung" (Fr772), which has rightly long been read as one of Dickinson's key comments about her poetic fame and literary immortality. While Jean McClure Mudge connects the "attar of the rose" with Dickinson's carefully copied and hand-bound manuscripts which she preserved in the cherry bureau in her bedroom/workroom (112), the metaphor should be broadened to include letters as well as poems.

When Dickinson's first editors, T. W. Higginson and Mabel Loomis Todd, chose to label Dickinson's hand-sewn manuscript books "fascicles," a term associated with a kind or manner of flowering, they linked her art to another cultural context drawn from antebellum women's culture: gardening and the language of flowers. Cadman explains how the word "fascicle" connects Dickinson to a rich social context "that included access to the earth, systems of symbolic languages, customs among white, middle-class women, and principles of science which the poet felt free enough to accept or reject" (134). Dickinson's frequent allusions in her letters and poems to the Victorian language of flowers demonstrate that she was well aware of how words and activities associated with gardening could function as a kind of symbolic language. She employs flower imagery and the traditions associated with it, as she does the language of cooking, visiting, and cherishing keepsakes, to say essential things about her aesthetic aims. Dickinson's sophisticated use of metaphors drawn from the domestic vocabulary of gardening offers us the richest insight into her poetic aims and processes.

Young women in Victorian society, Emily Dickinson among them, received special encouragement to perfect their skills as gardeners as another means of self-improvement, as well as a way to nurture others with gifts from their gardens and conservatories. Lydia Sigourney concurs in her *Letters to Young Ladies*, writing that

> [T]he tending of flowers has ever appeared to me a fitting care for the young and beautiful. They then dwell, as it were, among their own emblems, and many a voice of wisdom breathes on their ear from those brief blossoms, to which they apportion the dew and the sunbeam. While they eradicate the weeds that deform, or the excrescences that endanger them, is there not a perpetual monition uttered, of the work to be done in their own heart? (89)

Catharine E. Beecher's advice manual, which contains a much more extensive discussion about the benefits for young women of cultivating flowers and fruits than either Bennett's or Sigourney's, also stresses the benefits of gardening to a young woman's maturation and character, for it is a useful habit that "is greatly promotive of health and amusement" (251) because it necessitates rising early and developing habits of order and neatness. Yet in Beecher's eyes growing fruit or flowers has social benefits as well, for she tells parents: "Benevolent and social feelings could also be cultivated, by influencing children to share their fruits and flowers with friends and neighbors, as well as to distribute roots and seeds to those, who have not the means of procuring them" (251–52). Emily Dickinson followed Beecher's advice by regularly and enthusiastically sharing the fruits of her horticultural labors with others as part of her participation in the custom of gift-giving described above.

Emily Dickinson cultivated flowers, both outside in her garden and indoors in her small conservatory/greenhouse. She was also one of many young women in Victorian America who made a hobby of collecting, pressing, and then carefully mounting and labeling sample blossoms in her herbarium. Dickinson's herbarium is one of the treasures preserved in the rare book vault at Harvard's Houghton library, and a facsimile edition was produced in 2004. It contains hundreds of carefully pressed specimens, most of flora native to the Amherst area, all meticulously labeled with their botanical names. A teenaged Emily Dickinson writes enthusiastically about the plants she grew in her conservatory as well as her ongoing herbarium project in a May 7, 1845 letter to Abiah Root: "My plants look finely now. I am going to send you a little geranium leaf in this letter, which you must press for me. Have you made you an herbarium yet? I hope you will if you have not, it would be such a treasure to you; 'most all the girls are making one. If you do, perhaps I can make some additions to it from flowers growing around here" (L6).

Dickinson's extant letters reveal that she also followed Victorian custom by sending flowers with letters, a habit begun early and sustained all her life. Indeed, the crumbled remnants of dried, pressed blossoms still fall from between the pages of some of the manuscript letters housed in the Houghton Library special collections. Comments in her letter texts still point readers toward her enclosures even when the tokens themselves have long disintegrated entirely. In a postscript to one 1846 letter to Abiah Root, for example, the young letter-writer explains, "I send you a memento in the form of a pressed flower, which you must keep" (L12). Most of the year she is able to send flowers gathered from her garden. Dickinson reminds Louise Norcross of how extremely lucky she is to receive a garden blossom very late in the year 1869 when she writes that "Maggie [Margaret Maher, a household servant] 'dragged' the garden for this bud for you. You have heard of the 'last rose of summer.' This is that rose's son" (L337). When garden blossoms were unavailable, Dickinson often substituted hothouse flowers from her small conservatory. As she explains the distinction in a letter to Mrs. Edward Tuckerman: "I send you inland buttercups as out-door flowers are still at sea" (L437).

Since flowers spoke so significantly to her, Emily Dickinson often used flowers to speak for her. Comments in letters, as well as the pressed blossoms that often accompanied them, indicate that she regularly used the Victorian language of flowers as a kind of visual and verbal shorthand—a practice Judith Farr explores in *The Gardens of Emily Dickinson* while placing the poet's gardening and flower imagery in social and cultural contexts. The language of flowers, which Claire Powell describes as "essentially a Victorian cult" (14), is a language without words, for the flowers function as nonverbal texts with which Dickinson knew that her female correspondents, in particular, were likely to be familiar. In one letter, Emily Dickinson suggests to Elizabeth Holland that her ten-year-old daughter Annie, by drawing and sending a picture of a flower in a letter, could tell her all she needed to know about whether her mother was ill or well: "[I]f you are *well* – let Annie draw me a little picture of an erect flower; if you are *ill*, she can hang the flower a little on one side!" (L269). Similarly, she comments on the language of flowers in a letter to a neighbor, Mrs. Edward Tuckerman, explaining, "Vinnie asked me if I had any Message for you, and while I was picking it, you ran away" (L741).

Emily Dickinson knew that both writer and reader must be familiar with the code before these messages without words could communicate their meanings. Like her predecessor, the eighteenth-century letter-writer Lady Mary Wortley Montagu, who once observed that since there was no flower without a sentimental meaning, it was possible to send letters of passion, friendship, or civility, or even of quarrel or reproach, "without inking the fingers" (Powell 19), she understood that much could be communicated *nonverbally* if both sender and recipient understood the flowers and their contexts. Writing to Eugenia Hall, she reminds her reader of this point: "Let me thank the little Cousin in flowers, which without lips, have language" (L1002). And again, to Fanny and Loo Norcross she explains, "The career of flowers differs from ours only in inaudibleness. I feel more reverence as I grow for these mute creatures whose suspense or transport may surpass my own" (L388). Someone like "Master," on the other hand, who seems not to have understood the shorthand, would have been unable to decipher the floral message, as the draft of one of Dickinson's letters to him suggests: "You ask me what my flowers said – then they were disobedient – I gave them messages. They said what the lips in the West, say, when the sun goes down, and so says the Dawn" (L187). She refuses to explain or gloss the flowers' messages in words; this reader is consigned to being an outsider.

Dickinson's use of the language of flowers as a kind of code started early, for as Emily Fowler Ford recalls in her memoir of Emily Dickinson, her group of girlfriends at Amherst Academy assigned one another flower names. Lavinia was dubbed "the *Pond Lily*," Ford reports, and explains that Emily Dickinson named herself "the *Cow Lily*," because of the "orange lights in her hair and eyes" (Leyda I, 229). As an adult woman, Dickinson continued to rely on the language of flowers to provide those who knew her with essential insight into her character, habits, and creative processes. One well-known example of this strategy is central to T. W. Higginson's account of her entrance when he met her for the first time in her Amherst parlor. Handing him two day lilies, "she said," as he recalls, "'These are my introduction' in a soft frightened breathless childlike voice" (L342a).

Even at her own funeral, for which the poet left explicit instructions, Dickinson expected those in attendance to be able to "read" the Victorian flower code in order to understand fully the symbolic significance of the ceremony. Higginson's description of the service, for example, includes comments describing not only the deceased's "perfect peace" but also the fact that she was buried with "a little bunch of violets at the neck & one pink cypripedium; the sister Vinnie put in two heliotropes by her hand 'to take to Judge Lord'" (Leyda II, 475). Barton Levi St. Armand interprets each flower's coded meaning for contemporary readers in *Emily Dickinson and Her Culture*, his study of Dickinson's Victorian context. Violets, he reports, stand for "Faithfulness, Watchfulness, Modesty and Rural Happiness"; cypripedium, a native American wild orchid, connotes "Capricious Beauty"; heliotropes suggest "Devotion unto death and beyond" (75).

Dickinson puts the language of flowers to symbolic uses in many of her letters that ruminate on those moments in which human beings are transformed from one state to the next, from this world to the next, from life to death to eternal life. As Deborah Cadman explains, the language of flowers provided a particularly appropriate way to express faith in immortality, renewal, and rebirth because "as living things grown in women's gardens or found in certain habitats, flowers move from hand to hand, sometimes offering the possibility of another cycle of making and remaking if the original gift included bulbs, cuttings, or seeds" (8). Flowers become associated in Dickinson's mind with her ideas about immortality. In a letter to Mr. and Mrs. E. J. Loomis, for example, she writes, "My acquaintance with the Irreparable dates from the Death Bed of a young Flower to which I was deeply attached" (L945). Similarly, she uses the language of flowers to write about the death of her young friend Sophia Holland, the first death to affect her deeply: "She was too lovely for earth & she was transplanted from earth to heaven" (L11). Later, allusions to flowers are often found in Dickinson's elegiac verses. In a March 1874 letter, for example, both the poem that ends the letter and the flowers that apparently accompanied them are intended to memorialize Charles Sumner. As she explains in her consolatory letter to Mrs. Jonathan L. Jenkins: "I am picking you a flower for remembering Sumner" (L411). The letter's last three lines are printed as a poem:

> When Continents expire
> The Giants they discarded – are
> Promoted to endure –
> (L411; Fr1321)

Over and over in her later letters Emily Dickinson continues to transform the Victorian language of flowers into metaphors for the written products of her creative imagination, offering gifts of words to her readers in both poems and letters as a way to describe herself. Judith Farr concurs, noting in her study of Dickinson and her gardens that the poet often "spoke of the written word as a flower" and just as often "spoke of a flower when she meant herself" (11).

The transformation starts when, like the letters themselves, the flowers enclosed begin to substitute for her own presence, as in an 1851 letter to Emily Fowler (Ford) where Dickinson writes, "My flowers come in *my* stead, today, dear Emily. I hope you will love to see them, and whatever word of love, or welcome kindly, you would extend to *me,* 'do even so to *them.*' They are small, but *so* full of meaning, if they only mean the *half* of what I bid them" (L61).

In the 1859 poem "South Winds jostle them" (enclosed in an 1862 letter to Higginson), as in the letter passages cited above, the speaker focuses on describing the crucial moment in which possession of both the letter/poem and the bouquet of flowers it describes is transferred from writer to reader. The speaker deliberately and self-consciously presents her poem to the reader:

> South Winds jostle them –
> Bumblebees come
> Hover – Hesitate – Drink – and are gone –
> Butterflies pause – on their passage Cashmere –
> I, softly plucking,
> Present them – Here –
> (Fr98E; L261)

By waiting until the final two lines to allow the "I" to intrude directly into this impressionistic word picture of a flower garden, the poet calls attention to the act of presentation, the way in which both the flowers and the written text of the letter/poem physically connect her to distant readers. She calls attention to the transformation by simultaneously presenting both the flowers and the written words that describe them to her readers. Finally, the speaker completely collapses the distinction between natural object (the flower) and artistic construct (the written text) with the use of the single pronoun "them."

In an 1862 letter to her distant cousin Eudocia C. Flynt, Emily Dickinson conflates the flower/letter metaphor even further. She writes:

> You and I, did'nt finish talking. Have you room for the sequel, in your Vase?
> All the letters I could write,
> Were not fair as this –
> Syllables of Velvet –
> Sentences of Plush –
> Depths of Ruby, undrained –
> Hid, Lip, for Thee,
> Play it were a Humming Bird
> And sipped just Me –
>
>   Emily.
>
>   (L270; Fr380A)

The images of wealth and luxury describe not only the blossoms from her garden but also the richness and sustaining power of the poem, which becomes the letter text. Similarly, in a poem that almost certainly accompanied a gift of flowers from the poet's garden, Dickinson's speaker explicitly associates the poem's "I" with the flower, writing:

> I hide Myself within my flower,
> That fading from your Vase,
> You, unsuspecting, feel for me –
> Almost a loneliness.
>
>   (Fr80B)

MacGregor Jenkins recalled in his personal remembrances of his boyhood neighbor Emily Dickinson, "Occasionally, Emily wound a verse around the stem of a flower sent a friend, perhaps part of a larger bouquet, suggesting more than unity with it;" and he interpreted this conflation of poetic persona and blossoms as Dickinson's way of showing those who received her gifts of words that "blossom and poem emerge from her center, the fruit of profoundest culture of heart, mind, and hand" (257). In an early poem, she actually constructs a flower-self out of words:

> A sepal – petal – and a thorn
> Opon a common summer's morn –
> A flask of Dew – a Bee or two –
> A Breeze – a'caper in the trees –
> And I'm a Rose!
>
> (Fr25)

Like the rich, nonverbal language of flowers or other social codes associated with the domestic tasks of cooking, sewing, and paying social calls, the lyrical "Syllables of Velvet – / Sentences of Plush" depend upon suggestion and indirection rather than direct statement to communicate to readers.

Dickinson's skillful use of the complex, nonverbal Victorian flower code also connects her work to Romantic and Transcendentalist notions about how nature offers the writer complex, cryptic, nonverbal texts to try to interpret. As Dickinson explains in a letter to Elizabeth Holland, the robins in her yard "are writing *now*, their Desk in every passing Tree" (L890). Dickinson's comment here echoes Emerson's doctrine of correspondence, which he sets forth in Part IV of his 1836 *Nature*. Emerson's choice of the word "correspondence" draws upon the language of letter-writing, for he equates the relationship between human beings and the natural world in which they live with epistolary exchanges. According to his theory and Emily Dickinson's practice, writing is a kind of exchange between two individuals or two realms that links separate yet interconnected worlds and minds.

The Victorian flower code thus provides the poet with a powerful metaphor for her creative imagination, a subtle and efficient way for her to refer to her identity as a literary artist and the cryptic encoding that characterizes her poetic voice and style. As Brita Lindberg-Seyersted reminds us, Dickinson offered many of her poems and letters as "artistic products" (21), thus clearly connecting her creative writing with other gifts she sent as tokens of affection. One of her most sustained explorations of the metaphor occurs in the following poem, which skillfully conflates the Victorian flower code with broader ideas about germination, creativity, artistic growth, and posthumous fame:

> This is a Blossom of the Brain –
> A small – italic Seed
> Lodged by Design or Happening
> The Spirit fructified –

Shy as the Wind of his Chambers
Swift as a Freshet's Tongue
So of the Flower of the Soul
It's process is unknown –

When it is found, a few rejoice
The Wise convey it Home
Carefully cherishing the spot
If other Flower become –

When it is lost, that Day shall be
The Funeral of God,
Opon his Breast, a closing Soul
The Flower of Our Lord –

(Fr1112)

In the opening stanza of the poem, the speaker highlights the spiritual dimension of the artistic process, language that echoes Dickinson's ideas explored earlier about the sanctity and sacredness of letter-reading and letter-writing. The opening line, "This is a Blossom of the Brain," is itself a rhetorical gesture of gift-giving; both the blossom, which Dickinson might send from her garden, and the lyrical language of the poem itself are offered to her reader as gifts and as tokens of her affection. Dickinson also uses the word "italic," a term associated with printing and handwriting, to connect the realms of nature and poetry. Stanza two continues the association between nature and language's expression of it and stresses the mysteriousness of both creating a poem and growing a flower from a seed or bulb to a beautiful blossom. In both instances the speaker is in awe, for "[i]t's process is unknown." The final two stanzas of the poem comment on how few people who receive the poet's "Blossom[s] of the Brain" will recognize their value, perhaps an oblique comment on Dickinson's ideas about how few her readers were during her lifetime and a gesture toward her hope for posthumous fame. Clearly the speaker considers her legacy of language to be her best hope for immortality. The prospect of being ignored or unappreciated is equated in the final stanza with "[t]he Funeral of God."

Later in her life, Emily Dickinson most often sent bulbs with letters to friends and relatives instead of cut flowers. As she explains to Joseph Chickering in a July 1885 letter: "In childhood I never sowed a seed unless it was perennial – and that is why my Garden lasts" (L989). Unlike cut flowers, perennials could renew themselves, grow, and bloom again the following spring because the bulbs, only temporarily dormant, had the potential to live again, even long after the person who planted them had perished. Similarly, written words could ensure a kind of immortality for the person who wrote them once they reached readers' hands and hearts. Dickinson offers her blooms, the "Result" of her creative efforts in the form of both letters and lyrics, and reminds her readers that these "Blossom[s] of the Brain," require careful cultivation on the part of both the one who wrote them and those who receive them if they are to reach fruition. By sending letters and poems to distant readers through the mail, she hopes to ensure a kind of immortality through her words.

The images in a poem like "This is a Blossom – of the Brain" connect the natural world and the poet's role as creator of letters and lyrics with the sacred and the spiritual. Over and over in her letters Emily Dickinson describes the act of letter-writing as a private, sacred activity best done at her small writing desk upstairs, away from others in the peaceful sanctuary of her bedroom and most often long after the rest of the household is fast asleep. Jeanne Holland rightly recognizes the sacred, ritualistic nature of Dickinson's attitude toward her correspondence in her "Scraps, Stamps, and Cutouts: Emily Dickinson's Domestic Technologies of Publication." She writes: "Dickinson's sacred ritual was the circuit of letter-writing, poetry-making, and reading, which, for her, constituted one activity. . . . She resisted the inflexibility of print through the ritualized methods she used to exchange her poems with a select body of readers" (*Cultural Artifacts* 136). The poet's introductory comment in a letter to Elizabeth Holland is typical, for here Dickinson sets the scene and describes the circumstances surrounding her letter's composition: "I have stolen away from company to write a note to you; and to say that I love you still" (L179). Communion with a beloved, physically distant friend requires solitude and solicitude.

Reading letters received from others is, for this writer, an equally private and sacred activity, certainly not an experience willingly shared with others despite the Victorian custom of reading letters aloud to friends and family members. In her personal letters to family and friends Dickinson insists that her words are intended only for their designated recipient, that "rare Ear, / Not too dull" (Fr945). Even in her earliest letters to her brother Austin and her school friends the young correspondent repeatedly reminds her readers not to share the letters they have received from her with others. She considers the relationship between writer and reader to be a sacred trust. Nor should those who write to her direct their epistles to more than one reader. In an 1866 letter to Elizabeth Holland, she chastises this friend for having sent a letter addressed jointly to her and her sister Lavinia, icily noting: "A mutual plum is not a plum . . . . Send no union letters" (L321).

Dickinson's rules for reading the correspondence she receives from others are equally stringent; she insists on solitude in which to savor a letter from a friend. The poem below, written from the perspective of the letter recipient, describes the proper method:

> The Way I read a Letter's – this –
> 'Tis first – I lock the Door –
> And push it with my fingers – next –
> For transport it be sure –
>
> And then I go the furthest off
> To counteract a knock –
> Then draw my little Letter forth
> And slowly pick the lock –
>
> Then – glancing narrow, at the Wall
> And narrow at the floor
> For firm Conviction of a Mouse
> Not exorcised before –
>
> Peruse how infinite I am
> To no one that You – know –
> And sigh for lack of Heaven – but not
> The Heaven God bestow –
>
> (Fr700)

The speaker writes of letter-reading as something akin to a religious experience—a cherished activity that transports the reader out of her small room and gives her an experience she describes in the last stanza as a kind of "heaven on earth." Those who would read over her shoulder (invade her privacy) are even less welcome than a mouse would be in this speaker's private chamber. Anyone not the sole designated recipient is characterized as an eavesdropper who, by reading or "overhearing" an intimate epistolary conversation, violates all rules of propriety by "picking the lock" of a letter.

In a prose fragment written on a fragment of an envelope, Dickinson once again warns against violating the privacy of personal correspondence by using the same metaphor of illegal breaking and entering. Breaking the seal of a letter not addressed to you is like breaking a confidence or invading privacy: "As there are Apartments in our own Minds that – (which) we never enter without Apology – we should respect the seals of others" (Prose Fragment 21: *Letters* III, 914). The seal on the letter's envelope, this writer insists, should provide protection, just as a lock on a door should keep unwelcome intruders out. As she reads, writes, and sends letters and poems, and receives communications back from others, these domestic-based gift exchanges take on greater and greater significance for the poet and come to represent ideas and processes much larger and much more universal than themselves. Dickinson's behavior might be described, as the feminist theologian Kathryn Allen Rabuzzi writes in *The Sacred and the Feminine: Toward a Theology of Housework*, in terms of a "performer [who] is caught up in something much larger than herself." Like the "flow" in sports, it becomes impossible to separate "performer from performance." As Emily Dickinson participates in her poetics of kinship, she effects "a transformation of the ordinary, profane world" (97).

Dickinson's sources of inspiration, then, spring primarily from the women's culture that surrounds her, which Elizabeth Phillips effectively describes as "a life of family, friends, neighbors, acquaintances, 'the help,' the quick and the dead; involvement with current events and crises at home or in the country; sermons, visits, and teas, housekeeping and caring for the sick, talk and gossip, writing notes and letters, reading everything in sight, gardening, a closeness to nature and nature's creatures, and the observance of local color and customs. Taking part in all that life, she also took it in and emerged as a poet" (211–12). The success of Emily Dickinson's poetics of exchange and kinship depends, in large part, upon her recipients' willingness to recognize that her words are gifts that, like gifts of food or flowers, deserve to be cherished as tokens of the writer's affection. Like the perennials from her garden, Emily Dickinson believes that her letters and poems, her "Blossom[s] of the Brain," will bloom as long as there are readers to receive them, listeners with "that rare Ear / Not too dull."

KAREN DANDURAND

"Saying nothing . . . sometimes says the Most"
Dickinson's Letters to Catherine Dickinson Sweetser

The occasion that confronted Emily Dickinson as a writer of consolation letters in January 1874 was the most challenging she had ever faced. The books and magazine articles that advised letter-writers on the correct way to deal with various situations certainly did not cover this circumstance. What does one say to a woman whose husband has disappeared, with his disappearance being prominently featured as a news item in the major New York City newspapers? Among the possibilities advanced were that he had been murdered, that he had suffered amnesia following a head injury resulting from a fall a few days earlier, that he had committed suicide, or—perhaps most difficult to deal with for the letter-writer—that he had deliberately left his wife and family.[1] Dickinson chooses to articulate the inadequacy of words for the situation—or more precisely, the efficacy of choosing not to speak: "Saying nothing, My Aunt Katie, sometimes says the Most" (L408). Ironically, perhaps, in this opening sentence— the only sentence of the letter apart from the poem that follows—she adopts the position of silence, which is personified in the poem and called a "sorer Robber" than death:

> Death's Waylaying not the sharpest
> Of the Thefts of Time -
> There marauds a sorer Robber -
> Silence - is his name -

No Assault, nor any menace
Doth betoken him.
But from Life's consummate Cluster,
He supplants the Balm.

(Fr1315)

The letter quoted in its entirety above is the second of ten extant letters Dickinson wrote to Catherine Dickinson Sweetser, whom she addresses most often as "Aunt Katie." (In more than half of the letters, a formal salutation is omitted; instead the first sentence incorporates either a phrase of direct address or a third-person reference to "Aunt Katie.") The first two letters, in 1870 and 1874, are consolatory letters written on the death of Catherine's oldest child and disappearance of her husband, respectively. That no other letters survive from that decade (one dated 1876 in *Letters* is misdated and belongs instead to 1880) does not mean that no others were written; perhaps these two letters were preserved with notes of sympathy and support received on these two sad occasions. Other letters not kept in those special groupings perhaps did not survive, or have not yet come to light. Several of the later letters to Kate Sweetser also touch on consolatory themes, offering sympathy or thanking her for expressions of sympathy she has conveyed. The eight letters written between 1880 and the end of Dickinson's life in 1886 are concerned in large part with a shared love of flowers and gardening. They also include literary and biblical allusions—the former to sources that show an expectation of literary sophistication in the addressee, and the latter in ways that take the biblical texts outside orthodox usage. Like the earlier letters, they emphasize the familial relationship between them and their roles within their own immediate families. The letters evidence a depth of emotional connection and empathy, as Dickinson writes in the earliest extant letter, on the part of one "who knows how deep the Heart is and how much it holds" (L338).

These letters have previously received no sustained critical attention. In two important studies of Dickinson's letters as literary productions, one or more of the letters to Catherine Sweetser is considered, but the letters are not treated as a group. William Merrill Decker discusses the earliest extant letter from Dickinson to her aunt, the 1870 letter of condolence on the death of Henry Sweetser. Marietta Messmer comments briefly on four letters to Catherine Sweetser in her extensive analysis of Dickinson's letters, but none of them is treated in its entirety and they are not treated in relation to each other since Messmer's strategy is to look at common elements in letters to various correspondents. It is not

her purpose to look at these letters in the context of Catherine's life or her relationship with Dickinson. In his *Life of Emily Dickinson*, long the standard biography, Richard B. Sewall discusses Dickinson's only letter to Joseph A. Sweetser
but not those to Catherine. Finally, in his exhaustively researched and thoroughly documented biography, Alfred Habegger gives extensive attention to
Dickinson's letters, not only as sources of biographical information but as pieces
of writing; he includes Letters 408 and 478 to Catherine and the only extant
letter to her husband, Joseph Sweetser (L190). But while he does look at the
letters in their historical and biographical contexts, on which he offers valuable
information, the much larger scope of his project precludes an in-depth examination of this group of letters.

Catherine Sweetser's life story, as it is reflected in letters she wrote, as well as
in other Sweetser and Dickinson family papers and various records, is an important part of the context of Dickinson's letters to her. When Catherine has
been noticed by Dickinson scholars, it is usually for the extraordinary fact of
her husband Joseph's unsolved disappearance in 1874 that, as discussed above,
was the occasion for Dickinson's second condolence letter to her aunt. But
Catherine's life also was dramatic in other less public respects, and her experiences are markedly those of a woman in the patriarchal society of nineteenth-
century America. Two letters written to male relatives illustrate those experiences: in 1835, when she was twenty-one, she wrote from the Ohio frontier to
her older brother Edward, asking that he support her implicit wish to postpone
her trip east to be married to Joseph Sweetser; and in 1869 she wrote to her
husband, pleading with him to come see their infant granddaughter and visit
their daughter Mary, from whom he was estranged because he had disapproved
of her marriage to her cousin Charles Sweetser. I am not suggesting that Dickinson was privy to these letters (though, years after it was written, she may have
read the earlier one, which was among Edward Dickinson's family papers); but
in the later decades of her life, she was probably aware, at least generally, of
situations they reflected, and this awareness gives depth to the understanding
and empathy she expresses in her letters.

In the spring of 1834, Catherine went with her mother and younger sister
Elizabeth to join her father, Samuel Fowler Dickinson, in Cincinnati, Ohio,
where he had taken a position at the newly established Lane Seminary, of which
Lyman Beecher was the first president. Among Catherine's closest friends in
Ohio were Lyman Beecher's daughter Harriet, who married Calvin Stowe the
year after Catherine's departure to go back east, and son Henry Ward Beecher,

who joined his family after his 1834 graduation from Amherst College. A key-note of Catherine's letters from Ohio to her family and friends was her home-sickness for New England and especially for her home in Amherst. This is a prominent theme in her May 12, 1835 letter to her brother Edward. In the first part of that letter, she expresses great unhappiness with her life in Ohio, but she does not seem particularly eager to make the trip east to get married. She suggests pointedly to Edward that there is still time to postpone her trip—and the wedding—if he thinks that is what she should do. Then the letter breaks off. When she returns to writing it, she says she has been out picking wildflowers with Henry Beecher. She rhapsodizes about the flowers, which she wishes she could send instantly to her sister-in-law Emily Norcross Dickinson and about how beautiful it is in Ohio: "Henry Beecher & I have been this afternoon for flowers & I never saw any more beautiful. Tell Emily that I have *every spare dish* filled with them . . . I wish I could just tie up a bunch & toss them fresh over the mountains into her flower pitchers" (ms. letter, Houghton Library; qtd. in Leyda I, 28). In closing the letter, she again urges Edward to let her know immediately if he thinks she should delay her trip. After her departure, Henry writes her an impassioned letter bemoaning her absence and pledging his undying affection (Rugoff 251). That at the time he was apparently already committed to marrying Eunice Bullard—whose brother Asa Bullard was the husband of Catherine's sister Lucretia—did not seem to dampen his enthusiasm. Evidently Edward did not respond supportively to Catherine's implied wish to delay her trip. Even if, as Habegger suggests, he had disapproved of her entering into the engagement to Joseph Sweetser (45–46), perhaps he thought it best that she be safely settled in marriage with the young businessman rather than becoming involved with the more charismatic Beecher, who at that time would not have seemed destined for the worldly wealth he achieved as writer, lecturer, and pastor of a well-to-do Brooklyn congregation.

Catherine returned to Amherst in June 1835 and was married to Joseph Sweetser later that year, at the home of her sister Mary Newman in Andover, Massachusetts. In a marriage that lasted almost forty years before Joseph's disappearance, they had seven children and, after more modest circumstances in the early years, enjoyed an affluent lifestyle. In terms of worldly wealth, Joseph was very successful, eventually providing his family not only with a "beautiful residence . . . at Poughkeepsie, on the Hudson" (Leyda II, 126), but also an apartment in a fashionable New York City neighborhood. In the spring and summer of 1853, Catherine and Joseph Sweetser had the means to take an extended trip to Europe (L106; Habegger 423). However, a memorandum Catherine wrote on their twenty-third anniversary in 1858 seems at least ambivalent (Sweetser Family Papers), and the decade that followed would bring problems within the family.

Charles Sweetser, orphaned nephew of Joseph Sweetser, who was raised in the Amherst home of Joseph's brother and the Dickinsons' neighbor Luke Sweetser, was at the center of these problems, first involving his business partnership with Catherine and Joseph's son Henry and later his marriage to their daughter Mary. Letters Charles wrote to his cousin Henry and to his Uncle Joseph in April 1866 indicate that he forced Henry out of their partnership in the *Round Table*, citing the strained finances of the business as necessitating the change. Yet he continued to turn to his uncle for career and business advice, as he had since before he graduated from Amherst College in 1862, and for financial help in later enterprises (Sweetser Family Papers 990, 991, 995). Joseph Sweetser's opposition to his daughter's marriage to her cousin is understandable given Charles's repeated failures in business and his seeming inability to stay with any job or business venture for very long. But it also is reminiscent of the disapproval Joseph expressed more than thirty years earlier concerning the 1834 marriage of Emily Norcross Dickinson's sister Lavinia Norcross to her cousin Loring Norcross. Referring to what he describes as "*so near* a brother and sister made nearer by the holy rites of matrimony," Joseph says, "Certainly I do not view it in the light of a proper match" (Leyda I, 26). Although I have found no record of his views on the marriage a few years later between Timothy Dickinson (Edward and Catherine's brother) and his cousin Hannah Dickinson, it seems likely that Joseph would have disapproved even more strenuously, since Timothy and Hannah were doubly cousins: their fathers were brothers and their mothers were sisters. Despite Joseph's misgivings, Charles and Mary Sweetser were married in October 1867 at the Sweetser home in Poughkeepsie. Charles appeared to be on good terms with his uncle/father-in-law, whom he addressed as "my dear father" in a December 11, 1867 letter reporting that he and Mary had "heard Dickens twice & with real pleasure" and that they were "hoping that you and mother and Kate may be down this week to use our tickets and occupy our superb seats. . . . Mary and I are having happy, happy times – the winter flies on silver wings" (Sweetser Family Papers 997). But over the next year the relationship between Joseph and Charles became increasingly strained so that by the time Charles and Mary's daughter was born in late August 1869, Joseph was estranged from his daughter and son-in-law. Catherine, delighted with her new status of grandmother, wrote to Joseph describing their grand-daughter: "a real little beauty" whose "hair is dark & eyes deep blue – She has surveyed her Grandmother this morning with apparent satisfaction" (Sweetser Family Papers 959). Joseph evidently did not respond to his wife's urging to come to see the baby, and over the next year the estrangement between him and Charles and Mary grew. When Charles was quickly declining in health, Joseph refused to give him any further financial assistance. When Charles died of tuberculosis on January 1, 1871, in Florida, a letter from an Amherst resident to his wife suggests that his plight had become the subject of local gossip: "When Charlie lost his health and had not a cent in the world, he went to Florida, his wife wanted to go and take care of him but her father [said] . . . if she wished to go to her husband, do so, but never come back to him again, & he should help her no more. . . . She could not go to her husband, so he died . . . among strangers." The comment that follows may suggest that Joseph's actions incurred wider condemnation: "How very sad this is, and how inhuman it seems, when there is so much money in the Sweetser family" (Leyda II, 165). The family circle from which Joseph Sweetser suddenly disappeared only a few years later may not have been as happy and peaceful as one would assume based on their material circumstances.

This brief discussion of the story of Catherine Sweetser and her family brings us to the years when Dickinson's earliest surviving letters to her aunt were written, but before looking at them, there is another part of the context to examine: Dickinson's references to Catherine Sweetser in letters to other correspondents. Dickinson mentions her aunt in four letters in the late 1840s and the 1850s, and, although more than a decade separates them from the first of her extant letters to Catherine, these letters, to Austin Dickinson in 1848 and 1853, and to Joseph Sweetser and Susan Dickinson in 1858, also form an important part of the context of Dickinson's letters to her aunt. Catherine is referred to variously as "Aunt Catharine," "Aunt Kate," "Aunt Sweetser," and—in the reference that is most distant—indirectly in the phrase "Uncle Sweetser and his wife." The earliest of these four letters, written to Austin on June 25, 1848, when Dickinson was at Mt. Holyoke Female Seminary, is neutral in tone. She refers to a young woman "who has been teaching school in Brooklyn & is quite intimate in Aunt Kate's family" and reports, "She said Aunt Catharine was coming to Amherst, next week" (L25). Dickinson makes no connection between her aunt's expected visit to Amherst and the news that she herself has gotten permission to go home the same week. In the other letter to Austin and in the letter to Susan Dickinson, her tone is sarcastic or ironic, and she portrays her aunt as someone who is an outsider to their Amherst circle. The most significant of the four letters, written to Catherine's husband, Joseph Sweetser, suggests that Dickinson's relationship with her Aunt Kate had evolved to a new level of equality and intimacy. Surprisingly, this letter seems to have been written after the letter to Susan referred to above—perhaps indicating that what she says about "Aunt Sweetser" in that letter has more to do with her relationship with Susan than with her actual attitude toward her aunt.

Dickinson's comments on her aunt in the 1853 letter to Austin and the 1858 letter to Susan are used to construct a bond of intimacy between Dickinson and her correspondent that depends on other people being depicted as outsiders. In the letter to Austin, Catherine and Joseph Sweetser's children play a more direct role than do their parents. They are part of a larger group of relatives who will be staying in Amherst and whose presence, Dickinson implies, will be as unwelcome to Austin as it will be to her: "Uncle Sweetser and his wife are going to Europe in May, and Elisabeth and their children are coming to Amherst to board at Mr Newman's for the summer! Such intelligence needs no comments" (L106). Although the Sweetser cousins and Aunt Elizabeth have not yet arrived and so are not mentioned there, a comment on the Newmans in a letter to Austin dated April 21, 1853, is consistent with Dickinson's treatment of all of them in Letter 106: "The Newmans seem very pleasant, but they are not *like us*. What makes a few of us so different from others? It's a question I often ask myself" (L118). This idea of the younger Dickinsons as people who are different from others and share a special bond with each other is extended to Susan Gilbert even before she becomes a member of the Dickinson family. In a letter to Austin earlier the same month, Dickinson includes Sue along with Vinnie in a group where she and Austin are central: "I cant help wondering sometimes if you think of us as often as we all do of you. . . . I think about this a great deal . . .tho' I dont talk with Vinnie or Sue, about it. . . . I think we miss each other more every day that we grow older, for we're all unlike most everyone, and are therefore more dependent on each other for delight" (L114).

In the letter to Susan, written on a Sunday evening in fall 1858, when Susan is visiting her sister Martha Smith in Geneva, New York, Dickinson gives a humorous account of happenings in Amherst. For example, commenting on the status of various family members, she writes, "Carlo – [is] comfortable – terrifying man and beast, with renewed activity – is cuffed some – hurled from piazza frequently, when Miss Lavinia's 'flies' need her action elsewhere. // She has the 'patent action,' I have long felt!" (L194; ; OMC29). She then mentions the morning and afternoon sermons, at the latter of which her aunt Catherine Sweetser was present but her aunt Lucretia Bullard was not: "Aunt Sweetser's dress would have startled Sheba. Aunt Bullard was not out – presume she stayed at home for 'self-examination.' Accompanied by father, they visited the grave yard, after services. These are stirring scenes!" "Aunt Sweetser," like "Aunt Bullard," is the object of Dickinson's wit. The use of their last names distances her aunts, making the relationship less intimate and placing them in the older generation. In saying that "Aunt Sweetser's dress would have startled Sheba," Dickinson suggests that her aunt was more dazzlingly arrayed than "King Solomon in all his glory." According to the biblical account, Sheba was greatly impressed by the splendor of Solomon's court and particularly noted that his subordinates and even his servants were richly dressed. Sheba herself is portrayed as a rich and powerful woman who crossed the desert with a large retinue of attendants and a long caravan of camels loaded with gold and spices to visit King Solomon's court. Her wealth and power, reflected in her clothing and ornaments, are emphasized in the popularization of the image of the Queen of Sheba. In saying that her aunt's "dress would have startled" the legendary queen, Dickinson suggests that it certainly shocked people in Amherst. Juxtaposing her comment on Catherine Sweetser's dress with her report on Lucretia Bullard's "self-examination," Dickinson sets up a contrast between the two aunts: Lucretia, the staid Boston matron examining her soul in the tradition of the evangelical Protestantism represented by her husband, the Reverend Asa Bullard, secretary of the Massachusetts Sabbath School Society; Catherine, wife of a prosperous merchant, her taste in dress reflecting fashionable and worldly New York society, and perhaps her trip to Europe five years earlier. "Aunt Sweetser" hardly seems the "Dear Aunt Katie" to whom Dickinson writes or the "Aunt Kate" she writes about in her letter to Joseph Sweetser.

Although she refers in Letter 190 to an earlier letter she wrote him, this is the only extant letter from Dickinson to the man Alfred Habegger calls "her most literary uncle" (352). It seems surprising that she is writing to Joseph Sweetser rather than to her aunt; that she sends her love, by way of Joseph, to a group that presumably includes her Aunt Kate—"Please give my warmest love to my aunts and cousins"—may indicate that Kate and her children are visiting another of Dickinson's aunts. Perhaps they are visiting with the Bullards in Boston before they come to Amherst; Dickinson seems to indicate, in the sentence before the one just quoted, that she expects a visit from them soon: "It seems very pleasant that other ones will soon be near." The direct reference to Kate comes toward the end of the letter: "We formed Aunt Kate's acquaintance, for the first – last spring, and had a few sweet hours, as do new found *girls*." Of course Dickinson knew her Aunt Kate long before "last spring"; after all, Dickinson and the adolescent Catherine Dickinson lived in the same house for the first few years of the young Emily's life. But in saying, "We formed Aunt Kate's acquaintance," she describes a new relationship between them, comparing their "few sweet hours" to time shared by "new found *girls*." She puts them on an equal basis and positions them as if they are in the same generation, though maintaining the family relationship of aunt and niece. Dickinson will retain this relational paradigm—aunt and niece who are also confidential friends—in her letters to her aunt, whom she most often addresses or refers to as "Aunt Katie," perhaps deliberately combining the respectful title "Aunt" with the more girlish form of Catherine, or Kate, by using the "ie" ending.

The earliest extant letter from Dickinson to her Aunt Kate, as noted earlier, was written on the occasion of the death at age thirty-three of Henry Sweetser, the oldest child of Joseph and Catherine, on February 17, 1870—the day that was also Kate's fifty-sixth birthday. (There is no reference to this fact in the letter and no indication that Dickinson was aware of it, although she may have realized the added pathos of Kate's son dying on her birthday.) Dickinson begins with an explanation of why she did not write immediately: "When I am most grieved I had rather no one would speak to me, so I stayed from you" (L338). As she will in the letter four years later, she asserts the power of "saying nothing": "But when I am most sorry, I can say nothing so I will only kiss you and go far away." Here "saying nothing" is only a temporary position to avoid disturbing her aunt before she is ready to hear words of consolation: "I thought by today, perhaps you would like to see me, if I came quite soft and brought no noisy words."

To accomplish the purpose of this letter, that is, to offer consolation to her aunt, any doubts Dickinson feels about immortality—what she had called "the Flood subject" in an 1866 letter to Thomas Wentworth Higginson (L319)—must be put aside. She takes a stance of unquestioning faith in the promise of an eternal life and a reunion in Heaven. By a series of assertions of absolute certainty, she offers comfort to the grieving mother: "I know we shall certainly see what we loved the most. It is sweet to think they are safe by Death and that that is all we have to pass to obtain their face. // There are no Dead, dear Katie, the Grave is but our moan for them." The poem that is incorporated in the letter at this point (a quatrain unique to her correspondence with this aunt, appearing nowhere else in her manuscripts) dwells on the moment of "Our final interview"—presumably in Kate's case the last time she saw her son before he died "in his sleep." The experience Dickinson imagines her aunt has gone through is made universal by the use of first person plural pronouns:

> Were it to be the last
> How infinite would be
> What we did not suspect was marked
> Our final interview.
>
> (Fr1165)

The only instance when there is the hint of questioning is in the final paragraph that follows the poem, where she writes, "Henry had been a prisoner. How he had coveted Liberty *probably* his Redeemer knew" (emphasis added); here, rather than doubt about Henry's immortal state, she allows for a possible lack of total omniscience on the part of deity—but asserts it is more likely that "his Redeemer knew." William Merrill Decker notes that "Dickinson's condolence draws upon two commonplaces of such messages: that we are sure to see the deceased in an afterlife, and that death, in this instance, has come as a release from suffering" (167). In regard to the use of commonplaces—and Decker certainly acknowledges that she goes well beyond them—this letter contrasts markedly with the 1874 letter, discussed earlier, for in that circumstance there were no commonplaces to draw on. Whereas here expressions of certainty about immortality can be emphasized as an appropriate way of consoling, in the later situation there is no certainty.

Because of the occasions that prompted them and so their specific purposes, the two letters written in the 1870s stand apart from the eight that Dickinson wrote to her Aunt Kate in the 1880s. These later letters, while sharing some characteristics with the two earlier ones, are more closely connected with each other in subject matter and themes. A topic that is at least touched upon in all but one of the letters—and a central focus of some of them—is a shared love of flowers. Dickinson comments on her own garden and asks about Kate's, sometimes in metaphorical terms but with the sense she is still referring not to figurative but to actual gardens that are invested with deep significance. In a late letter, where she thanks her aunt for sending flowers that were "still fragrant" when they reached her, one is reminded of the wish Catherine expressed in her 1835 letter that she could send flowers from the Ohio meadow to her sister-in-law Emily.

Though not so frequent as references to flowers, as noted earlier, several letters also include biblical and literary allusions and quotations. It seems clear that Dickinson expects her aunt to recognize these references and understand their import. As noted above in the discussion of her letter to Joseph Sweetser, Dickinson formulates the relationship between Kate and herself in the paradigm of young women who are intimate friends. At the same time she emphasizes their familial relationships, not only between the two of them, as aunt and niece, but as they are part of the larger Dickinson family and each is part of her own immediate family. In contrast to the first two letters, where no other members of either family are mentioned (except Henry, in the first), the 1880s letters often refer to other members of her own and her aunt's households.

Letter 478, though written four years later than the date Johnson and Ward had assigned, remains apparently the earliest of the eight letters to Kate in the 1880s. As Habegger has also pointed out, it belongs not in 1876 but in 1880 (587–88, 734). (The manuscript of this letter is missing, and this no doubt contributed to the misdating; as will be seen, the identification of William Adams as "Dr. A---" facilitates accurate dating.) Dickinson writes this letter following Kate's August 1880 visit to Amherst and opens by referring to her inability to see Kate before she departed because others were there saying good-bye, describing it as a situation beyond her control: "When I found it beyond my power to see you, I designed to write you, immediately." She offers an explanation why she did not write sooner, putting the delay in a positive light. First, Judge Lord arrived for a visit and, she says, he "was my father's closest friend," and so spending time with him is not just a personal preference but a matter of filial duty. The second reason she gives for her delay is similar to that in her 1870 letter where she offered sympathy on Kate's loss of her son. Here she writes, "Seeing [in a newspaper] the death of your loved Dr. A---, I felt you might like to be alone." As Habegger notes, "Dr. A---" is the Reverend Doctor William Adams (587); Adams was pastor of the Madison Square Presbyterian Church from its founding in 1854 until he resigned in 1874 to become president of the Union Theological Seminary ("Rev. Dr. Adams Dead"). An obituary says he was "one of the best known Presbyterian clergymen, not only in this country, but in the world." The description of his preaching in that death notice suggests that his sermons would have appealed to Dickinson, though there is no evidence she ever heard him: "His sermons were strong, and their language was so simple that they struck home to every hearer who could understand and appreciate plain Anglo-Saxon. . . . He never used superfluous words" ("Rev. Dr. Adams

Dead"). In addition to being pastor of the church Joseph and Catherine Sweetser attended, he was also their personal friend. It is interesting that the consolatory quotation Dickinson offers on the death of this clergyman comes not from the Bible but from Shakespeare: "Beloved Shakespeare says, 'He that is robbed and smiles, steals something from the thief.'"

The last paragraph of this letter is perhaps the most interesting, not only in what it reveals about Dickinson's social practices but also for the language she chooses, as well as for her reference to the long-unidentified "Uncle Underwood." When it became clear that she would not be able to visit with her aunt before Kate's departure, she sent in by Maggie a glass of sherry and a flower, and also perhaps some delicacy to eat. (One is reminded of Dickinson's comment in another letter to Kate when her younger sister, Elizabeth Dickinson Currier, is visiting in Amherst: "Aunt Libbie just looked in on us, and I go to make her a Dish of Homestead Charlotte Russe" [L897]). Kate's question conveyed by Margaret Maher—"Maggie said you asked should you 'eat the flower'"—seems to refer to a flower set on a tray or plate as garnish. In reply now, Dickinson refers her aunt to "the bees" as "the only authority on Etruscan matters." What Dickinson means by her reference to "Etruscan matters" remains obscure, as does the assertion that "the bees" are "the only authority" on them. Interest in this ancient civilization among historians and archaeologists had grown in the second half of the nineteenth century and awareness of it had spread to the popular culture. Perhaps there was a specific reference to the Etruscans with which they were both familiar.[2] In support of her apology that, according to Vinnie, "the sherry I sent you was brandy," she evokes a memory from the past that combines references to flowers and the natural world with the literary world of ideas and words: "I did not intend to be so base to the aunt who showed me the first mignonette, and listened with me to the great wheel, from Uncle Underwood's 'study,' and won me in 'divers other ways' too lovely to mention." The man she refers to as "Uncle Underwood" is Kingsley Underwood, her great-uncle and Kate's uncle by his marriage to Clarissa Gunn, sister of Emily Dickinson's paternal grandmother. After she returned from Ohio following her husband's death in April 1838, Lucretia Gunn Dickinson spent extended periods of time, including the last months of her life, at the Underwood home in Enfield, Massachusetts, where she died in May 1840. By the time Lucretia came to stay in their home, Kingsley Underwood, ten years older than his wife, was in his late sixties but still vigorously engaged with national political issues, though he lived in a quiet country town. His poems, which ranged from personal topics to fiery abolition themes, appeared regularly at this time in the *Hampshire Gazette*, a weekly newspaper published in Northampton. Habegger notes that Emily and Lavinia visited with their grandmother at the Underwood home for a few days in September 1838 while their parents went to Boston (107). He suggests that the memory of being with Kate in "Uncle Underwood's 'study'" may refer to a May 1840 visit, when presumably they were in Enfield for Lucretia's funeral (although there is evidently no record they were there then). It is impossible to know when the experience recalled in the letter took place, but there might well have been more than one occasion when Dickinson and Kate visited the Underwoods together during one of Kate's many stays in Amherst. One possibility is late June or early July 1848, when they were both to be in Amherst, as noted in Dickinson's letter to Austin quoted above; both Clarissa and Kingsley Underwood were still living at that time—she in her late sixties, he in his late seventies.

Dickinson's reference to "Uncle Underwood's 'study'" evokes both the literary and the natural worlds in conjunction. By putting the reference to his "study" in quotation marks, Dickinson indicates that it does not designate a conventional study, a room furnished with a desk, tables, bookshelves, and, of course, books. The designation "study" does suggest it was a place where he went to read, think, and develop ideas for poems, perhaps jotting down notes and drafts on scraps of paper. The "study" where Dickinson and her Aunt Kate "listened . . . to the great wheel" was probably not a room in the Underwood home but some alternative space—perhaps out in the natural world near the Swift River and within sound of the millwheel—a space referred to as his "study" by Kingsley himself or by others. Perhaps it was a spot similar to the lake Thomas Wentworth Higginson wrote about in his essay "My Outdoor Study." Dickinson was familiar with Higginson's essay, which appeared in the *Atlantic Monthly* in September 1861 and was reprinted in his *Outdoor Papers*; she had placed that book strategically on a table in the parlor before his August 1870 visit. It is possible the term "study" was not used by Kingsley Underwood or others in his time but that it is applied retrospectively in this letter by Dickinson to evoke the combined literary and natural setting she shared with Kate at that moment in the past.

What appears to be the next letter (L668) followed the one above more closely than any other two letters in the series, if Johnson and Ward's dating is correct. In some respects, it is fairly conventional in its topics—for example, expressing concern about the health of her correspondent ("I hope you were well since we knew of you") and reporting on the health and general state of her own family ("Mother has had a weary Cold, and suffers much from Neuralgia"; "Vinnie knows no shadow ... and courageous Maggie not yet caught in the snares of Patrick"). She closes the letter with best wishes for her correspondent's family ("I hope your Few are safe") and in the final sentences expresses a wish for a response "when you feel inclined." But while the general purpose of these statements may follow convention, her expression clearly goes beyond the conventional.

Dickinson's construction of the letter is more complex than a description in terms of conventional letter-writing models suggests. She begins by setting up a subtle parallel as a means to assert a bond of sympathy between her aunt and herself: "Aunt Katie and the Sultans have left the Garden now, and parting with my own, recalls their sweet companionship." While "Aunt Katie" might be taken to identify some flower that like the "Sultans" is gone from Dickinson's "Garden," I think that is not the case. Rather she is drawing attention to the similarity in their situations: gone from Kate's garden are Kate's "Sultans" and Aunt Katie herself, just as Dickinson and her flowers (referred to in the phrase "parting with my own") are gone from Dickinson's "Garden." The "sweet companionship" she "recalls" is that between Katie and her sultans, brought to mind by her own loss of the flowers with which she had a similar relationship. The trope of flowers as companions, as sentient beings with human qualities, is developed further in the sentences that follow and reappears toward the end of the letter, in which straightforward statements not involving flowers are interspersed, including those quoted above. The flowers in Dickinson's garden also are personified. She reports that her own sultans "were not I think as exuberant as in other Years" and conjectures it may have been because "the Pelham Water shocked their stately tastes." She says her flowers, or specifically her sultans, were "cherished avariciously, because less numerous," bringing to mind her statement in a letter to Samuel Bowles in the late 1850s: "My friends are my 'estate.' Forgive me then the avarice to hoard them!" (L193). She even gives the gardens, both her own and Kate's, the ability to be "willing to die": "I trust your Garden was willing to die – I do not think that mine was – it perished with beautiful reluctance, like an evening star." One is reminded of the earnest "desire" she expressed to Edward Everett Hale to know whether Ben Newton "was willing to die" (L153), and her more recent assertion in a letter to Higginson that "Mr Bowles was not willing to die" (L553).

After this, the letter shifts to the seemingly conventional concerns noted above, but putting them within the context she has created gives them an added depth of feeling. Straightforward statements are juxtaposed with more emotionally weighted ones: "I hope you were well" with "There are Sweets of Pathos, when Sweets of Mirth have passed away"; "Mother has had a weary Cold" with "The 'Ravens' must 'cry,' to be ministered to – she need only sigh." Two references to Kate's recent visit, presumably the visit referred to in the previous letter, function to connect her even more closely to the place and the people about whom Dickinson is talking. Her mother, Dickinson writes, "I trust is no feebler than *when you were here*" and, after her comments on Vinnie and Maggie, she concludes, "Perhaps it is quite the *Home* it was *when you last beheld it*" (emphasis added). "Home" in reference to the Dickinson Homestead would have had great resonance for Kate. She was the first of her generation to be born there (the year after the house was completed), as Dickinson was the first of her generation (since Austin was born before Edward and Emily Norcross Dickinson took up residence in their half of the Homestead). When Kate visits Dickinson and her family in Amherst, she is returning to her own first home; until she left it when she was twenty years old, it was the only home she had ever known. Dickinson brings the letter to a close by evoking the flower trope of its opening, joining a reference to Kate's family and a reference to Kate's flowers: "I hope your Few are safe, and your Flowers encouraging." The final sentences, as noted above, hint her desire for a reply and link Kate to her sultans to the degree that in the last short sentence Kate herself seems to be a flower: "News of your Sultans and yourself, would be equally lovely, when you feel inclined. Blossoms have their Leisures."

Letter 746 begins by enthusiastically acknowledging a letter from Kate; again, the sultans are prominently featured. Dickinson sets herself up as the representative of the "Household," expressing their unanimous opinion "that Aunt Katie never wrote so lovely a Letter." The "Household" is whimsically delineated not in terms of its human members—mother, Vinnie, and Maggie, in addition to Dickinson herself—but as consisting of "the Geraniums down to the Pussies." Whereas in some of the other letters she gives specific excuses for not writing sooner, here she asserts that the intention that Aunt Katie's letter "should be immediately replied to by each member of the Family" was not carried out because "unforeseen malignities prevented," without explaining what they were. She then turns to the "Sultans," a subject featured in Letter 668, which, if the dating of both is correct, was written more than a year earlier. In the previous letter, references were to Kate's and to Dickinson's sultans; here, Vinnie is brought into their company: "Vinnie lost her Sultans too – it was 'Guiteau' Year – Presidents and Sultans were alike doomed." The reference to Charles Guiteau's assassination of President Garfield is strikingly different in tone from two references the year before in letters to Elizabeth Holland and Louise and Frances Norcross (L721,

L727). As flowers and gardens in the previous letter were endowed with human qualities, here she puts the flower on a level with the president, setting up the play on words in the last sentence of the letter: "With love for your Health, and the promise of Sultans and Viziers too, if the Monarchs come"; "Monarchs" is both a collective term for "Sultans and Viziers" and a reference to Monarch butterflies.

Referring to what Kate evidently had humorously described in her letter, Dickinson writes, "We were much amused at your 'Gardener.' // You portrayed his Treason so wittily it was more effective than Loyalty. He knew that Flowers had no Tongues." That she puts "Gardener" in quotation marks suggests that, like "Study" in Letter 478, the word is not to be taken in a conventional or literal sense. The tone of the reference to his "Treason" is similar to that in two letters that refer to her nephew Gilbert as a "beguiling Villain" (L664; OMC223; L665), both assigned by Johnson and Ward to 1880. The "Gardener" is, I suggest, a child, perhaps a grandson of Kate, and his "Treason"—like Gilbert's villainy—some act in defiance of adult authority that Kate has described humorously in her letter.

As the letter draws to a close, Dickinson, in keeping with letter-writing conventions, does express her concern for her correspondent's well-being and solicits concern in return, using plural rather than singular first-person pronouns so as to include "each member of the Family," and Vinnie specifically: "We trust you are safe this Norwegian Weather, and 'desire your Prayers' for another Snow Storm, just over our Heads." The letter ends with the sentence quoted above.

Letter 828 is one of the shortest of the letters written to Kate in the 1880s and the only one that makes no reference to flowers. Dickinson responds to a request from her aunt to have the Bible that had belonged to Kate's father, Samuel Fowler Dickinson, and had been in the possession of Edward Dickinson. The brevity of the letter is explained by Dickinson's closing, "in *haste* and fondness" (emphasis added). It differs from the other letters in that it is primarily concerned with fulfilling a specific request; the nature of that transaction and the parties to it suggest a deviation from conventional gender roles that seems surprising for the Dickinson family. Dickinson shows no hesitation in granting Kate's request but explains that there must be a slight delay: "I have found and give it in love, but reluctant to entrust anything so sacred to my Father as my Grandfather's Bible to a public Messenger, will wait till Mr. Howard comes, whom Mrs. Nellie tells us is due this week" (referring to John Howard Sweetser, son of Dickinson's late neighbors Luke and Abby Sweetser, who had been in business with his uncle Joseph in New York). Her opening words seem to indicate that Dickinson is the sole person deciding about the disposition of the Bible, and that disposition does not follow what would seem an expected and conventional line of inheritance. Dickinson's agreeing to give the Bible to her aunt bypasses the expected patriarchal control of family heirlooms, especially striking in that Dickinson represents the Bible as until then following a male line of descent, from her grandfather to his oldest son, her father. Apparently Kate's request for the Bible was directed to Dickinson, not to Austin, who, in addition to being the oldest child and only son, was the administrator of his father's estate. Turning from the transaction that is its main business, the letter acknowledges something Kate has said about Edward and Emily Norcross Dickinson, presumably in her letter asking for the Bible: "Thank you for loving my Father and Mother – I hope they are with the Source of Love," here expressing not the certainty about immortality of the 1870 letter but "hope." Noting her concern for her aunt's well-being—"You did not tell me of your Health – I trust because confirmed," the letter closes conveying "Vinnie's affection" and her own "fondness."

Letter 892 follows Judge Lord's death on March 13, 1884, and a letter from Kate on that occasion. In addition to Lord's death, Dickinson's letter focuses on an event in honor of Kate about which she has written, which Dickinson acknowledges by saying, "Thank you for telling us of your triumphs"—perhaps a celebration marking her seventieth birthday, which was February 17, 1884. Although I have found no evidence of such an event, it seems likely there was at least a family party, if not a larger one. In this letter, flowers per se are not a focus, though "Aunt Katie's Rose" of the opening phrase represents Kate's life, which has "had many Thorns"; as the sentence goes on, the Rose becomes representative of Kate herself: "it is still a Rose, and has borne the extremities of a Flower with etherial patience, and every deference to her is so sweetly deserved, we do not call it courtesy, but only recognition." This seems to refer to specific recognition that Kate has been given. The next sentence suggests a looking back over Kate's long life: "It is sweeter that Noon should be fair than that Morning should, because Noon is the latest, and yet your Morning had it's Dew, you would not exchange." Dickinson follows the reference above to Kate's "triumphs" by quoting from Milton's "To the Lord General Cromwell": "Peace hath her Victories, no less than War." This seemingly obscure quotation evidences the level of literary sophistication she assumes from Kate.

As mentioned above, the other primary focus of this letter is the death of Judge Lord. Dickinson thanks her aunt "for speaking so tenderly of our latest Lost." Of course, what Kate had written we cannot know, but it is worth noting that she had probably known Otis Lord when he was a young man, especially if her brother Edward's friendship with Lord had its roots in that time. Kate was only two years younger than Lord, and she and her family were still living in Amherst when he was a student at Amherst College from 1828 to 1832. That Dickinson shares with Kate some of what Lord wrote in his last letter to her—significantly choosing his report on early spring flowers—shows the closeness she feels to her aunt and perhaps acknowledges her aunt's own connection with Lord. By sharing something as valuable to herself as one of Lord's last statements, she also acknowledges and validates the sympathy that Kate has given. Then, bridging what would seem a substantial gap between the two topics of her letter—Kate's "sweetly deserved" "triumphs" and the death of Lord—she writes, "In this place of shafts, I hope you may remain unharmed." Kate is, after all, nearly as old as was Lord, a fact emphasized by the milestone birthday she has recently passed. Dickinson follows this, in closing the letter, by referring to Kate's children and her relationship with them (which would seem in keeping with the conjecture that they have recently honored her on her seventieth birthday): "I congratulate you upon your Children, and themselves, upon you. // To have had such Daughters is sanctity – to have had such a Mother, divine." She then draws a contrast with her own situation: "To *still* have her, but tears forbid me. My own is in the Grave."

The next two letters, 897 and 952, are related in that they both are devoted in large part to thanking Kate for a gift of lilies. The editors' notes to these letters suggest that the first, which they date spring 1884, acknowledges bulbs, and that the second, which they date November 1884, acknowledges lilies (presumably from those bulbs), which Dickinson says in the first letter that she anticipates in fall: "The hope to meet them in person, in Autumn, thro' your loving Hand, is a fragrant Future." We cannot know whether bulbs were received and acknowledged in the first letter, as Johnson and Ward surmise. In any event, it is important to note that Dickinson specifically acknowledges her aunt's *words* rather than an enclosure: "*Your account of the Lilies* was so fresh I could almost pick them" (emphasis added). Like the opening of Letter 746, this is praise of Kate's skill as a letter-writer. As in almost all of these letters, Dickinson expresses wishes for Kate's health and well-being: "I hope you are well as you deserve, which is a blest circumference"—the only time the word "circumference," which carries great import for Dickinson, appears in these letters.

Letter 952 begins by acknowledging that "[t]he beloved lilies have come." Whether they have come because bulbs sent in spring have reached fruition or because Kate has sent the flowers is open to question, but the answer is not essential to reading the letter. The lilies seem a memorial for Emily Norcross Dickinson, though whether Kate's timing was deliberately for this purpose cannot be known. The sentence quoted in part above continues, "and my heart is so high it overflows, as this was mother's week, Easter in November," referring to the anniversary of her mother's death on November 14, 1882. She memorializes not only her mother but also her father and nephew Gilbert: "Father rose in June, and a little more than a year since, those fair words were fulfilled, 'and a little child shall lead them' – but boundlessness forbids me." At this point the letter breaks off with an ellipsis before turning to other subjects. R. W. Franklin indicates that in Mabel Loomis Todd's transcript of this letter, the manuscript of which is missing, a poem follows:

> Though the great waters sleep
> That they are still the deep
> We cannot doubt.
> No vacillating God
> Ignited this abode
> To put it out.
>
> (Fr1641E)

Unlike the poems in her letters to Kate in 1870 and 1874, which exist in no other version, Franklin notes there were seven manuscript copies of this poem, all written in the years 1884 to 1886. The certitude of this poem is offered to reassure herself and Kate. She then turns to Kate's health, which has evidently been precarious: "It is very wrong that you were ill. . . . It is sweet you are better." That her illness was serious is suggested by the sentence that follows: "More beating that brave heart has to do before the emerald recess." She extends her concern and love to the rest of Kate's family—and to her flowers, which again are personified: "With sorrow for Emma's accident, and love for all who cherish you, including the roses, your velvet allies."

Letter 991, which Johnson and Ward date conjecturally "1885?" and place as Dickinson's last letter to Kate Sweetser—although it cannot be so dated with certainty—is a fitting conclusion to the series of letters, with its emphasis on flowers and its benediction and blessing. Again, Dickinson is thanking Kate for flowers she has sent that were "still vivid and fragrant when they reached my fingers." Without a formal salutation, it begins, "Aunt Katie never forgets to be lovely, and the sweet clusters of yesterday only perpetuate a heart warm so many years." The occasion for the flowers is not specified. Perhaps Kate sent them because she had learned that Dickinson was ill, as suggested here by her saying, "were the wrist that bears them bolder, it would give reply." Habegger indicates that Dickinson suffered a prolonged illness that lasted from October 1885 into the following year (624–25). However, her reference in the second sentence to Kate's similar remembrances over the years may suggest that, like the lilies of Letter 952, these flowers were sent to commemorate some event—perhaps Dickinson's fifty-fifth birthday on December 10, 1885. (If her phrase "a memory that adheres so long" refers to a particular anniversary that Kate has marked by sending flowers, Emily Norcross Dickinson's death would seem too recent to be a likely reference.) Dickinson writes, "Tropic, indeed, a memory that adheres *so long*" (emphasis added). Having explained the brevity of her letter due to physical weakness, she gives, in lieu of the "reply" for which her wrist is too weak, a tripartite benediction: "a kiss and a gratitude, and every grace of being, from your loving niece."

Then using a modified biblical quote, she commends Kate to angelic protection: "'I give his angels charge!'" As Messmer points out, Dickinson uses the same passage in three other letters, each time with a change from the original and at least slight variations from the other instances; she notes that "each time it is she herself who takes charge of 'God's' angels." This is, Messmer suggests, an instance of Dickinson "appropriating the voice of divine authority" (164). In this final message, perhaps the most significant variation from the three other letters in which she uses the same biblical quote comes in the correction that follows it: "Should I say his flowers, for qualified as saints they are." So these letters end where so many of them were focused, with the flowers that she here leaves as guardian angels watching over her Aunt Katie. In the closing sentence she brings Vinnie into the circle as she draws attention back to the flowers Kate has sent: "Vinnie's and my transport."

NOTES

1. Information on this unsolved disappearance appears in Alfred Habegger's *My Wars* (561) and in Jay Leyda's *Years and Hours* (II, 216) as well as contemporary newspaper articles, "A Missing Merchant" and "Disappearance of Mr. Sweetzer." As the news heading indicates, even the family's surname appears variously in print. The same is true for Aunt Kate's first name, which Richard Sewall and R. W. Franklin spell "Catherine" and Habegger, Thomas Johnson, and Leyda spell "Catharine."

2. See Judith Farr's essay in this collection.

JANE DONAHUE EBERWEIN

Messages of Condolence

"more Peace than Pang"

"What shall I tell these darlings," Emily Dickinson wondered at the start of her January 1863 letter to Louisa and Frances Norcross shortly after their father's death left her cousins orphaned at ages 20 and 15 (L278). This had to be an earnest question, not just a rhetorical one; though her foregrounding the challenge she faced in conveying solace on paper to loved ones so overwhelmingly bereaved suggests that she approached this delicate task with artistic sensibility. Within Dickinson's social culture, to write a prompt letter of condolence was obligatory. Nineteenth-century guides to etiquette left no doubt that "all who can should write to a bereaved person" (Sherwood 204) and that such letters should be "sent immediately" (Tomes 269). When one shared in the grief, the work of condolence proved even harder: "If the affliction which calls for [such letters] is one which touches you nearly, really grieving and distressing you, all written words must seem tame and cold, compared with the aching sympathy which dictates them" (Hartley 122).

Yet even if Dickinson had turned to one of many booklets providing models for social and business correspondence, she would have found few examples of letters of condolence. Instead of providing examples of that delicate yet routinely necessary epistolary sub-genre, editors often made the puzzling choice to reprint the letter an English nobleman wrote on the eve of his execution even though purchasers of their guides would be most unlikely to face imminent beheading. Such books often neglected to provide models for expressions of sympathy that might help someone seeking the right words or tone when reaching out to a bereaved friend. Yet women, especially, bore a Christian duty to act as agents of comfort. In William Buell Sprague's *Letters on Practical Subjects to a Daughter*, Dickinson could have read of her obligations to that vast majority of the human race who "at some time or other, become the objects of sympathy from being openly buffeted by the storms of adversity" (211). Her friend Josiah Holland recommended piety as the prerequisite for women who believed, as all should, that "you carry within your own bosom light for the dying, hope for the despairing, consolation for the bereft" (161).[1] It was also widely acknowledged that women tended to excel men in epistolary skills because of their deeper social sensitivities and skill in conversation.[2]

Although compilers of the ubiquitous letter-writer guides avoided providing any formula for condolences, they warned of likely pitfalls.[3] Beyond the usual faults of misspelling, poor grammar or punctuation, and blotted pages, there was danger of reopening the mourner's wounds or even raising doubts about the eternal prospects of the deceased.[4] Mrs. John Sherwood, who wrote on etiquette for *Harper's Bazar* late in Dickinson's lifetime, dismissed efforts to justify afflictions by second-guessing God's perspective as "the wine mixed with gall which they gave our Lord to drink; as He refused it, so may we" (209).[5] Goals the writer should strive for included brevity, sincerity, and that combination of performative skills that Karen Halttunen sums up as "*controlled* communication of *proper* sentiments" (121). Ideally, such a letter could become an instrument of mercy. Sherwood reminded her Gilded Age readers that "often a phrase on which the writer has built no hope may be the airy bridge over which the sorrowing soul returns slowly and blindly to peace and resignation" (212). The odds must have been better and the duty to try even more imperative for that "truly accomplished woman" Dr. Holland characterized in *Titcomb's Letters* as "one whose thoughts have come naturally to flow out in artistic forms, whether through the instrumentality of her tongue, her pen, her pencil, or her piano" (112)—all of which were Dickinsonian tools.

Fully aware of her gifts by 1863 and trusting that the afflicted "will weep less, if we weep on [their] account" (Taylor 108), Emily Dickinson followed up her question, "What shall I tell these darlings," with varied attempts at solace (L278). In non-theological language, she reminded Loo and Fannie of Christian hope, suggesting the comfort their wearied father would find in heavenly reunion with his wife. Beyond that, she showed them how their family in Amherst wept with

them and offered them at least "half" a home before ending with offers "of comfort, or of service" and assurance of her love. A poem, "It is not dying hurts us
so" (Fr528A), recurred to themes and images of her opening paragraph.

One among many letters of condolence Emily Dickinson wrote from childhood to just days before her death, this letter marks a transition from sentimental and even formulaic early attempts at comfort to the mature writing that is
typically more heart-felt yet distilled. In the rhetoric text from which she had
studied at Mount Holyoke, Samuel P. Newman maintained that "it should ever
be impressed on the student, that, in forming a style, he is to acquire a manner
of writing, to some extent, peculiarly his own, and which is to be the index of
his modes of thinking" (xi), and the style Dickinson eventually developed as a
writer of condolence letters became distinctively, even inspiringly, hers. Her
masterpiece is her first letter to Susan Dickinson on Gilbert's death (L868;
OMC234), a letter Richard Sewall praised as "perhaps the finest she ever wrote
anybody" (*Life* 204) and of which Benjamin Lease writes "there are few more
moving letters in the English language" (xvi). Long practice in crafting messages
of solace prepared her to meet that heart-crushing test. Examining Dickinson's
letters of condolence as a particularly revealing sub-genre of her literary performance helps us to appreciate subtleties of her social awareness even while calling attention to artistic experimentation and development. These letters also
provide rich sources of insight into Dickinson's thoughts on life, death, and
immortality—often rendered in metaphors central to her imagination. Sometimes these letters reflect the genteel Christian culture in which she was raised;
often they deviate from it. Like the "Martyr Poets" of one of her poems, she
"wrought [her] Pang in syllable" to achieve for others "the Art of Peace" (Fr665).[6]

Long before that 1863 letter to grieving cousins, Dickinson had attempted to
comfort friends through letters. Although no copies remain of her earliest efforts, we know from two 1845 letters to Abiah Root that she was in correspondence with Sarah Norton after that friend lost her mother (L6, 8). Reports to
Abiah about Jane Humphrey's widowed sister (L15, 20) and Abby Wood's dying
brother (L31) indicate other occasions for such outreach. When she extended
sympathy in the 1840s, it was generally within the context of a chatty letter as
if she had taken too much to heart the exhortations found in epistolary guidebooks to write as one would converse. An 1846 letter buried condolences within
the larger framework of Emily's uncomfortable response to Abiah's announce-
ment of her religious conversion (L11). Formulaic invocations of God's will and
regret for blighted human hopes in the case of Abiah's late friend, E. Smith,

allowed the unconverted Emily to display her command of conventionally pious rhetoric, though her extended reminiscence about her own grief when Sophia Holland died conveys a hint of rivalry between these friends both in writing skill and spiritual sensitivity, competitiveness that soon disappeared from Emily's correspondence.[7]

Dominant themes of those early letters were the loneliness she attributed to mourners and the pity she felt. "I pity her very much she must be so lonely without her mother" (L6), she wrote of Sarah Norton, and she alerted Abiah that Abby "must be very sad, and need all comfort from us. She will be left *alone* – wont she?" (L31). Other themes include submission to God's will, though that reference, in the letter to Abiah about E. Smith, may simply echo her correspondent's piety (L11). Concerns about her own death and projected loss of friends recur often in these letters. Her tone, occasionally platitudinous in her earliest efforts at consolation, tended toward sentimentality—to speculations on grievers' sad feelings and a typically adolescent display of her own. When reporting in 1850 about her response to Leonard Humphrey's death, she even acknowledged to Abiah, "I am *selfish* too, because I am feeling lonely" (L39). Oddly, in view of her earlier confidence to Abiah about Sophia Holland's death scene, she claimed, "this is my first affliction, and indeed 'tis hard to bear it"; three years later she would exclaim to her brother, "Oh Austin, Newton is dead. The first of my own friends" (L110).[8]

A comment to Abiah in an 1847 letter from Mount Holyoke that Eliza Coleman had sent "a long letter giving me an account of [her sister Olivia's] death, which is beautiful & affecting" indicates that Emily, while still valuing amplitude as an epistolary merit, had started paying attention to style (L18). Her April 3, 1850 letter to Jane Humphrey marks the point in her life when she declared, probably with reference to poetic aspirations, "I have dared to do strange things – bold things, and have asked no advice from any – I have heeded beautiful tempters, yet do not think I am wrong" (L35). Yet it is, at least initially, a letter of consolation—sent upon learning that Jane's father was near death and mailed the day he died. She must have guessed that Jane would read it in bereavement, and she reached out immediately to assure this friend of her loving presence: "The voice of *love* I heeded, tho' *seeming* not to; the voice of affliction is louder, more earnest, and needs it's friends, and they know this need, and put on their wings of affection, and fly towards the lone one, and sing, sing sad music, but there's something sustaining in it." She knew that Jane might expect to hear of "Heaven, and the Savior, and 'rest for the weary,'" but Emily recognized that she, still unconverted, could not deliver that message so convincingly as others. She, too, was coping with loneliness, not the isolation of the orphan but that of the unsaved in the midst of the 1850 First Church awakening. From anticipation of the great transition from life to death Jane was about to witness, the letter raised questions about the transformation new converts claimed to have experienced and then boasted of Dickinson's own turn in startling new directions. Aside from the usual newsy postscripts, this letter ends on an appeal for remembrance by Jane that feels strangely tactless in a letter destined to be read by a daughter in mourning: "Dont put us in narrow graves – we shall *certainly rise* if you do, and scare you most prodigiously, and carry you off perhaps! 'This is the end of earth.'"

By contrast, Dickinson's letter, ten years later, attempting to console Mary Bowles on losing a stillborn child, provides a model of tactful control; she recognizes the mother's unique need yet offers to share the suffering and perhaps ease it (L216). Other letters that demonstrate artistic and social maturation include those to Edward Dwight on his wife's death (L243, 246); yet her April 1860 letter to her sister when their Aunt Lavinia died rambles painfully and focuses more on Emily's loneliness for their aunt and for her too-long-absent sister than on Vinnie's need for comfort after long care-giving service (L217).

As Polly Longsworth has observed, "It wasn't until the death of her father in June 1874, a shock so devastating, so unnerving and mysterious, that the tenor of the poet's understanding shifted to a new key" (4). Personal experience taught her the needs and capabilities of the afflicted and helped her to recognize what attempts at consolation might prove comforting—and when. Despite the many neighborhood losses she recounted in early letters to friends and her brother— to whom she reported that Vinnie had "reserved the *deaths*" for her as letter-filling substance (L53)—Dickinson's most direct and bitter experiences of bereavement came late and in relatively quick succession from her father's sudden death in 1874, through Samuel Bowles's in 1878, Dr. Holland's in 1881, Charles Wadsworth's and her mother's in 1882, her nephew's in 1883, Judge Lord's in 1884, right up to Helen Hunt Jackson's in 1885. Letters reporting to friends the impact of her father's collapse and death and Judge Lord's stroke document the traumatic impact of life-changing news and the inability of the person in such a state of shock to process information beyond grateful awareness of arms and voices offering support (L414, 752). Anyone extending condolence, then, should recognize that love may be appreciated even "though I could not notice it" and though the griever feels that the "mind never comes home" (L414). Even when sympathy might be rebuffed as intrusion, it must still be proffered. When her Aunt Kate Sweetser lost her son, this sensitive niece admitted "when I am most grieved I had rather no one would speak to me, so I stayed from you, but I thought by today, perhaps you would like to see me, if I came quite soft and brought no noisy words" (L338), and words on paper might be softer and easier to turn away or return to later than those spoken. Experience taught her, as well, the value of brevity: "One who only said 'I am sorry' helped me the most when father ceased – it was too soon for language" (L730).[9] Still, words brought solace after the first interlude of grief. Detailing the little events of her mother's last day, eating "Beef Tea and Custard with a pretty ravenousness that delighted us" (L779), reminded Dickinson how deeply mourners needed validation of their efforts to sustain the life that faded. Florence Hartley's observation in *The Ladies' Book of Etiquette* that "early stages of great grief reject *comfort*, but they long, with intense longing, for sympathy" (124) found reinforcement in her own experience of loss, and each grief taught her to cling more thankfully to remaining friends.

Dickinson's responses to griefs of her friends document her growing social sensitivity, even in years of seclusion; they also demonstrate participation in her century's genteel culture of mourning while simpler practices of her youth yielded to Gilded Age formalities. Aware of mourners' burdens, she respected their need for shelter while also recognizing how confronting pain might speed the way to healing. When Margaret Maher's brother was killed in an 1880 mining accident, she nudged her Norcross cousins to help out by writing a condolence letter: "If the little cousins would give her a note – she does not know I ask it – I think it would help her begin, that bleeding beginning that every mourner knows" (L670). Judging when to introduce such attempts at comfort called for social tact, as Dickinson acknowledged in a letter to Thomas Wentworth Higginson when his wife died in 1877. "I had feared to follow you, lest you would rather be lonely, which is the will of sorrow," she acknowledged, but had been encouraged by newspaper reports to guess this man of letters might be receptive to the two notes she sent immediately after the death (L519).

Evidence here that there had been a sequence of notes reflects Dickinson's tendency in mid-life to extend condolences gradually rather than try to sum up all memory, comfort, and acknowledgment in one letter. In fact, the sequences of letters she sent to such friends as Higginson, Mary Bowles, and Elizabeth Holland more or less followed etiquette of the times regarding visits to the bereaved. Characteristically referring to her letters in terms of being with people—assuring Mrs. Holland, for example, that "you knew we would come as soon as we knew" (even though she would have been, by 1882, about the last mortal Elizabeth would expect to find at her doorway), Dickinson recognized that she must be cautious not to intrude on a mourner's need for privacy (L775). Guides for behavior in times of grief mandated that calls be made as soon as word of the death reached those the family attempted to contact and within a month following the funeral by other acquaintances. Nothing exempted friends from this obligation even though only intimate friends should actually expect to see any of the bereaved on this first visit of ceremony. Most inquirers would simply leave a card to show sympathy and willingness to be of service, perhaps writing a few lines or just leaving it with the bottom left corner turned in to indicate condolence. Even at the funeral, women among the chief mourners might remain out of sight and, if they followed the body to the grave, would stand at a great distance heavily veiled in black.[10] So Dickinson's first note to Mary when Samuel Bowles died in January 1878 contained only a few lines expressing grief, and she waited for the widow's reply to judge what more might follow (L532). The second note acknowledged hesitation to intrude on private sorrow yet foregrounded the urgency impelled by love: "I hasten to you, Mary, because no moment must be lost when a heart is breaking" (L536). Writing "to be willing that I should speak to you was so generous, dear," she acknowledged that Mrs. Bowles could rightly have ignored that first response, just as she could have refused to see Emily Dickinson if this friend had ventured into her crape-marked home. Relieved to find that "the broken words helped you," she wrote at somewhat fuller length about grief, rest, the value of work, and her memories of "Mr. Sam," while responding gratefully to his widow's inquiries for her ailing mother.

Even more reflective of the stages of visitation following death is Dickinson's sequence of 1881 letters to Elizabeth Holland, a closer friend than Mary Bowles and one with whom she could be more open and comfortable. The first letter, in this case, was a bit longer but still not detailed. It testified to the Dickinsons' collective shock on receiving the telegram: "We read the words but know them not. We are too frightened with sorrow" (L729). In their shock, their condition paralleled trauma in the Holland household. She moved on to a quick reference to heaven as "but a little way to one who gave it, here," thereby testifying to her household's confidence in the Doctor's eternal well-being while softening the experience of sharp division between mortal life and immortality. Her main message at first, however, was one of love and shared grief: "How can we wait to take you all in our sheltering arms?" She could not write more just yet because "the heart is full – another throb would split it – nor would we dare to speak to those whom such a grief removes." Letters followed in rapid succession, however, each its own kind of brief, supportive visit. Dickinson's second letter declared her desire to help—"if I can rest them, here is down – or rescue, here is power" (L730)—yet offered her mother's anguished "I loved him so" as Dr. Holland's "tenderer eulogy." In her third letter, she followed up on that initial reference to heaven, not relying on religious formulas, however, and even recognizing how unreal such hopes would seem just then. "After a while, dear, you will remember that there is a heaven – but you can't now. Jesus will excuse it. He will remember his shorn lamb" (L731). Thoughts of eternity could only prove consoling in Dr. Holland's case, luckily: "The *safety* of a beloved lost is the first anguish. With you, that is peace." Still in October came a fourth letter-visit, encouraging the widow to "the duty which saves," which is the obligation to carry on for others until "power of life comes back" (L732). By now, Dickinson had received a letter from Elizabeth, to which she responded "How sweetly you have comforted me." She cherished details of the Doctor's last day and lovingly remembered comfort Mrs. Holland had extended to her when her father died. More letters followed with sympathetic words and gentle remembrance as shared griefs intensified bonds uniting close friends.

Such letters reflect Emily Dickinson's awareness of how grief becomes a long and evolving process. The bereaved need sympathy but cannot, at least initially, imagine healing; friends, intuiting this, refrain from pressuring them to deny their suffering. An 1862 letter to her former minister, Edward Dwight, voiced concern for the widower without expecting him to have reached stoic self-control or even pious submission. "I do not ask if you are 'better,'" she wrote, "because split lives – never 'get well' – but the love of friends – sometimes helps the Staggering – when the Heart has on it's great freight" (L246). To her minister cousin Perez Cowan, she held out gentle hope that "as Days go on your sister is more Peace than Pang" (L332). Acknowledging the reality of "Pang," Dickinson never claimed to know the way to "Peace," yet she stayed faithfully by friends as they moved—numbly at first and then bruisedly—through long, circling, and unpredictable waves of grief. Without claiming to be an effective instrument of comfort, she held out hope, as in this message to Higginson: "Do not try to be saved – but let Redemption find you – as it certainly will – Love is it's own rescue" (L522). Through such expressions of tender attentiveness, she became for her correspondents—as Joan Kirkby finds she remains for today's readers—"the philosophical friend with and through whom we may think through our own relations to death, to our specific dead, to the beloved dead" (134).

Respect for friends' ways of finding peace led Dickinson to reject rigors of Gilded Age etiquette with its mandates on how much black must be worn and for how long in socially correct periods of mourning. She might have found herself in sympathy with Mrs. E. B. Duffey's advice that mourning garb should be worn only so long as it reflected the family's actual desire for protection against life's pleasant routines, though she would have avoided the language of obligation Duffey used in declaring "it is our duty to ourselves and to the world to regain our cheerfulness as soon as we may, and all that conduces to this we are religiously bound to accept" (223). One can imagine the sharp Dickinsonian contempt for Amherst neighbors who criticized Susan for her lengthy black-shrouded display of grief for Gilbert (Sewall, *Life* 205), but then she responded with unhesitating support when Mrs. Holland defied conventions by celebrating her elder daughter's wedding only two months after being widowed. Her December 1881 letter of felicitation recognized the special poignancy of such timing. Although worried about the pain that another parting, even a joyous one, might bring her friend, Dickinson exulted that "Few daughters have the Immortality of a Father for a bridal gift" (L740). One of the absolute rules of letter-writing decorum held that one must never combine letters of condolence with those of congratulation, but the Hollands' complicated lives made such restrictions untenable for one whose letter-visits reflected multiple events and conflicting moods. Just a year after Dr. Holland's death, Dickinson sat down in cheerful spirits to congratulate her friend on her younger daughter's engagement only to receive word that Elizabeth's brother had died. So she began with her familiar declarations of presence and shared sorrow before moving on to concerns for Elizabeth's fortitude after such a succession of blows; still she ended "with tender thought of Kate in her joyful Hour," aware that peace and pang inevitably reinforce each other in one home (L775).

Also unusual in terms of social conventions was Dickinson's tendency to form new epistolary friendships upon losing persons close to her. Rather than writing to the most directly bereaved survivors in cases where she did not know those persons, she addressed others. It was Benjamin Newton's minister, Edward Everett Hale, to whom she sent to learn circumstances of his death and to whom she confided memories of a friendship she might not have wanted to discuss with his widow. Even while reaching out in love to Mary Bowles, she initiated a correspondence with Maria Whitney as another mourner like herself, writing "I have thought of you often since the darkness, – though we cannot assist another's night" (L537).[11] Letters to Benjamin Kimball, Judge Lord's executor, repeat this pattern, though the most remarkable of these correspondences was with two brothers, James and Charles Clark, who served as her ties to Charles Wadsworth after James Clark sent her a volume of Wadsworth's sermons.

His gift stimulated her quick and grateful response. "I have never before spoken with one who knew him," Dickinson wrote of her "Philadelphia," "and his Life was so shy and his tastes so unknown, that grief for him seems almost unshared" (L766). She had met this Northampton minister just once, in company with Wadsworth, so their tie was slight and he might have misconstrued her outreach. The combination of passionate, almost adoring esteem and love for Wadsworth with her obvious lack of personal knowledge of his family life would have raised doubts. Among forces that kept this correspondence alive and comforting, however, was Dickinson's sincere concern for Clark's own endangered health and the bond she and Lavinia came to feel with these mutually supportive brothers. Perhaps because she remained the family member responsible for writing about or in response to deaths, Dickinson's condolence letters tended to balance first-person singular and plural diction. She wrote in her own voice when recalling Wadsworth's last visit, but she conveyed sympathy in her sister's name also and sometimes her mother's. Her first letter to James Clark began "Please excuse the trespass of gratitude. My Sister thinks you will accept a few words in recognition of your great kindness" (L766), and the one she wrote in response to his words of comfort when their mother died said "we have spoken daily of writing you" (L788). Writing as her family's representative, she tended to speak of the dead in familial roles, often asking special remembrance to whatever person stood in relation to the deceased in one of her own roles as sister or daughter even if writing directly to the spouse.

This collective voice that distinguishes many of Dickinson's letters of condolence, like the social conventions guiding this sort of writing then and even now, prompted her to stress themes generally appropriate to such messages. In addition to conveying assurance of friends' supportive presence to the afflicted, she acknowledged shared grief in cases where she felt herself bereaved, telling Mrs. Stearns when her son died that "my heart breaks – I can say no more" (L694) and confessing in one of her last letters to Higginson that "fervor suffocates me" as she tried to return solace he offered while they both grieved for Helen Jackson (L1042). At other times, she forged a bond with mourners by reminding them of parallel experiences of grief, as in a letter to a neighbor that begins "I had the luxury of a Mother a month longer than you" and ends "To have *had* a Mother – how mighty" (L1022). That adjective, "mighty," illustrates a tendency in these letters to exalt the dead—even those unknown to her—with enhancing diction. The bereaved might take comfort in feeling that their lost were "Noble" (L577) or "fathomless" (L766) or even that their expressions had conveyed "ascension" (L967). Such diction suggested that the deceased already experienced a kind of glorification while living, a prelude to heavenly exaltation now enjoyed. Memories of friends tended to reinforce confidence in their eternal well-being, as when Dickinson told Mary Bowles how the purple tones of winter sunsets reminded Amherst friends of her husband and recalled to her personally an occasion when "the beautiful eyes rose till they were out of reach of mine, in some hallowed fathom" (L536). Remembering Josiah Holland, she envisaged him leading family prayer (L731), and the "unforgotten once" of her meeting James Clark convinced her that "to have seen him but once more, would have been almost like an interview with my 'Heavenly Father,' whom he loved and knew" (L826).

Among the expected topics of inquiry in such letters were circumstances of the death and funeral. Emily Dickinson often pressed to know "Did she know she was leaving you?" (L517), though she was prepared to wait until mourners were ready to share such memories, trusting that "some one will tell me a very little, when they have the strength" (L731). This was the sort of information she herself shared in responses to letters of condolence on her father's, mother's, and nephew's deaths, and social convention called for such revelations. According to one etiquette counselor, near relations of the deceased could be excused from supplying such narratives only if earlier letters, during the illness, had provided an account (Hervey 166). What is impressive about Dickinson's response to such deathbed narratives is her gift for distilling sweetness and even promise from topics others would find morbid. Particularly striking is the elation with which she replied to Elizabeth Holland's account of her husband's sudden, painless, yet conscious departure: "How lovely that he spoke with you, that memorial time! How gentle that he left the pang he had not time to feel! Bequest of darkness, yet of light, since unborne by him. 'Where thou goest, *we* will go' – how mutual, how intimate! No solitude receives him, but neighborhood and friend" (L732).

Even the most ebullient celebrations of a dead friend's glorified "State – Endowal – Focus" (Fr476), however, could do little immediately to assuage the pain of absence; so Dickinson typically reached out to the bereaved with acknowledgment of their affliction and even with reference to earlier losses whose pang would be reactivated. Her observation to Mrs. Holland that "October could not pass you by" (L775) conveyed her sensitivity to each friend's particular seasons of grief; so did her tendency to observe anniversaries of deaths and thank those whose outreach to her and Lavinia helped them through cycles of remembrance. Consoling Martha Gilbert Smith on the death of her husband, Dickinson remembered the little boy and girl who preceded him, urging Mattie to "Smile – for their sake, dear, to whom you have added a 'Father in Heaven'" (L577). Dickinson's letters validated loved ones' service and suffering, whether she hoped Charles Clark would not be "too far exausted from your 'loved employ'" (L826) or thanked neighbors for kindness to her dying mother. Grateful that their mother had savored the last foods her daughters prepared for her and called out at last for Lavinia in a way that recognized that younger daughter's staunch nursing comforted Dickinson and prompted her to commend others for their ministries of love. The funeral and visits to the grave thereafter afforded the bereaved additional opportunities to express that love, and Dickinson tended to associate such ministry with flowers—whether those bestowed on the dead for them to carry in their caskets or those carried back from the gravesite months afterward and given by friends to the family.[12]

When faithful care ended with the invalid's death, however, Dickinson made sure to comfort the afflicted with assurances of continuing love. To Susan, overwhelmed with loneliness for her son, Emily wrote "You asked would I remain? // Irrevocably, Susan – I know no other way" (L874; OMC239). When Edward Dwight feared she would soon forget both him and his late wife, she replied, "I trust she is more my friend – today – when I cannot see her – and learn it from her own sweet lips" (L246). Writing to Benjamin Kimball, she recalled Judge Otis Lord's reply to her question of what she could do for him in his absence: "'Remember Me,' he said. I have kept his Commandment" (L968).

The love that drew her to the bereaved brought concern for their healing, and Dickinson found many ways to coax friends toward renewed engagement in the work and pleasures of this life. One way she did that was by reminding them of a supportive community, making sure they knew how many people cared for them. In the letter to her Norcross cousins written soon after the letter I discussed earlier, Dickinson relayed kind inquiries of Amherst acquaintances and offered a sequence of news notes reminding these orphans of earlier visits in hopes of enticing them to return: "Would it interest the children to know that crocuses come up, in the garden off the dining-room?. . // Will it please them to know that the ice-house is filled, to make their tumblers cool next Summer. . . ? // And that father has built a new road round the pile of trees between our house and Mr. S's?" (L279). That new road would secure these girls a quiet refuge to sew shirts for soldiers, reminding them that they still had work to do that could make things better for somebody. Similarly, she reinforced Mary Bowles's attempts to resume activity, describing work as "a bleak redeemer" (L536). When a grieving Susan undertook to prepare Thanksgiving dinner only weeks after burying her child, Emily urged her to "reserve an Apartment for two Cocks" in the oven (L874; OMC239). In a letter to Perez Cowan that sought to check his tendency to look forward to his own death as a way of following his sister, Dickinson encouraged him to keep working and to maintain human contacts, commending him for remembering their mutual cousin's wedding in the midst of his grief: "Others," she declared, "are anodyne" (L332).

Language, too, could be anodyne, whether her own words, those she reported for others, or even those from the bereaved who reciprocated her own attempts to comfort. "Your sweet 'and left me all alone,' consecrates your lips," she told Mrs. Bowles upon receiving a note from that newly widowed friend (L536). Sometimes the simplest responses, like her mother's "I loved him so" (L730), spoke eloquently; yet grander rhetorical attempts occasionally planted themselves in the mind. Sharing condolences for Helen Hunt Jackson with Higginson, Dickinson alluded to a trope from a funeral sermon for Helen's father delivered when she and Emily were children: "'From Mount Zion below to Mount Zion above'! said President Humphrey of her Father – Gabriel's Oration would adorn his Child" (L1042). The question she first framed when moved to comfort the orphaned Norcross girls, "What shall I tell these darlings," remained a constant challenge that grew increasingly formidable as Dickinson discovered the power of language to intensify pang as well as summon peace (L278). "What a Hazard a Letter is!" she exclaimed on reading of Jackson's death, "When I think of the Hearts it has scuttled and sunk, I almost fear to lift my Hand to so much as a Superscription" (L1007). Yet she knew her pen must serve as her chief instrument of healing.

Dickinson's predictable response to anxieties about language entailed striving to utter "one liquid word" to ease sorrow (L859). Where her earliest letters of condolence had been talkative, self-absorbed, and diffuse, sometimes burying acknowledgment of grief in a pile-up of unrelated information, her mature ones are brief, tactful, and focused on the recipient at whatever stage of grief the author expected to find her reader. Some are classified by Johnson as letters only on the basis of salutation and/or signature; otherwise they are poems or fragments of poems. This message, for example, went to the widow of William Stearns, president of Amherst College:

> Love's stricken "why"
> Is all that love can speak –
> Built of but just a syllable
> The hugest hearts that break.
> Emily. (L463; Fr1392)

It is a message of shock, shared grief, and awareness of the ways language fails us; though—as Dickinsonian distilled wisdom, it also reminds us of what words can accomplish when deployed by a poet.

By the time Dickinson wrote her most brilliant and compassionate condolence letters, she was too far beyond apprenticeship to pay much attention to school-day guidelines on composition. Yet she had clearly intuited her way to insights collegians of her generation found in Newman's guide to rhetoric, where he identified metaphor as the figure of speech best suited to the "writer whose style is concise," who conveys "a vividness and distinctness in his views," striving "by a single and sudden effort to exhibit these views to others" (189–90). Such a writer's "turns of expression" would be recognized for brevity, boldness, and even grammatical ellipsis. Here is a point where distinctions between Dickinson's prose and poetry collapse; her words of consolation rely on metaphors that are the same in both genres and that remain so strikingly consistent throughout her decades of writing that they must be recognized as profound expressions of her consciousness. Not wholly distinctive to this author, however, many of her metaphoric clusters belonged to scriptural and literary tradition and drew on her century's sentimental culture of mourning.

Metaphors of human life as a journey arise almost universally when people review any one person's history or note general patterns, and Christians typically represent this trek in terms of pilgrimage toward heaven. So Dickinson often refers to the dead as travelers who have reached their destination, to which Jesus or their own beloved dead summon them. From the perspective of mourners, though, "Dying is a wild Night and a new Road" (L332). Their share of life's journey grows nightmarish in the disorientation of loss and loneliness, and Dickinson habitually figures their calamity in terms of being lost themselves in the wilderness or at sea. After her mother died, she notified Maria Whitney with a plea for support: "While we bear her dear form through the Wilderness, I am sure you are with us" (L777), much as she had offered her own strength to Higginson when she wrote "The Wilderness is new – to you. Master, let me lead you" (L517). When that dark journey plunged the mourner into the sea (for Dickinson, often a symbol of boundless, uncontrollable force equivalent to death), she acknowledged desperation.[13] From her 1860 condolence to Mary Bowles on the death of her baby, declaring "the waves are very big, but every one that covers you, covers us, too" (L216) to her 1883 letter to Susan after Gilbert's death—"Moving on in the Dark like Loaded Boats at Night, though there is no Course, there is Boundlessness" (L871; OMC236), Dickinson drew on this imagery to suggest the panicky bewilderment of the mourner in crisis. Although the quotations above represent the writer herself among those caught in the threatening tide, Dickinson sometimes volunteered piloting skills developed through experience. "You must let me go first, Sue," she urged Susan after a sister died, "because I live in the Sea always and know the Road" (L306; OMC113).

Sometimes such metaphors reflected the condition of the dead rather than their mourners. When her own mother died after being long protected by attentive daughters, Dickinson marveled "that the one we have cherished so softly so long, should be in that great Eternity without our simple Counsels, seems frightened and foreign" (L779). The dominant imagery of Dickinson's letters at this time, however, relates to her mother's flying: "It never occurred to us that though she had not Limbs, she had *Wings* – and she soared from us unexpectedly as a summoned Bird" (L779). These lines to Elizabeth Holland drew on a pattern of metaphor she had developed in that 1863 letter to the Norcross cousins, especially in the concluding poem that represented grief by figuring the dead as birds who fly south in winter and their survivors as left shivering in the cold (L278; Fr528A). Decades later she repeated that concluding message in words of comfort to Charles Clark, when Dickinson hoped "the winged Days that bear you to your Brother, are not too destitute of Song" (L880), and an 1884 letter to Elizabeth Holland included a poem, "Quite empty, quite at rest" that represented her own bereaved condition as that of a robin surrendering herself to the uncharted sky and venturing "Crumbless and homeless" in search of "Birds she lost" (L890; Fr1632). For the dead, however, bird-like power of flight conveyed ideas of power, escape, and freedom. More explicitly than usual, Dickinson called attention to the symbolic force of this metaphoric pattern in words of gratitude to a neighbor: "The last Gift on which my fleeing Mother looked, was Mrs. Hills' little Bird. I trust this Morning, a Bird herself, she requires no Symbol" (L778).

One reason why the dead fly from earth, of course, is that they have become weary, as Uncle Loring Norcross had been as well as her mother. Dickinson's letters made frequent use of culturally familiar imagery of tiredness and sleep. It comforted her as she struggled to compose her thoughts after her father's sudden departure to think that "almost the last tune that he heard was, 'Rest from thy loved employ'" (L414). Such metaphors remind the reader of the lost one's steadfast work in this wearying world and help to reconcile friends to the passing of one for whom life had become burdensome. It seemed a special blessing to Dickinson that her cousin Henry Sweetser died peacefully after long captivity as "prisoner" in a broken body, and that "his Redeemer ... brought him his Ransom in his sleep" (L338). The hope, surely, was that awakening to bliss succeeded death's sleep, so she clung to thoughts of Judge Lord who, "after a brief unconsciousness, a Sleep that ended with a smile, so his Nieces tell us, ... hastened away, 'seen,' we trust, 'of Angels'" (L890).

Those trusting words gave way at once, though, to the question "Who knows that secret deep" about the fate of the beloved dead and to her anguished response, "Alas, not I" (L890). When one studies her letters of condolence for perspective on her "Flood subject" of immortality (L319), conflicting evidence emerges. Such writing forced Dickinson to confront her own thoughts about the soul's destiny, but it often challenged her to do so in times of personal crisis. Moreover, she intended these letters to comfort sorrowing friends rather than disturb them; she had to keep in mind what a particular reader would find helpful. At times, chiefly in relatively early letters like those already cited to Abiah Root, she represented heaven as a place of judgment yet also of reunion (L11) or of endless domestic contentment such as she imagined for Fannie and Loo's parents (L278). Yet her letter to Vinnie when their favorite aunt died confessed uneasiness with such imagery and her continued bewilderment. "Blessed Aunt Lavinia now," she began bravely, but then admitted "all the world goes out, and I see nothing but her room, and angels bearing her into those great countries in the blue sky of which we don't know anything" (L217). Biblical passages to which she alluded told a mixed story. She found a measure of hopefulness in Christ's "Come unto me," when inviting a small child (L620) and in his promise to reward works of mercy (L729), but she confessed to James Clark the problem of the mourner left behind when she wrote, "No Verse in the Bible has frightened me so much from a Child as 'from him that hath not, shall be taken even that he hath'" (L788). Invoking the story of Lazarus, she identified with the grieving Mary, who confronted Jesus with the charge "'If thou had'st been here, our Brother had not died'" (L895).

Worth noting, however, is that the challenges Dickinson raised to Christian hopes tended to arise chiefly in letters to clergymen and their families. Perhaps she knew that they would get more than their share of platitudes from such unreflecting believers as "prate – of Heaven" (Fr476). She probably trusted that their faith held firm enough to withstand her questions and may even have hoped that they would help her confront the question "Is immortality true?" that she eventually directed to the Rev. Washington Gladden (L752a). Writing to her minister cousin, Perez Cowan, she contrasted their situations, noting, "You speak with so much trust of that which only trust can prove, it makes me feel away, as if my English mates spoke sudden in Italian" (L332). Even while fantasizing reunion above for Charles Wadsworth and James Clark, she asked Clark's brother with startling bluntness, "Are you certain there is another life? When overwhelmed to know, I fear that few are sure" (L827). Yet to interpret such questions as proof of disbelief stretches evidence too far. There are counterbalancing statements such as her assurance to Aunt Kate Sweetser that "I know we shall certainly see what we loved the most" (L338). When Maria Whitney wrote of "disillusion," Dickinson rejoined, "that is one of the few subjects on which I am an infidel. Life is so strong a vision, not one of it shall fail" (L860).

Communicating with friends at times when she and they struggled to imagine what, if anything, the dead experienced beyond this life's circumference, Dickinson responded with gently non-judgmental acceptance of each one's trust or doubt and with reverent awareness of mystery. Writing to the faith-supported Cowan, she cautioned against too much readiness for death, while acknowledging that his attraction to that topic linked him to her: "I suppose we are all thinking of Immortality, at times so stimulatedly that we cannot sleep," she declared, even as she declined to draw any firm conclusion from such guesswork. "Secrets are interesting, but they are also solemn – and speculate with all our might, we cannot ascertain" (L332). To the doubting Maria Whitney she wrote, "We cannot believe for each other – thought is too sacred a despot, but I hope that God, in whatever form, is true to our friend" (L591). The letter she wrote to Louisa and Frances Norcross in the wake of her mother's death may be recognized as an oblique message of condolence to Emily Norcross Dickinson's nieces, consoling them with the gentleness of their aunt's passing and with the image of her face in the casket expressing peaceful beauty. It also provided

Dickinson with opportunity to report on her own physical, emotional, and spiritual state in the midst of affliction and to express gratitude for the sustaining love on which she relied from these cousins. It is here that we find the closest approach to a Dickinson credo when she averred, "I believe we shall in some manner be cherished by our Maker – that the One who gave us this remarkable earth has the power still farther to surprise that which He has caused. Beyond that all is silence" (L785).

It was this lifetime experience of speculating on mysteries of immortality, cultivating metaphoric artistry, and nurturing social sensitivities that allowed her to touch hearts of suffering friends in ways that brought "more Peace than Pang" that prepared Emily Dickinson to write the most awe-filled and wondrous letter-poem of her life when her eight-year-old nephew died.

> Dear Sue –
> The Vision of Immortal Life has been fulfilled –
> How simply at the last the Fathom comes! The Passenger and not the Sea, we find surprises us –
> Gilbert rejoiced in Secrets –
> His Life was panting with them – With what menace of Light he cried "Dont tell, Aunt Emily"! Now my ascended Playmate must instruct *me*. Show us, prattling Preceptor, but the way to thee!
> He knew no niggard moment – His Life was full of Boon – The Playthings of the Dervish were not so wild as his –
> No crescent was this Creature – He traveled from the Full –
> Such soar, but never set –
> I see him in the Star, and meet his sweet velocity in everything that flies – His Life was like the Bugle, which winds itself away, his Elegy an echo – his Requiem ecstasy –
> Dawn and Meridian in one.
> Wherefore would he wait, wronged only of Night, which he left for us –
> Without a speculation, our little Ajax spans the whole –
>> Pass to thy Rendezvous of Light,
>> Pangless except for us –
>> Who slowly ford the Mystery
>> Which thou hast leaped across!
>   Emily. (L868; OMC234; Fr1624A)

Herself prostrated by grief and the fumes of disinfectants pervading Gilbert's sickroom next door, Dickinson rose from her bed to write what Thomas Johnson identified as "the most moving letter . . . in all her many years of correspondence"

(*Biography* 43), the letter Polly Longsworth singles out as most eloquently conveying Dickinson's "struggle for control, her reach for art in coping with death" ("Might" 7) and that Patrick J. Keane praises as "a work of art in which every rift is loaded with ore" (171). Much as he admired Dickinson's artistic achievement here, however, Richard Sewall faulted her attempt at condolence in that "Sue, the grieving mother, is hardly in it at all" (*Life* 205). Brilliant in its expression of Gilbert's vibrant essence, the message struck him as oddly detached from its audience. Such letters on loss of children, with which Dickinson had by then accumulated considerable experience, may be the hardest of all to write in that the parents' loss overwhelms them. When the Cowans buried their daughter, Dickinson had inquired, "Will it comfort my grieved cousin to know that Emily and Vinnie are among the ones this moment thinking of him with peculiar tenderness, and is his sweet wife too faint to remember to Whom her loved one is consigned?" (L620). Perhaps the letter Florence Hartley printed in a guide to nineteenth-century women's social behavior would have been truer to expectations; Hartley rightly praised this as "one of the most touching letters of condolence ever written," ascribing it to "a literary lady to a sister whose youngest child had died" (123–24):

> Sister Darling:
>   I cannot write what is in my heart for you to-day, it is too full. Filled with a double sorrow, for you, for my own grief. Tears blind me, my pen trembles in my hand. Oh, to be near you! to clasp you in my arms! to draw your head to my bosom, and weep with you! Darling, God comfort you, I cannot.
>
>   S.

Emily Dickinson, feeling that same "double sorrow," may well have embraced Susan in her visit to the dying child, and she certainly kept her in mind over the next weeks and year as a succession of loving letters and poems beautifully testifies (L869, 870, 871, 874, 938; OMC235–40). There could be no one all-purpose letter of condolence in response to such tragedy; yet this "Vision of Immortal Life" distills the essence of Emily Dickinson's "Art of Peace" (Fr665).[14]

It may be worthwhile to consider temptations the writer avoided. Dickinson dispensed with the sentimental bathos of the gift-book verse about parental grief for a dead boy that she had sent in 1856 to Mary Warner (L183).[15] Also omitted is any attempt to answer "Love's stricken 'why'" (Fr1392) or to advise submission to God's will. Never one to inflame a mourner's grief or suggest that the bereaved or the deceased deserved affliction, Dickinson responded to this sorrow in which she herself shared by offering a positive perspective quite distinct from routine condolences her brother and his wife would have received.[16]

The most amazing artistic feature in Dickinson's condolence-elegy for Gilbert is her ability to sustain a tone Lease calls "ecstatic, triumphant" (xvii). If one were to look for a prelude to this among her letters, it would be in one to Elizabeth Holland a few weeks after Josiah's death, when she responded to the widow's account of his passing with exclamations of sympathetic joy:

> How gentle that he left the pang he had not time to feel! Bequest of darkness, yet of light, since unborne by him. "Where thou goest, *we* will go" – how mutual, how intimate! No solitude receives him, but neighborhood and friend.
>
> Relieved forever of the loss of those that must have fled, but for his sweet haste. Knowing he could not spare *them*, he hurried like a boy from that unhappened sorrow. Death has mislaid his sting – the grave forgot his victory. Because the flake fell not on him, we will accept the drift, and wade where he is lain. (L732)

Some of the same stylistic features occur here that we find in her elegy for Gilbert—the staccato bursts, the exclamations, and the allusions. So do images of venturesome boyhood and contrasts between the freedom of the one who escaped and the bewilderment of those left to marvel at his flight across seas they must "wade" or "ford." Also striking is her attention to fascinating secrets that call to mind "a wild Night and a new Road" (L332) and God's tendency to "surprise" (L785).

Writing of Gilbert, Dickinson drew on image patterns familiar to her from other letters of condolence. Journey imagery evokes the child's impulsive rush toward fulfillment. "He traveled from the Full," leaping with "sweet velocity," and now "spans the whole." His journey takes him through "Fathom" and "Sea," but the way she figures him as a "Passenger" suggests a pilot. Boldly leaping across the dreaded flood of death, Gilbert leaves his survivors attempting to "ford" that sea. Perhaps she was thinking of Christ walking on the water and Peter's faltering steps, upheld only by faith, or of the death-in-life experience she had represented in "After great pain" as characterized by mindless, automatic motion when "The Feet, mechanical, go round – / A Wooden way / Of Ground, or Air, or Ought" (Fr372). The idea of trying to ford an ocean evokes impressions of infinite horizontal expanse as well as unmeasurable depths that overwhelm the mourners; while Gilbert, by happy contrast, is represented in images of ascension related to Dickinson's familiar metaphors of birds and flight: "Such soar, but never set"; "I . . . meet his sweet velocity in everything that flies." Absent here is imagery of weariness or sleep. She memorializes the boy in terms of energy, play, light, and even noise—still intensely alive. When comforting the Higginsons three years before on their infant's death, Dickinson had referred to "the flight of such a fraction" (L641), but there is nothing fragmentary in her portrait of Gilbert, whom she represents in circle symbolism as "No crescent" but one who "traveled from the Full." Oxymoronic phrases capture the contradictions inherent in her rapturous response to untimely death: "menace of Light," "ascended Playmate," "prattling Preceptor," and "our little Ajax." Alliteration and meter convey a subtly poetic awareness of design underlying the seeming disorder of this child's sudden soaring.[17] Metaphoric patterns familiar to readers of Dickinson's poems include those of light and darkness, times of day, and circles. The overwhelming impression she evokes is one of unstoppable dynamism, to which the reader responds with gratitude and awe.

One other celebrated Dickinson letter, her last, gives final perspective on Emily Dickinson's gift for consolation. Like the letter with which I began this discussion, this was written to her Norcross cousins, and it is the most intensely distilled of her messages:

> Little Cousins,
> Called back.
> Emily.
> (L1046)

In a way, this can be considered a condolence letter in that she had reason to believe Loo and Fannie would read it at about the same time a telegram alerted them to her passing. It would find them needing comfort. Although there is no reason to suppose that any of the Dickinsons relied on the ubiquitous letter-writing guides for epistolary models, this might be her contribution to the subgenre too long represented by "the Earl of Stafford to his Son, just before his Lordship's execution" or "Mrs. Rowe's to her Mother, on the Approach of her Own Death"—both frequently reprinted. Characteristically, Dickinson wrote with greater concision and ambiguity and with no attempt at preaching.

There is no ambiguity in the salutation, though: "Little Cousins" affirms both affection and kinship, as does the first name as signature. Yet "Called back" raises questions. Unlike most of today's tourists who find this phrase on her gravestone, her cousins would have recognized her allusion to Hugh Conway's popular gothic novel. This reference might have reminded them of pleasure they and

Emily had taken in frequent discussions of books they were reading. If one probes the reference further, one comes up against the oddities of *Called Back*, whose protagonist undergoes a succession of strange adventures. In the central chapter, itself titled "Called Back," Gilbert Vaughan returns with his amnesiac wife to the scene of a hideous murder. By confronting that trauma, the couple eventually enters a beautiful new life. Might Dickinson have been signaling to Fannie and Loo that sickness had called her back to physical and emotional crisis? If so, the book suggests a hopeful outcome of some sort, though not necessarily eternal. Yet another connotation of "Called back," the idea of being summoned home to heaven, may have been on Martha Dickinson Bianchi's mind when she chose this inscription for her aunt's grave, and it probably comforted the Norcross cousins also. What they and the rest of us feel in reading this letter is what Dickinson conveyed over and over in letters of condolence—that "delicate art" in which Sewall claimed "no one surpassed her" (205): death remains a tantalizing mystery but some sort of life endures along with love. If there can be "a bliss of sorrow" (L827), Emily Dickinson calls us back to that revelation.

NOTES

1. Conduct books, generally intended for young readers, tended to stress morality and piety rather than teach rules of etiquette; Sarah E. Newton distinguishes them as "codifying society's idealized expectations in regard to proper behavior in life, as opposed to behavior in society" (4). Whether addressed to women, men, or both (like Josiah Gilbert Holland's *Titcomb's Letters to Young People, Single and Married*), these guides set forth gender-specific goals for character development. Jack Capps's *Emily Dickinson's Reading* identifies the Rev. William Buell Sprague's *Letters on Practical Subjects to a Daughter* as an 1862 gift from Edward Dickinson to Emily. Other good examples include Eliza Leslie's eminently practical *Miss Leslie's Behaviour Book* and Catharine Maria Sedgwick's democratically inflected *Means and Ends; or Self-Training*. Carolyn De Swarte Gifford has reprinted two books by the Rev. Daniel Wise, *The Young Lady's Counsellor* and *Bridal Greetings* in *The American Ideal of the "True Woman" as Reflected in Advice Books to Young Women*, which has an informative introduction. Conduct books for women have provided valuable source material for Barbara Welter's *Dimity Convictions: The American Woman in the Nineteenth Century* and Sarah E. Newton's *Learning to Behave: A Guide to American Conduct Books before 1900*. Still valuable, especially for its bibliography, is Arthur M. Schlesinger's *Learning How to Behave: A Historical Study of American Etiquette Books*.

2. Sprague, for example, acknowledged with regard to epistolary skill that "I must do your sex the justice to say that in this respect they greatly exceed ours" (53), and the anonymous compiler of *The Letter Writer's Own Book* advises male readers to "study the letters of women in preference to those of men" (xii). Marietta Messmer comments

in *A Vice for Voices* on gender expectations with regard to writing of letters, noting that men's praise of women in this respect generally corresponded to impressions that women wrote from the heart, almost mindlessly, while men wrote from their minds (29–30).

3. Harry B. Weiss, whose bibliography in *American Letter-Writers 1698–1943* provides an invaluable guide to these books, describes them as intended for "those who wanted to write eloquent, polite, and effective letters on all sorts of subjects, but who lacked the skill to express themselves adequately" (3). Like etiquette guides, they were especially helpful for those hoping to rise from relatively low social levels. Although it seems improbable, therefore, that Emily Dickinson or any of her family bought or consulted such books, they remain useful as indicators of conventional practice in her time. Many included advice on epistolary style as well as models to be adapted. Oddly, though, many compilers of these letter-writers settled for reprinting outdated English prose models, including pieces by Samuel Richardson and Samuel Johnson, even when claiming, like the editor of *The Complete Letter-Writer*, that examples they provided would prove suitable for anyone "from the boy at school to the Secretary of State" (4). I am grateful to Oakland University's interlibrary loan office and to special collections staff at the Boston Athenaeum and Boston Public Library for access to representative letter-writing books and guides to social behavior.

4. Florence Hartley, for instance, cautioned readers against negative judgments: "To throw out hints that the sorrow is sent as a punishment to an offender; to imply that neglect or imprudence on the part of the mourner is the cause of the calamity; to hold up the trial as an example of retribution, or a natural consequence of wrong doing, is cruel, and barbarous. Even if this is true, (indeed, if this is the case, it only aggravates the insult); avoid such retrospection" (123).

5. Lavinia Dickinson subscribed to *Harper's New Monthly Magazine*, a sister publication. Emily Dickinson, then, might have had some knowledge of Sherwood's writing for *Harper's Bazar* as well as of advice Robert Tomes included in *The Bazar Book of Decorum* (1873), which preceded Sherwood's popular guide. Esther B. Aresty identifies Sherwood as "the star of all the etiquette writers who undertook to guide the manners of affluent hopefuls" from the last decades of the nineteenth century into the twentieth (261). (The magazine's name was spelled *Harper's Bazar* from its establishment in 1867 until 1929, when the more familiar spelling of *Bazaar* was adopted.)

6. Although Dickinson's letters of condolence are among the most poignant and powerful of her writings, they have only recently begun to attract focused critical attention. Valuable insights into her ability to speak to those who suffer may be found throughout Cindy MacKenzie and Barbara Dana's *Wider Than the Sky: Essays and Meditations on the Healing Power of Emily Dickinson*, especially essays by Polly Longsworth ("'The Might of Human Love': Emily Dickinson's Letters of Healing") and Joan Kirkby ("'A crescent still abides': Emily Dickinson and the Work of Mourning"). Longsworth counts "some sixty surviving letters of solace for the human trauma that [Emily Dickinson] herself found hardest to comprehend or to bear" and identifies consolation as key to Dickinson's sense of vocation (3). Kirkby focuses on the experiences

of today's readers who find that "in the presence of death, Dickinson is a wise compan-ion; no one has written so much about death and dying—and the difficult fact of re-maining behind" (136). Although Elizabeth Petrino focuses chiefly on poetry in *Emily Dickinson and Her Contemporaries*, the second section of that book deals with child elegies and epitaphic verse from a perspective that shows Dickinson questioning "the easy consolation promised in the Victorian period" (125). My own emphasis on letters of condolence reveals a more tender and hopeful manner of writing when Dickinson helped friends deal with their losses than Petrino finds in many of the poems she ex-amines, especially those adopting the voices of dead children. Other readings pertinent to this topic include major Dickinson biographies by Richard Sewall, Cynthia Griffin Wolff, and Alfred Habegger for perspectives they offer on Dickinson's relationships with particular correspondents as well as her own experiences with loss. Studies of nineteenth-century attitudes toward death and practices associated with mourning are illuminating, especially chapters 2 and 4 of Barton Levi St. Armand's *Emily Dickinson and Her Culture: The Soul's Society*. As documentation throughout this essay demon-strates, I have found studies of Victorian social conventions and women's culture espe-cially useful in establishing cultural context.

7. Marietta Messmer's chapter 3, "The 'Female' World of Love and Duty," provides valuable insight into the changing nature of Dickinson's epistolary friendships with Abiah Root, Jane Humphrey, and Elizabeth Holland as well as that with Susan Gilbert Dickinson. Correspondence with Susan has been freshly edited and examined by Ellen Louise Hart and Martha Nell Smith in *Open Me Carefully: Emily Dickinson's Intimate Letters to Susan Huntington Dickinson*.

8. George Mamunes's book, *"So has a Daisy vanished": Emily Dickinson and Tuber-culosis*, provides harrowing information about the waves of deaths, some sudden and others following long struggles for recovery, that struck the United States in Dickin-son's youth and proved especially lethal among young adults. Mamunes believes that Emily Dickinson herself suffered from tuberculosis and had ample reason to imagine herself among the early dead.

9. On the other hand, a comment to Perez Cowan qualifies this notion: "We bruise each other less in talking than in writing, for then a quiet accent helps words themselves too hard" (L332). Evidently, Dickinson cultivated such a quietly soothing manner in her letters.

10. Emily Dickinson's seclusion during family funeral services in the Homestead may, then, have been more "proper" and even conventional than Lavinia's participation. Accounts of her parents' funerals and even her own suggest less formality than eti-quette books proposed. Among nineteenth-century books I have found helpful in out-lining expectations for funerals and for the etiquette of mourning are Mrs. E. B. Duffey's *The Ladies' and Gentlemen's Etiquette*, Sarah A. Frost's *Frost's Laws and By-Laws of American Society*, Florence Hartley's *The Ladies' Book of Etiquette*, and Mrs. John Sherwood's *Manners and Social Usages*. Religious rather than social counsel for the bereaved and those assisting them "to *submit* and *submit with cheerfulness*" may be found in the Rev. Timothy Alden Taylor's *The Solace* (38) and Orville Dewey's *On the*

Duties of Consolation. Karen Halttunen provides detailed, informative analysis of gen-teel mourning behavior as "the most elaborate expression of a dominant middle-class culture by the mid-nineteenth century" in *Confidence Men and Painted Women* (125).

11. Alfred Habegger establishes unusually detailed context for this correspondence with Whitney in *My Wars Are Laid Away in Books*, especially pages 577–84. Joan Kirkby places this outreach in the broader context of Dickinson's behavior as vicarious friend: "She offers love and friendship to one she does not know because it is fellowship and creaturely feeling for which we yearn in the presence of death. And it is in this spirit that friendship is proffered and thus, through community with the dead (their shared love of Bowles), community with the living is born" (137).

12. Readers of Judith Farr's *The Gardens of Emily Dickinson* will not be surprised to find references to flowers in many of Dickinson's condolence letters and in letters re-counting her family's responses to grief. Her mother, quoted earlier as telling how Uncle Loring "held his bouquet sweet" at his funeral, herself "carried Violets in her Hand to encourage her" at burial (L278, L779). Messages to Charles Clark recall "the little flower which was my final ministry to your Brother" (L884), though the Dickin-son sisters regretted learning too late of James's dying: "Had we known in time, your brother would have borne our flowers in his mute hand" (L827). Annual flowering of red flowers Gilbert had loved renewed his memory (L938). The clover blossom Farr mentions finding pressed in Emily Dickinson's Bible at Harvard's Houghton Library (96–97) may well be the one for which the poet thanked Elizabeth Holland, who brought it back to her from a visit to Edward Dickinson's grave (L732). Farr writes that "for Dickinson . . . flowers were metaphors, of both her own self and others. . . . They had souls and played a role in the Christian mystery of death and resurrection" (23). Her discussion of floral symbolism at family funerals (136–38) suggests that the Dick-insons made use of their culture's "language of flowers" but avoided formal restrictions on their color (always white for a child) or their wreath- or cross-shaped arrangements (Duffey 221; Frost 133).

13. I have discussed sea images and related metaphoric clusters expressive of Dick-inson's symbolic treatment of death as circumference more fully in Part III of *Dickin-son: Strategies of Limitation*.

14. In chapter 3 of *Emily Dickinson and Her Contemporaries*, Elizabeth Petrino ex-amines this letter in the context of verse elegies for children, especially those of Lydia Sigourney. Of particular interest is the attention she pays to a related group of consola-tory letters, those Gilbert's grieving aunt sent over the next several years to Kendall Emerson, her nephew's playmate (84–85). Patrick J. Keane establishes a different liter-ary context, that of William Wordsworth's "Intimations Ode." Although his emphasis in *Emily Dickinson's Approving God: Divine Design and the Problem of Suffering* is on the poet's generally grim confrontation with the problems of loss and pain, he declares that "in its visionary ecstasy, this letter-poem, even taking its immediate function to console into consideration, seems antithetical to the bleak, coldly understated vision" of the poem he uses as the centerpiece for his book, "Apparently with no surprise" (Fr1624).

15. See St. Armand, *Culture* 41.

16. "The Letter Writer" section of *Collier's Cyclopedia* offers a reasonably good example of condolences that might have been sent by neighbors and friends in the 1880s:

Norwalk, Conn., June 3, 1882

My Dear Julia:

If God has plucked the bright blossom from your home it is for a purpose none of us dare divine. He alone can pour balm upon your crushed heart. The holy joy is yours of knowing that angel eyes now watch for your coming, and that your beautiful boy will receive you when "life's dark day is done."

If the tenderest or much-loving sympathy could soothe you, dear Julia, learn that you have it from your

Friend,
Laura (Robinson 192)

17. Marietta Messmer scans phrasing in this letter, noting that a major section "alternates between catalectic iambic tetrameters and trimeters, thus falling into a variant of Dickinson's common hymn measure" (37).

ELEANOR HEGINBOTHAM

"What are you reading now?"
Emily Dickinson's Epistolary Book Club

When eighteen-year-old Emily Dickinson wrote to Abiah Root, "What are you reading now?" and then reported on her own list (L23, May 16, 1848), she engaged in what was to be her lifelong activity: reporting on her own reading and eliciting suggestions from her network of friends. As do book enthusiasts today who, in increasing numbers, gather to cheer each other on in the pursuit of the latest award-winning book or of the classic title missed or well remembered, Dickinson and her epistolary comrades formed their version of a book club. Yes, there were *actual* book clubs in Amherst, about which more later, but primarily as Dickinson and her friends studded their letters with literary judgments and recommendations, they formed various conformations and branches of a "virtual" book club; in doing so, they behaved much as do their latter-day counterparts: sometimes they showed off; sometimes they reported on texts as suggestions of personal revelations; sometimes they borrowed the language of their favorites to deepen and convey expressions of sympathy, disdain, affection, and fear. Reading Dickinson's reading as part of an epistolary book club provides insight into the way the developing mind and tastes of Emily Dickinson reached out to the minds of those included in the circle. And, because at least half of the record of this book club exists and is available in the three-volume Johnson/Ward collection, it is no stretch to say that in corresponding as they did, the members of this elite club shaped future scholarly attention to the reading world of Dickinson's generation.[1]

126

Such attention began almost immediately when Dickinson's niece described the intensity of her aunt's reading *manner* (literally, her posture and rapt concentration) and when the granddaughter of Dickinson's dear friends, the Hollands, recalled their conversations about books. Subsequently Jay Leyda pointed to what has become almost a truism: that Dickinson "was no more and no less insulated" from the world than other artists and that, in fact, "the more continuous her exchange with other minds and temperaments, the wider and more varied became her reading" (Leyda I, xx). Along with such specialized books as those by Jack Capps and Benjamin Lease on the Dickinson library, most major scholars note what Dickinson sought in reading and in writing about reading. Richard Sewall, for example, who focuses on the inspiration Dickinson received from her reading, also cites the competitive spirit of the book-related letters (675); David S. Reynolds calls such literary conversations revelations of Dickinson's "deep, frustrated desire for popularity" (167); Susan Howe speaks of the voracity of Dickinson as a reader: "I knew that kind of an ear is an ear that has come through reading" (Gardner 145); and, recently, Mary Loeffelholz's exploration of the "Schoolroom" and the "Salon" offers the broader practices by which women readers in the nineteenth century shared poetry with each other. This essay, in effect, updates the notion of a "Schoolroom" and a "Salon" to the phenomenon of contemporary book groups, both scholarly as in single-author associations and popular as in those that meet in public libraries and living rooms.

What Loeffelholz says of the "Elocutionary Reader" and the "Reading Book" of the nineteenth century—that they "chaperone[d] poetry with explanatory prose" (29)—was unnecessary in what I am calling Dickinson's book club. Famously familiar from youth with Shakespeare, Milton, the Romantics, the narratives of the Bible and, later, with contemporary journals and novels, Dickinson did not need the approval of or the elucidation by teachers, mentors, and friends, but she did seem to delight in and invite their *company*. Their company implied expectations of reciprocity, reciprocity to which she paid attention. Early on, the "club" included, of course, her brother Austin, as well as her friends: Abiah Root, Jane Humphrey, and Susan Gilbert. Many of these early letters are lengthy ruminations that ranged from painfully introspective to hilariously funny. Gradually it morphed into another "club," including a wide range of people of all ages and expertise: her Norcross cousins, the scholarly Holland family, editor Samuel Bowles and his wife Mary, editor/mentor Higginson, and others. Dickinson adjusted her tone and her choice of topics for each.

The range of tone and topics is, for the most part, appropriate to book clubs. Admittedly, in his introduction to the collected letters, editor Thomas H. Johnson speaks of Dickinson's literary references as "desultory, often cryptic, or enthusiastic" (*Letters* xxi), and. Richard Sewall says that "it is hard to imagine [Dickinson] as participating in any sustained literary discussion, either in conversation or in correspondence" (*Life* 620). Re-framing the conversations in the context of what we today call book clubs allows the scholar to see as perfectly appropriate what Johnson calls "desultory" and what Sewall implies are superficial discussions. How many such groups probe as deeply as graduate seminars after all? Re-visualizing such literary conversations as practices within a democratic, mutually trusting book club might put them in a new, more modest but no less important perspective. Through such a frame we might profitably review exactly what Dickinson *does* say and ask—as well as what she does not—about selected authors in the context of her friendships with her book club members.

An excellent early example of an "enthusiastic" and somewhat "desultory" tone is the aforementioned "what are you reading" letter to Abiah Root, written after Dickinson had been recuperating at home during her Mount Holyoke year. Back at school, she wrote a long letter, as had been her wont, to one of the "intimate 'circle of five'" friends of her early years (Leyda II, 477). Although Martin Orzeck sees the Dickinson/Root correspondence as "at times a virtual chronicle of loss, absence, and loneliness" (135), this passage, a first foray of the reading club, is bubbly with Dickinson's interest in the reading of her friends and her joy in sharing her own endeavors. She minimizes the influence of school-assigned reading, instead speaking of the "feast" she had just had at home during her sick leave: "Two or three of them I will mention: *Evangeline, The Princess, the Maiden Aunt, The Epicurean*, and *The Twins and Heart* by Tupper, complete the list" (L23, 1848).[2] This varied fare seemed independent of Dickinson's curriculum, but it may have had other influences. Jay Leyda tells us that the *Express* of March 30 of that year had recommended the first two of these works. If Dickinson read the *Express*, she had two months to obtain the recommended books and report on them, however briefly, to Abiah in the mid-May letter. However high-spirited and affectionate the letter, it shows another quality of many participants in book clubs, including Dickinson, that "competitive" spirit noted long ago by Richard Sewall (673). There is a certain bravado in the list she gives Abiah, as there would be in a similarly breathless letter to Susan (L85, 1852) and in a later letter to Higginson (L261, 1862). She had shown the same competitive spirit about writing poetry in her letter to Austin ("Brother

Pegasus"): "I've been in the habit *myself* of writing . . . so you'd better be some-what careful, or I'll call the police!" (L110, 1853). Competition, implied or stated, did not diminish but was part of that yearning for company that these letters to her "epistolary book club" reveal.

Perhaps in her early years, at least, Dickinson's competitive spirit had an actual site; perhaps she *did*, in fact, attend an actual physical gathering. A letter to her brother, written when Dickinson was in her early twenties, suggests that possibility. In it, she tells Austin, in Boston at the time: "The Reading club seems lonely – perhaps it weeps for you" (L43, 1851), and in the next letter she men-tions it again, this time as though she were a member of it:

> Dont take too much encouragement, but really I have the hope of becoming before you come quite an *accountable being* . . . Why not an 'eleventh hour' in the life of the *mind* as well as such an one in the life of the *soul* – greyhaired sinners are saved – simple maids may be *wise*, who knoweth? . . . Our Read-ing Club still is, and becomes now very pleasant – *Stebbins* comes in to read now, and *Spencer*. (L44, 1851)

The Reading Club, it seems from Dickinson's neighborly gossip, which included family Amherst College contacts Milan Cyrus Stebbins and John Laurens Spenser (Johnson's notes), was not terribly serious. As the letter continues, she reports that the book talk disintegrated into dancing. Of interest, too, in 1851 is sister Lavinia's note on March 21 that "The reading circle commenced this evening" and on May 30 that she "attended *reading club* in evening" (Leyda I, 195 and 199; Sewall 249). Whether or not Dickinson attended with Vinnie we do not know, but she knew of such groups not only through her sister, who reports on a number of mutual family book recommendations (Leyda I, 195), but also through her Norcross cousins who "participated in the Concord Saturday Club, a small group devoted to the study of literature, whose members included Louisa May Alcott, William Ellery Channing, and Ralph Waldo Emerson" (Pollak and Noble 24). Most certainly, Dickinson and her young friends attended a Shake-speare Club. Dickinson's friend Emily Fowler told Mabel Loomis Todd of the crisis when the men raised the question of taking "all the copies of all the mem-bers and mark[ing] out the 'questionable passages,' at which time Emily took her famous departure, saying, 'there's nothing wicked in Shakespeare, and if there is I don't want to know it,' and she flounced out" (Todd 128).

Dickinson replaced such parlor meetings with meetings in letters, beginning with those written between 1849 and 1851, when she was home in a town burgeoning with ideas and while Austin and many of her childhood friends were scattered. However much fun she had "flouncing" out of actual meetings, now she had reason to try out her responses to a host of ideas and experiences in letters, thereby beginning her version of a literary book club. Particularly with Austin, she was often funny. As Martha Nell Smith discusses, a high-jinks of a letter to her brother depends for its fun on his knowing "Tired of the World," a *Punch* cartoon published in *Harper's*; it was a drawing of children discovering the sawdust inside their toys. Ending a long disquisition on the family's concern for Austin's soul and for her own temporary truancy, Dickinson refers to the cartoon, knowing her brother will have seen it. "I had written a *sincere* letter, but since the 'world is hollow, and Dollie is stuffed with sawdust,'" said the young Emily Dickinson, "I really do not think we had better expose our feelings" (L42, 1851).[3]

Such jokes and coded messages became triangulated, involving Emily and her future sister-in-law Sue: Sue and Austin, Austin and Emily, Emily and Sue. Austin, for example, had already recommended Ik Marvel's *Reveries of a Bachelor* to his sister when he and Susan Gilbert carried on their own epistolary book club. Writing from Boston to Susan in Baltimore (both were teaching) in October 1851, he said, "You ask what to read – I hardly know what to tell you – the world is full of books – some of them good ones. . . . For myself, I take most pleasure in looking over *old* books." Among the books he names that are scattered over his table waiting to be read are *Bachelor's Reveries*, Dana's *Prose and Poems*, Coleridge's *Table Talk*, and Hawthorne's *Mosses from an Old Manse*, and he recommends Sue's reading of Irving's *Life of Columbus* (Leyda I 218). By including the mammoth Irving work with two contemporary novels Austin might be showing a little bit of the family's competitive spirit. That month Emily also wrote to Sue, and she, too, talked about *Reveries* (L56, 1851).

Lost today to all but literary scholars, *Reveries* by Donald Grant Mitchell, who wrote under the name "Ik Marvel," was so important to the Dickinson book circle that it deserves special note. It may have come to the attention of Dickinson's friends when the December 16, 1851 edition of the *Springfield Republican* advertised *Reveries of a Bachelor, or Book of the Heart* as "a book most heartily to be beloved, or most contemptuously to be despised; a book with which many hearts will link themselves in sweetest sympathy, and which many hearts will regard as worth just its amount of blank paper" (Leyda I, 185). By February 22, Vinnie recorded in her diary that she had finished reading it (Leyda I, 194). By the following October, Emily, too, must have read it, for she wrote to "Susie," implying that both knew the book well. They might, she said, have "'a Reverie' after the form of 'Ik Marvel,'" a comment that Virginia Jackson places in the context of the Sue/Emily intimacy (Jackson 121). In that letter to Susie, Emily also passed along word of the author's second book: "Do you know that charming man is dreaming *again*, and will wake pretty soon – so the papers say, with *another* Reverie – more beautiful than the first" (L56, 1851). The next year the subject of Ik Marvel's marvels was still fluttering between the book club members. In a family letter Emily enclosed a note to her brother, comparing the author's new book, *Dream Life*, with *Reveries*, calling the later "not near so great a book" as the first, "yet I think it full of the very sweetest fancies, and more exquisite language I defy a man to use" and continuing her letter in a flight of fancy about the author (L75, 1852). Although, of course, not an analysis of either of the novels, this is hardly a "desultory" comment; it is, in fact, the kind of teasing comment a member of a book club might make. That triangulated book club had at least one more round of conversation on Ik Marvel. At least to these ears, Emily's letter to Austin a month later on "a glorious afternoon" is not only *about* but also a parody of *Reveries*: "the sky is blue and warm – the wind blows just enough to keep the clouds sailing, and the sunshine, Oh *such* sunshine." Compare Dickinson's style with that of Marvel's "Fourth Reverie," which begins, "It is a Spring day under the oaks – the loved oaks of a once cherished home. . . . in the sweet valley of Elmgrove," followed by four more pages of earnest magniloquence (149–56). Dickinson continued her letter to Austin: "It seems to me 'Ik Marvel' was born on such a day; I only wish you were here. Such days were made on purpose for Susie and you and me" (L80, 1852).

Ik Marvel's ramblings about yearning and loss from the seat by the fire (pictured in the drawing that is the frontispiece to the book), offered an over-the-top vocabulary for a sort of manic-depressive moodiness. When Dickinson reported on her father's judgment of "these 'modern Literati'" a full year later ("there were 'somebody's *rev-e-ries*,' he did'nt know whose they were, that he thought were very ridiculous" [L113, 1853]), one suspects that she had come to that conclusion herself.

Other letters from those early years reflect a lively convergence of social interests with reading recommendations. Dickinson reports to Jane Humphrey, for example, that she has received a volume of Emerson from Benjamin Newton, an early preceptor and her father's legal assistant (L30, 1850), and in a letter to her "Dearest of all Dear Uncles," Joel Warren Norcross, she slips in references to three widely different literary works: a popular character (Mrs. Caudle) in a

Punch story, Bryant's "Thanatopsis," and Milton's *Paradise Lost* (L29, 1850). During these years the Dickinson sisters looked forward to their copies of *Harpers*, they entertained visiting "tutors," and they attended Lyceum lectures. As Dickinson was becoming "wise" (L44, 1851), she was reaching beyond herself and her family to enlarge the circle of the epistolary book club.

Although earlier and smaller editions of Dickinson's letters have been superseded by the Johnson/Ward authoritative edition, they are of great interest to those reading over the shoulders of the book club members. Their editors either knew Dickinson or knew those who knew her well. These early editors of Dickinson's letters—Martha Dickinson Bianchi, reporting on an adored aunt; Mabel Loomis Todd (Dickinson's first "editor") and her daughter Millicent Todd Bingham, celebrating the poet in the community; and Theodora Van Wagenen Ward, granddaughter of the Hollands (later collaborator with Johnson), musing on Dickinson as friend—all privilege Dickinson as a reader and as one wishing to share her reading.

Of the early editors, Bianchi, who knew Dickinson most intimately, reminds the reader that *her* record (as opposed to that of Mabel Loomis Todd's earlier publication) "is made up from family letters hitherto withheld, deathless recollections, and many sentences overheard from her own lips" (foreword, *Life and Letters*). Bianchi notes Dickinson's lifelong connection with other writers; for example, she reports that even as a baby, her aunt had connected with the future author Helen Fiske (later to be Helen Hunt Jackson), when, apparently, the parents arranged a play date (*Life and Letters* 15). Bianchi judges Jackson as "a hopeless coquette from her youth up" in contrast to Aunt Emily, "reserved, a charmer of charmers" (74). More seriously she includes the letter from Dickinson to Jackson after both had become writers, Jackson publicly with her great novel of California's painful past: "Pity me, however, I have finished 'Ramona.' Would that like Shakespeare it were just published" (Bianchi 372; L976, 1885).

She notes that her aunt had been "the humorist of the comic column" in a school publication, "Forest Leaves" (*Life and Letters* 28). And, perhaps to counter the more racy stories told by Todd, she focuses on the intelligence and taste of her aunt—and her literary wisdom. Bianchi recalls such conversations as this one that turned family visits into a very private book club. She recalls her aunt's excitement when she (Martha) read Eliot's *The Mill on the Floss*: "You have been with Maggie and Philip in the Red Deeps, Matty!" Her aunt's ardor about texts was clearly contagious: "We touched on many vital things then. . . . She had a way of alluding to and talking about the characters in books familiar to us both, as if they were people living right about us – the three Brontë girls were nearer to her than most" (*Face to Face* 41). For Aunt Emily, as for most book club members, there were too many books, too little time. Her aunt, she said, felt with Browning that "Time, why, Time was all [she] wanted!" (46).

According to her niece, Dickinson's time was as fully occupied with reading as with writing, and both were active, not passive, pursuits: "Aunt Emily was busy, always busy. When she read, she was next busiest to when she wrote . . . she would sit straight up under the big reading lamp on the table" (*Face to Face* 46). Bianchi uses her own collection of letters and those of five others to show that even Aunt Emily's love interests also involved books, stating that Emily had "quite a spicy affair with a young law student in her father's office . . . who was bewitched with her." This person "brought her many books, among which were the first copies of the Brontë girls' strange stories, from 'Jane Eyre' to 'Wuthering Heights' and the 'Tenant of Wildfell Hall'" (*Life and Letters* 70). She speaks of Dickinson's correspondence with editor Thomas Wentworth Higginson as "literary philandering" (71), and she emphasizes the book club elements in Dickinson's friendship with Samuel Bowles: "It was his custom to bring to her the manuscripts of famous writers, before publication, and when he entertained [various well-known authors, including Charles Dickens], he would share his impressions of them first-hand with her; often reading her notes to him to those he considered able to follow her meteoric flights" (*Life and Letters* 81–82). Bianchi summed up Dickinson's life in terms of such literary exchanges: "Her books and friends went together in her later life; books first, perhaps" (*Life and Letters* 67).[4] From a long list of her aunt's favorite writers, Bianchi features "perhaps differently from all the rest" those who have been the subject of much subsequent criticism on Dickinson and which will be subjects of this essay: "the Brontës, all three . . . [and] Shakespeare always and forever, Othello her chosen villain, with Macbeth familiar as the neighbors" (*Life and Letters* 80).

These literary figures appear also in the prefatory remarks to the collection of sixty letters published by Theodora Van Wagenen (later Ward), granddaughter of the Hollands, whose home Dickinson first visited when she was 23 and Mrs. Holland was 33.[5] Elizabeth and Josiah Holland presided over a true—not a virtual—salon. Besides the fact that Dr. and Mrs. Holland were in a position to introduce Emily to the works of contemporary writers, many of whom Josiah Holland had published, their home was itself a center of culture and reading. According to the Hollands' granddaughter, the "parlor was a center where new books were shared and discussed, and music was a part of her daily life" (Ward,

Letters 19). Dickinson wrote to "Sister Holland" the rest of her life, often paraphrasing or archly commenting on Milton, Dickens, Shakespeare, and family friends of the Hollands like Henry James and William Dean Howells. In one letter, for example, she tells her friend, "Your Letters have the peculiar worth that attaches to all prowess, as each is an achievement for your delicate Eyes . . . I would not like to outlive the smile on your guileless Face. Doctor's 'Child Wife' – indeed – if not Mr Copperfield's," she says, and almost giddily continues, upping the literary ante from Dickens to Shakespeare: "Congratulate the Doctor on his growing Fame. / 'Stratford on Avon' – accept us all!" (L487,1877). Indeed, even for such "desultory" but lively references, the Hollands must be counted as major members of Dickinson's epistolary book club, as the granddaughter noted with such affection.

For her part, Mabel Loomis Todd includes in *her* volumes of letters members of the community like Emily Fowler Ford who recounted young Emily's sense of humor. She was, recalled Ford, "sparkling with fun . . . she certainly began as a humorist." Ford was in that exclusive actual as opposed to epistolary book club for some time as she recounts: "after we left school we met to discuss books" (Todd 123ff.), among which Emerson seemed particularly important to the little group working on *Forest Leaves*, the hand-written literary magazine in which Dickinson's script "was very beautiful—small, clear and finished" (Todd 127).

Such handwriting no doubt appeared, too, on the many letters to the Norcross cousins, gathered by Todd. Book lovers themselves, the cousins were dear to Dickinson and were, in fact, the object of her very last note before death. One (Miss Fanny) a librarian, the other (Miss Louisa or Louise or Loo), a teacher, both were ideal members of Dickinson's epistolary book club. In a letter from Dickinson's last years we hear the same eagerness—almost the same words—as in the youthful letter to Abiah. In January 1885, she says, "Loo asked 'what books' we were wooing now – watching like a vulture for Walter Cross's life of his wife [George Eliot]. A friend sent me *Called Back* [by "Hugh Conway" (1883)]. It is a haunting story, and as loved Mr. Bowles used to say, 'greatly impressive to me'. . . . Holmes's *Life of Emerson* is sweetly commended, but you, I know, have tasted that" (Todd, *Letters* 270; L962). In 1875 she quotes Charlotte Brontë to tell the Norcross cousins ("Dear Children") that their pleasure in meeting a friend she sent their way was a relief: "Charlotte Brontë said 'Life is so constructed that the event does not, cannot, match the expectation'" (Todd 256; L442), and the next year, August 1876, she cites the Brontës again.

As Todd reported long before Johnson's volume recorded it, the devoted and book-loving Norcross cousins are those to whom Dickinson makes her most famous literary reference: "What do I think of *Middlemarch*? What do I think of glory – except that in a few instances 'this mortal has already put on immortality.' George Eliot is one. The mysteries of human nature surpass the 'mysteries of redemption,' for the infinite we only suppose, while we see the finite'" (Todd, *Letters* 254; L389, 1873). In an earlier letter she is particular about *Middlemarch*: "Mr. C[hurch] alone knows. I am deeply indebted to Fanny, also to her sweet sister *Mrs. Ladislaw*; add the funds to the funds, please" (L401, 1873; quoted in Todd, *Letters* 250). What context? what funds?: that information is lost to us, but it is clear that as members in full of the book club, the sisters will see parallels between *Middlemarch*'s saintly but previously deluded protagonist, Dorothea, and her fine and equally saintly second husband, Will Ladislaw. In their choice of respondents and their editorial comments Todd, Van Wagenen [Ward], and Bianchi were the first to show (though, of course they did not use the words) the widening scope and the continuing enthusiasm of Dickinson's epistolary book club.

As all three of those letter collections attest, Dickinson's habit of exchanging literary observations with her friends began in adolescence, when Shakespeare seemed much on her mind. At fifteen, partly posing but also partly probably already intoxicated with the language of Shakespeare, she borrowed it for an autumnal letter to her friend Abiah Root. Whoever smiles at the elaborateness of this, should remember his or her own poses as a teenager trying to impress another: "The summer is past and gone, and autumn with the sere and yellow leaf is already upon us" (L8, 1845). The closeness to *Macbeth*'s "My way of life / Is fall'n into the sere, the yellow leaf" shows that even then she had easy familiarity with Shakespeare and knew her friend had the same. Years later, she would tell a friend, "He has had his Future who has found Shakespeare" (L402, 1873). Apparently she found her future often. Because Shakespeare's words, sprinkled throughout her poems, have elicited so much scholarly discussion,[6] this focus on her use of such allusions in letters may be brief. What stands out to the reader of the book club letters, if I may call them that, is that Dickinson seems always to trust the recipient, the other member, to understand such a comment as "He that is robbed and smiles, steals something from the thief" (L478, 1876). This nearly exact line from *Othello* went to her aunt Catherine Sweetser in relation to a loved one's death, a death that Mrs. Sweetser, we surmise, accepted with stoicism. As elsewhere when she chooses Shakespeare's words to help her express herself, Dickinson does so with just enough exactitude to reveal that she has internalized the plays, incorporating them into her experience so much that she can retrieve them at the appropriate moment. Such is the case in her use of line to Mrs. Sweetser from *Othello*; the original was close: "The robb'd that smiles steals something from the thief."

Abiah Root, Elizabeth Holland, Maria Whitney, Mary and Thomas Wentworth Higginson, and many more members of the "book club" were trusted by Dickinson to understand the regret, treachery, stoicism, and ardor of *Macbeth*, *Othello*, *Coriolanus*, *Julius Caesar*, *King Lear*, *The Merchant of Venice*, *A Midsummer-Night's Dream*, *Romeo and Juliet*, and *The Tempest*. The most significant epistolary partner, with whom Shakespeare's lines became almost objective correlatives, was the person whose letters simply had to cross the Dickinson hedge. Dickinson's famous remark to Sue that "with the exception of Shakespeare, you have told me of more knowledge than any one living" (L757, 1882) was not only high praise for Sue, but it also implied that the two knew Shakespeare well enough to use his lines and his characters as intermediaries and perhaps as codes in their over-the-hedge conversations. Dickinson drew on lines and characters from the Bard in communications with Sue, just as she did lines from *Othello* to Mrs. Sweetser and from *Macbeth* to Abiah. Shakespeare, the focus of that club from which Dickinson "flounced out" in girlhood, is the only *dramatist* whose work she quoted (or misquoted) in letters to the book club companions. For the most part, she mined the poets, but she often mined them for their drama.

Even Milton, whom she echoed often in her poetry, appears in Dickinson's letters to her book club friends more often for dramatic reasons rather than theological/philosophical/poetic. Dickinson, who relished literary biographies, turned to that of Milton's wife as depicted in Ann Manning's *The Maiden and Married Life of Mary Powell* (1852) when she congratulated Dr. Holland on his new house, saying "God bless it! You will leave the 'maiden and married life of Mary Powell' behind" (L181). Twenty years later Milton is on her mind for deeper reasons. To Mrs. Henry Hills, she wrote: "to be loved is Heaven, and is this quite Earth? I have never found it so" (L361).[7] Dickinson's Milton was partly a cultural staple, partly a result of the emphasis at the Amherst Academy, where Milton was on the "acceptable" list of poets for young people (Sewall, *Life* 353), and partly the result of her own interiorizing of the little book in the Dickinson library, in which someone (perhaps Emily) has marked some of the feistier passages with telltale faint vertical lines. Whatever Dickinson took away from Milton, she knew she could share appropriate lines with like-minded, literate friends.

Just so, she seemed to count on her friends' knowing Edward Young's "Night Thoughts." Again, Abiah Root, who had studied literature with Emily at Amherst Academy, received slight misquotations of Young (L11, 1846), but Dickinson more often called on the poets of her own century in exchanges with book-smart friends. It would be good to know how many of those to whom she wrote were equally able to use poems in letters with anything close to the fluency with which Dickinson drew on the once-removed Romantics, Wordsworth, Keats, Byron (curiously not Shelley, at least not in the available epistolary evidence); the Victorians, including Tennyson; Americans like Longfellow; and, above all, the Brownings in faraway Italy. All, of course, were on the "must read" list for culture-seekers of her generation, but that was not the only reason that Emily Dickinson appropriated them to share with other members of her epistolary book club. A March letter to Mrs. Holland calls forth seasonal imagery on a February slipping into March: "Here is the 'light' the Stranger said 'was not on land or sea'" (L315, 1866). Johnson notes that this is actually a double reference; the line around which Dickinson places quotation marks is from Wordsworth's *Elegiac Stanzas*, but she has also wittily "quoted" Longfellow's "Paul Revere's Ride" by placing the number "1" over "land" and a "2" over "sea." To the Norcross cousins she writes of missing them through alluding to Wordsworth's Lake Windermere as if they are all together there: "I think of your little parlor as the poets once thought of Windermere, – peace, sunshine, and books" (L400, c. 1873). Had she been reading a biography of a Lake Poet or relative, one wonders, or had the cousins spoken of the lakes in a lost letter?

Byron obviously interests and is appealing to Dickinson for the drama inherent in his work—especially "The Prisoner of Chillon"—and in his person. Chillon became a metaphor for Dickinson, who used it in a letter to Lavinia while she (Emily) was confined for eye treatment in Cambridge (L293, 1864). Other references, curiously, all went to her male friends. To the still mysterious "Master" she seems to refer to their situation—or hers—as that of prison, saying "'Chillon' is not funny" (L233, 1861), and to Samuel Bowles, she says, "Dear friend. / If I amaze[d] your kindness – My Love is my only apology. To the people of 'Chillon' – this – is enoug[h] I have met – no othe[rs.] / Would you – ask le[ss] for your *Queen* M[r] Bowles?" (L249, 1862). Twenty years later she said to Higginson on hearing of the death of Helen Hunt Jackson, "perhaps she will learn the Customs of Heaven, as the Prisoner of Chillon of Captivity" (L1042, 1886). If the anguished situation of the prisoner who, tied to a post, watches his brothers die one by one, was more fraught with danger than hers, the image must have touched Dickinson deeply, and it had seeped into the culture sufficiently that Dickinson trusted her correspondents to know it and be touched by it as well. Byron's own life—particularly his club foot—also interested Dickinson, and she must have thought her book club letter recipients would know of it. Writing to Mrs. Holland about the Hollands' son, evidently hobbled as Byron was, Dickinson asks, "How is your little Byron?" and says, "Hope he gains his foot without losing his genius. Have heard it ably argued that the poet's genius lay in his foot" (L227, 1860).

While the references to Milton, Thompson, and Byron reflect Dickinson's use of serious texts for serious messages, she could also enlist poetry for irony. In a strange, fanciful letter to her Uncle Joel Norcross, twenty-year-old Emily, sick and therefore home from school, muses over people going to their final judgment, using a snippet of Bryant's "Thanatopsis" (L29, 1850).[8] In the same league are familiar lines from Longfellow, which serve as analogues to her mood and also, perhaps, as self-conscious literary ornamentations. At least three times—to Austin in October 1851, to Susan in April 1852, and to Emily Fowler (Ford), January 1853—she slightly misquotes from "The Rainy Day," a passage trite in our day and probably in hers: "when the day is dark and drear and the wind is never weary" (L54, L88, and L98).

When Higginson, who was, according to Sewall, "the one she talked to most about books" (567), asked for her favorite poets, Dickinson did not name the pompous Young or the naughty, anguished Byron or even the most highly regarded of them all, Shakespeare. She said: "For Poets – I have Keats – and Mr and Mrs Browning" (L261, 1862). Yet references to Keats come late in the extant letters. To Forrest F. Emerson after the death of Gilbert and also the death of "Helen of Colorado" she speaks of Keats's death, witnessed so vividly by his faithful friend Joseph Severn: "Dear Clergyman / Should she [a mutual friend] know any circumstances of her [Jackson's] life's close, would she perhaps lend it to you, that you might lend it to me? Oh had that Keats a Severn!" (L1018, 1885). Dickinson depended on Forrest Emerson's knowing that, according to his friend, Keats's dying words were, "'Severn, lift me up, for I am dying. I shall die easy. Don't be frightened. Thank God it has come" (Johnson, *Letters* 891). She also trusted that the Norcross cousins would recognize Keats in the letter that begins, "I scarcely know where to begin, but love is always a safe place." In it she talks of being "very sick," and, perhaps inspired by *Endymion* itself or by a Higginson essay, "The Life of Birds," asks "Was your winter a tender shelter – perhaps like Keats's bird, 'and hops and hops in little journeys'? / Are you reading and well, and the W[hitney]s near and warm?" (L1034, 1886). Particularly considering *Endymion*'s opening—"A thing of beauty is a joy forever"—the passage, like most of Dickinson's bookish allusions, *is* relevant to the situation; it shows an understanding of the work of the whole from which she has snatched a line (*Endymion* privileges the imagination); and the reference relies on reciprocity as Dickinson chooses a line from a poem or a biographical tidbit that the recipient will be likely to know.

Perhaps Mrs. Browning's much publicized and romanticized marriage and, even more, her death, made this reciprocity even more possible in the case of the many Browning references. There seem to be no obvious nods to the Brownings in extant letters before the death of Elizabeth Barrett Browning, but after that time there are anguished references for the rest of Dickinson's life. As her niece reported and as her letter to Higginson indicates, Dickinson revered the Brownings almost as much as—if not more than—she did Shakespeare. Just as she asked Mrs. Todd to "touch Shakespeare" for her, she requested that Samuel Bowles make a similar pilgrimage during the summer of 1862 (the year of her explosion of poetic energy): "Should anybody where you go, talk of Mrs. Browning, you must hear for us – and if you touch her Grave, put one hand on the Head, for me – her unmentioned Mourner" (L266, 1862). There was a difference, of course: Dickinson did not have Shakespeare's picture on her wall (she did have Barrett Browning's). She did not suggest that a friend (Mary Bowles, Samuel's wife) name a child for Shakespeare as she did six months after Elizabeth's death: "will you call him Robert – for me. He is the bravest man – alive – but *his* Boy – has no mama – *that* makes us all weep – dont it?" (L244, 1861). And Shakespeare was not the subject (as probably was Barrett Browning) of an aesthetic declaration: "This was a Poet" (Fr446).

Almost as often as she used Shakespeare as a communal objective correlative, Dickinson linked Barrett Browning to her well-read addressees. Appropriating (probably) a queenly passage in *Aurora Leigh*, Barrett Browning's narrative in verse about a woman poet, Dickinson wrote to the Norcross sisters (apparently in answer to a lost letter of which this is part of the conversation): "Women, now, queens, now! And one in the Eden of God" (L234, 1861). Much has been written about the profound influence of Barrett Browning on Dickinson's poetry; as she was crafting those lyrics, she was also drawing on the poet in the shared reading with her friends.[9] While images from *Aurora Leigh* and the spirit of the feisty eponymous heroine are embedded in the poems, Dickinson's focus in her *letters* to her book club partners more often reflected (as do most book club discussions) the *plot* of *Aurora Leigh*. As usual, Dickinson assumed her correspondents would recognize such oblique references as the one to the Norcross cousins in which she compared a relative of theirs to a lay-a-bed character in the narrative poem. Cousin Harriet, she reported in a frisky letter to the "Dear Children," as she called her cousins, "will hate to leave it [her bed, in which she had been reclining from March to May after a broken hip] as badly as *Marian Erle* did" (L372, 1872). Dickinson enjoyed her own little joke—one based on Marian Erle (*Aurora Leigh* 108–17)—so much that she repeated it and elaborated on it in another letter to the Norcross cousins (L696, 1881). Although most who have discussed the influence on Dickinson of this long Barrett Browning narrative in verse do so by focusing on the very serious *poems* the scholars believe to have been influenced by the poignant story of the wishful writer Aurora Leigh and those around her, one might note in *the letters* the lighter uses to which Dickinson put these ribbing references to the unhappy Marian Erle. Just so, she appeared to take a jocular tone in her references to another deeply serious Barrett Browning poem: "Caterina to Camoens." Twice she uses the line that is a refrain in Barrett Browning's rather sing-song poem (a bit, alas, like Poe's "Raven") about a maiden with lovely eyes who dies. Once in an apology to Mrs. Holland (it seems for an Austin delay) she explains that Austin "is overcharged with care, and Sue with scintillation." She apologized, too, for the letter: "I hope I have not tired 'Sweetest Eyes were ever seen'" (L491, 1877).

She also assumed that another correspondent, the editor Thomas Wentworth Higginson, to whom she had written of her literary preferences, would appreciate a portrait of Elizabeth Barrett Browning: "Persons sent me three – If you had none, will you have mine?" (L271, 1862). Earlier that summer, in her obsequious response to his apparently surgically sharp criticism, Dickinson had expressed interest in the poem he had just recommended: "You spoke of Pippa Passes," she says; "I never heard anybody speak of Pippa Passes – before." Browning's *Bells and Pomegranates*, of which the poem was the opener, had been published in 1841, twenty-one years earlier. "To thank you, baffles me. Are you perfectly powerful?" She signed it with the stance slightly (to these ears) tinged with satire: "Your Scholar" (L268, 1862). That stance aside, in the next nine years of correspondence with him, she apparently did not purchase or otherwise find the book in which "Pippa Passes" appeared, telling him in 1871 that she "never saw" *Bells and Pomegranates*, but, nodding to Browning's wife, she said that she had "Mrs Browning's endorsement" of it. Rather, she praised the poems of *Mrs. Hunt, Mrs. Browning*, and the prose of *Mrs.* Lewes (L368, 1871, italics mine).

Although she did not give Higginson the satisfaction of thinking he may have led her to Robert Browning, she had, in fact, been following the narrative poet. To the Norcross cousins again, she mentioned "that Robert Browning had made another poem" (L298, 1862; Johnson believes she was referring to *Dramatis Personae*). She had quoted twice from *Sordello*: once to Louise Norcross she had referred to an illness, saying, "I am not so well as to forget I was ever ill, but better and working. I suppose we must all 'ail till evening'" (L337, 1869). After the exchange about Browning with Higginson in 1871, she used the same allusion she had sent to her cousins (L477, 1876), and four years later she alluded to Browning's "Evelyn Hope" to the Norcross sisters: "and love, you know, is God, who certainly 'gave the love to reward the love,' even were there no Browning" (L669, c. 1880). Four years later, mourning the death of Otis Lord, she wrote to her cousins again, quoting closely (as Johnson shows us in his notes to the letters) from Browning's "Love Among the Ruins"; the next year she quoted from *By the Fireside* and called Robert "the consummate Browning" (L966, 1885); and less than a year before her own death, she wrote to William S. Jackson in sympathy for his loss of Helen Hunt Jackson with a paraphrase of Browning's "The Last Ride Together" (L1015, 1885). By that time, there was a vigorous Browning Society (an *actual* book club), at which Higginson was to appear. Dickinson, herself close to death, wrote in response to the notice in the *Springfield Republican* that Higginson was too ill to read there: "Deity – does He live now? / My friend – does he breathe?" (L1045, 1886; Johnson 905).

Many book clubs discuss poets as Emily (and we must think her friends as well) did with Shakespeare, Milton, Tennyson, Wordsworth, Longfellow, and the Brownings. There were more. Dickinson's letters, for example, also include two other poets whose work Higginson had recommended: Maria Lowell, (Bianchi, *Life and Letters* 276) and Julia Ward Howe (L405a, 1874). Few book clubs explore essays; nor did Dickinson's—other than Ruskin in the early letter to Higginson as she tried to impress him, and Emerson, author of "a little Granite Book you can lean upon" (L481, 1876), who had dined across the hedge at Sue and Austin's. As with most contemporary reading groups, however, she spoke most often of *novels*. Her interest in novels was a small protest against her father's sternness. In spite of his advice to his future bride to read novels by Lydia Maria Child, Maria Sedgwick, and others (Pollak, *Parents* 16–17, 121), on the whole, novels did not meet with the approval of the patriarch—or so Dickinson told Higginson (they "joggle the Mind" [L261]), but Emily kept reading them and talked about them with her friends. In addition to the obvious—Dickens and the Brontës—Dickinson and her friends also read what Mr. Dickinson called "these 'modern Literati.'" (L113, 1853). According to his daughter, Edward Dickinson included "Uncle Tom" and "Charles Dickens" in the list of disapprovals—along with the aforementioned Ik Marvel. Dickinson mocked her father, saying that to him such "'modern Literati'. . . are *nothing*, compared to past generations, who flourished when *he was a boy*" (L113, 1853).

Of course, the "modern" writers then are often classics now. Although Stowe does not appear in the extant conversations between the "book club" members, others whom the stern father may have scorned do. Used "as personal resources" and as examples of Dickinson's desire "to recognize a supportive society of contemporary authors" (Eberwein, *Strategies* 84–85),[10] other writers in her own golden literary period are among Dickinson's subjects: Nathaniel Hawthorne, George Eliot, Harriet Prescott Spofford, among others. In fact, her references to their stories are, says David Reynolds, evidence of Dickinson's "radical" taste, along with her fascination with the "lurid" contents of the *Springfield Republican* (176), and they are evidence of "the breadth of her awareness of the most experimental tendencies in contemporary American culture" (Reynolds 189).

Among the *British* novelists who may have fed such radical interests was Charles Dickens, whose vivid attacks on the inequalities of his society, genius for idiosyncratic characters, startling narrative power, and, not least, gothic qualities obviously entered Dickinson's imagination, her poetry—and the letters to her friends. Charles Dickens became famous the year after Emily Dickinson's birth. *The Pickwick Papers*, which made him the most popular author of his day in England and only somewhat later and somewhat less so in America, was published in 1837. As early as 1844 Edward Dickinson had added Dickens's 1842 *American Notes* to his library (Leyda I, 84), and as the family grew, many novels were passed across the hedge between the two Dickinson homes. With the rest of the family, Emily obviously read and appropriated the books, sometimes for parody as the aforementioned "Dollie" cartoon pointed out by Martha Nell Smith demonstrates. Smith has also written of Dickinson's potential parody of pathetic Little Nell and other sentimental Dickens characters. "Poor Torn Heart," according to Smith, was sent with a picture of Little Nell to Sue "so that the seraphs popped up – like a pop-up greeting card" (Smith, "Cartoonist" 78). Jay Leyda tells us that she also cut out the title of Dickens's *The Mystery of*

Edwin Drood (II, 158). Those playful practices aside, other letters clearly show Dickinson's love of Dickens.

In the middle of young Emily Dickinson's long note to Jane Humphrey, Dickinson puts Jane's absence in terms of "The immortal Pickwick himself," who "could'nt have been more amazed when he found himself soul – body and – spirit incarcerated in the pound than was I myself when they said *she* had gone – gone!" (L30, 1850). In the next extant letter, this one to Abiah Root, Dickinson quotes the end of Dickens's latest book, *The Haunted Man*, characteristically turning the line, "Lord, keep my memory green," into her own "keep your memory green" (L31, 1850), indicating that she had interiorized it, not researched it. The next year she has fun with the penurious, loquacious landlord of David Copperfield, Mr. Micawber. Writing to Austin about the Gilbert "twins," she referred to the twins and the wife of Mr. Micawber to reassure Austin of her watchfulness over his interests: "'I will never desert Micawber,'" she says, "however *he may* be forgetful of the 'Twins' and me, I promised the Rev Sir to 'cherish' Mr Micawber, and cherish him I *will*, tho Pope or Principality, endeavor to drive me from it" (L49, 1851). The Micawber twins remark to Austin is one of a number of times Dickinson used Dickens's plots as touchstones for her developing relationship. A note to Sue from Emily in 1853 cited two close friends in *David Copperfield* as metaphors, perhaps, for their friendship, knowing that literate, teacher, soon-to-be-sister-in-law, Sue would understand a reference to the "*clandestiny*" of Miss Mills, good friend of Dora Spenlow, David's future wife (L107, 1853). Dickinson includes another reference to *David Copperfield* in an 1859 letter to Mrs. Holland. Apparently someone had done a favor anonymously on behalf of Mrs. Holland, as Dickinson says, "I did not suspect complacency in 'Mr Brown of Sheffield'!" (L204)[11]

As these examples attest, Dickinson does not attribute or explain references to Dickens's novels; she obviously expects that the recipient of a letter will understand such a coded name as "Marchioness," when she signs herself that way to Samuel Bowles (L241, 1861). Whether because the novel was so culturally familiar or because she had already had some conversation about this minor character in *The Old Curiosity Shop*—the novel in which, to name her once again, Little Nell touches hearts—she playfully signs with the label (the only name of) the drudge who marries the terrible Dick Swiveller. Such casual comments may not resemble the deeper discussions of a book club, but they show a desire to connect with others with mutual knowledge of a text, with mutual appreciation for it, and often with wit.

While Dickinson often called on Dickens for fun, she reveals and seems to expect others to have a deep passion for the Brontës and George Eliot, with whom this essay will end. However, first, her own compatriots. As she sang "New-Englandly," so she read with Yankee eyes and communicated mainly with others who were still in New England. In a home thoroughly connected through books and journals with American writers, she devoured *Harper's*, the *Atlantic*, and the *Springfield Republican*. Sometimes under their influence, sometimes not, she sought out books by fellow Americans, often speaking more directly—less symbolically or metaphorically—about her own countrymen and women's literary works. To be sure, there are some conspicuous exceptions. For example, in the aforementioned letter to Austin (L113, 1853) she mentioned two of them, one the moody Ik Marvel, the other Harriet Beecher Stowe. As previously noted, a number of letters show her familiarity with and interest in the former. However, it seems almost impossible for her not to have read Stowe, whose book changed American history in the 1850s. *Uncle Tom's Cabin* would have interested Dickinson, probably, at least as much for the attack on the clergy as for its passionate assault on the institution of slavery, and she must have followed the stage adaptation performed in Amherst in 1854 (Leyda I, 320). Dickinson must also have followed Stowe's defense of Lady Byron that appeared first in the *Atlantic Monthly* in 1869, especially (as Christopher Benfey reminds us) when, in 1871, Stowe lived several blocks away from the Homestead with her daughter, an Amherst minister's wife (Benfey, *Summer* 116, 151). Although, as Benfey suspects, Emily Dickinson probably met Stowe, extant letters have no other references to the novelist than that in the playful letter to Austin about their father's resistance to fiction (L113). Why, one wonders, did the more obscure Ik Marvel elicit so much more conversation among the members of this book club? Perhaps Stowe was too popular—and too political. Perhaps the silence, if it was silence, was simply the result of there being nothing left to say about Stowe.

Nor did she mention in known letters another close neighbor, Louisa May Alcott, whose work was bursting on the consciousness of the reading public after Alcott's account of nursing the war wounded and for her sentimental, autobiographical novel, *Little Women*.[12] It is hard to imagine that Dickinson and her circle did not know of and probably read Susan Warner's *Wide Wide World*, the best-seller of 1850. For that matter, few comments survive about any of the women writers whom Nina Baym includes in her *Guide to Novels by and about Women in America 1820–1870*. Guessing that only a fraction of the letters

Dickinson wrote survived between the covers of the three volumes edited by Johnson, we wonder what she thought about and how she shared the book she asked Susan to lend her: Rebecca Harding Davis's *Life in the Iron Mills*. A note across the hedge in April 1861 says, "Will Susan please lend Emily [this book]" (L231, 1861).[13] Such gaps are all the more strange since both Dickinson's "preceptor," Thomas Wentworth Higginson, and the Hollands' friend William Dean Howells encouraged and published women writers. In fact, American women novelists were succeeding in the marketplace so much that Hawthorne famously called them "That d____ mob of scribbling women."

When Dickinson did read American women contemporaries, her comments to her epistolary book club indicate that she absorbed their work personally for their affect rather than analytically for their style and technique. When she speaks of the work of Elizabeth Stuart Phelps, Harriet Prescott Spofford, and Helen Hunt Jackson, she is sharing her emotional response to the books that apparently affected her nerves and moods. The few comments that survive in extant letters suggest that there must have been discussions outside of the letters and in letters that are missing. David Reynolds notes Dickinson's affinity to the popular "literature of misery," such as Sara Parton's *Fern Leaves*, which, according to Reynolds, she read aloud to her father (185). According to a note from sister Lavinia to their brother Austin, Vinnie also read the book to their father, even the "spicey passages," as he "advis[ed] me to put in all the little words as they wouldnt hurt me," said Vinnie (Leyda I, 286). Dickinson may have learned about Parton, a.k.a Fanny Fern, through Helen Hunt Jackson, who once lived in the same boarding house with Parton (Sewall, *Life* 577). Ten years later a note to Louise Norcross offers another tantalizing possibility: "Of Miss P--- I know but this, dear. She wrote me in October, requesting me to aid the world by my chirrup more" (L380, 1872). The manuscript of this letter was destroyed, but Johnson and Leyda think it probable that "Miss P" was Elizabeth Stuart Phelps, who had won the admiration of Higginson and John Greenleaf Whittier for her reformist zeal and her cutting-edge prose. Dickinson's next sentence to Louise smacks of satire about such earnest muck-raking: "She [Miss P] did not write to me again – she might have been offended, or perhaps is extricating humanity from some hopeless ditch." If that surmise is correct, it could explain the absence of discussion among the book club correspondents of the prolific work of writers with reforming spirits: Stowe, Alcott, Davis, and Phelps. On the other hand, the books Dickinson *did* respond to, she read "hungrily, uncritically, and with her whole being" (Sewall 671).

Sewall adds to that comment that her tastes were "banal." That word would be harsh for the popular Harriet Prescott Spofford, but Spofford is an example of a writer whose popular appeal did not keep Dickinson from reading her work and talking about it with the members of her book circle. In February 1860's *Atlantic* she read Spofford's "The Amber Gods," which caused her to ask Sue to "Send me everything she [Prescott Spofford] writes" (Sewall 671). Spofford's name surfaces the next year in Dickinson's early report to Higginson on her favorite authors. In a separate paragraph from "You inquire my Books," she makes a perhaps playful point of her father's judgmental censorship and of her independence from that judgment. "He "buys me many Books – but begs me not to read them," she reported, "because he fears they joggle the Mind." But she follows this probable fib with the comment, "I read Miss Prescott's 'Circumstance,' but it followed me, in the Dark – so I avoided her" (L261, 1862). The story by Harriet Prescott Spofford, one of Higginson's mentees, according to Sewall (566), had appeared in the *Atlantic* two years earlier, and it truly was frightening. Now anthologized in such standard collections as the *Heath Anthology of American Literature*, it can still terrify a reader with its unnamed protagonist surviving a wilderness of snow and a wild beast/Indian Devil whom she subdues by singing, only to be rewarded when rescued by finding that she has no safe harbor after all; her home is burned to the ground, and the remains show evidence of that Devil. That was just the beginning of the novelist's career, a writing life that would last until 1921. Dickinson also read Prescott Spofford's critique of another woman writer, Elizabeth Sheppard, which ran in the June 1862 *Atlantic*. In fact, says Leyda, she cut out the headline on the article (Leyda II, 60). It would be interesting to know where that clipping went; is there a book club letter from Dickinson talking about Spofford talking about Sheppard?

The most famous of Dickinson's contemporary American women writer epistolary partners—though not a subject for the book club—was her Amherst childhood neighbor and exact contemporary, Helen Fiske Hunt Jackson. This complicated relationship requires an attempted play-by-play description. One letter from Dickinson to Jackson—"Pity me ... I have finished Ramona" (L976, 1885)—is scant evidence that Dickinson reciprocated the enthusiasm Jackson showed for Dickinson's poetry. Just so, there is no evidence that Jackson's work—her novel *Ramona*, her story/novella, *Mercy Philbrick's Choice*, her comprehensive sociological report on Native Americans, or her precise, regular sonnets—was a topic between Dickinson and her other friends, with the important exception of Higginson.[14] Especially one wishes to know Dickinson's reaction to *The Republican* Book Column's revelation that Helen Hunt Jackson was the "Saxe Holm" who had written *Mercy Philbrick's Choice* in a new volume of *The No-Name Series* because some see Dickinson in Jackson's depiction of the remarkable village spinster Mercy.

What *is* well documented amounts to another version of triangulation within the reading circle. Before the flurry of entreaties by Jackson for Dickinson to publish, Higginson had joined what might have been a simple neighborly friendship, telling Dickinson in 1869 that they had a mutual friend in Jackson, whom he did not name, and who, he said, "could [not] tell [him] much" (L330a, 1869). In that letter he scolds Dickinson for what he perceives as her isolation and invites her to visit one of several flourishing discussion groups (read salons or book clubs) in Boston, which he playfully said "all ladies" visit. Three years later, writing in response to an *Atlantic* article by Higginson, Dickinson joins him in praise of her childhood neighbor, saying that "Mrs Hunt's Poems are stronger than any written by Women since Mrs— Browning, with the exception of Mrs Lewes" (L368). Higginson's enthusiasm persisted. In December 1874, he wrote, "Pray read the enlarged edition of Verses by H.H. – the new poems are so beautiful" (Leyda II, 214). This praise of one poet to another by a mutual mentor would not set the teeth on edge so much if Dickinson had not habitually enclosed her own poems in letters to Higginson. In her recent extensive exploration of the Higginson / Dickinson relationship, Brenda Wineapple reports what Dickinson may never have realized, that the distinguished editor frequently "praised her [Dickinson's] poems to friends" and "boasted that he had 'letters from Emily Dickinson containing the loveliest little delicate bits of poetry imaginable'" (185). Whatever he said to others, to her he was never as definite in praise as was Mrs. Hunt. One suspects that Dickinson read (as we do) the patronizing tone in Higginson, who had written publicly praising her contemporaries like Helen Hunt while he told Dickinson a tad tepidly, "I certainly feel that I have known you long & well, through the beautiful thoughts and words you have sent me" (L405a, 1874).

If she harbored any wistful envy, however, Dickinson did not reveal it in letters. In 1875, she politely congratulated Jackson on her second marriage (L444) in a four-line poem that apparently puzzled Jackson so much that she returned it to Dickinson for an explanation with a scrawled (facetious?) warning: "This [note] is *mine*, remember. You must send it back to me, or else you will be a robber" (Johnson's note on L444, 1875). The next year Jackson began her crusade to induce Dickinson to publish, especially to contribute to the *No Name* series, something that happened, probably because of Jackson, in spite of Dickinson's resistance (see, for example, L476, 1876). The three-way relationship in this case was quite different from that of other triangulated friendships. Dickinson was not the enthusiast asking for material, praising it, quoting, or paraphrasing it. Instead, the praise just missed the right target. Higginson praised Jackson to Dickinson and praised Dickinson to Jackson and others; Jackson, whom Johnson calls "the only contemporary who believed that Emily Dickinson was an authentic poet" (*Letters*, 947), praised Dickinson to Higginson and, of course, in extraordinary if general words, to Dickinson; and Dickinson, who had hoped for praise from Higginson, responded with cool self-control to the passionate pleas of Jackson to arrange publication and equally stoically to the apparent lack of direct support from Higginson. Dickinson's only extant reference to Jackson's powerful and often beautiful California novel, *Ramona*, was what she remarked to the author herself—that she did not want the book to end. Her only reference to the poems that Higginson had been urging Dickinson to read was sent to him and referenced his enthusiasm: "Mrs Jackson soars to your estimate lawfully as a Bird" (L622, 1879). She apparently did not recommend either the novel or the poems to other members of her book club. This must sound captious against Sewall's generous comment that perhaps "one of the best things [Higginson] did for" Dickinson was "sharing her poems with Helen Fiske Hunt Jackson" (*Life* 577). In his later essay Sewall clearly altered that statement, noting that perhaps the match Higginson had engineered was not the best. Thinking, probably, of Jackson's energy, time, and intellectual passion spent on the plight of American Indians, Sewall notes that Jackson "was a crusader. Emily, clearly, was not" ("Perfect Audience" 203).[15] Dickinson and Jackson, who played together as children, hovered in each other's consciousness until toward the end of their lives when Dickinson wrote to Jackson to express sympathy for her wounded leg (L976, 1885) and shortly thereafter wrote to William S. Jackson in a brief but touching burst of sympathy at his wife's death (L1015, 1885).

The lack of discussion of Jackson's novel is the more interesting by comparison with another American poet and novelist for whom Dickinson did form a private fan club. Like Jackson, but in his case on a much larger world-fame scale, Henry Wadsworth Longfellow was primarily known as a poet, one whom Dickinson seemed to love and whose epics and lyrics she had committed to memory. She seemed to know such work as the aforementioned references to Paul Revere's "one if by land" directive, to the epic "Evangeline," and to lyrics like the "rainy day" poem. She continued to sprinkle nearly exact Longfellow poetry lines through her letters,[16] but it was clear, too, that Emily Dickinson read and wanted to share with her friends Longfellow's novel, *Kavanagh*, one that has also been read as having parallels in Dickinson's life. Unlike her one recorded comment on *Ramona*, Dickinson mentions Longfellow's novel at least six times to her epistolary book club members. In the long, affectionate letter to Jane Humphrey she quotes the book: "Kavanagh says 'there will be mourning – mourning – mourning at the judgment seat of Christ' – I wonder if that is true?" (L30, 1850). Brief as it is, the reference implies that Dickinson trusted that Jane, who had moved to teach in Warren, Connecticut, also knew the novel.

Now known almost entirely only because it figures so prominently in Dickinson's letters, *Kavanagh*, first published in 1848 and reprinted many times thereafter, concerns the manners of a dreamy, impractical novelist, Churchill, who seeks a subject for his genius, not realizing that the subject is right before him: the close friendship of Alice Archer, whose "grey eyes seemed to see visions," and the vivacious, self-confident Cecilia Vaughan. One is lonely, cooped up in sickness with her mother; the other entertains suitors, among them the ridiculous Mr. Hawkins and the earnest preacher, Kavanagh. Thanks to a mistake made—however unlikely this might sound—by carrier pigeons, the eponymous character marries the wrong one of these two close women friends. Although the novel may seem silly to some contemporary readers, two years after its publication Dickinson quoted the minister Kavanagh to Jane with that brave question "I wonder if that [the possibility of mourning in heaven] is true.?" Dickinson's question, of course, is radical, just as the whole novel may be considered "revolutionary"; as David Reynolds points out, Longfellow's depiction of the two ministers in the novel privileges the "imaginative" clergyman over the orthodox one (Reynolds 168–69). Reynolds calls Alice a "gloomy, dreamy girl who sublimates her hopeless infatuation for Kavanagh in poetic visions"; she is, some say, akin to the novel's fan, Emily Dickinson. Dickinson, of course, did not meet her own Kavanagh until four years after she read the book, but she alluded to the plot and cast herself as Alice in a letter to her future sister-in-law and best friend Susan Gilbert, reflecting some jealousy of Sue's sister Martha who had just joined Sue: "You do not hear the wind blow . . . your little 'Columbarium is lined with warmth and softness,' there is no 'silence' there – so you differ from bonnie 'Alice'" (L38, 1851). The next year she reports to Austin that their house guest "had finished 'Kavanagh' and would return it immediately" (L68, 1951). Two years later, Sue away again, Emily wishes her back quickly with a little rhyme from the novel (L102, 1853).

By the last of her many references to the characters of Longfellow's novel two decades later in a letter to Mrs. Holland (L619, 1879), Dickinson also speaks of Henry James, apparently sharing James's fun with moral reformers: "I fear I must ask with Mr Wentworth [an upright character in *The Europeans*, serialized that year], "Where are our moral foundations?"" From Henry Wadsworth Longfellow to Henry James, Dickinson read selectively the work of diverse fellow Americans. When she received Higginson's *Short Studies of American Authors* for Christmas in 1879, she wrote her own review of "American Authors": "Of Poe, I know too little to think – Hawthorne appalls, entices – / Mrs Jackson soars to your estimate lawfully as a Bird, but of Howells and James, one hesitates" (L622, 1879).[17] She does not mention fellow poet Walt Whitman in this letter, but many suspect the truth of avid reader Dickinson's assertion in an early letter to Higginson: "You speak of Mr Whitman – I never read his Book – but was told that he was disgraceful" (L261, 1862).

There is more solid evidence in the book club letters—besides that he "appalls," as she told Higginson—that she did indeed read Hawthorne from early in his career. Missing Austin, she had compared their sibling love to that of Clifford and Hepzibah, hedging at the end of her fanciful re-creation of the *House of Seven Gables* to say, "I dont mean that you are *him*, or that Hepzibah's *me* except in a relative sense, only I was reminded" (L62, 1851). As was her wont, she also followed news about Hawthorne the man. Worried about the wounded Higginson during his service in the Civil War, she asks, "Are you in danger?" She adds to her letter a version of "The only News I know / Is Bulletins all day / From Immortality" (Fr820B), but one bit of news from Concord she knows is that "Mr Hawthorne died" (L290, 1864). Fifteen years later, worrying that she is losing track of literary news, she writes to Higginson again to say that she is sorry not to have seen the Hawthorne essay that he evidently recommended to her (L593, 1879). She does not mention Melville by name in letters to Higginson, but she had probably read *Typee*. To the Norcross cousins she had written "I got down before father this morning, and spent a few moments profitably with the South Sea rose. Father detecting me, advised wiser employment, and read at devotions the chapter of the gentleman with one talent" (L285, 1863). This snippet suggests, first of all, that the exotic Melville book was part of an ongoing conversation with Fanny and Loo, the rest of which is lost. Further, there may be an element of wit in that "one talent" comment; along with the parable to which she was probably literally referring, she suggests that by contrast Melville is multi-talented.

Longfellow, Hawthorne, and Melville are not surprising topics for a book club of Emily Dickinson's vintage, but Dickinson also read, interacted with, and discussed with friends the true "modern Literati." Particularly because of the family friendships with editors, she was aware of and discussed with her friends the writers who ushered in American realism. One such editor/author about whom the Norcross cousins and Dickinson wrote was the gifted James Russell Lowell, who was in the middle of his run as editor of the *North American Review*. It was in the *Atlantic*, however, that Dickinson encountered a Lowell essay that she recommends to Loo: "Read Mr. Lowell's *Winter*. One does not often meet anything so perfect" (L337, 1869). In addition to his editing and encouragement of younger writers, Lowell had already published his own distinguished prose and poetry such as *A Fable for Critics*. Contemporaries and mutual shapers of the literary life on the East Coast, Lowell and Higginson intersected often; once it was through Emily Dickinson when she wrote to Higginson a note that, one infers, must have accompanied a gift of something by Lowell (Johnson thinks it may have been *Three Memorial Poems*): "Is the Year too elderly for your acceptance of Lowell, as a slight symbol of a Scholar's Affection?" (L486, 1877). She also spoke of Lowell in a letter of sympathy to a new widower, family friend Richard Mather, in what appears to be a thank-you note for thanks from him: "The few words of Lowell's seemed true to me – I hope you have felt like reading them," followed by one of the most profound passages on death Dickinson ever wrote (L523, 1877). She quoted Lowell, too, to the Dickinson's former pastor, Jonathan Jenkins, the next year (L564, 1878). Ironically, although in this letter *she* was writing to comfort him (and his wife, who had just been injured), *Jenkins* would officiate at her funeral just eight years later.

The other influential editor of the period, William Dean Howells, provides a contrast to Higginson, who (however great an influence on and friend to Dickinson he was) never read her with the understanding of Howells. Higginson himself acknowledged his own slowness to understand Dickinson's genius in his *Atlantic* article on the occasion of the first editions of the poems. Although, as he says, there was "on my side an interest that was strong and even affectionate," it was "not based on any thorough comprehension." He also acknowledged that he was probably a disappointment to her, that there was "on her side a hope, always rather baffled, that I should afford some aid in solving her abstruse problem of life." Quoting the article, Millicent Todd Bingham, Mabel Todd's daughter, adds: "Though he became her 'safest friend,' Mr. Higginson's affectionate interest was tempered with caution, not to say bewilderment. And he was silenced by her austere integrity – so high, so solitary" (*Ancestors'* 167–68). On the other hand, when, in the tenth year of his editorship of the *Atlantic*, Howells received the Todd/Higginson edition in 1894, his enthusiasm was immediate: "What a rare and strange spirit she was!" Howells wrote (Bingham, *Ancestors'* 310). In fact, Higginson might have learned something from Howells, whose1891 "Editor's Study" column picked up, almost for the first time, the "Terribly un-sparing" quality of "these strange poems" as the "perfect expression of her ideals." Most of all, Howells anticipated the readings of Dickinson as a modernist: "the fact that the artist meant just this harsh exterior to remain, and that no grace of smoothness could have imparted her intention as it does" (Bingham, *Ancestors'* 96). More to the point of the living Dickinson's active book club, Dickinson ap-preciated Howells as much as he did her in his postmortem appreciation. His writing, if not his name, crept into a surprising number of important Dickinson letters—more, actually, than did those contemporary writers who have been more thoroughly discussed.

Dickinson's interest in Howells may have begun as early as 1867, when Emily gave his early book *Italian Journeys* to Susan (Leyda II, 127). How good it would be to know to what extent Emily rummaged in the gift before she gave it. She may well have noted, too, the item in the April 1872 *Republican* concerning Howells's qualifications for becoming editor of the *Atlantic*. Dickinson probably read his contribution to *A Masque of Poets*, published in 1878, and we know that she *did* read him later. To Mrs. Boltwood, a cousin of Emerson and an Amherst neighbor, Dickinson sent a pie with a note that shows her reading of and appreciation for a novel of Howells that had been unfolding serially in *Scribner's* beginning in January: "Though a Pie is far from a flower, Mr Howells implies in his 'Undiscov-ered Country,' that 'our relation to Pie' will unfold in proportion to finer relations" (L629, March 1880?). The next year she was obviously interested in Holland's publication of Howells's *A Fearful Responsibility*, for she quoted a conversation with him in a brief, funny note to Sue: "Doctor – How did you snare Howells? Emily – / 'Emily – Case of Bribery – Money did it – Holland'" (L714, 1881).

Reading Dickinson reading her American sisters and brothers through the years, promoting their work in letters to others, drawing attention to the char-acters and plots she loved most and the aphorisms she quoted so often reflects her New England sensibility, but she also had a deep, deep English sensibility that manifested itself strongly in her passion for George Eliot and the Brontë sisters. What Karen Richard Gee calls Dickinson's "passionate and lifelong" interest in George Eliot began with Eliot's early books while Dickinson was still in her twenties and lasted throughout her life. Although she did not comment on Sue's 1859 Christmas gift, *Adam Bede* (Leyda I, 376), there was no doubt of her growing love for the works of George Eliot. By 1862 Dickinson knew *Mill on the Floss* well enough to drop a funny detail in a letter to yet another editor in the family circle, Samuel Bowles, who later recommended to Susan "a noticeable, discriminating, fresh" article on George Eliot that Sue probably shared with Emily (Leyda II, 169). To stress the durability of her remembrance of Bowles, Dickinson used Eliot's description of the "best Brocade" that was strong enough to "stand alone" (L277, 1862), and ten years later she repeated to Higginson a phrase that became the title of one of Millicent Todd Bingham's books on the poet: "truth like Ancestor's Brocades can stand alone" (L368, 1871). Thirteen years later, responding to a dramatic story from Mrs. Holland, who had been chased from her home by a sewer rupture, Dickinson turned, in melodramatic but light tone, to Maggie Tulliver's flood catastrophe in *The Mill* (L888, 1884).

In the intervening years Dickinson talked Eliot with her epistolary partners, but the nature of the novels and the events in her life created a different tone for her references: one of awe. Dickinson's most famous book club letter may be the one she writes in answer to what they must have asked: What did she, Emily, think of *Middlemarch*? It is worth looking at the sentences that surround the "What do I think of glory" line. The mood of the whole letter is euphoric, verging on manic. It is almost as though Dickinson has become Dorothea in the moment of her epiphany, stretched out on the ground, feeling its pulse below her in the novel's magnificent end. Dickinson tells Loo and Fanny, "Spring is a happiness so beautiful, so unique, so unexpected, that I don't know what to do with my heart" and "Life is a spell so exquisite that everything conspires to break it." As she had appropriated a humorous detail from *Mill* with those stiff brocades and used them to lighten her letters, in this case she reflected the hard-won joy of Dorothea. The letter continues after the "glory" line: "What do I think of glory – except that in a few instances this 'mortal has already put on immortality.' George Eliot is one. The mysteries of human nature surpass the 'mysteries of redemption'" (L389, 1873). That letter was written to the Norcross cousins in April. By November the family had obviously all absorbed Eliot's greatest novel. Dickinson's grief over her father's death the next year (June 1874) seems connected to her deepening appreciation of George Eliot's gravitas and sweeping insights into human emotions.

It was then that Dickinson turned to her treasured friends in that reading circle to talk seriously and often of Eliot. She sent Higginson a note and offered to send him "the last Books that my Father brought me" (L449, 1876). One of those was George Eliot's poems, probably, says Johnson, *The Legend of Jubal and Other Poems*, published in 1874. The next month she promised to send Higginson *Daniel Deronda* "when it is done" (L450, 1876). It had not completed serialization in *Harper's* yet, but when it was published in book form, she did indeed send Higginson a copy with her own "Immortality," one of the few poems she titled (L457, 1876). When Higginson went to England two years later, she continued to talk about George Eliot: "Perhaps you have spoken with George Eliot. Will you 'tell me about it'?" (L553, 1878). The sentence followed references to Shakespeare and to the Dresden Madonna. References to Eliot's characters continued throughout Dickinson's life. In July 1880, when Dickinson wrote to tease Mrs. Holland about not answering a previous letter, she compared her aunt, who must have written a self-pitying letter, to "Aunt Glegg" (L650, 1880). The next April *The Republican* printed a note on "George Eliot's face," which may have been what prompted Dickinson to write—again to Mrs. Holland—that "Vinnie is eager to see the face of George Eliot which the Doctor promised, and I wince in prospective, lest it be no more sweet. God chooses repellant settings, dont he, for his best Gems?" (Leyda II, 347; L692). That fall, Dickinson cut the portrait of George Eliot out of the November issue of *The Century* (Leyda II, 357).

George Eliot, a.k.a. Marianne Lewes, died on December 22, 1880; six days later, midway through another letter to Mrs. Holland, Dickinson announced: "Grieving for 'George Eliot' – grieved for Dr Smith, our Family Savior, living Fingers that are left, have a strange warmth – It is deep to live to experience 'And there was no more Sea'" (L683, Christmas 1881). Thinking back on that grief, she wrote to the Norcross cousins. The manuscript of the letter has been destroyed (along with all others to these recipients), and we wonder what preceded these words and what letter from the Norcross cousins came back to Dickinson in response to this remarkable passage:

> The look of the words [stating the death of George Eliot] as they lay in the print I shall never forget. Not their face in the casket could have had the eternity to me. Now, *my* George Eliot. The gift of belief which her greatness denied her, I trust she receives in the childhood of the kingdom of heaven. As childhood is earth's confiding time, perhaps having no childhood, she lost her way to the early trust, and no later came. Amazing human heart, a syllable can make to quake like jostled tree, what infinite for thee? (L710, 1881?)

Probably Dickinson's anguish for Eliot's doubt was rooted in an article on George Eliot's faith in an 1873 issue of *The Republican* (Leyda II, 204). Obviously, too, Dickinson's urgent fascination with the life of the creator of the great books would shortly after Eliot's death be sharpened by the publication of Mathilde Blind's *Life of George Eliot* in 1883. Dickinson, who was voracious for news of Eliot, exchanged notes with editor Niles, who by this time was wooing her for publication, over the several biographies recently issued (L813 and 813A, 1883). She either remembered or continued to read the *Jubal* poems and expected that her neighbor Nellie Sweetser did, too, for she spoke of the "Choir invisible" in praising the Sweetser boy's singing (L951, 1884). The next year, in the context of an impending biography of Bowles, she wrote to Maria Whitney to remember him and his (puzzling) story: "the Highwayman did not say your money or your life, but have you read Daniel Deronda [published in 1876] / That wise and tender Book – I hope you have seen – It is full of sad (high) nourishment" (L974, 1885).

At the time she was devouring news of Eliot, she was also talking to her friends about Currer and Acton Bell. It, too, was a lifelong relationship. Dickinson began her discussion about the Brontës early in her life and early in their success. A year after its publication, Dickinson returned a copy of *Jane Eyre* to her father's law clerk, Elbridge Bowdoin, one of those with whom the young Emily "went to ride" (Leyda I, 208). Dickinson expressed awe: "If all these leaves were altars," said Dickinson to Bowdoin, apparently including some actual leaves, "and on every one a prayer that Currer Bell might be saved – and you were God – would you answer it?" (L28, 1849). Dickinson knew that her Amherst-educated correspondent Bowdoin would be aware of the news that "Currer"/ Charlotte Brontë was ill. Brontë would not, in fact, "be saved" for long: she died five years later. The Brontës and their characters lived in Dickinson's imagination and in the letters she wrote to reading friends. Plucky, intelligent, self-directing, and oft-disappointed Jane had been absorbed by Dickinson and had become so familiar that in an 1876 letter to Mrs. Holland, enclosing a letter for her friend to redirect to Charles Wadsworth, she quotes directly from the end of the novel. She asks if her "little Load" is "too heavy," and answers her own question by quoting Rochester: "'I find your Benefits no Burden, Jane'" (L475, 1876).

As the years progressed, Dickinson would learn a great deal about the Brontë sisters and would incorporate biographical references in the letters to members of the reading circle. For example, in the Christmas season after Dr. Holland died, Dickinson used a quotation from the introduction to *Wuthering Heights*, telling Mrs. Holland, "Fearing the day had associations of anguish to you, I was just writing when your token came ... Reminded again of gigantic Emily Brontë, of whom her Charlotte said 'Full of ruth for others, on herself she had no mercy.' The hearts that never lean, must fall. To moan is justified" (L742, 1881). Two years later, she told Mrs. Holland, "I wish the dear Eyes would so far relent as to let you read 'Emily Brontë' [probably A. Mary F. Robinson's life of Emily Brontë, published in Roberts Brothers' Famous Women Series] – more electric far than anything since 'Jane Eyre'" (L822, 1883). Dickinson also read the poetry of the Brontës. In 1884 she asked her brilliant friend Maria Whitney (to whom she wrote at least seventeen letters, most of them referring to mutually beloved books) if she had read Emily Brontë's "marvellous verse" (L948), and she offered a copy of the collected poems to Bowles, who "denied" the gift (Leyda II, 28). Thomas Niles, however, did not rebuff the gift of "The Currer, Ellis, & Acton Bells Poems," which Dickinson sent him in place of those he had requested: her own poems (L813B, 1883). Finally, on an "exquisite" day in May three years later at the Dickinson home, T. W. Higginson read Brontë's "Last Lines" at Emily Dickinson's funeral (Leyda II, 474–75; Sewall 575). The leader of the book club was—for a time—silent. In the 1890s she would speak again through the Higginson / Todd volumes.

Whether or not Dickinson was ready to publish her own work (debatable) or to have it published after her death (less debatable), she was most certainly ready to publish in letters to her friends her enthusiasm over her own *reading*. Her choice of excerpt and recipient is interesting. For example, Sewall explains how "the list of the books Emily mentioned in her letters to Higginson is re- markable neither for range nor for novelty" (Sewall 569). The epistolary book club that included the Norcross cousins, however, elicited more interesting, less predictable selections. As Sewall says, "It is clear that the three cousins read the same magazines (*Harper's* and the *Atlantic*) and enjoyed the same novels." Ex- cept, as Sewall notes, for *The Vicar of Wakefield* and *Don Quixote*, they shared only new novels (Sewall 638), as do most current book clubs. Next to the read- ing itself, the intense process described so vividly by her niece, the sharing of it seemed of urgent importance to Emily Dickinson. That, of course, was a Vic- torian convention. Agnieszka Salska speaks of that convention and notes, "From the very beginning, cultivation of emotional intensity seems to constitute the common ground of Dickinson's letter writing and poetry" (Salska, "Letters," *Handbook* 166). One such evidence of emotional intensity—Dickinson's line to T. W. Higginson that "To live is so startling, it leaves but little room for other occupations" – makes the round of greeting cards and calendar quotations, but the rest of that sentence is just as important, "though Friends are if possible an event more fair." She ends the brief letter with a couplet, also well known, "Menagerie to me / My Neighbor be" (L381, 1872).

Those who think of Dickinson as the myth behind the garden boundary need only look at the letters to see how through friends, those in the neighborhood and those scattered across the world to whom she wrote her letters, her life had indeed become an "event." The letter with which this essay began – the one to Abiah Root in which she asked "What are you reading now?" – was an early pass at membership in the select but huge book club that formed around Emily Dickinson most of her life. The youthful exuberance and broad, less developed revelation of the young Emily to Abiah had changed by the time, almost thirty years later, when she thanked Mr. F. B. Sanborn for a book, perhaps one by or about Shakespeare: "I am glad there are Books. / They are better than Heaven for that is unavoidable while one may miss these. / Had I a trait you would accept I should be most proud, though he has had his Future who has found Shakespeare" (L402, 1873). Dickinson knew she was fortunate to live in a home filled with books and stimulating journals and to have friends who were similarly endowed. She wrote to the Norcross cousins about a mutual friend and houseguest who "fed greedily upon *Harper's Magazine*," and she imagines life without such a magazine: "Suppose he is restricted to Martin Luther's works at home. It is a criminal thing to be a boy in a godly village" (L234, 1861). Her village was as wide as her library, a library most decidedly *not* restricted to Martin Luther's works—a funny comparison on her part—and her "brain" was "wider than the sky." That she could share it with scores of correspondents and then (through the wisdom of those who saved and the labor of those who edited her letters) with "the world," makes her—and us—lucky neighbors.

NOTES

1. Because Lavinia Dickinson burned all the letters *to* her sister, with few exceptions, readers must speculate based on Dickinson's responses what exactly those letters might have contained.

2. Apparently Abiah was to know that the list includes long narrative poems by Longfellow and Tennyson, a prose romance by Thomas Moore, a novel by Marcella Bute Smedley, and a boxed pair of novels by Martin Farquar Tupper. That Emily Dickinson does not identify the authors in the letter suggests that all were part of the culture known to her book club friends. However, both Longfellow and Tennyson had been reviewed in the *Hampshire and Franklin Express*, which recommended both Tennyson's mock epic ("good humored satire") and Longfellow's Acadian epic (a "plaintive, touching, melancholy tale" (Leyda I, 142)

3. Smith points out that, as elsewhere, "Dickinson assumes Austin's conversancy with contemporary popular literature. Then she gleefully uses their mutual literacy to encode and express some of her most irreverent feelings [for parents and ministers, topics in the letter] even as she claims to hide them" ("Cartoonist" 100). See the cartoon from *Punch* in Leyda I, 201.

4. Among those on her list were the following: "George Eliot's works she called 'that lane to the Indies Columbus was trying to find.' Longfellow, Tennyson, the Brownings, Socrates, Plato, Poe, and the Bible sift through her conversation; Keats and Holmes, Ik Marvel, Hawthorne . . . Howells and Emerson, Sir Thomas Browne, De Quincey, George Sand, Lowell" (*Life and Letters* 80).

5. This was a remarkable family: Josiah, who eventually became the founder and editor of *Scribner's Monthly*, had fought at Vicksburg, joined the *Springfield Republican*, founded and edited *Scribner's*, and become a successful author in his own right. Among other works, he wrote a major history of the area; a long narrative poem, which sold more than any other single poem in its day except "Hiawatha"; and several novels. With Emily's friend Elizabeth, he parented three children. Some thirty years after the Holland Srs.' deaths the grandchildren discovered the sixty letters.

6. Among scores of such studies Judith Farr and Paraic Finnerty, perhaps most intensely, have followed the lead of earlier critics Whicher and Sewall, in exploring the meaning of Dickinson's Shakespeare. See, also, the discussion of Dickinson's use of *Hamlet* (Heginbotham, "Dickinson's 'What if I Say'" 154 ff.), and Martha Nell Smith and Ellen Louise Hart's work on the "masking" quality of some of the Shakespeare references, particularly those to Sue (*OMC* xviii). Sue herself ended her obituary of "Miss Emily E. Dickinson of Amherst with this: "Keen and eclectic in her literary tastes, she sifted libraries to Shakespeare and Browning; quick as the electric spark in her intuitions and analyses, she seized the kernel instantly, almost impatient of the fewest words by which she must make her revelation" (*OMC* 267–68).

7. As in other cases, this was an appropriation, not a paraphrase or a glib quotation (L361, 1871). On Dickinson's Milton I have argued elsewhere that at least seven letters and scores of poems paraphrase or quote Milton; many more use his images for heterodox appropriations. See Heginbotham in the *Emily Dickinson Journal* (1998), in which I explore the possible significance of the marks in a tiny 1819 edition of *Paradise Lost* in the Dickinson library.

8. L29 is full of other literary references, and it is in itself a literary exercise. Dickinson recreates (or invents) a dream; Richard Sewall calls this letter "the most sustained bit of virtuoso writing (of what survives) she had yet done" (*Life* 384). In the fanciful letter – a mock soap-opera kind of story – she not only quotes Bryant's "drapery of the couch" as imagery but also alludes to *Paradise Lost*, to *Susannah*, to Hume's *History*, and to some cartoon figures, Mrs. Caudle and Mrs. Partington. The mystery in this list, at least to me, is *Susannah*. Could she be talking about Susanna Rowson, whose *Charlotte Temple* was a best-seller when it was published in 1790?

9. Among the important commentators on the influence of *Aurora Leigh* on Dickinson are Gilbert and Gubar (559–61); Jane Eberwein (*Strategies* 73–76); Denise

Kohn in *An Emily Dickinson Encyclopedia*; and Richard Sewall, who says that *Aurora Leigh* was a taste she shared with Samuel Bowles (*Life* 473). See, too, Virginia Jackson's influence tracing (187–88) and Jay Leyda's list of lines marked (II, 338). Another letter (L234, 1861) with its reference to a finally self-directing woman writer (Aurora Leigh) also alludes to another "queenly" writer, George Sand, who "'must make no noise in her grandmother's bedroom.'" Linking the two writers, about whom the Norcross cousins and Dickinson must have been writing, compounds the complexity of the reference. Gardner Taplin explores this link in his introduction to *Aurora Leigh* (xv). Jay Leyda tells us that Susan Gilbert acquired the 1852 edition of *The Poems of Elizabeth Barrett Browning* on January 1, 1853 (I, 259).

10. Eberwein's *Strategies* chapter on "The Precious Words" explores the reasons for Dickinson's responses to a variety of writers: to experience "the drama of suspenseful spiritual life" through John Bunyan (83); to "hope" through *Aurora Leigh* (85); to share "private anxieties" through Hawthorne" (85); to "nurture a tendency toward melancholy reflectiveness" through Longfellow (89); and more. Eberwein's more recent essay, "Is Immortality True?" in Pollak's *Historical Guide* shows the relationship between the literary resources and Dickinson's world and communal values.

11. Actually "Mr. Brooks of Sheffield" is the name that Murdstone calls David Copperfield as an alias. She gets it correctly in a penciled note to Ned written many years later (L549, 1878), and again in a note to Mrs. Holland still later (L820, 1883). She slips in another Dickensian reference to Samuel Bowles, who is suffering from sciatica (L241, 1866).

12. Dickinson could not have known that some of the stories in the *Atlantic* were those of her Concord neighbor and almost exact contemporary (1832–88), but she must have focused on a signed article/letter by Alcott in an 1866 *Republican*, correcting scandalous assertions about George Eliot (Leyda II, 118). Susan Dickinson had given Alcott's *Aunt Jo's Scrapbag* to Ned in 1872 (Leyda II, 195); and Alcott's name was one of those attached to the *Masque of Poets* in 1878 (Leyda II, 301). Dickinson knew of her.

13. How she reacted to the strong first-time publication by a thirty-year-old housewife from Wheeling, West Virginia, bears some study. Tillie Olsen's afterword to Davis's re-published *Life* tells us that when it appeared that April (1861) it brought "absolute News, with the shock of unprepared-for revelation. In the consciousness of literary America, there had been no dark satanic mills; outside of slavery, no myriads of human beings whose lives were 'terrible tragedy,'" and so forth (Olsen 88).

14. Among the few other incidental references to Jackson is a note to Maria Whitney that reports on a visit from the Jacksons (L573, 1878); another appears in Dickinson's thank-you note to Higginson for his *Studies of American Authors*, a work that included Jackson and Stowe (L622, 1879).

15. Along with Sewall's chapter on Hunt in his major biography and his later essay, see, for example, Georgiana Strickland's thorough discussion of the Dickinson/Jackson friendship in the *Emily Dickinson Journal*.

16. For example, also to Abiah, Dickinson alluded, as she would in letters to others, to "The Rainy Day"; she borrowed the words of Longfellow's tribute to his dead wife,

"Footsteps of Angels" (L36, 1850); she used Longfellow's version of Miles Standish and Priscilla in a letter to Mrs. Elizabeth Carmichael (L665, 1880); she expressed her affection to Mrs. Holland by saying that she was glad her friends were not flowers, for they would die, using a rather lugubrious Longfellow poem, "The Reaper and the Flowers" (L185, 1858). She kept up such references through her life, using one of Longfellow's most famous lines in a penciled note to Sue, presumably in relation to news from Egypt: "Had 'Arabi' only read Longfellow, he'd have never been caught – Khedive." Then, perhaps because this time she did not trust Sue with the shared memory, she added the single line – one of Longfellow's most famous, of course: "Shall fold their Tents like the Arabs, and as silently steal away" (L768, 1882).

17. The Poe comment seems to be one of her fibs to Higginson. Daneen Wardrop says that Dickinson had read "widely the work of American male gothic authors such as Nathaniel Hawthorne, Edgar Allan Poe, and Washington Irving" (10). She follows Johnson's lead in supposing that Dickinson's thank-you note to her young friend Henry Emmons (two years her junior), might have been in response to a gift of Poe; cleverly Dickinson says "I find it Friend – I read it – I stop to thank you for it, just as the world is still – I thank you for them all – the **pearl**, and then the **onyx**, and then the **emerald** stone" (L171, 1854; emphasis mine—she expected him to get the joke).

JUDITH FARR

Emily Dickinson and Marriage

"The Etruscan Experiment"

> "Will the sweet Cousin who is about to make the Etruscan Experiment, accept
> a smile which will last a Life, if ripened in the Sun?"
>
> Emily Dickinson to Eugenia Hall, mid-October 1885

What would it be like to receive a letter from Emily Dickinson? Thomas Wentworth Higginson always remembered where he was standing when he took one from a mailbox on April 16, 1862. The letter Dickinson sent (he would receive many more) was direct and determined but made an effort to be suppliant and polite to the literary figure whose advice she desired. Beginning without blandishments or even a classic salutation, she asked, "Are you too deeply occupied to say if my Verse is alive?" (L260). Higginson's was to become one of the earliest published accounts of being startled by a Dickinson letter. But there were many people to whom Emily Dickinson wrote amiably, heartily, confidingly, mischievously, consolingly, erotically, whose responses to her letters we lack. On occasion, therefore, one is free to speculate.

Suppose you were twenty years old and received a brief note from a lady (reputed to be brilliant if strange) whom you rarely saw and who signed herself "Somewhat Cousin Emily –" (L1002)? The note was accompanied by flowers which (the writer declared cryptically) "without lips, have language" and it was preceded by another longer letter that offered thanks as well as this request:

"May I know how to make the Music [you played], and the Cake [you baked]." This note was signed "Smilingly, Cousin Emily" (L1001). If you were Eugenia Montague Hall, praised by her family for good taste, you might be delighted to be thus singled out for your talent in singing and baking by one whose garden was a legend in her village and whose cakes and bread were almost equally famous.

If you were Eugenia, however, the diction of the letter-writer might remind you of an earlier time, a different letter. You were only eleven then and the same person had addressed you fondly as just "Genie" and shown much tact in writing to you intimately and fancifully of what you loved best: your flowers, your dolls. "The lovely flower you sent me," she had written then, "is like a little Vase of Spice and fills the Hall with Cinnamon – You must have skillful Hands – to make such sweet Carnations. Perhaps your Doll taught you. I know that Dolls are sometimes wise. Robins are my Dolls. I am glad you love the Blossoms so well. I hope you love Birds too[.] It is economical. It saves going to Heaven" (L455). The fondness you would surely have discerned in Cousin Emily's lines might have provoked fascination with her mode of utterance; after all, she didn't mind sounding preposterous (*everybody* knows dolls can't teach!); she didn't mind stretching the truth (birds reach the sky, maybe, but heaven is different from the sky!). You yourself might only be eleven but *you* never wrote in such an odd, eccentric, yet delicious way.

Then, in October 1885, you are no longer a child but a woman about to embark upon the vocation most women of your era think nobler than any other: marriage. Engaged to Mr. Franklin Lambert Hunt of Boston, you are to be joined in sacred matrimony at the home of your Montague grandparents in Amherst. On your wedding day you are handed a loving note from your now truly remote cousin, the reclusive Emily Dickinson. Do you recognize the style and reflect that only Emily would be likely to have employed it? "Will the sweet Cousin," the note asks, "who is about to make the Etruscan Experiment, accept a smile which will last a Life, if ripened in the Sun?" (L1021).

At present, these questions lack answers. Indeed, one is tempted to pose another more specific one: Would young Eugenia Hall Hunt, only twenty, have grasped the meaning of the term "Etruscan Experiment"? Why "Etruscan"? Why "Experiment"? In the flurry of her wedding festivities, did she simply put aside the note and attribute the Etruscan allusion and the simple gift of a "smile" to Cousin Emily's curiously unique way of expressing herself? Did she have time on that wedding day to wonder whether Cousin Emily was teasing her, trying to baffle her with such a word as "Etruscan"? (Yet would it not have been rather unkind of Emily to do so?) Or might the word have been somewhat familiar to Eugenia as the child of a Boston and western Massachusetts culture that kept up quite aggressively with newspaper, magazine and other literary reports on the arts? While she probably would not know all it signified, "Etruscan"—like "Greek" or "Roman"—might not have seemed to Eugenia an altogether mysterious word. Coupled with "Experiment," it may have invited contemplation.

At the very least, Eugenia must have been grateful for Emily Dickinson's kindness. For Emily's letters (especially in later life) were often treasured while her truly sociable habit of marking the special occasions of her loved ones was often deeply appreciated. When some critics dub Dickinson "unsociable," they misunderstand the poet's nature.[1] Perhaps deriving this definitive characterization from such a poem as "The Soul selects her own Society – / Then – shuts the Door" (Fr409) as well as from the legend of the Myth of Amherst, they transform a preference for exercising choice in human relations into total exclusivity. Emily Dickinson's letters reveal that she treasured a number of people as her society. She visited them often through language, especially when life itself had visited *them* with crucial experiences. In fact, her letters are an important corrective to the vision of Dickinson as an altogether reclusive hermit.

In 1883, she wrote that there were only two real subjects: "Love and Death" (L873). Those who mourned loved ones who died received richly sympathetic letters from Emily Dickinson, letters that probed the significance of passage from this world into eternity. These were matched in number and intensity by letters sent to the newly married or those about to be married, although gossips imagined Dickinson as a kind of Puritan nun, a spinster dedicated to a life of obscurity and to tending the hearth and health of others. Though she was unmarried herself, the idea of marriage, like the fact of death, obviously seemed to fire Dickinson's emotion. And anyone who encountered certain of her poems and letters realized that she appeared astonishingly familiar with the passion called "love."

As he sought to prepare readers for the posthumous publication of her *Poems* in 1890, Thomas Wentworth Higginson (who became her first editor) announced that despite their presumed formal delinquencies, they were "woven out of the heart's own atoms" (Buckingham 8). Especially because her first published volume contained such ardent lyrics of love and renunciation as "I cannot live with You –" (Fr706), subsequent reviewers assumed that Emily Dickinson must have experienced some grand romance, some compelling—apparently

unconsummated—love affair. The fact that, despite the vivid charm she exhibited as a young woman, she went to her grave unmarried had always energized
the speculation of her small New England village. Compounded with her mature habit of occasional seclusion, Dickinson's single state seemed a pattern of
omission and avoidance in need of various explanations: psychological, cultural,
sociological, religious, even literary. (Mabel Todd, for example, instinctively appealed to the last category by comparing Emily to Dickens's Miss Havisham.)[2]
Because she was unafraid to declare herself "The Wife – without the Sign!"
(Fr194) and to intimate in both her letters and poems an acute acquaintance
with the rituals of marriage, discussion of the possible "causes" of Dickinson's
single life has continued until the present day.[3] A few early biographers proposed that Edward Dickinson's objections to suitors like Dr. Josiah Holland or
George Gould may have kept his daughter from marrying.[4] Others thought she
feared displeasing her father by "crossing [his] ground" (L330) to live in another
man's home. Emily herself told Higginson five years before she died, "When
Father lived I remained with him because he would miss me," confessing hon-
estly "[Now] I do not go away, but the Grounds are ample – almost travel – to
me" (L735). A predilection for the single state was attributed to her, too, one
that was rooted in the culture of New England and thus had somehow
communicated itself to the literate genius who, she claimed, "s[aw] New
Englandly"(Fr256). Certainly she seemed as a young girl to be alarmed if chosen
friends married. A letter to her brother Austin that rings with joy about
youthful games and pleasures ends on a sober note by exclaiming "*BFN. is
married*"(L44). Thus Benjamin Franklin Newton's marriage—she used to call
her father's clerk her tutor and claimed he longed for her to be a poet—was
recorded in italics. She seemed to insist upon the gulf between her and him,
now fixed by his new state in life.

Today, especially among feminist scholars, it is often argued that Emily Dickinson "chose" to remain unmarried; indeed, that "remaining single in a society
that placed enormous burdens on wives [made] Dickinson . . . able to concen-
trate on writing poetry" (Martin, *Triptych* 115). This theory appeals to those who
admire the independence and unconventionality Dickinson exhibited, both as
a woman—in her aversion to organized religion, for example—and as a poet,
whose major poems achieve a bold originality in form and diction that set her
apart. To imagine that Emily Dickinson's state in life, like her artistic vocation,
was distinctly elected and that the limitations of such a life became its freedoms
allows one to conceive her as a dedicated artist. Such an artist would wisely

separate herself from any distraction—however radiant—that could interfere with her endeavors. The young Emily's readings in the *Atlantic Monthly* or *Harper's* might then be seen to have encouraged her in leading a life apart "in the stillness of [her] own inner world," "isolated from worldly surroundings" and "the pressure of all human relations."[5] This kind of life does not easily admit of marriage.

In fact, a life of solitude was often considered necessary to a poet of Dickinson's time, despite the hysterical adventures of Shelley (whom she probably read about in the *Atlantic* of January 1860 but never mentioned by name) or the violent indulgences of Byron (whose verse she admired). She could often have read that a mid-Victorian wife responsible for running a household was especially unlikely to find the solitude in which to create while her frequently consulted newspaper *The Springfield Republican* informed readers in a February 24, 1862 review of George Eliot's *Silas Marner* that "Happy marriage . . . take[s] the passion out of women geniuses." Martha Dickinson recalled her aunt exclaiming exuberantly that one turn of the key in the lock of her bedchamber door meant freedom (Leyda II, 483). While she said she "love[d]" "Little Ones . . . very softly" (L728), Dickinson never expressed a yearning to bear or rear children. Certainly her attitude to keeping a house *soigné* was almost comically disdainful: "I prefer pestilence" (L318). As a little girl, she was, Alfred Habegger observes, attracted to patriarchs like Moses and even to the "paternal order that mandated her own disabling exclusion as a female" (118). As late as 1878 at age forty-eight she wrote to her nephew Ned about being scolded by her mother "when I was a Boy" (L571). Susan Dickinson once told Samuel Bowles that Emily's knowledge of conditions suited to growing corn came from her roving days "when a boy," perhaps overhearing the conversation of her father's farm laborers. The boyish life held attractions: freedom to act, to learn, to initiate, to refuse. Meanwhile, it is clear from many of her letters in girlhood and even in early middle age that the ordinary domestic life of a married woman—especially housekeeping, church-going, entertaining—did not appeal to Emily Dickinson. Are these sufficient reasons to propose that she did indeed *choose* to remain unmarried?

One is obliged in this connection to recall the observation made by her sister and lifelong companion Lavinia about Dickinson's spinsterhood: "It was only a happen."[6] To be sure, we know that on one occasion at least, Emily Dickinson did choose to reject a marriage proposal. In 1880, in her forty-ninth year, she answered what seems to have been Judge Otis Lord's invitation to marry and live with him in Salem. "Dont you know," she told him archly, "[that] you are happiest while I withhold and not confer – dont you know that 'No' is the wildest word we consign to Language?" (L562). To say "No" is to assert one's will as decisively as possible; Dickinson may have recalled Emerson's observation in "The Poet" that a poet "speaks adequately . . . only when he speaks somewhat *wildly* [emphasis mine], or 'with the flower of the mind' . . . [and] with the intellect . . . suffered to take its direction from its celestial life" (332). Although she tempered her refusal by admitting that she shared Lord's passion, her words appeared to issue from profound self-awareness: "it is Anguish I long conceal from you to let you leave me, hungry, but you ask the divine Crust and that would doom the Bread." (Food was one of Dickinson's symbols for passionate love. Earlier, in 1859, she had written of married love, "Am told that fasting gives to food marvellous Aroma, but by birth a Bachelor, disavow Cuisine" [L204].) So, while she refuses him with tender regret, even imagining the "happy night" she might experience in gratifying their mutual longing, the poet addresses Lord with what Emerson might have called "wildness": instinctive determination. Should she yield Lord her "Crust"—her social identity as "Emily Dickinson"—in order to become "Mrs. Lord," she would be forced to surrender her inner self, the "Bread" of her personality, the quintessential spirit that imagined and made poems (L562). It is both ironic and touching that she declined to share Lord's home in phrases of homely imagery: the making of bread, her task in the Dickinson household.

On this occasion then, Emily Dickinson did indeed choose not to be married. After all, she was fewer than ten years away from death, her identity was fixed, and, as she also vouchsafed, "the 'Stile'" that confined her in spinsterhood was "God's." I doubt that Lord believed her when she promised, "when it is right I will lift the Bars" (L562). Nevertheless, this choice cannot prove the supposition that Dickinson *always* chose to remain single. What if—as Lavinia insisted—the "rewarding person" had come along? (Earlier, perhaps, and possessed of a great fortune, many servants, a cloistered set of rooms for her use alone, protective pride in her writing, and with no desire for a family over which she would be required to preside?) Emily, Lavinia claimed, had always hoped he might.[7] Certainly—at least in maturity—Dickinson demonstrated no aversion to romantic attraction or sexual joy. In adolescence she could—quite naturally—be sometimes timorous about rising to a man's requirements in the act of love. Still, "To be an affianced being," she told her brother Austin as he planned to marry Susan Gilbert, seemed to her "rather a serious thing" (L167).

I believe that it was not passion or sexuality but rather the change in identity and state necessarily brought about by a wedding ceremony and a marriage contract that could alarm and even alienate the young Emily Dickinson. Marriage, she announced in one of her first poems to be published posthumously, was a "soft Eclipse" (Fr225). To be married was on one hand a "comfort" since "the Girl's life" represented the "pain" of lack of rank and status. Once married, one became royal, a "Czar," since among the patriarchal Victorians, single women were rankless: perennial dependents. Nevertheless, a wife was customarily eclipsed by her husband, like the moon by the sun. Wentworth Higginson, seeking a title for this ambivalent poem, called it "Apocalypse," thus emphasizing its quality of revelation and disclosure. Yet it puzzled him. Higginson knew that the marriage of Elizabeth Barrett to Robert Browning appealed to Dickinson, so much so that she could envision herself as either of the partners, while the loneliness their child Pen might have experienced after his mother died excited in her a near-maternal sympathy, prefiguring her intense love for Gilbert Dickinson.[8] Since he asked her whether she would not come to Boston one day ("All ladies do"), her kindly and solicitous "Preceptor" never seems to have realized how truly enmeshed in a private world Emily Dickinson was (L330a; L265). Even if an extraordinarily empathetic man appeared, would she have been able finally to "cross [her] Father's ground" (L330) to another's?

One cannot seriously entertain any of these notions without remarking the development of Dickinson's vision of marriage. And I mean by "marriage," of course, what Dickinson herself would have done: a union of sentiment and legality, a social and emotional contract between man and woman, as historically and traditionally established. Marriage was certainly not the only union Dickinson contemplated or wrote about. The glory of romance had even more authority, she found, and—as experience would teach her—it might also (like marriage) aspire to permanence. The lasting charm of friendship was among her major themes while in several poems and letters, she contemplated the appeal, pathos, and sufferings of lesbian love. Still, the "unions" she celebrated were often described in relation to marriage. Thus, in one brilliant lyric "Ourselves were wed one summer – dear" (F596), she imagines the marriage or reception of "the Sign," of another woman who becomes a "Queen" in June, season of weddings. In this poem, the speaker herself, abandoned by the other woman when the latter marries, also becomes a queen like the new bride. But unlike the bride, *her* "Cottage" fronts on the North of sacrificial—intellectual—endeavor, not on the sunny south of natural "Bloom."[9] In poems like this one, marriage between man and woman constitutes election, even fruition, but also the surrender of the bride's original identity. As Dickinson dramatically expresses it: "Your little Lifetime failed;" that is, the bride's existence up to now is obliterated by her new position as wife (while the speaker herself endures the anguish of loss and unfulfilment). Dickinson's lesbian poems, several of which I discuss in *The Passion of Emily Dickinson*, adopt various attitudes toward heterosexual marriage while lesbian love she regards as possibly desirable but often, as in the grim "Like Eyes that looked on Wastes," a "Compact" in "Misery" (F693). Certainly Dickinson's lesbian poems take some of their power from the poet's ironic contemplation of the married state.

In this essay I propose to observe the development of Emily Dickinson's attitudes toward marriage as they appear chiefly in her letters. As important as the poems in revealing her inner self, Dickinson's letters are often highly wrought and disclose the development of a personal vision of life. As I have briefly indicated, the poems present an often theatrical, mysterious, sometimes even mystical idea of marital communion. But rhapsodic, apocalyptic, fervent, religious or comically flirtatious as they may be, her marriage poems do not precisely exhibit a sequence or growth of attitudes. Moreover, the voice of those poems is not the historic Emily Dickinson's; rather, it is that of "a supposed person" whose experiences are informed by, yet not identical with, her own (L268).[10]

Emily Dickinson's ultimate vision of marriage was expressed not long before her death in her letters and in her use of the phrase "the Etruscan Experiment" in her message to Eugenia Hall Hunt. This use of the word "Etruscan" together with Dickinson's offering of a verbal gift of "a smile which will last a Life, if ripened in the Sun" (L1021) has not been explicated. However, the words illumine the poet's view of marriage while incidentally providing another example of her frequently overlooked acquaintance with the visual arts.[11] The visual and decorative arts of the Etruscans—the ancient peoples of what is now Tuscany— were being closely studied in the late eighteenth and nineteenth centuries. Especially respected was Etruscan funerary art such as the famous "Sarcophagus of the Married Couple from Cerveteri" (see Illustration A), the reclining husband and wife clasping each other in a warm embrace and smiling brightly but inscrutably at the viewer.

We do not know whether Dickinson's cousin Eugenia was familiar with Etruscan art or with the Etruscan tomb sculptures of divine figures or married lovers who exhibit what historians call the mysterious "archaic smile" visible on

Illustration A. Sarcophagus of a married couple on a funereal bed. Detail of the couple. Etruscan, from Cerveteri, 6th century BCE. Terra cotta. Photo: Lewandowski/Ojeda. Louvre, Paris, France. Réunion des Musées Nationaux / Art Resource, NY

many famous Etruscan statues like the Apollo from the Portinaccio Temple of Veii (see Illustration B). Though the Apollo was not discovered during Emily Dickinson's lifetime but during the Tuscan excavation of 1916, I have chosen to depict it here as the most "extraordinary" example of the famed smile: "Where in Archaic art does one find a face quite like this?" (Brendel, 242). These sculptures were usually constructed of terra-cotta: a hard, durable kiln-burnt clay. When used to perpetuate the images of a husband and wife, such material implied their lasting commitment. If employed to depict divine figures, terra-cotta might suggest enduring authority. Whether or not her young cousin was familiar with Etruscan sculpture, I shall offer the hypothesis that it could not have been unknown to Emily Dickinson. By sending Eugenia "a smile which will last," Dickinson was alluding to the iconography of a civilization that flowered long ago and memorably in Etruria (Tuscany), thus wishing Eugenia enduring happiness. Her use of the word "smile" was probably a clue to her meaning, even as it was a symbolic tag by which to identify the Etruscans themselves.

Together with its allusion to the Etruscan civilization and culture, a significant aspect of Dickinson's letter to Eugenia is her use of the word "Experiment."
In 1878, in a message to Higginson—a widower who had remarried—Dickinson
named marriage "the Lane to the Indies, Columbus was looking for": that is, the
route to the paradisal Spice Islands of happiness (L575). During that period she

Illustration B. Apollo of Veii from the sanctuary of Portonaccio (detail of head). Etruscan, late
6th century BCE. Museo Nazionale di Villa Giulia, Rome, Italy. Scala / Art Resource, NY

also liked to allude to the Garden of Eden with its inhabitants, Adam and Eve, as a state of semi-divine pleasure. In a letter of 1885 sent to the son of her deceased but still beloved Samuel Bowles, she spoke of his brother Charles's recent engagement as Charles's new "Residence" in "Eden" (L1017). Thus, Eden, like the Spice Isles, had come to represent bliss to her while marriage stood for an *earthly* heaven. The Etruscan marriage sculptures wherein wife and husband's broad smiles are a chief focus of interest may have represented to her the attainment of such a state. In selecting the word "Experiment," however, she emphasized the idea of uncertainty, probably having reflected that successful marriage necessarily requires trial and effort. One of the important features of Etruscan marriage sculptures was the equal size of husband and wife. By comparison, the "pair sculptures" of ancient Egypt usually portrayed a giant husband dominating his tiny spouse. Thus, the famous statue of Demedji and Hennutsen (ca. 2465–2438 B.C.) represents Demedji, overseer of the King's fortresses, as huge while his wife Hennutsen—though a priestess of the goddess Hathor—is much smaller. The Etruscan vision of equality between husband and wife was embodied in the warm embraces of their pair sculptures. And equality called for a devotion inconsistent with condescension (see Illustration C). Since Emily Dickinson's letters show her to have been well aware that married women in her own society were often subjected to condescension in many ways, her mature selection of the Etruscan images is revealing.

However, it took Dickinson a lifetime as well as the deaths of her parents to envision such a marriage of equals. The young Emily's attitude to the married state was characterized by a mixture of fascination, awe, distaste, admiration, and genuine fear. The letters she wrote in her teens and twenties are at first those of the "shy and nervous" girl remembered by her schoolmaster,[12] the girl enamored of her home, her brother and sister, and the girls—Abiah Root, Jane Humphrey, Emily Fowler—who preceded Susan Gilbert as objects of Emily's lover-like devotion. When daughters were born to her neighbors, the fifteen-year-old Dickinson was so aware of the role played by girls in helping their mothers—and so alive to how steadily her own mother toiled—that she christened them "Embryos of future usefullness" (L7). This Emily resented housekeeping and when forced to assume her mother's chores, lamented "I am yet the Queen of the court, if regalia be dust, and dirt" (L 36). Her writing had to be set aside for "sweep[ing]" (L58).

Yet it was not housekeeping that deeply troubled her. She who confessed "how to grow up I dont know" and who wished she could remain always a child

Illustration C. Statue of Demedji and Hennutsen. Ca. 2465–2426 BCE. Limestone, H. 32⅛ in. (83 cm), W. 18⅞ in. (48 cm), D. 20⅛ in. (51 cm). Rogers Fund, 1951 (51.37). Photo: Bruce White. The Metropolitan Museum of Art, New York, NY, U.S.A, copyright © The Metropolitan Museum of Art / Art Resource, NY and that she and Susan might "ramble away as children" experienced profound anxiety at the thought that most women marry, that marriage might claim her friends, and that she herself might be separated from them by wedlock (L115; L94; OMC10). Letters written in her early twenties react to the vision of her friends marrying as if they were going to their graves, not the altar. Thus she wrote Susan Gilbert in 1852, "I have thought today of what would become of me when the 'bold Dragon' shall bear you . . . away, to live in his high mountain – and leave me here alone" (L70). Men (whom she speaks of as "all the whiskers," however "gallant") bring captivity and death-in-life to her girl-hood friends (L85; OMC6). In her not-altogether playful imaginings, her friends become sacrifices to powerful inhuman forces: thus the man who might take her Susan (her "love and rest") away from her is really a "Dragon" (L85, 70). But she was not unique among her friends in conceiving of weddings as little deaths. One girl wrote of another (Ann Fiske): "Is she to be *sacrificed* [emphasis mine] in October?" (Leyda I, 255). Sometimes, the young Emily was capable of reproaching new brides sharply for leaving *her* as well as their common earlier state as maidens bound by sentimental friendship in order to embark on the discovery of what they might experience as wives.

In one famous epistle of 1852 to Susan, the anxiety that accompanied Dickinson's youthful attitude to marriage and weddings is painfully manifest:

> Those unions, my dear Susie, by which two lives are one, this sweet and strange adoption wherein we can but look . . . how it will take *us* one day, and make us all it's own, and we shall not run away from it, but lie still and be happy!

> You and I have been strangely silent upon this subject, Susie, we have often touched upon it, and as quickly fled away, as children shut their eyes when the sun is too bright for them. . . . How dull our lives must seem to the bride, and the plighted maiden, whose days are fed with gold, and who gathers pearls every evening; but to the *wife*, Susie, sometimes the *wife forgotten*, our lives perhaps seem dearer than all others in the world; you have seen flowers at morning, *satisfied* with the dew, and those same sweet flowers at noon with their heads bowed in anguish before the mighty sun; think you these thirsty blossoms will *now* need naught but – dew? No, they will cry for sunlight, and pine for the burning noon, tho' it scorches them, scathes them; they have got through with peace – they know that the man of noon, is *mightier* than the morning and their life is henceforth to him. (L93; OMC9)

One need not study the many nineteenth-century texts, verbal and visual, in which women were described as flowers or urged to achieve the innocent dependency of flowers to recognize how easily this floral imagery must have occurred to the poet, herself a gardener whose intimacy with her flowers was both acute and well known.[13] In this paragraph, an unmarried girl is not without nurture; indeed, she is refreshed by "dew," the gentle affection of other girls. But when the sun, the "man of noon," the male, appears, she is "bowed in anguish": his power burns, scorches, scathes and humbles her. This is one of Dickinson's early ways of describing deflowering, the murder of virginity. Nevertheless, maiden-flowers (she declares) pine for the same sun that can ravish and sear. Their "peace," their tranquil independence, may be destroyed but they nevertheless thirst for the generative spell of the male; if one interrogates the metaphor, it implies that a flower—a woman—cannot become mature without sunlight. Yet the over-powering "message" of the girl Emily's letter is that love for men results in a woman's being not merely wilted but altered, subjected, "bowed in anguish." Such "bowing" is appropriate to a slave, not to a queenly woman-flower and certainly not to a sexual equal. The anxiety in Dickinson's accents here verges on terror.

Finally, her anxiety sweeps all before it and "Oh, Susie," she cries, "it is dangerous, and it is all too dear, these simple trusting spirits [girls], and the spirits mightier, which we cannot resist! It does so rend me, Susie, the thought of it when it comes, that I tremble lest at sometime I, too, am yielded up" (L93; OMC9). To be "yielded up" is to lose all autonomy (and, implicitly, the struggle not to capitulate). While an engaged girl might be dowered with a ring of pearl and gold, no matter how she might be congratulated and served, she will end as a wife violated in her person and her integrity; possibly, even, as a wife both violated and forgotten. It is hard to see how such a woman could "lie still, and be happy."[14]

This letter is characteristic of Dickinson's reactions to the prospect of marriage during her early twenties. If she could tell Jenny Humphrey in 1852, "I think of the grave very often," she could also excuse herself to friends for pondering how she might suffer when they, or she, are carried off by "a brave dragoon," her phrase in a letter to Emily Fowler (L86, 40). (Somehow, the "brave dragoon" of 1851 becomes the "bold Dragon" of her letter of 1852: either a "Freudian slip" or the result of having thought more rebelliously about him.) When Emily Fowler became Mrs. Gordon Ford, Emily Dickinson attended the wedding of her old friend. Later, she sent the new bride a description of her reactions: "Dear

Emily . . . I knew you would go away, for I know the roses are gathered, but . . . when it came, and hidden by your veil you stood before us all and made those promises, and when we kissed you, all, and went back to our homes, it seemed to me translation, not any earthly thing, and if a little after you'd ridden on the wind, it would not have surprised me" (L146).

In the theological sense, marriage can indeed be interpreted as "a translation" whereby two consent to become as one. But the young Emily Dickinson does not regard such an event joyfully as one might the reception of a sacrament, for instance, but as a form of transmogrification. Her girlhood friend might as well have become a witch and ridden on the wind; indeed, as a New England girl, Dickinson would have been aware that, in old Salem, witches were thought to ride on winds. (By marrying, then, her friend becomes a performer of spells and no longer within the sacred circle of untouched maidens. Did Dickinson unconsciously imply such a change?) In the same letter, she mournfully informs the new bride that she hopes she may be happy, wondering girlishly whether there might be a little cricket singing for her on the new domestic hearth! Next, tactlessly, even cruelly, she informs Emily Ford that in the aftermath of the wedding her father had recently come to visit the Dickinsons and "looked solitary": "I thought he had grown old. How lonely he must be – I'm sorry for him" (L146).

Such a message combines resentment—"you will not come back again"—with naiveté. The letter-writer appears to intuit none of the rightful claims of married love by which a wife must put her spouse before her parent, still loving both. As for the delight of a newly married bride and groom able at last to indulge their passion freely, she does not even imagine it. Here, the immature Emily Dickinson punishes Emily Fowler for becoming Emily Ford, a "translation" of which she is in awe but one that she resents as a form of betrayal. Many years later, Dickinson declined to receive Mrs. Gordon Ford (now a published though insipid poet) when she visited Amherst. Thereafter, her old friend struck off an affectionate elegy, published in 1891, entitled "Eheu! Emily Dickinson," which forgave the poet for "shrinking" from her. Ford's sonnet made clear, however, that not being willing to "touch a hand, or greet a face" was, *she* thought, unmannerly if not inhumane.

But time—indeed, a life-time—passed. In late summer of 1881, the fifty-year-old Emily Dickinson wrote to congratulate her old friend Elizabeth Holland on her daughter Annie's coming marriage. "Thank you," she jested affectionately, "for apprizing us of the sweet Disaster in your family" (L723). Dickinson was clearly still capable of toying "smilingly" (as she put it) with such hyperbolic nominatives as "Disaster" when considering how "Cupid" in his "Pink Coupe" could disturb a bride's family (L1001, 723). Events in her own life, however, now enabled her to emphasize the word "sweet." She had used it in her letter of 1852 to Sue, speaking of marriage as a "sweet and strange adoption" (L93; OMC9); but her emphasis then had been on "strange." Marriage was something foreign, dangerous, possibly fatal. Now, in 1881, the prohibitions and challenges of marriage had become colored for Dickinson by the pleasure she imagined such a bond could provide. The truth of the biblical proverb that "Love is stronger than Death" had been proved again and again by the fiery constancy of her own relationships: with Susan Gilbert Dickinson, with the journalist Samuel Bowles, with Judge Lord. Moreover, instead of penning scenarios about women who love, she had also come to "feel [more] sweetly toward the invading powers," men (L723).

It is, and was, almost universally assumed that Emily Dickinson's life altered around 1858. ("Altered" is the word she herself used to describe to Master how his love had affected her [L233]). Her devotion to Susan Gilbert had been so intense that, at the age of twenty-one, she was capable of writing to her in metaphors of that frightening convention called marriage and of lovers and weddings besides: "I feel so eager for you ... [I] feel that *now* I must have you .... Why, ... it seems ... as if my absent Lover was coming"; "come with me this morning to the church within our hearts, where the bells are always ringing, and the preacher whose name is Love – shall intercede there for us!" (L96, 77; OMC11, 5). However, in 1856 Susan married Austin Dickinson after a period of indecision that seems to have brought on a long illness. Despite the passage of many decades and several occasional ruptures between sisters-in-law, Emily would remain faithful to the fact of their early love. While ceasing to see much of Susan near the end of her life, the letters she sent to her could be confiding and might be signed "Faithfully," as if the writer needed to remind them both of the fidelity of their old attachment. One letter-poem to Sue is sublime for its comprehension of what love creates: a bond between lovers whose absolute adhesion never denies their individual identities:

> Show me Eternity, and I will show you Memory –
> Both in one package lain
> And lifted back again –
> Be Sue – while I am Emily –
> Be next – what you have ever been – Infinity –
>
> (L912, Fr 1658; OMC246).

As in the case of a time-honored wedding vow, memory bound their union though Emily wrote to her old correspondent with an erotic sophistication also taught by other affections.

As I have argued at length elsewhere, I think it unlikely that an encounter in 1855 (occasionally followed over time) with her "Dusk Gem" and "Man of sorrow," the Presbyterian minister Charles Wadsworth, transformed Emily Dickinson's life (L776).[15] Perhaps in defensive self-interest, Susan Dickinson spread the tale that secret, frustrated passion for Wadsworth caused Emily's reclusion and inspired her poems for that thrilling man of fire and authority whom she called "Master." However, her more than fifty letters to the Dickinson family's friend Samuel Bowles, editor of the *Springfield Republican*, contain imagery that is so complicit with that of her letters and poems for "Master" that the two lustrous figures may be identical. Each was her "Sun" (L908) and convinced her of the appeal of masculine charm, generosity, and good humor. "Struck, was I, nor yet by Lightning," she was able to write around 1864, imagining a defloration—the tearing and maiming of her "Mansion"—that was not frightening but glorious. In this poem, man and woman together see "the infinite Aurora / In the Other's Eyes" (Fr841).

While the "Master" canon speaks of her mature ability to find the idea of passion gratifying, Dickinson's letters of the late 1860s and 1870s also show developing awareness of what could be the beauty and benefits of married life. Her sister Lavinia had had a youthful romance with the self-centered Joseph Lyman who made love to and then cynically dropped her. Subsequently, Vinnie was depressed when the "wedding cards" of friends came to her "from some where every day" (Leyda I, 253). Emily's ambitions were triumphantly focused elsewhere—on writing poetry, on reading, on friendship (romantic or sociable), on horticulture. But Emily, too, showed curiosity about the marriages of friends and the "m[e]n [they] live [d] with," her pointed words to Helen Hunt Jackson, who demanded that she explain them, together with what the poet meant by saying that in marrying, Jackson had been "fl [u]ng to Dooms of Balm" (L601a, 444). Mrs. Jackson was unaware that "Doom" continued the poet's meditations on a wife's change of state or "translation" while "Balm"—healing, perfumed ointment—added a complicating idea: the power of marriage to rescue the married from privations like loneliness.

While the long, amiable union of Dr. Josiah and Mrs. Elizabeth Chapin Holland furnished Emily Dickinson with a benign example of the marriage bond, her own parents' union of forty-six years (1828–74) was more easily and intimately observed. It must have provided sharp stimulus to a young woman seeking to parse what should be the contractual relation of the sexes: how they appeared to be, how they ought to be.

Were Emily Dickinson's parents happy? Certainly they differed greatly in temperament. Edward Dickinson was (as Lavinia claimed) "the only one in the family to say 'damn,'" an attorney of parts whom Higginson rather unfairly deemed "thin dry & speechless" and who (Emily joked) "steps like Cromwell when he gets the kindlings" (L342b, 339). "Squire" Dickinson's reticence in the presence of a famous visitor who was a man of letters and his independent daughter's friend might have stemmed from a shyness that resembled Emily's "Cowardice of Strangers" (L735); it did not accord with his skill as a speaker in the House of Representatives or suggest the responsiveness to literature—Pope, Addison, Shakespeare, Young—that he exhibited in youth. Was he "dry?" Someone who could openly curse had his passions. Several critics tax Edward Dickinson harshly for failing to praise or even mention her physical charms in his courtship letters to Emily Norcross. He is frequently described as repellently cold in his addresses to her, a quiet, somewhat depressive but not spineless girl who loved flowers and family and was hesitant to leave her cherished home in order to marry.

True, Edward was so opposed to women's suffrage and the "scum" of "females" who promoted it that his sister Mary, a school teacher, wrote to rebuke him for it (Wolff 119). He was in favor of equal education for men and women but considered that their spheres should be different: man's, the world; woman's, the home. Having sent his daughter Emily to Miss Lyon's Seminary, he subsequently (one could easily argue) took limited interest in her interest in literature, promoting Austin's dilettantish efforts instead. On the other hand, it was Edward who built a conservatory so that his elder daughter could grow, and even experiment with, flowers rare in New England; it was Edward who wished her to visit Washington when he was in the House there, yet would not force her (already retiring) to do so. Edward Dickinson's attitude toward both his daughters seems to have been highly conditioned by fears for their safety. The letters he sent to his wife when Emily and Lavinia were children are full of anxiety lest either catch cold or, by getting her feet wet, contract one of the deadly diseases like tuberculosis that continually carried off members of their mother's Norcross family. Were they to marry, they would be subject to the prospect of death in childbirth. An anxious Victorian father would scarcely have envisioned any daughter's wedding without fear.

It is my belief that Edward Dickinson wooed Emily Norcross with a distinct measure of yearning. When he calls her "Dearest Friend," it is with the understanding that friendship is one of the highest kinds of "esteem"—another word he consecrates to her—between equals. He writes of "my regard for the virtues which my acquaintance with you has convinced me you possess" and if he does not praise her eyes or breasts in the fashion of a more carnal sweetheart of (let's say) Jacobean times, it is probably that he does not think such addresses proper, nor did he want to offend a modest and religious girl. In the case of his future wife as with his future family, Edward's chief care is their security and well-being: "I do not wish you to risk yourself on my protection," he tells Emily Norcross, unless "you are satisfied . . . of having your happiness secured." He is not ungenerous. And when he utters what have been considered contemptible sentiments such as "Let us prepare for a life of rational happiness," he is imagining what to them both would have been a noble and even beautiful prospect: the union in tranquility of a devoted pair. One should remember that Edward signs himself on the eve of his wedding: "My Dear, once more, good night . . . I am Yours entirely & forever."[16] A practical man, he was not without poetry (though his daughter Emily once complained that he seemed so). It was he who described himself greatly moved by the beauty of "moonlight evenings," telling Emily Norcross that "one of our Peach trees"—on their new property—was "in blossom" and that he was ravished by "such beauties" (Pollak 210). It was also Edward Dickinson who rang the Amherst fire bell once to call the town's attention to the splendor of the sunset.

But were the Dickinsons happy together? The courtship letters they wrote to one another—Edward's longer and much more frequent than the diffident, often provokingly reticent Emily's—are not the burningly passionate epistles their daughter would one day write to Judge Otis Lord. But they exhibit a deep affection in whose constancy this reader is moved to believe. Emily's mother was timid in the fashion of well-reared Victorian girls. Indeed, "timid" was to become one of her sharp-witted poet daughter's favorite compliments to women she admired.[17] Throughout Mrs. Dickinson's married life, she depended almost entirely on her husband's protective care. (Upper-class Victorians did not consider this kind of dependency weakness, moreover; rather, that the stronger partner should support his less aggressive but charming spouse was viewed as wise.) Jay Leyda's indispensable *Years and Hours of Emily Dickinson* records some occasions on which Mrs. Dickinson accompanied Edward on professional trips. (The poet recalled sadly after her death, "Mother has now been gone five

Weeks. . . . When we were Children and she journeyed, she always brought us something. Now, would she bring us but herself, what an only Gift" [L792].) If Squire and Mrs. Dickinson were necessarily separated, however—during his service in the House of Representatives, for example—they exchanged fond messages in which Edward counseled his wife to care for her health and assured her that he needed her amiable society. She in turn reported how painfully she missed his companionship and guidance. The sweetness of domestic life was a constant theme of their correspondence. Finally, when told that Edward Dickinson had died, his wife cried out, "I loved him so."[18] That she was not speaking truthfully seems unlikely in view of the degree of Mrs. Dickinson's grief; the poet herself was greatly moved by her mother's abandoned, broken lament.

Indeed, when her husband's "firm Light" was suddenly "quenched" in 1874, Emily Norcross Dickinson was struck an emotional blow from which she never quite recovered (L432). By the summer of 1875, the poet had become both her mother's nurse and the chronicler of her widow's bereavement. She wrote to Higginson, "Mother was paralyzed Tuesday, a year from the evening Father died," following this message with a second that mourned the perished intimacy of her parents' lives: "Mother was very ill, but is now easier . . . She asks for my Father, constantly, and thinks it rude he does not come—begging me not to retire at night, lest no one receive him" (L440, 441).

In nursing her for the better part of a decade thereafter, Emily Dickinson the poet was to acquire an affection and regard for Emily Dickinson, wife and mother: a respect that she had not apparently possessed in girlhood. Moreover, while she was to make the famous claim that her mother did not care for "thought," she was also to recall, "I was reared in the garden," noting the real contribution of her mother not only to her practical skills but to what became a sophisticated knowledge of botany (L261, 206).

Then, after Mrs. Dickinson died in 1882, the poet sorrowfully described to her favorite cousins Frances and Louisa Norcross the disappearance of a woman who was very unlike her formidable consort yet had now followed him into the same perplexing eternity: "she slipped from our fingers like a flake gathered by the wind, and is now part of the drift called 'the infinite'" (L785). By her long illness and in her wistful attachment to her dead husband, moreover, Mrs. Dickinson had become "a larger mother" than before and "very beautiful." Thus Emily grants to Lou and Fanny an inspired idea of married lovers united for eternity: "the grass," she writes, "that received my father will suffice his guest, the one he asked at the altar to visit him all his life." In these piteous

words, the separateness—personal and sexual—of her parents becomes nulli-
fied by the poet's visionary perception. Edward and Emily Norcross Dickinson
did not resemble the Etruscan husband and wife of "The Married Couple of
Cerveteri" by sharing equal domestic authority in their lifetimes. Nevertheless,
they exhibited equal concern for the social and emotional rituals of their home,
presenting themselves as a complementary pair. So O. A. Bullard's portraits,
done in 1840, suggest: "Mother" faces left and "Father" faces right, each within
the scope of the other's gaze.

Not long after her mother's burial, Emily Dickinson—who as the older
wrote most of the Dickinson sisters' social messages—addressed the already-
mentioned words to her cousin Eugenia Hall: "Will the sweet Cousin who is
about to make the Etruscan Experiment, accept a smile which will last a Life, if
ripened in the Sun?". Eugenia was soon to become Mrs. Franklin L. Hunt and
"the Etruscan Experiment" was clearly matrimony. As I have said, "Eden" had
served Dickinson eloquently for many years as a symbol of sensual love. In the
late 1880s, however, "Eden"—in a letter mentioned earlier, congratulating
Charles Bowles on his engagement—had also come to mean the happy condition of being ready to marry: "Eden has no number nor street," she informed
Bowles's brother Samuel, asking him to forward her good wishes (L1017). "Eden"
now expressed a positive conception of marriage; in 1871, Emily had written "to
be loved is Heaven" (L361), but heaven was not in her earlier view to be found
in married life. By the time she wrote to Eugenia, it was. The "Etruscan
Experiment" was an Edenic one.

Her letter was then followed in the same year and month by Dickinson's
eulogy for her deceased mother: "I had the luxury of a Mother a month longer
than you . . . Remembrance engulfs me" (L1022). In her final years, letters celebrating weddings and burials were often associated with or arrived hard upon
each other. In matters of love and death, the Etruscans occurred to her four
times. On each occasion she appeared to understand—and acknowledge—
significant features of their art and culture.

Her message mentioning the "Etruscan Experiment" and promising Eugenia
a "smile," for example, had been preceded by playful words to her Aunt Katie
Sweetser, a fellow gardener. These were written in 1876: "Maggie said you asked
should you 'eat the flower.' Please consult the bees – they are the only authority
on Etruscan matters" (L478). Some question had apparently arisen between
Emily and Mrs. Sweetser about the safety of consuming garden produce; so, in
this case "Etruscan matters" would seem to be agricultural expertise handed

down from the past as symbolized by the ancient inhabitants of Etruria, whose chief industries were farming, seafaring, and mining. This letter, like her greeting to the affianced Eugenia, is concerned with fertility, with "ripen[ing]," with the relation between human beings and the earth: all, considerations that marriage involves. And if she chose the Etruscans in such connections, was Dickinson aware that the ancient Roman writers praised Etruria highly as "rich in grain, livestock, everything else"? And what of the "smile" associated with Hellenized Etruscan figures?[19]

On two other occasions, Dickinson was to allude to the Etruscans in captivating poems of quasi-religious significance. A lyric included in the twelfth fascicle and written "about early 1862" in R. W. Franklin's calculation, describes the "sublime deportments" of ancestors who "Bent to the Scaffold" and suffered or died for causes, ancestors whose bravery transcends any the speaker (troubled for nameless personal reasons) can muster. In their martyrdom, these forbears "Beckon" to her with an "Etruscan invitation – / Toward Light" (Fr300). Her words suggest that Dickinson was familiar with the history of the Etruscan people as warriors and monumental builders. For more than 500 years until the supremacy of Rome, their superb civilization flourished. They were deeply interested in life after death (as is shown by Etruscan tomb paintings of the fifth century B.C., depicting the ceremonies of the afterlife: for example, the "Tomb of the Leopard" or the "Tomb of the Triclinum"). They are thus able, Dickinson's speaker thinks, to guide her toward the "Light" of another world. The last Etruscan city was claimed by the Emperor Augustus in 40 B.C. Although the Romans denied their influence, the Etruscan culture and social customs had great effect upon them, even as Herodotus argued. Especially in their sophisticated funerary art—the refined terra-cotta sarcophagi lids that showed human beings dining or conversing in the after-life—the Etruscans presented noble investigations of the problem of existence.

For that reason, perhaps, Dickinson appealed to the idea of the Etruscans again in another poem written in 1882, a poem gorgeous in the confidence of its seductive music. In it, Dickinson noted "The Moon upon her fluent Route" in the heavens, a moon "Defiant of a Road," she said (Fr1574). Meanwhile, she added, "The Star's Etruscan Argument / Substantiate a God." The stars, she claims, are ancient as the Etruscan civilization. Were they not the best witnesses of God's existence? In this poem as elsewhere in Dickinson's verse, a kind of eccentric imperative (or hortatory) mode coexists with the declarative; for the verb "Substantiate" means both "*does* substantiate, and "*may it* substantiate."

Whether or not God exists was a question of profound importance for Emily Dickinson, even as it was the subject of her penultimate letter (L1045). If the stars compose an "Etruscan Argument," it is that, as evidence, they were both ancient and dazzlingly persuasive.

I have already mentioned one aspect of Emily Dickinson's Etruscan "writings" which suggests that, in addition to their history, she was familiar with their elegant funerary art. These are what appear to be her allusions to the famous "archaic smile." Her gift to Eugenia of "a smile which will last a Life" calls to mind the "Sarcophagus of the Married Couple from Cerveteri" (ca. 520 B.C.), who smile with delight as they embrace each other on their funeral couch. It is a monument that portrays man and wife as equal in size and therefore of equal status. It was well known that Etruscan women were given far more authority and freedom than Greek women or even the Roman *dominae* and had "a different social status" as their partners' equals (Torelli 507, 511). Etruscan society had been steadily investigated since the fifteenth century when the Dominican friar Annio da Viterbo (1432–1502) claimed it had "very ancient roots, connecting it to the Scriptures." Piranesi was to devote two magnificent texts to the Etruscans in 1761 and 1769 while a great number of Etruscan objects were collected and preserved in the Vatican's Museo Gregorian Etrusco as a result of the extensive archaeological studies of the eighteenth century. The sarcophagus of the Married Couple was not purchased to be housed in the Villa Giulia of the Italian National Museum until 1895, however, after the political unification of Italy took place in 1861. It was then found among a heap of clay scraps in a warehouse near Cerveteri. Emily Dickinson could not have seen or heard of this Etruscan monument, continually reproduced in art historical works today as the best example of its kind. Yet there were other even earlier monuments that resembled it in the size and disposition of the married couples and in their contented smile. These she might have seen in reproductions of many other statues.[20] Indeed, by 1842, when Abraham Lincoln married Mary Todd, Etruscan marriage had become associated with mutual respect, joy, and fidelity. The wide ring Lincoln placed on his bride's finger was of Etruscan gold and bore the sentiment "Love Is Eternal."

Emily Dickinson had been nicknamed "Socrates" (while Abiah Root was Plato and Sarah Tracy, Virgil) in the group of five girls at Amherst Academy who showed their love for classical studies by reading the ancients in translation. During her education at the Academy and Mary Lyon's, she would probably have encountered discussion of the Etruscan civilization, especially since nineteenth-century excavations in Tuscany were by the 1840s making the Etruscans' origins—Hellenic or native to Italy itself?—a topic of disputation. That her three allusions to Etruria occurred in 1876 and the 1880s, however, suggests to me that during the lively period of American interest in Oriental—and Hellenic—inspired art, she saw photographic copies of the Etruscan funerary statues being collected in Tuscany and exhibited in the United States and abroad.

The concluding phrase of Dickinson's letter to Eugenia is important. It accords the undertaker of the Etruscan experiment a smile "which will last a Life, if ripened in the Sun" (L1021). That smile is evidently the metaphor of Emily's approval and good wishes but, given its proximity in her sentence to the word "Etruscan," it recalls the fact that Etrurian sepulchres depict married pairs smiling. Thus she sends a woman about to marry some advice: marriage itself must, like a fruit or flower, ripen in the sun in order to last the lifetime of the partners. At this point, the poet's many allusions to the phenomenon of sunlight with its primary meaning as the enabler of all earthly and human growth clarify the letter-writer's. Again and again, the sun is, for Dickinson the poet, passion itself or a superbly powerful force that incites it. So, the lover in "Struck, was I, nor yet by Lightning" "holds a Sun on" the speaker, and his passion for her enables her to "die" (the Elizabethan idiom denoting orgasm), leaving the unawakened life behind (Fr841). In her poem "Longing is like the Seed / That wrestles in the Ground," Dickinson explains that those who love, like plants, must practice "Constancy" "Before [they] see the Sun!" and are able to leave the buried life for one of fulfillment (F1298). To push through the ground toward the destiny of bloom, a seed—like a married pair—must be willing to conquer great burdens and challenges. Emily Dickinson's final "teaching" about marriage, if one may so describe it, was that it should partake of passion and even romance, sealed by the bond of commitment and undertaken with respect for each equal partner in the common undertaking.

What of her own inclinations? Did she really choose not to be married or was her unmarried state, in Lavinia's words, "only a happen?" To attempt an answer to this question, the words of the poet Emily Dickinson may again be justly called upon to illumine those of Dickinson the letter-writer. The latter was fond of sibylline utterance: so, she told Elizabeth Holland in 1884, "All grows strangely emphatic, and I think if I should see you again, I sh'd begin every sentence with 'I say unto you'" (L950).

But the poet Dickinson had herself revealed her attitude to being married twenty years earlier, around 1864. At a time when "Master" was still upon the scene and the love poems that exhibited much understanding of sex between man and woman grew apace in the fascicles, she nevertheless wrote:

> Given in Marriage unto Thee
> Oh thou Celestial Host –
> Bride of the Father and the Son
> Bride of the Holy Ghost –
>
> Other Betrothal shall dissolve –
> Wedlock of Will, decay –
> Only the Keeper of this Ring
> Conquer Mortality –
>
> (Fr818B)

One might be tempted to understand this poem as a description of how a professed nun could conceive of her vocation: one that transcended that of a wife and married her to God for all eternity. Yet I believe, rather, that Emily Dickinson wrote this poem to describe her own spiritual calling: that of poet. In a beautiful and significant lyric, written two years earlier, she confessed: "Alone, I cannot be – / For Hosts – do visit me" (Fr303). These were the angels of art, of inspiration. They would finally make her immortal. While human love always appealed to her and earthly marriage came to seem blessed, Dickinson had not been single for many years and was in fact already married: to the Muse who—more than any human person proposed by me or others—was her true Master.[21] That she never married another may have been in one sense "a happen." Yet had she done so, she would have violated that intense "Constancy" long pledged to a higher power.

NOTES

1. See Helen Vendler, "The Unsociable Soul" (34). Dickinson's letters inhibit such an interpretation. Similarly, Harold Bloom writes, "[Dickinson's] letters are [artful] prose-poems . . . . You cannot argue her attachments from her letters, which are high-fantastical" (*Best Poems* 575). But this is to deny the evident humanity that shines forth in her letters' language and in the frequency with which she wrote select correspondents like the Norcross cousins.

2. "One inevitably thinks of Miss Haversham [*sic*] in speaking of her" (Leyda II, 377).

3. Many readers hypothesize a distinct "cause" preventing Dickinson from marriage. Cynthia Griffin Wolff declares that "she rejected woman's traditional resort" in order "to discover some other role" (127). Wendy Martin finds that she made "a decision to remain single," possibly in accord with Emerson's precept that sublime vision

was accorded to the chaste (*Triptych* 151); Emerson himself was twice married, however. Janet McCann makes a distinction between Dickinson's attitude to marriage in
the poems (where it is seen as "the ideal [human] union and role" and her attitude to
marriage in the letters wherein she sees "the actual lives of married women [as] depress-
ing and enervating" (191). Jane Donahue Eberwein writes, "Directly or indirectly, Dickinson chose spinsterhood" but advances a few reasons why marriage would not have
appealed to her: for example, "the fragility of marital peace" evident in her brother's
household (*Dickinson* 29).

4. On September 15, 1882, Mabel Todd wrote in her journal that Amherst town
gossip was promoting the theory that "Dr. Holland loved [Emily Dickinson] very much
& she him, but that her [stern] father . . . would not listen to her marrying him" (Leyda
II, 377). Genevieve Taggard identifies Gould as Dickinson's lover throughout *The Life
and Mind of Emily Dickinson*.

5. Quoted by Judith Farr from January 1858 *Atlantic* article titled "Our Artists in
Italy" (*Passion* 24).

6. Lavinia described to Mrs. Caroline Healey Dall "false statements" made about
her sister's reclusion and about her so-called love disaster, saying that no such disaster
had ever occurred and that her retired life was "only a happen" (Sewall, *Life* 153).

7. Lavinia insisted that Emily was "always watching for the rewarding person to
come." Her remark that Emily "had to think," however, was somewhat at variance with
her vague observations about possible suitors (cf. Wolff, 118).

8. Dickinson's ardent respect and affection for Elizabeth Barrett Browning's
poems, especially *Sonnets from the Portuguese* and *Aurora Leigh*, began early in her
writing life, as she confesses in "I think I was enchanted" (Fr627). In the elegy for that
"Foreign Lady" which begins "Her – 'last Poems,'" she cries, "What – and if Ourself
a Bridegroom – / Put Her down – in Italy?" (Fr600). For Robert Browning, man
and poet, she preserved a deep reverence clearly mingled with personal attraction.
His picture hung in her bed-chamber, she urged Samuel Bowles's wife to name her
child after him, and one year before her death called him "the consummate Browning"
(L966).

9. Dickinson often associated herself with the North and what she construed as
northern characteristics or virtues. So she begged Higginson to "excuse the bleak simplicity that knew no tutor but the North" (L368), separating herself from those who
represented the quixotic allure of the South (Farr, *Gardens* 187–88).

10. Dickinson's famous remark to Higginson that when she stated herself as the
"Representative of the Verse – it does not mean – me – but a supposed person" wisely
encouraged him to grant her the necessary latitude or "Circumference" to imagine and
write about experiences other than her own (L268). At the same time, due to the coded
nature of her more cryptic poems, intended for specific persons and not necessarily for
a general reader, there are few poets to whose art biographical knowledge can be more
helpfully relevant. (See Farr, *Passion*, especially pp. 100–244).

11. Dickinson read John Ruskin's *Modern Painters*, admired Thomas Cole's paintings (probably *The Voyage of Life* in particular) so much that she twice signed herself

"Cole" in one letter (L214), and alluded to the iconography of other Hudson River artists like Church (a correspondent of Samuel Bowles and known to Austin). She wrote of Guido Reni, Domenichino, and other artists extolled in the nineteenth century, and probably profited from reading the *Art Journal* (to which Austin Dickinson subscribed) as well as magazines like *Scribner's* and *Harper's* which discussed art works and reproduced pictures by such painters as Winslow Homer. (See Farr, "Dickinson and the Visual Arts" 61–92.)

12. Recollection of Daniel Fiske (Leyda I, 81).

13. According to Susan Dickinson, "Love of flowers" was her primary characteristic, while their growth and appearances provided her with a multitude of apparently diverse subject matters (Farr, *Gardens* 3 and passim).

14. I have never seen a discussion of Dickinson's formula "lie still;" yet it is tempting to wonder whether she was familiar with the old jest about wedding nights on which Victorian girls were expected to "lie still and think of the British Empire." In the mature and vivid sexual poems such as "Struck, was I" (Fr841), lying still was not in question.

15. Most specifically in *Gardens*, 198–200, and also in *Passion*, 28–29 and passim.

16. "Esteem" is the word Edward uses continually to record his respect for Emily Norcross as an equal partner in their "friendship" (Pollak, *Parents* 4 and passim). His words of commitment appear on 211.

17. When she says her dying Aunt Lavinia "is such a timid woman," she seems to be praising her gentility (L207). Mrs. Julius Seelye's "timidity" is the mark of her generosity (L508). She grieved for the dead Mrs. Edward Dwight, whose "timid portrait" moved her to consider other women "bristling – and very loud" (L243, 246). Perhaps influenced by Dickens's and other favorite Victorians' preference for delicate heroines, Dickinson seems to regard timidity as a charming proof of femininity, but then "Beauty is often timidity" (L807).

18. Dickinson describes her mother's reception of the news of her husband's death to Elizabeth Holland, asking "Had he a tenderer eulogy?" (L730).

19. See Annette Rathje (*The Etruscans* 54). The Etruscans are not mentioned by Homer but "enter the Greek cultural universe with Hesiod" in the *Theogony*, according to Mario Torelli (*The Etruscans* 26). From the sixth century B.C. on, "Etruria came under increasing Greek influence." During its "Hellenisation," the archaic smile was probably imported from Greek statuary (Rathje 15).

20. In the important essay "Modern and National," in *Winslow Homer*, Nicolai Cikovsky, Jr., charts and explains the dissemination of artistic imagery in the nineteenth-century United States through brochures of exhibits and reproductions in books or magazines like *Harper's* or *Scribner's* to which the Edward Dickinsons subscribed. He observes, "By the later 1860s the products of [the American] image industry were so ubiquitously available that they became a mode of experience nearly equivalent to reality itself" (65). Thus, a painting by Cole or Church could be reproduced in the media or through subscription to a series, as in the case of James Smillie's engravings of *The Voyage of Life*. Emily Dickinson might have seen the archaic smile or an Etruscan funerary couple in any number of venues, especially since it is known that Austin and

Susan lent her their books and other reading materials. The explosion of interest in Oriental and Hellenic art in the American 1870s makes this especially likely.

21. I attempt to affirm this fundamental "marriage" to the Muse of poetry in my novel, *I Never Came to You in White*, which portrays the complex fire of genius as it appeared and developed in Emily Dickinson from her school days at Mary Lyon's Female Seminary to her final years. Frequently misunderstood, underestimated, or even traduced by the conventional, often envious people surrounding her in this fiction, the poet has a rich inner life with a "Mysterious Person" who sustains her from childhood to her death and who inspires her brilliant verse. In the novel's penultimate line, my fictional Emily Dickinson herself provides his name. She addresses him not as any human lover and not as the Calvinist God of her family but "O Muse" (216).

JAMES GUTHRIE

Heritable Heaven

Erotic Properties in the Dickinson-Lord Correspondence

The drafts of letters Emily Dickinson apparently wrote during her correspondence with Judge Otis Phillips Lord, justice of the Massachusetts Supreme Court, employ a wide range of legal terms and references. Elsewhere I have discussed the extent to which the drafts dwell upon matters related to property law, notably the areas of bankruptcy and trespass, as part of a larger campaign Dickinson conducted to negotiate the conditions of their romantic relationship.[1] I wish to expand upon that subject now by considering how her correspondence with Judge Lord makes similar use of concepts drawn from the practice of estate law. Although it may seem strange (or at least ironic) to focus upon the topics of wills, bequests, and heirs while examining what are essentially love letters, evidence suggests that Dickinson and the Judge found the language of estate law especially congenial for describing the future they hoped to spend together.

But first, a word of caution: over the past fifty years, the Dickinson-Lord drafts have generated considerable controversy, for several reasons.[2] To begin with, the "correspondence" really isn't one, in the truest sense: no reciprocating drafts, letters, or copies of letters sent by Lord to Dickinson are known to exist, presumably having all been destroyed by Lavinia Dickinson after her sister's death, in accordance with the poet's wishes. We do not know whether any or all of the forty-odd pencil drafts Dickinson wrote developed into letters she actually sent; we cannot be sure that each draft designated as belonging to the "Dickinson-Lord correspondence" was, in fact, intended for Judge Lord and not someone else; we do not know when several of them were written, nor can we confidently assign a chronologic order to them. The manuscripts themselves are in a rough and fragmentary state, and, to make matters worse, several were obviously mutilated, perhaps by different hands, on separate occasions.[3]

Without speculating unduly about why successive custodians of the manuscripts—a group comprising Lavinia Dickinson, Austin Dickinson, Mabel Loomis Todd, and Millicent Todd Bingham—should have wanted to censor them, I nevertheless agree with other readers who have been persuaded that the drafts were mutilated at least in part due to their sexual frankness.[4] Despite this possible bowdlerizing by friends or family, however, the manuscripts as they have come down to us remain astonishingly passionate.[5] A playful eroticism, often expressed through witty tropes pertaining to matters of law, is a hallmark of the Dickinson-Lord correspondence. In fact, the sheer prevalence of legal terms and concepts in these documents provides one of the more compelling reasons for regarding them as indeed constituting the remnants of a discrete (if not always discreet) correspondence that probably continued right up until the Judge's death in 1884.

A series of deaths, illnesses, and other family crises darkened both the Judge's and Dickinson's lives in the years immediately preceding the start of their relationship. Elizabeth Farley Lord, the Judge's wife, succumbed to cancer in 1877. Three years earlier, the poet's father, Edward Dickinson, had died while away from home in Boston, and on the first anniversary of his death, Dickinson's mother suffered a debilitating stroke. Although Dickinson withdrew more and more into the Homestead after her father's death, she maintained a network of old friendships that included the Judge, while simultaneously welcoming, albeit shyly, new acquaintances such as Mabel Loomis Todd. Mrs. Todd and Austin Dickinson eventually fell in love and conducted an adulterous affair that instigated the "war between the houses." Austin's infidelity entangled Emily Dickinson in a web of competing allegiances. Susan Gilbert Dickinson had been the poet's best friend virtually from girlhood, yet she remained steadfastly loyal to her older brother. Family loyalty probably induced Emily Dickinson to turn a blind eye on his activities, or she may have acted out of sympathy, for her own affair with the Judge could have overlapped with her brother's and Mrs. Todd's during a two-year period, from 1882 to 1884. The atmosphere in the Dickinson household at that time may have been regulated by a tacit policy of *quid pro quo;*

evidence suggests that Austin, and Lavinia, too, approved of and abetted their sister's liaison with Judge Lord.[6] But some members of the Lord family apparently viewed the Judge's romance with the poet as indecorous at best, perhaps because he had become a widower only rather recently, or because he was her senior by eighteen years.[7] That age gap, coupled with Otis Lord's close friendship with Dickinson's father, may have made the relationship seem faintly incestuous.

On October 19, 1875, before the affair got underway, the Judge was visiting the Dickinson family in Amherst when Emily Dickinson (then forty-two years old) and her mother made out their last wills and testaments. Somewhat ironically, perhaps, the Judge's wife, Elizabeth Farley Lord, affixed her signature to the poet's will as one of the three required witnesses (Leyda II, 236). Mrs. Dickinson's stroke undoubtedly lent some urgency to the family's efforts, and the Dickinsons may have had to delay drawing up the two wills for a while until she had recovered sufficient power of speech to make her wishes known. She left everything to her daughters: "I give devise and bequeath all the Estate which I shall die seized or possessed of to my two daughters, Emily Dickinson and Lavinia Dickinson, to them, their heirs and assigns forever" (Leyda II, 236). Drafting the two wills may have been part of a larger effort made by the Dickinsons to tie up loose ends of legal business left over after Edward Dickinson's death. In 1875 the entire country was still recovering from the Panic of 1873, and the family may have been seeking to ensure its future solvency by liquidating some of its real estate holdings. In May 1875, six months before the poet and her mother made out their wills and only one month before Mrs. Dickinson suffered her paralyzing stroke, the Dickinsons sold a strip of their prized Main Street haymeadow to the Hitchcocks, whose property abutted the meadow and who had already purchased an acre of it thirteen years earlier.[8] On the occasion of this second sale to the Hitchcocks, Emily Dickinson's name appears on the deed as one of the property's co-owners, presumably because she inherited a fractional interest as part of her share in Edward Dickinson's estate. The meadow was a valuable piece of land; originally eleven acres in extent, it was one of the few remaining undeveloped parcels in close proximity to Amherst's business district, the College, and the train station.

Emily Norcross Dickinson's will does not list her attorney son, Austin, as one of her beneficiaries, but there would probably have been no need to do so, since by October 1875 Austin was likely already acting in his capacity as administrator of Edward Dickinson's estate, having filed his application (signed by his mother and two sisters) to be so named in the Hampshire Court of Probate on August 3, 1874, on the heels of his father's death.[9] As administrator, Austin assumed the reins of virtually all of the Dickinsons' finances, although family members would have retained some degree of personal control over properties inherited individually—such as, for example, Emily Dickinson's share of the Main Street haymeadow. The task of fulfilling dual roles as administrator of the estate and partial heir to the Dickinson patrimony may have come to seem to Austin, then forty-six years old, sufficiently complex for him to seek legal advice from Judge Lord on the occasion of the Lords' visit on October 19, when the two Dickinson women's wills were signed and witnessed. Judge Lord, in addition to being a family friend of long standing, was also a highly respected attorney soon to be elevated to the state Supreme Court in December 1875, just two months after his consultation with the Dickinsons in Amherst.

We cannot, however, know exactly how much legal assistance the Lords actually rendered to the Dickinsons during that visit, aside from the helpful provision of Mrs. Lord's name to Emily Dickinson's will as signatory witness. Judge Lord may have lent a hand in drafting the wills so as to help Austin consolidate his control over the Dickinsons' future financial affairs. Both wills contain language carefully crafted to explain that the mother's and daughter's wishes are fully in accord with Austin's. "My only and much beloved son William A. Dickinson knows and appreciates the situation and circumstances of his Sisters," Mrs. Dickinson's will reads, "and his love for them, and for me will approve, and his judgment will sanction this disposition of my property by me, which is made in equal and in undiminished love to them all." A similar note is sounded in the poet's will: "Retaining for my only and dearly beloved brother William A. Dickinson in unabated vigor, the affection which I have ever had towards him, and knowing that his fraternal love towards me is undiminished, I am sure that his judgment concurs with mine in the disposition of my estate."[10] Both documents take pains to emphasize that Austin is not competing with his sisters for a share of the estate, helping to ensure that no court of law would ever have to bear the burden of settling future family squabbles over the Dickinson patrimony.[11]

Her father's and brother's high opinions of Judge Lord as man, judge, and attorney may have dispelled any initial reluctance the poet felt in embarking upon an affair with him after he became a widower two years later, in 1877. Austin's endorsement of Judge Lord is reflected indirectly by letter draft L560 (which Werner dates as written around 1880), in which Dickinson recounts for the Judge's benefit a conversation she had recently had with her nephew Ned, then around twenty years old. The draft begins with an offhand compliment, but her language soon introduces an unmistakable note of eroticism grounded in the same sort of mild dominance and submission fantasies that the poet and the Judge indulged in elsewhere in their correspondence,[12] as well as in a muted suggestion of incest or even pedophilia. These potentially embarrassing intimations are enfolded within and made innocuous by figures of speech and diction rooted in matters of law. After introducing her general topic—the unorthodox, individualistic, and private nature of Judge Lord's Christian belief—Dickinson goes on to quote her nephew:

> "Well – my Father [Austin] says if there were another Judge in the Commonwealth like him [Lord], the practice of Law would amount to something." I told him I thought it probable – though recalling that I had never tried any case in your presence but my own, and that, with your sweet assistance – I was murmurless.
>
> I wanted to fondle the Boy for the fervent words – but made the distinction. Dont you know you have taken my will away and I "know not where" you "have laid" it? Should I have curbed you sooner? "Spare the 'Nay' and spoil the child"?
>
> Oh, my too beloved, save me from the idolatry which would crush us both –

Dickinson's tropes seem tailored to entice and restrain the Judge simultaneously. She presents herself to him as an attorney who had "tried" a "case" in which he had lent her "sweet assistance," that is, in which he had acted the part of assisting counsel, or, alternatively, in which she had represented herself in front of him, a courtroom strategy that obligates a presiding judge to assist the *pro se* defendant during trial. Evidently the metaphorical suit had arisen out of a playful dispute regarding Lord's sexual conduct: he had made physical advances she discouraged, although later she wonders rhetorically whether she should have stopped him sooner—or, perhaps, have stopped him at all. But sparing her "Nay," she says, would have threatened to "spoil" Lord by making his conquest of her too easy. In alluding to classroom discipline and the rod of correction, Dickinson's diction implicitly assigns to herself a position she customarily ascribed to the Judge, that is, authoritarian and punisher of wrong-doers, while also portraying him flatteringly as a naughty schoolboy. Thus it is Judge Lord's "boyishness" that the draft finally emphasizes, not Ned's.

Dickinson's emotional ambivalence in L560 about how she should have responded to the Judge's overtures is echoed and reinforced stylistically. Her figural presentation of the Judge shifts from assisting attorney, to presiding judge, to miscreant, and the register of her epistolary tone fluctuates from casual conversation to impassioned plea. Her informally copulative punctuation consisting primarily of dashes (which are even more numerous in the manuscript itself) simulates breathlessness. Dickinson's letter is thus engineered to portray her as being only partially in control of herself, and in so doing it re-enacts the nervousness she had felt while in the Judge's presence, despite her best efforts to maintain her composure. She implies that her rebuff of him had not been in accord with her true wishes and suggests that her conflicted impulses are the result of a disorienting "idolatry" of him which, she melodramatically suggests, now threatens to overpower her completely. Suppressing her desires, which have become only more inflamed since their encounter, has caused her to verge upon behaving in sexually inappropriate ways, that is, by treating Ned, because he had praised the Judge, as the Judge's physical and sexual surrogate, whom she is tempted to "fondle." Although by making a "distinction" between Ned and the Judge, Dickinson does finally avoid committing an incestuous act, her hyperbole implicitly presents her as having become unhinged by desire, her caresses threatening to go everywhere.

Dickinson also confesses in L560 that Lord has "taken [her] will away," and now she does not know where he has "laid" it. Here she is likely injecting a bit of bawdy humor based upon their common experience in the composing of her will about three years earlier. Estate attorneys often advise clients to store their wills in secure yet accessible locations and to take care not to misplace them. Dickinson may have sought to amuse the Judge by attributing to him the same act of carelessness he had once warned her against committing; the fact that she encloses her reference in quotation marks may signal that she is repeating his advice verbatim. But the substance of the joke is, of course, that she is simultaneously presenting herself as a woman whose *will* to resist a man's sexual advances has temporarily deserted her. Such ribaldry would have been entirely to the Judge's taste: according to contemporary accounts, Otis Lord could be, despite his reputation for legal rigor and moral rectitude, delightfully risqué in relaxed conversation with close friends.[13] Dickinson evidently savored what she called the "May" in Lord's composition,[14] and this witty conflation of sexual and legal references exemplifies her tendency to *perform* for the Judge in their correspondence by appealing to his erotic and legal imaginations simultaneously.[15]

Because she wished to persuade Judge Lord to view her as his peer, not his subordinate, their difference in age presented Dickinson with a formidable obstacle. As in her implicit treatment of the Judge as a misbehaving schoolboy, one strategy she adopted in the drafts was to reverse their junior and senior statuses. Conceivably, she may have been inspired to do so by the inverted "May–December" nature of their affair: she associated his "boyishness" with the "May" in his personality, and her own birthday fell in December, as the Judge would have known. But Dickinson's effort to erase the years between them may also have been driven by a desire to change the way the Judge viewed her after having known her for forty years primarily as the daughter of his erstwhile best friend. The language in Dickinson's drafts often seems designed to encourage the Judge to think of her as a mature, independent woman rather than as dependent juvenile, and, as an adult, she would be entitled to an adult's legal rights and financial interests. Accordingly, Dickinson may have tried subtly to steer the Judge away from thinking of her as an heiress, a legal *legatee*, and toward regarding her as a property-owning *legator*, as when she had made out her own will, with his likely assistance.

Dickinson's efforts to persuade the Judge to think of her as a mature woman and not as a child may be discerned in draft L750. That document is unusual within the correspondence both for its length and for the fact that it may be dated quite precisely: Dickinson wrote part of it on Sunday, April 30, 1882, and the rest on Monday, May 1. Judge Lord was then nearby in Springfield presiding over a sensational manslaughter trial, and Dickinson was following the course of the proceedings as they were reported in the *Republican*. The Judge's proximity to Dickinson, coupled with his unavailability while court was in session, seemed a crime to her in itself: "though that Felons could see you and we could not, seemed a wondering fraud." Dickinson's draft plainly responds to a letter from the Judge, for she says at one point, "Your's of a Yesterday is with me." She begins her reply by deflecting an infantilizing reference to herself and to Lavinia that the Judge had evidently made: "His little 'Playthings' were very sick all the Week that closed." Here Dickinson's punctuation serves not only to show the Judge that she is quoting him, but also to invest his phrase with a deflating irony. Then Dickinson immediately continues, "and except the sweet Papa assured them, they could not believe – it had one grace however, it kept the faint Mama from sleep, so she could dream of Papa awake." Dickinson's substitution of the maturely maternal term "Mama" for the juvenile and slightly demeaning "Plaything" functions simultaneously to distinguish her from her sister and to erase the barrier of age between herself and the Judge. Rather than being a child, she identifies herself to him as potential fellow parent.

Yet Dickinson's implication that she could become a parent should be taken with a grain of salt, for at the time of their correspondence she and Lord were well beyond their childbearing years, and his health was becoming increasingly precarious. Instead, Dickinson's language should be understood as operating within the plane of possibility and the imagination. Her intention would seem to be to focus the Judge's attention upon cultural and societal traditions associated with marriage and family-building. Correspondingly, Dickinson's language in L750 subtly emphasizes the allied themes of sexuality, marriage, and fertility. She follows up an observation about a visit Judge Lord had paid to Amherst one month before, in April, with a topical observation about Emerson's then-recent death (on April 27). Initially she adopts a transcendental tone suitable to the occasion, but then her language veers instead toward suggestions of eroticism and fecundity: "the Ralph Waldo Emerson – whose name my Father's Law Student taught me, has touched the secret Spring. Which Earth are we in? // *Heaven*, a Sunday or two ago – but that also has ceased. // Momentousness is ripening. I hope that all is firm. Could we yield each other to the impregnable chances till we had met once more?" Despite Dickinson's ostensible purpose of memorializing the sage of Concord, her diction emphasizes ripeness, firmness, yielding, and fertility—that is, the stuff of life, not death. Here, "Heaven," rather than denoting the conventional Christian paradise or serving as a celestial metaphor for the Over-Soul, is put to work as a euphemism for the decidedly temporal pleasures she and the Judge had recently enjoyed during his April visit to her home in Amherst. Her word "impregnable" in particular stands out: it denotes both resistance to forcible entry and a susceptibility to being made pregnant. Such denotative ambivalence would have been entirely in keeping with Dickinson's rhetorical goal of emphasizing potentialities. Even if it were unlikely that she ever would actually become pregnant, and despite her occasional concern over the difference in their ages, she may have wished to remind Lord that she was younger than his wife, who had died childless.

Dickinson also surreptitiously emphasizes a theme of shared domesticity in L750 by using wordplay to tease the Judge about an incongruity she perceived between his public and private identities. She says that although moments they had recently spent together in Amherst were pleasant, "I have a strong surmise that moments we have *not* known are tenderest to you. Of their afflicting Sweetness, you only are the judge." Marta Werner, in her transcription of this document in her book *Emily Dickinson's Open Folios*,[16] renders the final word as being capitalized, "Judge," and if Werner's reading is accurate, Dickinson's reference here may denote the Judge personally, rather than judges in general. If so, then Dickinson may be subtly mocking Lord's judicial office in her two conjoined sentences by transferring his domain of expertise from the public trial bench to that of private sexual fantasy (i.e., "moments we have *not* known"). This playful subversion of the Judge's authority and eminence resurfaces later in the draft when Dickinson seeks to discover whether the Judge has already returned to Salem after the trial verdict and sentencing concluded. "I trust you are 'at Home,'" she writes, "though my Heart spurns the suggestion, hoping all – absence – but itself." The poet's quotation marks ironize "at Home," a stock newspaper expression, by pointing to what was, by her own logic, an implicit logical fallacy: her heart having become, she hoped, the Judge's *proper* home, he could not possibly be "at home" while away from her. With gentle sarcasm, then, Dickinson imports a phrase from society gossip pages to emphasize the private and domestic side of a man long known to all the Dickinsons who had metamorphosed, over the years, into a minor celebrity.

Dickinson's language about "homes" in L750 also helps direct the Judge's attention to legal issues connected with joint home ownership and co-habitation. In the "Monday" portion of L750 Dickinson resumes her previous day's discussion of the Judge's putative "homelessness" while he was away from her, writing, "I'm glad you are 'at Home.' Please think it with a codicil. My own were homeless if you were." For the second time in this document Dickinson draws upon the journalistic phrase "at home," and her quotation marks continue to invest the words with irony, since they could not be true so long as the lovers were separated from each other. As for Dickinson's reference to a "codicil," according to *Black's Law Dictionary*, a codicil is "A supplement or addition to a will that modifies, explains, or otherwise qualifies the will in some way." Codicils are apt to be required if and when a testator remarries and/or reasonably expects a new heir to be added to the family line. Dickinson's coupling of "home" with "codicil" encourages a consideration of houses as heritable estates. If, by the logic of her metaphor, she and the Judge already form a family unit, a "Mama" and a "Papa," a report that he is "at home" while she is not there with him would mean that she had become "homeless," not only in the sense that she has nowhere to live, but also that a property of enduring value had been wrested from her control.

Dickinson's diction and tropes subtly suggest that in order to address the problem of the poet's future financial security, the Judge should modify either his will
or his marital status.

Uppermost in Dickinson's mind at the time may have been the impending
dissolution of her own household in Amherst after her mother's death. Home,
always a core concept for Dickinson, signified comfort, security, and privacy. In
another letter draft associated with the Dickinson-Lord correspondence, the
poet wrote, "You spoke of 'Hope' surpassing 'Home' – I thought that Hope *was*
Home – a misapprehension of Architecture –" (L600). Yet the likelihood that
Dickinson and Lord would ever actually marry and live together was made
problematic by complications within their families. Dickinson had her unmarried sister's wishes and welfare to attend to, and the Judge had his own obligations to fulfill. After Elizabeth Farley Lord's death, three Farley nieces came to
live with him to help keep up the house and monitor his health. One of these
three young women, Abbie Farley, is remembered by a contemporary as having
heartily detested Emily Dickinson, and at least one biographer has speculated
that this hostility arose from a fear that if Lord and Dickinson were to marry,
the poet would share in the Judge's estate, either reducing the nieces' portion or
cutting them out altogether.[17] Because Dickinson and Lord must have been
acutely aware that their romance imperiled the Farley nieces' standing as potential beneficiaries, the couple would have been placed in the awkward position of
wishing that they could somehow respect the girls' legitimate expectations while
managing simultaneously to establish a sound financial footing for the few years
they might yet spend with each other.[18]

These factors conspired to relegate the possibility of Dickinson's joining the
Judge in Salem to the realm of speculation. Consequently, she and he may have
fallen into the habit of representing any time they *were* able to spend together,
such as his intermittent visits to Amherst, as an alternative form of home:
"heaven," or the "*Heaven*, a Sunday or two ago" they had known together (L750).
This idealized site of co-habitation would be gratifyingly free of mundane, ter-
restrial complexities such as propriety, property rights, and family responsibilities, yet retain temporal delights such as guaranteed physical proximity and
sexual intimacy. Dickinson's hypothetical heaven-home may also have been a
byproduct of a steadily declining interest in the conventional Christian heaven.
During virtually all her adult life Dickinson had remained skeptical of the value
of a heaven too dissimilar to the sensuously appealing, edenic Earth. The un-
satisfactory intangibleness of the conventional Christian heaven was a topic to

which she and the Judge apparently reverted often in their discussions and cor-respondence. Dickinson writes in L750, "[I]n Heaven they neither woo nor are given in wooing – what an imperfect place!" In the euphoria of the lovers' new-found physical attraction, perhaps the idea of a bodiless, sexless heaven began to seem insipid. Dickinson and the Judge may also have discovered common ground in a joint willingness to temper, especially in light of Emerson's liberal theology and of discoveries made only recently by Darwin, the rigorous Calvinist faith in which both had been raised.[19]

Evidence suggests that Dickinson and Lord framed their intensifying reli-gious doubt ironically as an argument about heaven's physical existence, and they began referring to paradise semi-facetiously as a parcel of real estate that could be deeded or willed. Such, at least, would seem to be the basis of figural language appearing in another Dickinson-Lord draft (L791), in which Dickinson writes, "I . . . cannot refrain from taxing you with an added smile – and a pang in it. Was it to him the Thief cried 'Lord remember me when thou comest into thy Kingdom,' and is it to us that he replies, 'This Day thou shalt be with me in Paradise'? // The Propounder of Paradise must indeed possess it." Here Dick-inson is commenting humorously upon Luke 23:43, Jesus' promise made to the thief while both were nailed upon the cross. She could reasonably assume that the Judge was familiar with long-standing controversies concerning this passage, which had been cited in arguments made both by those generally questioning the concept of scriptural inerrancy, and by Protestants specifically opposed to the Catholic doctrine of Purgatory. Although Jesus promises the thief in Luke that they will be reunited in heaven on that very day, the day of their deaths, scriptural critics pointed out that the Bible also describes both Jesus' body as lying in the tomb for three days and the concurrent descent of his soul into hell prior to his resurrection and ascent to heaven. Catholic orthodoxy held that the thief could not possibly have joined Jesus Christ that very day in heaven because the thief would first have had to expiate his sin in Purgatory; thus, according to the Church, the word "today" in Luke was not to be taken literally.[20] Chrono-logical inconsistencies generated by Luke 23:43 were sometimes resolved (or exacerbated, depending upon one's point of view) by various biblical interpreters' and translators' insertion of a comma, as in the King James version: "Verily I say unto thee, Today shalt thou be with me in paradise." Here, the comma preceding "Today" emphasizes Jesus' good faith in making his promise, which is a guaran-tee that the thief would join him in heaven *that very day*, with no period of preparation or expiation required of either sufferer after he had died.

Dickinson's humor derives from being even more literal-minded than biblical commentators had been, except that her literalness is legalistic, not exegetic: she treats Jesus' promise to the thief in Luke 23:43 as an oral contract. Her clause "The Propounder of Paradise must indeed possess it" implicitly presents Jesus as assuring the thief a share in an estate, heaven, which he himself stands to inherit. A legal "propounder" is, again according to *Black's*: "An executor or administrator who offers a will or other testamentary document for admission to probate." Thus Jesus speaks on the cross both as heir to an estate and as its legal administrator or "propounder," although no legal disposition of the estate has yet been made. From a fiduciary standpoint, then, Jesus' promise to share his future inheritance with the thief is as tenuous as the Bible's anachronistic ordering of events, and Jesus' offer may even be thought of as fraudulent, since no documentary proof of title to the property exists at the time of crucifixion. Finally, in her allusion to the contested passage from Luke, Dickinson may also have been referring indirectly to discussions she had been having with the Judge concerning language, in which he also took a passionate interest. The idea that inserting, moving, or removing a comma could change a sentence's, or a faith's, message so profoundly may have amused the Judge, who during a long legal career undoubtedly witnessed the same phenomenon occurring in any number of legal documents.[21]

In characterizing Jesus as "propounder" of a heavenly estate, the poet could draw again upon the Judge's familiarity with the Dickinson family's own legal situation, in particular with Austin Dickinson's petition to be named administrator of his father's estate. Austin's legal standing resembles Jesus' in that both are beneficiaries and administrators of an inheritance, simultaneously receiving and overseeing the distribution of a patrimony. In the aftermath of Edward Dickinson's having died intestate, Dickinson and Lord may have been acutely conscious of the importance of possessing tangible proof of ownership in an estate. Yet another, equally personal, legal frame of reference may be hinted at by Dickinson's quoting from Luke: "Lord remember me when thou comest into thy kingdom." That plea may be understood as meaning either "when you enter your kingdom" or "when you come into your inheritance." If the latter, "Lord" in the passage renames the legatee, who is putative heir to the kingdom of heaven. Whether Dickinson is referring here to the Lord of heaven or to Otis Phillips *Lord* is unclear, perhaps purposefully so. That Dickinson was capable of punning upon the Judge's name is suggested by her comment mentioned earlier, "you only are the Judge."[22] Thus in L791 she may be gently reminding Lord that if he were to offer her a heritable heaven such as his house in Salem—or his own body—he too had to be able to make good on his promise.

Dickinson's and Lord's habit of using "heaven" to signify an ideal condition of sexual freedom may also have derived from another mutually understood cultural frame of reference, *Antony and Cleopatra*. Shakespeare's frequently bawdy depiction of illicit middle-aged love was evidently a literary touchstone for Dickinson and the Judge, second only, perhaps, to the Bible. Dickinson's citation from Luke in draft L791 is followed immediately by the observation, "Antony's remark to a friend, 'since Cleopatra died' is said to be the saddest ever lain in Language – That engulfing '*Since*.'"[23] The poet's yoking of Luke to Shakespeare implies that she detected parallels between Jesus' promise to the thief and Antony's impassioned reaction to news of Cleopatra's death (a rumor spread by Cleopatra herself). Three similarities that may have suggested themselves to Dickinson are the inseparability of pledged pairs (Jesus and the thief, Antony and Cleopatra); the transformation of the phenomenal world by the presence or absence of the loved one; and temporal uncertainty. The phrase that Dickinson quotes falls in the midst of a soliloquy during which Antony realizes that during the few minutes which have elapsed after news of Cleopatra's purported death reached him, the world has been altered utterly, and he berates himself for delaying even briefly in following her to the grave:

> Since Cleopatra died
> I have lived in such dishonour that the gods
> Detest my baseness. I, that with my sword
> Quartered the world, and o'er green Neptune's back
> With ships made cities, condemn myself to lack
> The courage of a woman. . . .
>
> (IV xiv 55–60)

The transcendent sadness of Antony's phrase, Dickinson appears to be saying, derives from the temporal indeterminacy generated by the adverb "since," which may denote "ever since" or "because," or both. *Because* Cleopatra has died, Antony has no reason to go on living, and his sense of shame at remaining alive has grown stronger *ever since* he learned of her death. Moreover, his self-recrimination is ultimately pointless, because Cleopatra remains alive, a fact known to the audience, if not to Antony. Thus the "engulfing" quality of the word "Since" results from its compounding of chronology, causality, and tragic irony.

For devoted pairs, all time spent apart is experienced as null and empty, whether their separation is caused by distance or by death. The only consolation available for such couples was, Dickinson's drafts to Judge Lord suggest, the concept of heaven, whether a heaven on earth or one above. If on earth, Dickinson's "heaven" is cognate, as I have said, with a paradise of excess, a cockayne of unrestrained passion and uninhibited sexuality. At the back of Dickinson's mind, perhaps, was the very first scene in *Antony and Cleopatra*, in which the besotted lovers debate where to set the limits of their love (I i 15–17):

> *Antony.* There's beggary in the love that can be reckoned.
> *Cleopatra.* I'll set a bourn how far to be beloved.
> *Antony.* Then must thou needs find out new heaven, new earth.

Like Shakespeare's continentally mismatched African and European lovers, Dickinson and the Judge might aspire to carve out a "new" heaven on earth by blurring the edges of boundaries and bodies, locus and self.[24] Dickinson liked to employ geographic metonyms in referring to others, and to herself: she begins one of her letter drafts to the Judge by saying (probably in reference to a photograph of himself that he had given to her), "My lovely Salem smiles at me" (L559), and in a letter to Abbie Farley dated May 8, 1882, inquiring about the Judge's health, Dickinson asked: "Is he able to speak or to hear voices or to say 'Come in,' when his Amherst knocks?" (L751).[25] These conflations of person and place are reminiscent of Antony's designation of Cleopatra simply as the land she ruled, "Egypt."[26] Expressed metaphorically, then, Dickinson's and Lord's entire quandary was to align their two places of residence, or physical presences, despite the intervening distance.

Achieving such a confederated state required, however, a certain amount of diplomacy and careful negotiation from Dickinson, daughter of an attorney, and from Lord, a seasoned judge. In confronting middle age and its intricately woven networks of family loyalties, legacies, and responsibilities, the couple may have found it entirely natural and convenient to encode their obligations to each other and to others in the language of deeds, contracts, and wills. Such is the case, I think, in another long draft that is perhaps the most frankly erotic document in the correspondence (if not the entire corpus of her writing). Uniquely, this draft was folded to fit inside an envelope addressed by Dickinson to Judge Lord, then at Boston Court House. The draft presents the appearance of a letter virtually ready to be sent—and as such, it is all the more likely never to have been sent at all. Dickinson may have stayed her hand at the last minute, worried that her candor in the letter might, despite the "May" in his character, ultimately offend the Judge. Likely written in 1878 or 1879, the manuscript was mutilated at some point, so that both the draft's very beginning and its end are missing. Nevertheless, I think it reasonable to assume that the extant five sheets of the draft, numbered in order by Dickinson herself on their opposite sides, constitute the bulk of the draft as originally composed. Partly because the draft has been so radically altered—although there are other reasons[27]—I am drawing here upon Marta Werner's transcription of the draft, document A 740 in *Emily Dickinson's Open Folios*, rather than upon the text of Johnson's L562. Page one of the draft, its first one or two words cut away, begins as follows:[28]

> To lie so near your longing – to touch it as I passed, for I am but a restive sleeper and often should journey from your Arms through the happy Night, but you will lift me back, wont you, for only there I ask to be – I say, if I felt the longing nearer – than in our dear past, perhaps I could [new page] not resist to bless it, but must, because it would be right – The 'Stile' is Gods' – My Sweet one – for your great sake – not mine – I will not let you cross – but it is all your's, and when it is right I will lift the Bars, and lay you in the Moss – You showed me the word – I hope it has no [new page] different guise when my fingers make it – it is Anguish I long conceal from you to let you leave me, hungry, but you ask the divine Crust and that would doom the Bread –

Indeed, it is difficult *not* to read this passage as an extended sexual metaphor. Interpreting very freely, we might paraphrase what Dickinson says as follows: that she has lain close enough to the Judge to feel his genital "longing"; that if the lovers had freer access to each other and greater proximity, she might not be able to resist her impulse to "bless" his aroused state by having sex with him; that she has refrained thus far because of his public prominence and reputation, his "great sake," which scandal might compromise; that she intends to requite him sexually when the time is right; that he has already indicated his willingness to have sexual relations with her when he "showed [her] the word"; that when she herself is also ready, she will reply in kind, and she hopes that he will understand what she is saying when that moment arrives; and that she fears should they have sex sooner rather than later, his interest in her might wane. All of these messages are encoded in a series of images that would have resonated professionally with the Judge, particularly those concerning the legal status of rural properties. Dickinson's and the Judge's adjacent bodies, conjoined first in sleep, and later, potentially, by sex, are troped as neighboring country lots separated by a fence with a stile. The word *stile* is set off by quotation marks, as if it already possessed some shared signification, and it may be useful to consider for a moment what fence stiles meant to Dickinson and to Lord.

On New England farms, a stile ordinarily consisted of a step or a couple of steps on either side of the fence, and a single removable rail or bar at the top. Stiles could connect a single owner's pastures, or lands belonging to different owners. In the latter case, stiles possessed special legal significance, because they functioned as informal gateways to private property. Thus hikers would theoretically have needed to secure permission before using stiles to enter upon someone else's lands – although in day-to-day life, this requirement was probably ignored nearly universally. Yet property rights and the rules of trespass constitute only one dimension of the larger cultural context in which fence stiles would have been viewed in the contemporary rural imagination. They were also stereotypic locations for lovers' trysts, providing a place far from prying eyes where two people could sit side by side upon the fence rail. This cultural association of fence stiles with a lovers' rendezvous appears in contemporary popular and traditional song, as in these lines beginning a ballad that traveled from Ireland to America:[29]

> I'm sitting on the stile, Mary,
>   where we once sat side by side
> On a bright May morning long ago,
>   when first you were my bride.

Besides its usefulness as rustic love seat, the fence stile provided further opportunities for achieving physical contact when chivalrous men lifted their walking companions over the bar, and Dickinson's request to the Judge that he "lift [her] back" should she stray from their real or imagined bed may be grounded in this particular courting protocol. The courtesy of being lifted was also extended to children, as reflected in the concluding lines of Dickinson's early poem "'Arcturus' is his other name" (Fr117):

> I hope the Father in the skies
> Will lift his little girl –
> "Old fashioned"! naughty! everything!
> Over the stile of "pearl"!

Here, Dickinson's trope links fence stiles to the proverbial pearly gates while implicitly representing heaven itself as a farther field, a rural realm from which the speaker had previously been excluded, perhaps for having been "naughty."[30]

Summarizing, then, we could say that Dickinson associated fence stiles with rural lovers, childhood, property rights, and an entryway to paradise. Yet one additional possible context for Dickinson's deployment of the stile trope in this

letter draft to Judge Lord may be retrieved from the poet's own material circumstances: the legal disposition of the Dickinson meadow across the street from
the Homestead. As mentioned earlier, on at least two occasions the Dickinson
family sold some of this valuable parcel to the Hitchcocks, whose property at
the corner of College Street and School Street adjoined the meadow. The
longevity of the Dickinsons' friendship with all the Hitchcocks (the late Edward
Hitchcock, Sr., had been president of the College) suggests that both of these
business transactions were entirely amicable. Whether or not an actual fence
stile originally provided communication between their properties, the Dickinsons and the Hitchcocks were on cordial enough terms that their lands might
be thought of as having long overlapped each other figurally, if not physically.
Only five months before Dickinson and her mother made out their wills with
Judge Lord's likely assistance, the second sale to the Hitchcocks went through
on May 1. At that time, the meadow was one of the few tangible assets that we
know belonged, if only partially, to Emily Dickinson herself; the appearance of
her name on the bill of sale suggests that the strip sold to the Hitchcocks contained some land she considered specifically her own. Because this sale was one
of the rare instances in her lifetime during which she could legitimately think
of herself as a landowner, it stands to reason that Dickinson would have identified her own person closely with the meadow. Moreover, she was thoroughly
familiar with that property, having been able to gaze upon it from the vantage
of her bedroom window whenever she wished. Over time, Dickinson may even
have begun to consider the fraction of meadowland that she controlled as a
formal or informal dowry.

Participating simultaneously in the legal domain of rural property rights, in
the popular culture realm of sentimental romance, and in her own awareness of
herself as landowner, the metaphor of a fence stile would have given Dickinson
a convenient means of representing to Judge Lord the limits of lovers' claims
made upon one another. Yet the figure offers a further benefit: the opening
provided by a fence stile and the rising bar at its top render it peculiarly apposite
for designating female and male genitalia, whether used consciously or unconsciously. Passage between the neighboring properties is analogous to sexual
intercourse; in virtually equating property rights with sexual rights, Dickinson's
language makes a distinction between permitted and unpermitted entry. Entering someone else's property without permission constitutes trespass, another
legal topic that, as I have written elsewhere, Dickinson discusses in her correspondence with Judge Lord. In this particular letter draft, however, each of the

lovers is a potential trespasser: Dickinson, if she should stray at night from the Judge, and he, if he fails to secure her permission before making sexual advances. For her part, should she wander away from the Judge, she asks him to "lift" her back to the place where she properly, and perhaps legally, belongs, that is, by his side. The "there" to which she asks to be returned is, however, a location that remains as yet prospective, because the rest of her trope depicts herself and the Judge as currently occupying adjoining, separate lots, or beds, to which entry remains at least partially restricted.

By requiring the Judge still to stay on his side of the fence and by refusing, for the moment, to grant him full access to the lush pasture of her own sexuality, Dickinson would seem to be guilty of failing to reciprocate as a landowner after she has already imagined herself as straying beyond her own territorial boundaries and onto his land. Yet her trope presents her potential trespass as being accidental and unintentional, like sleepwalking, or like being lost—a commonly used defense against trespassing charges.[31] In any case, Judge Lord, troped as property owner, has already extended permission for her to enter his property, even while she has continued to forbid him access to hers. But she says she will some day give the consent required before lifting the "bar" to grant him full privileges to her body, troped as property, and her repetition of the word *lift* emphasizes the reciprocity of her action. Correspondingly, Judge Lord has already shown her "the word"; that is, he had given her verbal permission to cross the stile and enter upon his lands, and although Dickinson intends to repay him in kind, she professes anxiety about the format her consent will take, the "guise" it will have when her "fingers make it," perhaps by signing a legal document, perhaps by performing sexual favors.

When the Judge finally enters her property, he will do so not as interloper, but as legal co-owner. In her trope, Dickinson essentially invites him to assume the Hitchcocks' role in her family's actual property transaction, namely, that of an owner whose lands already adjoin hers, and who may achieve an even greater intimacy by *acquiring* her land.[32] Execution of the transaction awaits only her reciprocating affirmation that the property has been transferred to him—"it is all your's." Dickinson's use here of the present tense indicates that, from a legal standpoint at least, the Judge may be considered as already owning the property to which she nevertheless continues to forbid him free entry. If so, Dickinson is exposing herself to a legal liability, for an owner may not be denied access to his own lands. The ambiguity of Dickinson's figural language corresponds to the uncertainty of her legal standing. Apparently negotiations for the contested properties are virtually complete except for a few details remaining to be ironed out; in consciously contractual language, Dickinson promises she will fulfill her obligation to reciprocate sexually at a later date. For the moment, however, the Judge must continue to do his part by cleaving "nearer" to her, or, more particu- larly, by maintaining his "longing" for her close by, an issue made problematic both by his distance from her, in Salem, and by his travels around the Common- wealth on court business. The "nearer" the Judge maintains himself to her, Dick- inson seems to imply, the more likely it is that she will grant him full access to her enclosed meadow.

Dickinson's promise to the Judge to "lay [him] in the Moss" appears to guar- antee him sexual gratification after they have fully agreed on the terms of their relationship, yet her phrase may encompass more than just a roll in the hay. Besides rhyming with "cross" in the same sentence, the word "moss" inevitably also connotes burial, as in Dickinson's poem "I died for Beauty – but was scarce" (Fr448), in which she writes of buried companions conversing in their graves: "We talked between the Rooms – / Until the Moss had reached our lips – / And covered up – Our names." Thus, Dickinson's pledge to the Judge to "lay him in the moss" also seems a kind of midlife *liebestod*, one similar, perhaps, to Antony and Cleopatra's reckless, impassioned, and doomed romance. Read against the background of Dickinson's association of fence stiles with gateways to heaven, her promise to the Judge appears to entail not just sex, but also a fulfillment of last wishes. In this sense, her offer resembles both a promise made by the executor of an estate to carry out a testator's instructions—that is, he would be buried at the site he had stipulated—and a testator's bequest: "It is all your's," in that he would eventually inherit all she owned and thus would be interred finally on "their" land. In the context of Dickinson's and the Judge's larger figural discussion of heaven, wills, and estates, Dickinson is attesting that Judge Lord may believe, and rely upon, what she has been telling him, because she does indeed possess the real assets of which she has been the propounder. By consolidating several personal, legal, and cultural themes with which she knew the Judge would already be intimately familiar, Dickinson's tropes in this letter draft succeed in uniting property deeds and testamentary wills under a single figural umbrella. In this letter, probably never sent, Dickinson promises quite literally to give herself to the Judge like a piece of deeded or inherited land.

But of course Dickinson and the Judge never did marry, and he died in 1884, in Salem. Subsequently, Dickinson began corresponding with attorney Benjamin Kimball, Lord's executor and cousin, perhaps in part because, Thomas Johnson speculates, Judge Lord had made a bequest to her that Kimball was legally obligated to convey.[33] She told Kimball, "Your task must be a fervent one—often one of pain" (L967), knowing full well, having witnessed Austin's efforts, that the office of executor or administrator of an estate was sometimes not an easy one. She tried to encourage Kimball by saying, "To fulfill the will of a powerless friend supersedes the Grave," as if the act of executing a will, in addition to satisfying the law, overrode the finality of death by prolonging, if only on paper, the presence and personality of the deceased. In another letter to Kimball she said of Judge Lord (L968): "I once asked him what I should do for him when he was not here, referring half unconsciously to the great Expanse – In a tone italic of both Worlds 'Remember Me,' he said. I have kept his Commandment." In this sense, Emily Dickinson, too, faithfully executed Otis Lord's last wishes, and before she herself died in 1886, Dickinson evidently left instructions of her own, carefully carried out by her sister, that at her burial two heliotropes should be placed by her hands, "to take," as editor Thomas Wentworth Higginson noted in his diary, "to Judge Lord" (Leyda II, 475).

NOTES

1. "Law, Property, and Provincialism in Dickinson's Poems and Letters to Judge Otis Phillips Lord" in the *Emily Dickinson Journal*, substantively reprinted as chapter 7 in *Emily Dickinson's Vision*. Also, "Exceeding Legal and Linguistic Limits: Dickinson as 'Involuntary Bankrupt,'" again in the *Emily Dickinson Journal*.

2. Dickinson's love affair with the Judge, especially as it may be reconstructed on the basis of the letter drafts' contents, was first brought to light by Millicent Todd Bingham in 1954 in her book, *Emily Dickinson: A Revelation*. Among the various comprehensive Dickinson biographies, Richard Sewall examines the relationship in greatest depth.

3. Marta Werner's book *Emily Dickinson's Open Folios* includes an extensive discussion of textual problems generated by the Dickinson-Lord letter drafts. Readers should note that my discussion of the drafts here does not even attempt (with a single exception) to render the drafts in their original state, usually relying instead upon Thomas Johnson's "diplomatic" versions of them. Readers wishing to see more faithful transcriptions should consult Werner's book.

4. See, for example, Cynthia Griffin Wolff's comment, "The most striking thing in these letter drafts is the unmistakable element of sexual passion" (402).

5. Sewall, who speculates that Austin was chiefly responsible for scissoring the manuscripts, says, "It is surprising that so much was left in" (*Life* 654).

6. One indication of Austin's tacit approval would be his eventual delivery of the envelope containing the Dickinson-Lord manuscripts to Mrs. Todd. Lavinia's appro-

bation is implicit in her facilitation of the correspondence, for she sometimes served as intermediary between the Judge and her sister in their exchange of letters. Sewall speculates that Lavinia occasionally performed a similar service for Austin and Mabel Todd (654).

7. Abbie Farley, niece to Judge Lord, is reported to have said of Emily Dickinson: "Little hussy – didn't I know her? I should say I did. Loose morals. She was crazy about men. Even tried to get Judge Lord. Insane, too." It should be noted, however, that these sentences, which appeared first in Millicent Todd Bingham's *A Revelation* (23), are based upon hearsay. Farley was reported to have made the remark to Miriam Stockton, an acquaintance, who passed it along during an oral interview with Bingham. See also note 17, below.

8. This would be Mary L. and Edward "Doc" Hitchcock, Jr., who were contemporaries of the Dickinson siblings, and not Edward Hitchcock, Sr. The previous sale of a single acre of the meadow to the Hitchcocks was transacted on November 22, 1862. On that occasion, Emily Dickinson's name appears on the deed of sale as a witness, not an owner. For information about legal documents signed by Emily Dickinson, I am indebted to Alfred Habegger's biography (642–43). For a visual reference of the relative locations of the Dickinson and Hitchcock properties, readers should consult the 1873 Beers Atlas map of Amherst, published in 1873, reproduced in Polly Longsworth's *The World of Emily Dickinson* (88–89).

9. Edward Dickinson died intestate. His omitting to make out a will might seem strange in an attorney who had earned much of his living by setting up trusts and estates, but Habegger points out that Dickinson was probably just pursuing a carefully laid-out legal strategy, knowing that after his death, control of his estate would almost certainly pass into his attorney son's hands once a probate court had finished its deliberations (564).

10. A photostatic copy of Emily Dickinson's will appears on p. 112 of Longsworth's *The World of Emily Dickinson*.

11. After Emily Dickinson's death, a court of law did, however, become entangled in a Dickinson family dispute over the haymeadow. In his own will Austin left his portion in the meadow to his sister Lavinia with the understanding that after he died she would turn over a 53-foot-wide strip of the land to his mistress, Mabel Loomis Todd, as informal payment for her work in compiling and editing the first collection of Emily Dickinson's letters. After Austin died in 1895, Lavinia did sign a deed transferring the property to Mrs. Todd, but then reconsidered, later denying in court that she had understood what she was doing when she had put her name to the document. An account of the entire episode may be found in Longsworth's *Austin and Mabel* (399–425). See also note 32, below.

12. See Guthrie, *Emily Dickinson's Vision* 168.

13. According to a memorial to Judge Lord composed by the Essex County Bar Association, quoted by Bingham in *Emily Dickinson: A Revelation* (36–37), in his private life Judge Lord could be "piquant and racy in conversation."

14. After his death, Dickinson said of Judge Lord in a letter to Benjamin Kimball, "Calvary and May wrestled in his Nature" (L968).

15. Judge Lord may not have been the only correspondent for whom Dickinson tended to perform. Marietta Messmer writes, "Rather than sites for self-disclosures to an intimate friend, Dickinson's letters gradually become spaces for rhetorical performances, for entertaining an audience, and, ultimately, for controlled acts of self-representation *deliberately* tailored toward a specific recipient" (77).

16. See Werner's rendition of document A 744b in *Emily Dickinson's Open Folios*.

17. Cynthia Griffin Wolff writes, "The niece, Abbie Farley, was the chief beneficiary of Judge Lord's will, and since he was a man of considerable wealth, she stood to inherit a good deal so long as he did not marry. An intimate friend of Susan Dickinson's, Abbie Farley actively opposed the match; indeed, her hostility toward Emily Dickinson was so great that she destroyed everything the poet had written to Lord, letters and whatever poetry they may have contained" (403).

18. Draft L790 addresses the question of whether Dickinson would join Judge Lord in Salem: "You said with loved timidity in asking me to your dear Home, you would 'try not to make it unpleasant.' So delicate a diffidence, how beautiful to see! I do not think a Girl extant has so divine a modesty."

19. In draft L750 Dickinson mentions the author of *On the Origin of Species*, saying "we thought Darwin had thrown 'the Redeemer' away."

20. In his commentary upon Luke 23:43 in *The Anchor Bible*, contemporary biblical scholar Joseph A. Fitzmyer states confidently, "The joining of 'today' and 'in Paradise' in this verse creates a problem when one tries to relate it to the credal 'descent into Hell,' and even with 1 Pet 3:19–20. That, however, is a question about which Luke never dreamed" (1511).

On the subject of the legitimacy of Purgatory as part of church doctrine, the influential seventeenth-century English Puritan divine Thomas Watson preached, in *A Sermon Against Popery*,

> And, on the other hand, *Believers* when they die pass immediately to Heaven, *Luke* 23.43, *This day shalt thou be with me in Paradise. Christ Jesus* was now on the Cross, and was *instantly* to be in Heaven; and the *penitent Thief* was immediately to be with *Christ*: Here is no mention of any such place as *Purgatory*. The ancient and *Orthodox* Fathers were all against *Purgatory*; as *Chrysostom, Cyprian, Austine, Fulgentius.*

21. The contemporary legal scholar David Mellinkoff writes, in his book *The Language of the Law*, "A characteristic lack of adequate punctuation is a major obstacle to precision in legal writing, and has been for centuries" (366). Mellinkoff associates a change in attitude toward punctuation among members of the American legal community with a shift in opinion expressed within the pages of an authoritative work edited by another famous Amherst resident (and attorney), Noah Webster: "Punctuation-for-pause – accepted by Noah Webster – is displaced by punctuation-for-meaning in the unabridged second edition of his famous dictionary" (367).

22. I discuss another possible instance of Dickinson's punning upon the Judge's name in *Emily Dickinson's Vision* (165).

23. Páraic Finnerty says in his book *Emily Dickinson's Shakespeare* that Dickinson, in claiming that this line is the saddest in all of Shakespeare, is probably seconding the published opinion of T. W. Higginson, who wrote that "Shakespeare might have taken from them [i.e., the lines of Petrarch's Sonnet 251] his 'Since Cleopatra died,' – the only passage in literature which has in it the same wide spaces of emotion" (157).

24. See *Emily Dickinson's Vision* (168–69).

25. Similarly, Dickinson refers in L750 to the Rev. Charles Wadsworth, who had died recently, as "My Philadelphia."

26. As in the lines, "Egypt, thou knew'st too well / My heart was to thy rudder tied by th' strings, / And thou shouldst tow me after" (III xi 57–59). Páraic Finnerty says that in the Dickinson family's edition of the plays, the page margin by these lines is marked in pencil (140).

27. Another reason to use Werner's transcription rather than Johnson's is that Johnson, in L562, begins this document with text appearing on a separate scrap of paper, listed in Werner's book as A739: "Dont you know you are happiest while I withhold and not confer – dont you know that 'No' is the wildest word we consign to Language? // You do, for you know all things – " Although the topic of deferred sexual gratification may also be raised in A740, contra Johnson, I see no compelling reason why the two documents should be combined. Also, the pages of A740 present a different appearance from A739, being individually numbered, as well as written on sheets of stationery rather than upon scraps.

28. My reproduction of Werner's transcription necessarily omits many textual details, such as line breaks and letter spacing, present in Dickinson's autograph text.

29. The song is "The Lament of the Irish Emigrant," composed originally as a poem by Anglo-Irish writer Helen Selina Blackwood, Lady Dufferin (b. 1807, d. 1867). My text here is drawn from a version of the song in the Duke University collection of historic American sheet music.

30. See also the concluding lines of "I'll tell you how the Sun rose" (Fr204):

> But how he set – I know not –
> There seemed a purple stile
> That little Yellow boys and girls
> Were climbing all the while –
> Till when they reached the other side –
> A Dominie in Gray –
> Put gently up the evening Bars –
> And led the flock away –

Here, Dickinson's phrase "the other side" seems to suggest the further precincts of heaven. The word *bar* has, of course, other legal significations, as in *bar examination*.

31. See, for example, the passage in *Walden* where Thoreau describes exculpatory (and probably completely fictitious) explanations for his presence when property owners

found him walking uninvited upon their lands: that he had become so consumed in chasing a "hound, a bay horse, and a turtle-dove" that he lost track of his whereabouts.

32. The troublesome Dickinson meadow continued to intervene in the family's romantic lives and legal affairs. Martha Dickinson Bianchi, Austin and Susan Dickinson's daughter, was compelled to sell what remained of the meadow in 1917, following the financial collapse of her husband, Captain Bianchi, fraudulent Russian count and covert munitions purchaser for the czarist court (see St. Armand, *Culture* 149).

33. See *Letters* 861.

ELLEN LOUISE HART

Alliteration, Emphasis, and Spatial Prosody in Dickinson's Manuscript Letters

Emily Dickinson's letters in manuscript offer readers more information about prosody than the standard print editions can provide. Although "prosody" generally refers to the technical aspects of versification, prose also has a prosody. A study of the prosody of Dickinson's prose focuses on the way sound is organized in individual sentences. Here, for example, is the first page of a five-and-a-half-page letter she wrote in the early 1870s to Susan Huntington Gilbert Dickinson, her beloved friend, sister-in-law, and neighbor, who lived next door.[1]

> To miss you, Sue,
> is power.
> The stimulus
> of Loss makes
> most Possession
> mean.
> To live   lasts
> always, but to
> love is firmer
> than   to live.
> No Heart that
> broke but further
> went   than
> Immortality .
>   (OMC158; L364)[2]

This text is my print translation, or "diplomatic transcription," a rendering of manuscript lines in print or type that attempts to represent line breaks and proportionate amounts of space between words in visual lines.[3] Since the first volume was published in 1894, Dickinson's letters have been described as "poetic" by critics, readers, and reviewers. The letters are mixed genre texts. Many combine prose sentences and verse passages. Among the prosodic strategies of the prose is alliteration, a sound pattern most often defined as the repetition of initial sounds. But the category also includes assonance and consonance in the medial and final positions of a word. I use "alliteration" in both ways: to refer to all three sound effects as a category, and, specifically, to mean initial letter repetition. Context distinguishes between the two. I maintain that alliteration serves as a central acoustic, rhetorical, rhythmic structure in the letters and that this recognition is key to understanding how the prose is "poetic." Furthermore, I argue that Dickinson's letters use visual strategies of spatial arrangement to produce precisely articulated sound, to create rhythm, and to direct interpretation through emphatic stress.

The letter to Susan Dickinson quoted above provides an example of alliteration's centrality in the prose. The opening sentence, which is also the letter's first paragraph, begins with a phrase that plays on the recipient's name through the consonance of "s" and assonance of "u." The pattern continues and expands through the consonantal sequence of "m" and "s" in "miss," "Sue," "stimulus," "Loss," "makes," "most," "Possession," and "mean"; a thread of "l's" follows: "live," "lasts," "always," "love," and "live"; and then the final and medial "t's" in "Heart," "that," "but," "went," and "Immortality." The effect is to draw sounds together and build to the climactic point of "Immortality," the last word on the page, on a line by itself.

In these lines the visual accentuates the acoustic. Lineated sentences compound the effects of alliteration. Conventions of prose determine line boundaries by the length and width of a page, not by visual or rhythmic considerations. The opening sentence of Dickinson's letter, "To miss you, Sue, / is power," puts stronger stress on "miss," "Sue," and "power," weaker stress on "to," "you," and "is." Speech often favors a pattern that moves from a weak beat to a strong beat, the iambic pattern in verse. In speaking or reading, the heaviest stress frequently falls at the end of a line, and the next heaviest at the beginning, with less stress on a word in the middle. The line break in this sentence, with the consonance and punctuation, positions "Sue" in the final position of the line. Emphasis on Susan's name, her nickname, adds to the intimacy of the letter's opening. The sentence begins with a phrase starting with an infinitive, and line division suspends the thought, delaying completion, creating tension, and accentuating the effect of the startling statement that to miss someone you love, which would appear to be a kind of helplessness, is actually the opposite: it is power.

Since alliteration in the prose functions in similar ways in the poetry, commentary on Dickinson's verse is useful in understanding the prosody of the letters. In her guide to writing poetry, *Thirteen Ways of Looking at a Poem*, Wendy Bishop points out that "alliteration is partly a visual device" (406). In *Graces of Harmony: Alliteration, Assonance, and Consonance in Eighteenth-Century British Poetry*, Percy G. Adams concurs: alliteration is "noticeable" to readers "because the eye catches" initial letters so quickly (63). The patterning encourages reading and rereading, moving from one phrase to the next, backward and forward, returning to the first. Rhetorically, alliteration moves an argument point by point. Adams writes that the sound patterns not only have "an acoustic appeal" but "can be persuasive, emphatic, functional" (36); he finds that "the most distinctive use of vowel and consonant echoes in the age of Dryden and Pope was to aid the structure, the rhetoric, the idea" (186).

Throughout Dickinson's letters, as in the second sentence of the letter to Susan, "The stimulus / of Loss makes / most Possession / mean," alliteration contributes to an aphoristic quality, adding to the condensation, maximizing meaning, and facilitating memorization. "The aphorism is oracular," writes Northrop Frye, "it suggests that one should stop and ponder on it" ("Verse" 293). Visually, a scene or situation in a letter unfolds piece by piece, with details holding a reader's attention momentarily, inviting the reader to focus on each part of the accumulating whole. The letter to Susan continues by describing the scene at home, playfully and figuratively:

> The Trees keep
> House for you
> all Day and
> the Grass looks
> chastened.
> A silent Hen
> frequents the
> place with
> superstitious
> Chickens – ...

Popular nineteenth-century writers whose works were included in the Dickinson family library provided models of alliterative description. Dickinson was an avid reader of Charles Dickens, who writes in *Bleak House*, "well may the court be dim, with wasting candles here and there; well may the fog hang heavy in it, as if it would never get out," and "the Lord High Chancellor looks into the lantern that has no light in it" (xviii). The prose is "musical, sonorous," with "frequent concorded repetition of sound that constitutes assonance," explains Vladimir Nabokov in his lectures on the novel (xvii–xviii). Nabokov points to Dickens's "marked alliteration," and notes "a kind of incantation, a verbal formula repetitively recited with growing emphasis; an oratorical, forensic device" (xvii). Dickinson also read Poe, who begins "The Fall of the House of Usher" with the memorable phrase: "During the whole of a dull, dark, and soundless day."[4] Discussing "The Raven," in "The Philosophy of Composition," Poe identifies the "originality" of the verse as "some altogether novel effects arising from an extension of the application of the principles of rhyme and alliteration" (460). Dickinson's writing achieves some of its "originality" through similar means.

Much of the work on Dickinson's use of alliteration occurs only in studies of the poetry, and, with the exception of Percy Adams, these investigations have not been extensive, perhaps because this strategy for organizing sound is so often seen as simple. "Far more than . . . any poet before her," Adams claims, Dickinson "replaced end rhyme with consonance" (173). This analysis of Dickinson's prosody in a work entirely devoted to a study of alliteration is an anomaly. Many Dickinson critics identify her signature rhyme as "slant" rhyme and isolate the sound pattern from its larger context, which is a range of rhyme based on a spectrum of alliteration.[5] It is my view that alliteration in various positions in a line deserves much more attention in the analysis of Dickinson's rhyme. Here James Guthrie's discussion of range of rhyme in "Near Rhymes and Reason: Style and Personality in Dickinson's Poetry" is helpful: "Taken as a whole, rhyme can be regarded as a scale ranging from no rhyme at all to exact rhyme, with dozens of gradations in between that poets can employ to modulate their sound. . . . Typically, Dickinson used a network of related sounds to hold her poems together, combining assonance, consonance, and near and exact rhyme" (71).[6]

Commentary on alliterative verse in English gives insight into Dickinson's goals in her prose. Alliteration in the oral tradition of the Middle Ages played an important role in creating drive in long narrative poems. David Lawton, in *Middle English Alliterative Poetry and Its Literary Background*, refers to alliteration as a "systematic linking device" (28). In "Old English Language and Poetics," an introduction to his verse translation of *Beowulf*, Seamus Heaney explains that "where end-rhyme puts the most prominent aural feature at the end of the verse, alliteration creates a dynamic across the middle of the line" (xix). Robert B. Shaw, in *Blank Verse: A Guide to Its History and Use*, makes a similar point: alliteration in blank verse helps avoid "mid line slackening."[7] Adams in *Graces of Harmony*, notes that assonance and consonance provide poets with "a means of stressing the rhythmic peaks in a line of poetry" (29). Pope, he observes, excelled in his use of a wide range of consonance beyond other poets "after Dryden and at least until Emily Dickinson" (63).

Adams maintains that Dickinson "is not only unique with her invigorating images and quick twists of wit" but "is intriguing in her use of phonic recurrences" (172–73). He exemplifies his conclusion that she "often preferred [consonance] to end rhyme" with a discussion of "I like to see it lap the Miles" (Fr383), "where there is no end rhyme but in which two end words of each stanza consonate" ("up" and "step," "peer" and "pare," "while" and "Hill," "Star" and "door"). I would add to Adams's remarks that, notably, Dickinson considered changing "I like to see it" to "I like to hear it." The poem confounds the visual and aural: a fast-moving train looks and sounds like a horse, a perverse Pegasus, "neighing" like the orator Boanerges, complaining in "horrid – hooting stanza"—a phrase that plays with the idea that harsh and silly alliteration makes bad poetry, unlike Dickinson's skillful intricacy and control.

In Dickinson's poetry and prose, manuscript features draw attention to alliteration and contribute to emphasis. Through spatial arrangements that inscribe emphasis, Dickinson offers cues about which words in a line to stress. Readers have the option of following her suggestions or overlooking them. This is not a matter of achieving the "correct" reading. Although I argue here that standard print editions of the letters alter rhythm, I am not claiming that they defeat it. This is a matter of degree. My view is that in order to discover a full range of visual and acoustic effects, encounter certain subtleties and nuances of meaning, and appreciate rhythmic complexities, readers benefit, immeasurably, from access to the textual information that manuscript provides. My interest here is in emphasis set out by breaks and spacing; and my experience of reading is that this contrastive stress, in the prose and poetry, works in conjunction with other manuscript features, including capitalization and punctuation.

Dickinson capitalizes words with special significance to indicate their importance, a common practice in nineteenth-century writing that she adopted and exploited. In the opening page of the letter to Susan, "Loss," "Possession," "Heart," and "Immortality" are highlighted. Often letters appear in the form of a capital without being full sized, and an editor translating manuscript to print might opt for using a lower case letter; however, in manuscript the mid-sized letters draw attention in a manner similar to capitalization.

Discussions of the punctuation, the dash in particular, have been extensive but isolated in Dickinson studies, separated from analysis of their manuscript context. Often the mark is seen as an idiosyncrasy, an oddity of Dickinson's style.[8] Dashes serve multiple, sometimes oppositional purposes, as critics have shown: making syntactic connections, letting meaning resonate, allowing sound to echo, introducing silence, acting as a musical rest, or permitting a breath. However, focus has been on the mark when it could also be on the space itself that the dash is holding open. In the late writings, dashes appear less often, and line breaks and space between words are used more frequently. One reason is that without requiring punctuation, space itself comes to suggest pause and stress.

Muriel Rukeyser in *The Life of Poetry* maintains that silences are "part of the sound" (116). In discussing the biological relationships of rhythm to the body— walking and breathing—she calls for "inventing" punctuation: "we need a mea- sured rest" and "a system of pauses which will be related to the time-pattern of the poem" (117). Rukeyser points out that E. E. Cummings's use of space on the page "can provide roughly for a relationship in emphasis through the eye's dis- cernment of pattern" (117). This observation on Cummings approximates the way Dickinson replaces punctuation marks with space in her late writings. Per- ceiving spatial prosody as enhancing the effects of sound in Dickinson's verse and in her prose is, in part, determined by the reading practices of an individual. Whether the time that it takes for the eye to move from the end of one line to the beginning of the next registers as a pause depends on a reader recognizing or hearing the break. Interpretation of the line then depends on whether or not she allows herself to be directed by perceived emphasis. When Dickinson divides a verse line or a sentence, and when she leaves more space than is usual between words in a line, does a reader recognize those spaces as expressive features that set the emphasis and establish rhythm? Or does she read through the break?

Prosodists debate where in the reading process the writer ends and the reader begins. John Hollander points out that even in enjambed verse the word at the end of a line receives some sort of momentary foregrounding or emphasis, and that this is not a matter of the word marking the end but of the end mark- ing the word.[9] A word at the end of a divided line in Dickinson's verse or prose can take on a similar "sort of momentary foregrounding or emphasis." I find Catherine Addison's view in "Once Upon a Time: A Reader-Response Approach to Prosody," convincing. Addison argues that "rhythm depends essentially on movement and must be reenacted in real time in order to exist" (663) and that "the rhythms and patterns of sound in poetry" "cannot be conceived without the prior notion of a reader perceiving them" (655).[10]

Emphasis works as an interpretive strategy, a writer signaling meaning to a reader. A question from everyday conversation highlights the relationship of emphasis to interpretation. "Do you have money?" can be four different questions: "Do you have *money?*", "*Do* you have money?", "Do *you* have money?", and "Do you *have* money?"[11] Each question has a distinct meaning and brings to mind a different scene, situation, and circumstance. This example works especially well because of its emotional impact: anything to do with money is likely to elicit, to some degree, a heightened response. Between a writer and a reader, as well as between two people in conversation, emphasis is an emotional exchange. In *Poetry and the Fate of the Senses*, Susan Stewart, discussing the "Dynamics of Poetic Sound," points out that "in speech, stress can determine emphasis in ways that remain indeterminate to writing without the addition of supplemental discourse or diacritical marks: Did Isolt say hello to *Tristan?* Did Isolt say *hello* to Tristan?" (75). Stewart quotes Allen Grossman: "Stress is the inscription of the subjective or meaning-intending volition of the speaker (this is for the reader)" (75).

In Dickinson's letter to Susan, a pattern of infinitives is set and stress is varied: "to live," "to / love," "to live":

> To live   lasts
> always , but to
> love is firmer
> than   to live .

In the phrase "To live lasts," "to" and "live" are closer together, while "live" and "lasts" are farther apart. Pauses after "live" and "lasts" give the words greater emphasis, more impact. Both words receive emphatic stress, and the thought unfolds gradually: "to live," "to live lasts," "to live lasts always."

The degree of difference in blank space between handwritten words may be more identifiable at a glance in some instances and harder to gauge in others, but generally the eye can register the relative distances. It is also possible to measure the spaces with a ruler. (Some of Dickinson's manuscripts are on stationery that has a graph pattern, and a reader can count the number of small squares between words.) There are random elements in some visual lines, including dimensions of the sheet. The fact that patterns of arranged space exist by design in Dickinson's manuscript writings does not mean that every mark and space on a page is always positioned according to a consistent plan. Readers who observe and study manuscript features can learn to recognize the proportionate spacing and evaluate its interpretive significance, a reading practice I model here:

> No Heart that
> broke but further
> went   than
> Immortality .

Emphasis is conveyed in degrees through combined visual strategies. Here "Heart" is capitalized, and short lines (two or three words) promote a word in the middle of a line. Then, "Heart," "broke," and "but" make consonantal threads of final "t" and initial "b." The "t"'s continue in "went" through the climactic finish, "Immortality." This arrangement accentuates "Heart," then "broke," then "but": the uplifting second part of the thought—that the heart went further, not that the heart broke—is visually, dramatically set forth. There is a larger amount of space between "went" and "than," balancing the sound, pacing the revelation, and ensuring that "Immortality" is not divided. (There would have been room in the line above to place "Immor-," if Dickinson had wanted to do so.)

On the next-to-last page of the letter, in a passage with parallel subject-verb construction,

> I trust   that
> you are warm.
> I keep your
> faithful place.

spatial arrangements indicate a greater emphasis on "trust" than on "keep." Dickinson knows that while Susan is away, she is being loved where she is, while, at the same time, the place of their mutual love (at home in houses side by side) is secure.

A verse passage (Fr1202) that appears on the fourth page of this letter,

> Of so   divine
> a Loss
> We enter but
> the Gain,
> Indemnity for

Loneliness
That such a
Bliss has been.

promotes precise articulation of consonance and assonance: the medial and final
"t's" of "enter," "but," "Indemnity"; "so" and "Loneliness"; the "n's" in "divine," "enter,"
"Gain," "Indemnity," "Loneliness," "been." "But" has additional stress followed by
a pause and alliterating with "Bliss" and "been." "Loss," "Loneliness," and "Bliss"
are linked by consonance, and "Loss" and "Bliss" by their single syllable forms.
The result of the visual and acoustic connections is the heightened emotion of
the equations: loss is loneliness, yet loss and loneliness are bliss.

In this stanza, with a 3.3.4.3 pattern of beats, measured lines one, two, and
four consist of one- and two-syllable words with a weak beat followed by a
strong beat.[12] The third measured line, with three- and four-syllable words,
varies the pattern without changing the number of beats: stress falls on the
second syllable of "Indemnity" and the first and third syllables of "Loneliness."
In conventional lineation a more prominent stress among strong beats falls on
the last word of a measured line, particularly in verse that rhymes. The lines
quoted above rhyme abab: "Loss" and "Loneliness," "Gain" and "been." However,
because divided lines "distribute centers of the verse," "divine" receives more
stress.[13] The syllables of "Indemnity" may be drawn out emphatically in a short
line, and there is a longer than usual amount of space before the word that follows it. The result of these arrangements is the passion of the reversal: the loss
is divine; the loneliness is redeemed.

Dickinson's prosodic strategies have roots in the mid-nineteenth-century
theory and practice of elocution and grammar. In *The Teaching of English: From
the Sixteenth Century to 1870*, Ian Michael explains that "19th century readers
read prose out loud, lots of it, so readers heard, learned, were familiar and comfortable with prose rhythms and the concept of prose having rhythm and the
rhythm being important" (138). Nineteenth-century education taught students
that reading out loud was an essential skill. Training was formalized and extensive. Elocution textbooks instructed students in articulation and delivery. Along
with syntax, orthography, and etymology, grammar studies included instruction
in prosody and versification. Dickinson would have encountered the concept of
"accent" studying grammar as well as elocution.

In the mid-nineteenth century, "accent" had several meanings, as it does in
prosody today: according to Paul Fry, accent may be metrical; lexical ("the

accentual pattern customary to the word because of derivation or the relationship of prefix and suffix to root"); or refer to "the variable degree of emphasis
given syllables according to their sense in context" (3). Three nineteenth-century
usages are exemplified in Harriet Beecher Stowe's 1859 novel, *The Minister's
Wooing*. One refers to pronunciation and inflection in speaking a language.
With a touch of ridicule, Stowe describes a French-speaking visitor to Newport,
Rhode Island, Madame de Frontignac, as conversing with a "sweet, lisping
accentuation of English" (130). "Accent" can mean syllable stress. "With a vigorous accent on each accented syllable," a dress-maker sings lines from a hymn by
Isaac Watts: "From *the* third heaven, where God resides, / That holy, happy
place" [emphasis Stowe's] (120). And "accent" is "emphasis" in an emotional context where the speaker delivers words with particular conviction. Mary Scudder,
the novel's main character, explains to the flirtatious Senator Aaron Burr during
an evening spent attending a high society social gathering that this is her first
time at this kind of event but that she sometimes hears of such occasions: "'And
you do not attend?' said the gentleman, with an accent which made the inquiry
a marked compliment" [emphasis Stowe's] (127).

In several instances Dickinson appears to use "accent" to mean emphasis.
Writing to Thomas Higginson in 1869 she notes that she and Higginson are
"indebted in our talk to attitude and accent" (L330), and in 1876 she writes:

> I almost inferred
> from your accent
> you might come
> to Amherst –
> I would like
> to make no
> mistake in a
> presumption so
> precious – but a
> Pen has so
> many inflections
> and a Voice
> but one, will
> you think it
> obtuse, if I ask
> if I quite
> understood you?
> (L470)[14]

Dickinson acknowledges that speech distinguishes emphasis, and handwriting cannot "inflect" a word so that the writer's intention is clear.

Another reference to "inflection" comes in a poem that begins, "Many a phrase has the / English language – / I have heard but one" (Fr333). The phrase is described in terms of the contrasting sounds of nature's language: "Low as the laughter of the Cricket," yet "Loud as the Thunder's Tongue"; "Murmuring" like the tide, yet "Saying itself in new inflection" like a "Whippowil." Ordinarily spelled "whippoorwill," the bird's name echoes its call. The misspelling is closer to a phonetic spelling, playful and ironic in a poem that comments on "Orthography." Derived from the Greek for "correct writing," or spelling, the word may also refer to accurate pronunciation. In more word play, "Orthography" "breaks in" or dawns on the speaker/poet, who breaks the word, and the line:

> Breaking in bright Orthogra -
> phy
> On my simple sleep –

Division draws attention to the pronunciation of each individual syllable in the poem's only four-syllable word. Fitting the complete word onto the line would have been possible with crowding. The first line of the final stanza, "Not for the Sorrow, done me," crowds "done me" to fit it in. Drawing out the syllables of "Orthogra -/phy" may give the word a playful, possibly pedantic quality, as if the speaker were a student envisioning the spelling. The poem plays with the idea of upholding a standard of correctness that is irrelevant to nature's message. Sound captured through writing can be ambiguous, until an "inflection," an accent, clarifies the situation, here bringing the listener to tears, "Not for the Sorrow, done me – / But the push of Joy."

Eighteenth- and nineteenth-century literary theory connects emphasis with emotion. A textbook used at Amherst Academy during the years Dickinson studied there was *Elements of Criticism*, by Henry Home, Lord Kames, a work first published in England in 1762. Susan Dickinson's personal copy of the book, with penciled notations and underlinings, is at Harvard's Houghton Library. Kames writes that "an accent considered with respect to sense is termed emphasis," that accents "contribute to the melody by giving it air and spirit," and that they contribute "to the sense by distinguishing important words from others" (293).

"On the right management of the emphasis," defined as "stronger and fuller sound of voice," "depends the life of pronunciation," writes Lindley Murray, an American-born grammarian whose *English Grammar* replaced Noah Webster's manual in popularity and influence after 1795 to become the most widely used grammar in American schools. "If no emphasis be placed on any words, not only will discourse be rendered heavy and lifeless, but the meaning often left ambiguous. If the emphasis be placed wrong, we shall pervert and confound the meaning wholly" (211). For Murray, English grammar encompasses the following, in four sections: first, "the form and sound of the letters, the combination of letters into syllables, and syllables into words"; second, "the different sorts of words, their various modifications, and their derivation"; third, "the union and right order of words in the formation of a sentence"; and fourth, "true pronunciation of words, comprising accent, quantity, emphasis, pause, and tone," and "poetical construction of sentences," that is, "the laws of versification" (204).

"There are two kinds of pauses," Murray explains: "first, emphatical pauses; and next, such as mark the distinctions of the sense" (215). "The emphatical pause is made, after something has been said of peculiar moment, and on which we desire to fix the hearer's attention. . . . But the most frequent and the principal use of pauses, is, to mark the divisions of the sense, and at the same time to allow the speaker to draw his breath; and the proper and delicate adjustment of such pauses, is one of the most nice and difficult articles of delivery" [here "nice" means "precise"] (216). In a manner similar to my earlier discussion of the variety of meanings that the question, "Do you have any money?" might have, depending on the emphasis, Murray interprets variations of stress in the biblical line, "Judas, betrayest thou the son of man with a kiss?" He claims that, without accents, "the hearer would be under the painful necessity, first, of making out the words, and, afterwards, their meaning" (212). "In solemn discourse, the whole force and beauty of an expression often depend on the emphatic word," Murray asserts, "and we may present to the hearers quite different views of the same sentiment, by placing the emphasis differently" (211).

Nineteenth-century elocution manuals mirror the concerns of grammarians, first with pronunciation, then with accent, or interpretive stress. Ebenezer Porter's *Rhetorical Reader, Consisting of instructions for regulating the voice, with a rhetorical notation, illustrating inflection, emphasis, and modulation, and a course of rhetorical exercises* (the central text for elocution classes at Amherst Academy when Dickinson was a student there) defines emphasis as "a distinctive utterance of words which are especially significant, with such a degree and kind of stress, as conveys their meaning in the best manner" (38). Porter writes that "emphasis is governed by the laws of sentiment, being inseparably associated with thought and emotion. It is the most important principle, by which elocution is related to the operations of the mind," and "the soul of delivery" (38).

The goal for the practice of "Articulation," followed, in order, by instruction in "Inflection," "Accent," "Emphasis," and "Modulation," is summed up in the term "distinctive utterance." This concept appears repeatedly in the manuals of the most influential elocutionists, including the work of poet and prosodist Isaac Watts. Thomas Sheridan, in his *Course of Lectures on Elocution* (1803) claims that "the first, and most essential point in articulation, is distinctness," and "the chief force of indistinctness is too great precipitancy of speech" (34). "Precipitancy" is a term derived from "precipice," meaning "headlong." Elocutionists use this language to warn against rushing inattentively through a sentence, slurring words and falling away from the heights of elevated expression.

In *Elements of Elocution* (1810), John Walker, whose *Critical Pronouncing Dictionary* was also used at Amherst Academy, cautions against "hurrying over" unaccented syllables, which "though less forcible, ought to have the same time as those that are accented" (272). Dickinson's concern for the integrity of sound through her attention to the spacing becomes a means of protecting the "distinction" of each syllable. In this way she avoids "precipitancy" and adds to the effectiveness of her alliteration.

In "Hearing the Visual Lines: How Manuscript Study Can Contribute to an Understanding of Dickinson's Prosody," I argue that, in the poems, spatial arrangements introduced for acoustic and expressive purposes are not "accidental." The same is true for Dickinson's prose. Early nineteenth-century instruction manuals for penmanship make clear that leaving unequal amounts of space between words was not the norm for successful handwriting: rather, it was a sign of a writer who needed more training. Copybooks accompanying instruction manuals consist of lessons and practice exercises that teach students to write neatly and clearly and to place words at regular intervals. The 1881 edition of *Gaskell's Compendium of Forms, Educational, Social, Legal, and Commercial; Embracing a Complete Self-Teaching Course in Penmanship and Bookkeeping, and Aid to English Composition; Including Orthography, Capital Letters, Punctuation, Composition, Elocution, Oratory, Rhetoric, Letter Writing, etc.,* in a section called "Spacing," states that "the spaces between letters and between words should be as uniform in manuscript as in print. The rule is to leave just space enough between the words to write the small m; between letters just enough to avoid crowding" (32). The 1873 edition of *The Payson,*

Dunton, and Scribner Manual of Penmanship remarks that, "It is a very common fault to place the words too far apart" (37).[15] Dickinson's intention in placing some words further apart than others is to create what John Walker refers to as "contradistinction," a strategy for articulation he links with emphasis: "Wherever there is contradistinction in the sense of the words, there ought to be emphasis in the pronunciation of them," and "wherever we place emphasis, we suggest the idea of contradistinction" (199).

Walker's description of *Elements of Elocution* highlights the significance of emphasis to the study defined by Samuel Barber in *The Elocutionist* (1829) as the "branch of rhetoric which relates to DELIVERY" [all capital letters in the original]. His title page notes that "the principles of reading and speaking are investigated ... with directions for strengthening and modulating the voice ... to which is added a complete system of the passions, showing how they effect the countenance, tone of voice, and gesture of the body: exemplified by a copious selection of the most striking passages of Shakespeare: the whole illustrated by copper-plates explaining the nature of accent, emphasis, inflection and cadence."

In a passage especially illuminating in relation to prose—and to spatial prosody in Dickinson's letters—Walker discusses similarities between cadence in prose and meter in verse. Using terms from classical prosody, he writes: "The ancients thought harmonious prose to be only a loose kind of numbers [meter], and resolved many passages of their most celebrated orations into such feet as composed verse. In modern languages, where accent [used here to mean stress] seems to stand for the quantity [time taken to pronounce syllables] of the ancients, we find harmonious prose resolvable into an arrangement of accented syllables, somewhat similar to that of versification. The return of the accented syllable, at certain intervals, seems the common definition of both" (250–51).

Grammarians, literary theorists, and elocutionists all assert the key role of pauses in emphatic and rhythmic prose. For Walker a pause is necessary to pronounce a sentence "with clearness, force, and variety" (3). Kames notes that in a line of writing that is "most spirited and lively," "the accent being followed instantly by a pause, makes an illustrious figure; the elevated tone of the accent elevates the mind; the mind is supported in its elevation by a sudden unprepared pause, which rouses and animates; and the line itself, representing by its unequal division an ascending series, carries the mind still higher" (296). Porter explains that the "rhetorical pause" "occurs sometimes before, but commonly after a striking thought is uttered, which the speaker thus presents to his hearers, as worthy to command assent, and be fixed in the memory, by a moment of uninterrupted reflection" (59).

The correspondence to Susan Dickinson reads as a history of Dickinson's use of alliteration and her spatial prosody. In a section of "To miss you, Sue, / is power," line breaks and spacing allow readers to reflect on each detail after detail as the scene unfolds and emotion builds:

> The Forests
> are at   Home –
> The Mountains
> intimate at
> Night and arrogant
> at Noon , and
> lonesome Fluency
> abroad , like
> suspending Music.

Alliteration links elements of the landscape and helps create rhythmic phrasing: the medial and final "t"s in "Forests," "at," "Mountains," "intimate," "at," "Night," "arrogant," and "at," with "Noon" following "Night" and "l's" linking "lonesome," "Fluency," and "like." In the last line, "suspending" repeats the "d" of "abroad," while "Music" introduces new vowel sounds, bringing the music of the passage to a close. The rendering of the lines, "Intimate at / Night and arrogant / at Noon," creates rhythm through pauses, consonance, and parallel phrasing. In *The New Book of Forms: A Handbook of Poetics*, Lewis Turco writes on the sonic level of prose prosodies: "The oldest prosody in the world is based not upon counting syllables, but on grammatically parallel language structures" (8).

A passage in another letter to Susan from the early 1860s repeats syntactical patterns:

> It would be best to
>   see you – it would
> be good to see the
> Grass, and hear the
> Wind blow the wide
> way in the Orchard –
> Are the Apples
> ripe – Have the
> Wild Geese crossed –
> Did you save the
> Seed to the
> Pond Lily?
>   (*OMC*103; L294)[16]

Phrasing builds rhetorical momentum: "It would be best," "it would be good"; "to see," "to see," "and hear." Then Dickinson sets pauses at different points to vary rhythm and emphasis: "It would be best to / see you – it would / be good to see the / Grass," followed by the next chain of consonance: "Wind blow the wide / way." The second half of the passage continues the parallel language structures with three questions, rhythmic repetitions: "Are the Apples," "Have the Wild Geese," and "Did you save." Alliterative threads continue: "Geese crossed," "save the / Seed," and "Seed to the / Pond," while "Lily" stands out as a break in the pattern.

In "To miss you, Sue, / is power," alliterative passages range from the oracular to the quotidian, from the playful to the passionate. Dickinson handles the sound structure with extraordinary precision and skill, using it for any mood or emotional context. She is a great comic poet, as other studies have shown.[17] Whereas some alliterative humor may be rather silly ("Peter Piper picked a peck of pickled peppers"), Dickinson uses alliteration with subtlety to create and enhance wit and word play, as in the following lines:

> To look that
> way is Romance.
> The Novel "out,"
> pathetic Worth
> attaches to the
> Shelf .

"Out" means away, as Susan is "out," and also "checked out," as a book from a library. "Romance" is adventure, and puns on romance novel, a story of the heart. Susan's life and travels are an adventure. Dickinson's adventure is her love for Susan and the experience of missing her. The consonant blends in "pathetic Worth," the somewhat awkward sound of repeated "th," add playful humor to the emotional dynamics.

The letter's romantic closing takes play to the realm of the erotic:

> I trust that
> you are warm.
> I keep your
> faithful place.
> Whatever Throng
> the Lock   is
> firm upon your
> Diamond Door.
>   Emily.

With "I" and "trust" closer together, "trust" and "that" further apart, followed by the line break, the phrase is slowed, and the thought's completion held off. This dramatizes the intimacy. "I trust [pause] that," followed by, "I keep your," relatively evenly spaced, varies a pattern. Assonance enhances "faithful place" and connects "Throng" with "Lock." The alliteration of "Diamond Door" adds to the power of a mysterious trope that is similar to the figure of a locked door in the poem, "The Way I read a Letter's – this - / 'Tis first – I lock the Door" (Fr700). Here the speaker encloses herself in a secure place where she will not be disturbed or observed in the private act of reading, moving as far away from the door of the room as possible to "pick the lock" of the letter. "Then – glancing narrow, at the Wall – / And narrow at the floor," she checks for an intruder who might spy or interrupt. The room, like the shape of the letter's page, is narrow, and the speaker presents her perception as "narrow"—etymologically associated with the Greek "narce" or "stupor." But when she opens the letter's door, she "peruse[s] how infinite" she is, and "sigh[s] for lack of Heaven – but not / The Heaven God bestow." She longs for the heaven of human love. In Dickinson's letter to Susan, the "Diamond Door" represents that love in the form of Susan's infinite and heavenly space.

Dickinson's lifelong correspondence to Susan (her most substantial, diverse, and wide-ranging body of work) continued through four decades; it provides ideal evidence for studying the rhythms of the prose, tracing prosodic shifts, and following alliterative patterns as they establish tone and develop themes.[18] "Sweet and soft as summer, Dar- / lings, maple trees in bloom and / grass green in the sunny places" (OMC21; L178), Dickinson writes Susan and her sister, Martha, from Washington, D.C., in 1855.[19] Spanning the years of Dickinson's writing, alliteration conveys nature's beauty and the pleasures of experiencing the natural world. The structure of sound and emphasis builds a language of intimacy shared with Susan, an enduring emotional texture. In the early letters, Dickinson plays on the sounds of Susan's name and nicknames: "Sue," "Susie," "Sweet," and "Sister." For example, she begins an April 1852 letter with "So sweet and still, and Thee, Oh Susie, what / need I more, to make my heaven whole?" (OMC7; L88).

Underlining is a method of emphasis in the early letters:

Oh my darling one, how long you wander
from me, how weary I grow of waiting
and looking, and calling for you; . . .
. . . you'll never
go away, Oh you never will – say, Susie, promise me again, and I will smile faintly – and

> take up my little cross again of sad – <u>sad</u>
> separation. How vain it seems to <u>write</u>, when
> one knows how to feel – . . .
>
> (OMC3; L73)

Before the more prevalent use of space to indicate contrastive stress, Dickinson underlines:

> Were it not for the <u>weather</u> Susie –
> <u>my</u> little, unwelcome face would come
> peering in today – . . .
>
> . . . <u>Dear</u> Susie – <u>happy</u> Susie – I rejoice
> in all <u>your</u> Joy – . . .
>
> (OMC1; L38)[20]

This method continues throughout the correspondence but with less frequency after the mid-1860s. (In the poetry, Dickinson abandons underlining almost entirely after the early 1860s.)

Lindley Murray in *English Grammar* cautions against the error of "multiplying emphatical words too much": "it is only by a prudent reserve in the use of them, that we can give them any weight." Murray concludes: "To crowd every sentence with emphatical words, is like crowding all the pages of a book with Italic characters, which, as to the effect, is just the same as to use no such distinctions at all" (215). George Saintsbury, in *A History of English Prose Rhythm* (1912), complains that italics can become a "refuge of the forcible feeble," that "italic signposts" overemphasize: "the rhythm, if it is real, will supply the required emphasis unfailingly" (354). These seem to be the conclusions that Dickinson drew.

Through the mid-1850s alliteration intensifies expression of plaintiveness and longing:

> I miss you, mourn for you, and
> walk the Streets alone – often at
> night, beside, I fall asleep in tears,
> for your dear face, yet not one
> word comes back to me from that
> silent West. If it is finished, tell
> me, and l will raise the lid to
> my box of Phantoms, and
> lay one more love in; but if
> it <u>lives</u> and <u>beats</u> still, still lives
> and beats for <u>me</u>, then say me

<u>so</u>, and I will strike the strings
to one more strain of happiness before
I die. . . .

(OMC20; L177)

Consonance and assonance promote precise articulation and serve as rhetorical strategies for persuasion: final and initial "t"s in "yet not one / word comes back to me from that / silent West. If it is finished, tell . . ."; the thread of "tell," will," and "still, still"; the "l's" in "lid," "lay," "love," and "lives"; the archaic, poetic inversion "say me so," with the continuing chain of "s"s—"strike," "strings," and "strain"; and the culminating "I," "strike," and "I die."

Assonance functions as internal rhyme in this 1854 letter:

Few have been given me, and if
I love them so, that for <u>idolatry</u>,
they are removed from me – I
simply murmur <u>gone</u>, and the
billow dies away into the boundless blue . . .

(OMC22; L173)

Rhymes of "me," "<u>idolatry</u>," and "me," punctuated by a comma, line break, and dash, respectively, create rhythm, as do the consonating "have," "given," "love," and "removed." "<u>Gone</u>," followed by a comma and a pause, coming after the rhymes and breaking the chain of medial "v," provides acoustic variety, setting up a dramatic climax that resonates through the figure of the "billow [dying] away into the bound- / less blue" with its thread of consonating "b" and "l" to "bl."

Spatial prosody in the correspondence begins in the early to mid-1860s. In earlier letters words are usually evenly spaced, with some exceptions, and most lines adhere to prose conventions with the width of the sheet determining length of lines. Still, there are instances of line division serving expressive purposes in these early letters, for instance, in this passage from the letter quoted immediately above:

We have walked very
pleasantly – Perhaps this is the
point at which our paths
diverge – then pass on singing
Sue, and up the distant hill
I journey on.

(OMC22; L173)

The consonance of "we" and "walked," of "pleasantly," "Perhaps," "point," "paths," and "pass" leads to an alliterative double reading set up through line division: with the break functioning as a comma, "singing" is a verb, "pass on singing"; "singing" is also an adjective, becoming part of the name: "singing Sue." Word play here works to mask and mediate emotional tension, through which Dickinson holds out hope that the women's separation is temporary.

From the mid-1860s on, lines in letters have three or four words, and later two or three. More frequent line breaks and the increasingly prominent strategy of varying the amount of space between words intensify strategies of emphasis.

> Sister,
>   We both are
> Women, and there
> is a Will of God –
> Could the Dying
> confide Death,
> there would be no
> Dead – Wedlock
> is shyer than Death.
> Thank you for
> Tenderness –
>   (*OMC*III; L312)

Consonant sequences advance the reasoning: "We," "Women," "Will," and "Wedlock"; "Could" and "confide"; the chain of final, initial, and medial "d": "God," "Could," "Dying," "confide," "Death," and "would"—and then the doubled effect of consonance and assonance: "Dead," "Wedlock," "Death," and "Tenderness." In conventional prose form, "We both are Women, and there is a Will of God," the heaviest stress would fall on the last words of the clauses, "Women" and "God." Line division accentuates "both," drawing attention to the bond between the women. The three-syllable "Tenderness," alone as a line, varies the cadence. This word marks a turning point, a move from aphorism to direct personal statement: "I find it is the only / food that the Will / takes." Alliteration serves an emphatic, rhetorical purpose here, too: "find," "food."

The letter continues with affection and play:

> I am glad you go –
> It does not remove
> you . I seek you
> first in Amherst ,

> then turn   my
> thoughts without
> a Whip – so well
> they follow   you –

In the first two lines of this passage the words that are centered—"glad" and "not"—stand out. Susan might expect to read the opposite of what is said:"I am sorry you go. It removes you." This is what Dickinson means, and she also means the opposite, because Susan is everywhere in her heart, mind, and imagination. "First" and "Amherst" rhyme; their positions, first and last words in a line, add to the rhyme's effect. Consonance—"first," "Amherst," and "thoughts without"; "without," "Whip," and "well"; "well" and "follow"—moves the turning thoughts in overlapping patterns.

Lines of verse close the letter (Fr898):

> An Hour is a Sea
> Between a few, and me –
> With them would Harbor
> be –

Whereas meter may or may not be disambiguating, inscribed emphasis can be more directive. In this verse, three metrical lines form four visual lines:"Hour" and "Sea" hold the beats in the first line; the second syllable of "Between," "few," and "me" take beats in the second. The third line is ambiguous: a beat may fall on "With" or "them." The measured line puts the stress on "them." The shorter visual line, which does not carry through to the rhyme at the end, encourages a slower, more nuanced reading, supporting a stronger stress on "With." Alliterating "would" also emphasizes "With." Line division avoids crowding "Harbor" and "be," and prevents a slurring or unwelcome echo of "b" sounds in "Harbor be"; but the most important result of the measured line's division is to have "be –" alone as a line, the final line. The one-syllable, two-letter word creates visual irony, which Dickinson adds to by scripting it in an understated hand.[21] "Be –" rhymes and resonates, and completes the definition of home and existence: to be safe, to be alive, is to be with Susan.

The emotional intensity and rhetorical persuasion achieved through the combination of alliteration and expressive manuscript features highlight Dickinson's profound ability to bring the comic to the tragic—even when she consoles Susan on the occasion of the death of Susan's son, Gilbert, in October 1883, in a letter that begins, "The Vision / of Immortal / Life has been / fulfilled."

Here, lines resonate with consonance ("Immortal," "Life," "fulfilled."). Playfully, in the spirit of the lost boy, she writes:

> ... Now my
> ascended Playmate
> must   instruct me.
> Show us, prattling
> Preceptor, but the
> way   to   thee!
>   (OMC234; L868)[22]

In another letter following Gilbert's death,

> Dear Sue –
>   A Promise
> is firmer than
> a Hope, although
> it does not hold
> so much –
> Hope never knew
> Horizon –
> Awe is the first
> Hand that is
> held to us –
> Hopelessness in it's
> first Film has not
> leave to last –
>   (OMC236; L871)

alliteration's play defeats hopelessness.

In conclusion, the lines of the manuscript page to Susan that begin my argument and appear in this print translation,

> To miss you, Sue,
> is power.
> The stimulus
> of Loss makes
> most Possession
> mean.
> To live   lasts
> always, but to
> love is firmer

than to live.
No Heart that
broke but further
went   than
Immortality .

are rendered by Thomas Johnson in "Letter 364":

To miss you, Sue, is power.
The stimulus of Loss makes most Possession mean.
To live lasts always, but to love is firmer than to live. No Heart
that broke but further went than Immortality.

I hope to have shown here that this is not what Dickinson wrote. Standard print editions of the letters limit our understanding of their prosody and nuanced meanings. The richest, most productive way of experiencing Dickinson's writing is through manuscript images,[23] a way of reading that adds to our informed appreciation of the letters and contributes to our deep pleasure in their passion and their play.

NOTES

1. According to editors Thomas Johnson and R. W. Franklin, Susan Dickinson received the letter in 1871 while visiting her sister, Martha Smith, in Geneva, New York. Johnson's Letter 364 is dated "September 1871"; previously, he dated the verse passage in the letter (J1179) "about 1871." Franklin dates his Fr1202 "about September 1871."

2. *Open Me Carefully* (*OMC*) #158 renders line breaks as they appear in the manuscript letters; however, at the time this book was published the editors accepted the publisher's restrictions and did not have the option of representing differing amounts of space between words in a line. This is the case for all *OMC* documents.

3. "Diplomatic" comes from "diploma," referring to a document "doubled," or folded in half.

4. This line appears in Barton and Hudson's 1997 *Contemporary Guide to Literary Terms* to show that "consonance can likewise be used to great effect in prose" (8).

5. Brita Lindberg-Seyersted's *The Voice of the Poet: Aspects of Style in the Poetry of Emily Dickinson* makes a valuable contribution to the study of sound patterns in Dickinson's poetry. See Lindberg-Seyersted's commentary on "approximate" and "near" rhyme, alliteration in particular poems, and alliteration in a letter to Susan Dickinson on the occasion of Gilbert's death, L868 (20). In *Positive as Sound: Emily Dickinson's Rhyme*, Judy Jo Small's discussion of "rich consonance" is brief, but illuminating. See Small, 14–15, 201, and on 227, note 13. Small cites Timothy Morris's count of consonantal and assonantal rhymes (see 15). She greatly adds to our appreciation of Dickinson's "auditory imagination" and "musical aesthetic" (30). Focusing on Dickinson's prose,

Marietta Messmer, in *A Vice for Voices: Reading Emily Dickinson's Correspondence*, arrives at the significant conclusion that "rhetorical tropes" in the letters are "frequently combined with alliteration, anaphora, internal rhyme, assonance, [and] consonance" (36; see also note 12, on 202).

6. There are other aspects of this essay I find problematic, however, particularly the imprecise and impressionistic reasons Guthrie offers for Dickinson's choice of near rhyme, attributing the "self-referential" pattern to an "eccentric personality" (75).

7. See Shaw, 71–78, for an illuminating discussion of alliteration in the blank verse of Milton, Keats, Browning, and Tennyson.

8. An exception is Paul Crumbley's *Inflections of the Pen: Dash and Voice in Emily Dickinson*. In a chapter titled "Dash and Voice in the Letters," Crumbley traces patterns in punctuation in relation to the writer's polyvocalism, finding stylistic shifts as the correspondences progress.

9. See Hollander's chapter 5, "'Sense Variously Drawn Out': On English Enjambment," in *Vision and Resonance: Two Senses of Poetic Form*.

10. As Braid and Shreve, the editors of *In Fine Form: The Canadian Book of Form Poetry*, point out, prosody "is a field in which few things are entirely agreed upon" (20). The idea of expressive manuscript features and emphasis inscribed through spatial prosody contributing to the rhythm of Dickinson's prose is likely to be controversial, particularly among readers sensitized to the debates in Dickinson scholarship over the line breaks and the role of the manuscripts in reading the poetry. Some Dickinson critics argue that focus on the visual results in "an end to the music." John Shoptaw, in "Listening to Dickinson," claims that "since Dickinson wrote for both the eye and the ear," "too much faith in the manuscripts can make us forget this simple fact: we might open our eyes only at the cost of closing our ears" (21). This argument is similar to Domhnall Mitchell's position in *Measures of Possibility: Emily Dickinson's Manuscripts*. Like Mitchell and Christina Pugh in "Ghosts of Meter: Dickinson, After Long Silence," Shoptaw is concerned that manuscript study induces readers to "forfeit the aural experience of her poems for the graphic delights of her manuscripts" (21).

Cristanne Miller writes in "The Sound of Shifting Paradigms, or Hearing Dickinson in the Twenty-First Century," that "the formal experiments of nineteenth-century American poetry are overwhelmingly centered on sound play, especially rhythmic (generally metrical) variation, rhyme, and alliteration and assonance," that "by the early twentieth century, . . . the tendency to perceive poetry as primarily aural was changing," and that "critical expectations for and perceptions of poetry [gave] increasing attention to visual elements of the poem" (202–3). My position follows Miller's in the assessment of nineteenth-century developments in poetry but then departs from hers in its argument that manuscript allows Dickinson to use the visual to create aspects of the aural.

My aim is to take issue with Miller, Mitchell, Shoptaw, and Pugh, in Miller's words, "over the extent to which visual features of her manuscripts should dominate perceptions of her poetic" (203). My position is not that the visual "dominates" the aural, but that the visual leads to and creates the aural. I also hope to show that arguments for reading Dickinson's poems and letters in manuscript are not "based on a twentieth-century paradigm" (Miller 204), but that Dickinson's manuscript prosody is rooted in eighteenth- and nineteenth-century theory and practice of grammar and elocution.

11. In his discussion of accent in the *Princeton Handbook of Poetic Terms*, Paul Fry uses a version of this question that sounds more stilted: "Have you the money?" (3).

12. See my discussion of meter and four-beat verse in "Hearing the Visual Lines: How Manuscript Study Can Contribute to an Understanding of Dickinson's Prosody," particularly the long quotation by my co-author Sandra Chung on Dickinson's use and variations on the form (354). See also Derek Attridge, *The Rhythms of English Poetry*.

13. I am indebted to Tilly Shaw, retired from the University of California at Santa Cruz, for the succinct phrasing of this analysis (personal conversation, 1995).

14. This is my print translation of the manuscript lines.

15. I make this case for Dickinson's poetry in similar terms, using the same sources, in a somewhat longer form in "Hearing the Visual Lines." There I also provide a more extensive discussion of Dickinson's training in elocution at home and at school and explain at greater length the role of elocutionary theory and practice in nineteenth-century education and public life.

16. The second line of this passage is indented because Dickinson regularly avoided writing over the imprint of an embossment in a sheet of writing paper.

Since *Open Me Carefully* was published, I have assigned a capital "S" to "Seed." Upper- and lower-case letters can be difficult to distinguish, since their appearances are often very close in size and form. Determination of capitalizations in Dickinson's writing may be subject to editorial interpretation, and interpretation can change over time, as is the case with this correction.

17. See *Comic Power in Emily Dickinson*, co-authored by Suzanne Juhasz, Cristanne Miller, and Martha Nell Smith.

18. Part of my rationale for selecting from this correspondence to make my arguments is that images of the documents I discuss can be accessed online through the Dickinson Electronic Archives (www.emilydickinson.org). Readers with Internet access have the opportunity to compare manuscript images with my type translations and form their own conclusions.

19. *OMC* #21 presents the text but does not render the line divisions of the manuscript. Publisher's space limitations did not allow for lineation of lines in the letters of the 1850s, since these letters are longer than those of any other decade. When I quote the 1850s letters here, my line breaks are based on my unpublished print translations. This is the case for the following additional *OMC* documents, in order of their appearance here: 7, 3, 1, 20, 22.

20. *OMC* misses the underlining of "your," which is corrected here.

21. See the manuscript image at Dickinson Electronic Archives.

22. *OMC* #234 misses the underlining of "me," an example in a late letter of Dickinson underlining a word to add particular emphasis.

23. In *Radiant Textuality: Literature after the World Wide Web* (2001), Jerome McGann asserts that "the genres that determine the aspirations of [Dickinson's] work are scriptural rather than bibliographical: commonplace book writing, on one hand,

and letter writing, on the other" (63). He points out that "it has taken 100 years for scholars to realize that a typographical edition of Dickinson's writings—whether of her poetry or even her letters—fundamentally misrepresents her literary work" (62). McGann's pioneering achievement in electronic editing has supported the inspired work of manuscript scholars Martha Nell Smith and Marta Werner in their electronic publications of Dickinson's writing.

Through advances in technology (and as copyright permissions allow), more electronic editions and digital archives of Dickinson's writings will continue to become available, providing readers with essential access. (See, for example, "Emily Dickinson's Correspondences: A Born-Digital Textual Inquiry" by Rotunda New Digital Scholarship, University of Virginia Press, 2008 (ed. Martha Nell Smith and Lara Vetter, with Ellen Louise Hart as consulting editor). In addition to archives and editions, easy distribution by e-mail of high-quality manuscript images for casual as well as scholarly use has been a critical development. Next, audio files will make it possible for readers to view an image of a manuscript letter or poem and its standard print edition, while listening to recorded readings of both; listeners will thus be able to evaluate different performances, then record their own readings for comparison.

MARTHA NELL SMITH

A Hazard of a Letter's Fortunes

Epistolarity and the Technology of Audience in Emily Dickinson's Correspondences

Why not call them "pletters" or "loems"? That is how my witty partner articulated the "problem" Thomas H. Johnson describes in his introduction to *The Letters of Emily Dickinson*: "Indeed, early in the 1860's, when Emily Dickinson seems to have first gained assurance of her destiny as a poet, the letters both in style and rhythm begin to take on qualities that are so nearly the quality of her poems as on occasion to leave the reader in doubt where the letter leaves off and the poem begins" (xv). Indeed, when determining how to report and arrange Dickinson's own commentary on letters, Johnson's practice shows just how vexing editorial work can be, especially when bound by rigid distinctions that determine some groups of words be designated as prose, some as poetry. "[A] Letter is / a joy of Earth – / it is denied / the Gods" Dickinson wrote stockbroker Charles H. Clark, friend of Charles Wadsworth, late in her life (A730, L963).[1] Also in January 1885, she wrote the same words to Mabel Loomis Todd's parents: "A Letter is a / joy of Earth – / It is denied / the Gods" (A776, L960). Following the lead set by Todd's editing (*Letters* 1894 and 1931), Thomas H. Johnson designated the lines to the Loomises as poetry (J1639) but those to Clark as prose, saying of the letter to Clark, "The conclusion of the second paragraph, arranged as verse, is in a letter to the Loomises (no. 960)" (L963n). The only difference in Dickinson's presentation is that she breaks the first two lines to the Loomises after the article "a" while in the letter to Clark, she breaks the lines after "is." Why the lines to Clark would be seen as prose while the lines to Mr. and Mrs. Loomis were seen as poetry is not clearly explained, especially as R. W. Franklin regards the lines in each as poetry (Fr1672). However presented generically, the meaning of those words is indisputable, at least in relation to Emily Dickinson's letters, to which this collection of essays is devoted. My essay is one part of a think piece, a biography, if you will, of the lives of Dickinson's "letters" over more than a century for her posthumous readers. Through this analytical description, I will use comparison of letters to her primary correspondents, Susan Huntington Dickinson and Thomas Wentworth Higginson, to show how different were not only the content but even the containers in which Dickinson placed her letters to respective audiences. When the words of her epistles are translated into print (in Johnson's *Letters* and in my own *Open Me Carefully*, for example), any meaningful sense of these containers is lost, and I argue that much can be gained in learning about Dickinson as a writer when a reader takes these containers into account in critical analysis of her work.

Besides being a companion to the essays gathered in the archive of this volume, this piece is also a companion to *Emily Dickinson's Correspondences: A Born-Digital Textual Inquiry*, a critical edition of selected poems, letters, and letter-poems that focuses on the diversities of Emily Dickinson's surviving written record and that encourages innovation in interpretation, in reading, and in scholarly editorial practices. Printed translations of Emily Dickinson's manuscripts homogenize her various writings so that all letters appear to be of the same ilk, as do all poems. Yet editions that divide letters from poems and poems from letters elide important aspects of the positions of Dickinson's poems within epistolary contexts and vice versa. Poems are blended into or embedded in the prose in letters; poems are written on separate sheets and enclosed with letters; poems are written and sent as letters, with salutation and signature ("Introduction," *Emily Dickinson's Correspondences*). In other words, poems are often part of letters, and poems are often letters or are contextualized by their mutual enclosure in an envelope with a letter, but this practice is erased and made difficult to comprehend when they are stripped from their original context. Unlike *Open Me Carefully* or Johnson's *Letters*, *Emily Dickinson's Correspondences* is designed to expose readers to the different kinds of her writings; it features views of every sort of variation in the Dickinson corpus of surviving manuscript writings. The goal of that mode of presentation of her writings is to make it possible for more readers to engage in deeper, broader inquiries about the writing practices of this revered American poet, questions such as, "What was Emily Dickinson writing and sending to her contemporaries? What kinds of practices did she enact in her letter-writing? How are poems integral to, and integrated in, her letters? How might poems in letters, and letter-poems, differ from poems in bound manuscript books?"

Nearly a quarter-century ago, I first argued that Emily Dickinson's careful distinction between the terms "publish" and "print" served as witness to the fact that she published her poetry in coterie fashion by using her letter-writing to at least ninety-nine correspondents as her primary distribution medium. Thus *Rowing in Eden: Rereading Emily Dickinson* extended R. W. Franklin's under-noticed observation in *The Manuscript Books of Emily Dickinson* (xii) about her "need for self-publication" while it tested hypotheses and conjectures generated by my own study of her manuscripts through which I systematically examined her self-publication to different audiences. Through its comparative focus on the correspondence with Thomas Wentworth Higginson in conversation with that to Susan Huntington Dickinson, "A Hazard of a Letter's Fortunes" extends and revisits some of the critical investigations of my first book, which focused on the importance of manuscript study and on the most voluminous of her correspondences, that to Susan.

As Sharon Cameron astutely observed, everyone who knew Emily Dickinson or knew of her knew that she "was a writer" (Cameron, *Choosing* 53). Many were aware that she was writing poems, and the record shows that at least two of her contemporary audiences, Susan Dickinson and Thomas Higginson, gave her feedback on her writing. The epistolary exchange between Susan and Emily Dickinson over the writing of "Safe in their Alabaster Chambers" (Fr124) shows Emily writing four different (presumably) second stanzas in an effort to suit Susan, who at one point declared, "You never made a peer for that verse [the relatively stable first beginning "Safe in their Alabaster Chambers"], and I guess you[r] kingdom does'nt hold one" (Hart and Smith, OMC61).[2] Susan Dickinson appears, however, to have expressed a preference for the verse beginning "Light laughs the breeze" over the one beginning "Grand go the Years," which is the second verse of the poem version that Dickinson sent to Higginson. Some have read these facts—Susan's stated preference and then Emily's choice of a version to send to an esteemed man of letters—as evidence that Emily did not respect Susan's opinion. One can never settle whether or not that kind of spec-ulation is accurate, for there are too many unanswerable variables: did Emily receive Susan's preference as bad advice? Or, did she and Susan discuss which version might be more palatable to Higginson and opt for the "Grand go the Years" rather than the "Light laughs the breeze?" Or, did Susan change her mind about her preference, communicate that by telling rather than writing, and Emily follow that revised opinion? Or, perhaps, did Emily send whichever version she was working on at the time to Higginson? The questions could go on, practically indefinitely, and to speculate whether Emily's choice of a version to send to Higginson constitutes commentary on her regard for Susan's opinion seems futile. What is not futile, however, is to consider what we might call the "technology of audience" and its influence over a poet's choices. To use "technology" in this way may surprise some readers. Technologies are tools, and in this case "audience" might be considered a means by which a writer frames her presentation and thus a tool that influences the shape of that presentation.[3] In this case, the audience is Thomas Wentworth Higginson and the poet Emily Dickinson, and examining her self-presentation and her presentation of her writings to him offers insights into her work as a writer.

In her correspondence with Higginson, one sees that her pose is not simply coy, as has often been remarked. Repeatedly Dickinson moves to represent herself as literary, well read, and worthy of attention as a writer. As Cameron observes, "her defiant letters to Higginson, in which she solicited his opinion only to challenge it, to argue with the literary conventions she claimed she wanted to learn, make it possible to suppose that her alternative way of writing poetry required a private space in which conventions could be revised without the revision's being contested" (*Choosing* 53). For nearly a quarter of a century Dickinson wrote almost seventy letters and forwarded 102 poems to Higginson, a prolific writer frequently published in the *Atlantic Monthly*, "a magazine of literature, art, and politics." Liberal in many of his political opinions, advocating for the disenfranchised, Higginson was an abolitionist; in the Civil War, he was a Union colonel. Yet all evidence shows that she refused his advice regarding her poetic technique and practices.

"Known to be especially sympathetic to the status of women in general and to women writers in particular" (Johnson, *Poems* xxv), Higginson was a logical choice for self-publication beyond family and friends. When Dickinson first wrote Higginson in April 1862, she had just seen his "Letter to a Young Contributor" in the *Atlantic Monthly* (www.emilydickinson.org/higgyc/yc1.html) and had surely observed his "hospitality to 'new or obscure contributors' and his insistence that editors are 'always hungering and thirsting after novelties'" (Sewall, *Life* 539). His evaluation of Whitman shows that Higginson considered himself a literary authority but also that he was quite conventional: "It is no discredit to Walt Whitman that he wrote 'Leaves of Grass,' only that he did not burn it afterwards. A young writer must commonly plough in his first crop" (Leyda II, 127).[4] A fellow of prestigious scholarship and a steward of publishing, Higginson was part of a group that wanted to establish "a standardization of American authors—the creation of a canon of Great Names in our literature" (Jones 86). America was still forming; an ocean separated its English founders from the lands of their heritage, and, having created a constitution of their own, Americans yearned to claim a culture all their own. America's popular poetry had been "critically scorned since the early nineteenth-century, when the sale of men's verse first fell behind women's" (Watts 5). An article printed in the *Woman's Journal* and reprinted in the *Springfield Republican* just after his 1870 visit to the Homestead shows that Higginson was quite serious when he set himself up as someone who could teach women how to write:

> I wish I could possibly convey to the young women who write for advice on literary projects, something of the meaning of this word "thorough" as applied to literary work. Scarcely any of them seem to have a conception of it. Dash, cleverness, recklessness, utter impatience of revision or of patient investigation, these are the common traits. To a person of experience, no stupidity is so discouraging as a brilliancy that has no roots. (Leyda II, 153)

Regarding himself as an authority on women writers, Higginson generalizes from his experience. Unfortunately, his generalizations are quite cliché-ridden: "Imperial intellect" is of man, and "tender affections" are of women ("Cupid and Psychology," *Women and the Alphabet* 222). Provincial, he would banish most female influence from notions of "true" poetry, on account of women's tendencies toward "recklessness."

Dickinson's letters to him show that he called her wayward, dark, uncontrolled, and tameless in taste. The facts of their relationship, according to her, were that he asked "great / questions accidentally" (BPL Higg 65; L352). Unlike Susan Dickinson's, his words gave no drunkenness. To him Dickinson declared, "Domingo comes / but once" (BPL Higg 52, L265), while to Susan she wrote:

> To be Susan
> is Imagination,
> To have been
> Susan, a Dream –

What depths
of Domingo
in that torrid
Spirit!
    (OMC233, L855)

Dickinson did not understand his "precept," "always" (BPL Higg 55, L271). He told his sisters that she was a "partially cracked poetess" and talked enough about her to his friends that when the "Woolseys . . . wrote some funny things for different guests" at the Warings' "novel wedding festival," "one imaginary letter" to him was from his Amherst correspondent who sometimes signed her missives "Your Scholar" (BPL Higg 54, L481n). With the help of his wife's commentary, he elaborated on his January 1874 description to his sisters:

> I saw my eccentric poetess Miss Emily Dickinson who *never* goes outside her father's grounds & sees only me & a few others. She says, "there is always one thing to be grateful for—that one is one's self & not somebody else" but [my wife] Mary thinks this is singularly out of place in E.D.'s case. She (E.D.) glided in, in white, bearing a Daphne odora for me, & said under her breath "How long are you going to stay." I'm afraid Mary's other remark "Oh why do the insane so cling to you?" still holds. I will read you some of her poems when you come. (L405n)

According to an acquaintance of Dickinson's, Higginson declared that her poems "reminded him of skeleton leaves so pretty but *too delicate*,—not strong enough to publish" (Leyda II, 193).

Oddly, in an August 1870 letter to his wife, Higginson describes this woman who had certainly persuaded him of her "Kangaroo" character, or difference, in very conventional terms (BPL Higg 54, L268):

> A step like a pattering child's in entry & in glided a little plain woman with two smooth bands of reddish hair & and a face a little like Belle Dove's; not plainer—with no good feature—in a very plain & exquisitely clean white pique & a blue net worsted shawl. She came to me with two day lilies which she put in a sort of childlike way into my hand & said "These are my introduction" in a soft frightened breathless childlike voice—& added under her breath Forgive me if I am frightened; I never see strangers & hardly know what I say—but she talked soon & thenceforward continuously—& deferentially—sometimes stopped to ask me to talk instead of her—but readily recommencing. (BPL Higg 126, L342a)[5]

Higginson notices that seeing "Miss Dickinson (twice)" was "a remarkable experience, quite equalling my expectation," but seems not to have recognized that his image of her life simply "accords with the standard biography of other women poets of the period," as Cheryl Walker has noted (99). For example, Edward Dickinson, portrayed as a stern, almost "tyrannical" symbol of "power and intellect," strongly resembles Lucy Larcom's father. Dickinson's white dress costume and reclusive posture were, as Walker has shown, standard fare for poetesses. Higginson was familiar with Longfellow's *Kavanagh*, in which the "too sensitive" Alice Archer harbors a secret sorrow and avidly reads poetry, and he hailed the work of Helen Hunt Jackson, whose Mercy Philbrick perpetuated nineteenth-century clichés about women writers; he was certainly aware as well of Margaret Fuller, whose biography, as Walker and Albert Gelpi point out, to some extent parallels Dickinson's (Walker 100, 166; Gelpi 184–85).

Yet Higginson does not seem to have noticed that she "posed" [her brother's word] in their interactions. As the poet has continued to peek through all the myths with which we have "sicklied" her over (Alice James, quoted by Lubbers 42), the hostess at the end of his description much more closely resembles the gregarious woman "so surrounded by people" whom Annie Holland saw at a Homestead reception (Leyda II, 115) than she does the stereotypical notion of a poetess he first portrays. But, George Monteiro reminds us, if he did not recognize her show for him, and

> If he did not fully understand Emily Dickinson's genius or even dream of the magnitude of her achievement, his instincts in the end were good. In 1890, we tend to forget, there simply was no one more qualified to introduce Emily Dickinson's poetry than Higginson. Posterity has so far deemed it that Higginson's part in the publication of Emily Dickinson's poetry—although he was far from suspecting it—was his most significant contribution to the cause of American letters. (xi–xii)

It appears Dickinson was not so far as he was from suspecting his role, for when she guessed he might do this, she exhibited foreknowing gratitude in a letter that she drafted to Higginson (no copy was found among his papers): "Thank you for Greatness – / I will have deserved it in / a longer time" (A807, L353).

Perhaps the key to understanding Higginson's treatment of women and then of Dickinson is to remember the assumptions he apparently makes about women's tractability: women are thorough in areas where it is "expected" (demanded) of them, "in their housekeeping and their dress and their social observances" ("Thorough," *Women* 223, 228). He asserts not only that he knows what makes great poetry, but also that women will, if they want to be great— not merely "popular"—poets, accord their writing practices with his judgments. Behind "almost all these letters" women write him, Higginson declares "there lies a laudable desire to achieve success." He then asks, "How can this be answered, my dear young lady, when you leave it to the reader to guess what your definition of success may be?" From his answer it appears he assumed these women writers' first priority is to join the ranks of those published in *Ladies American Magazine* and *Godey's Lady's Book*. Citing the example of Mr. Mansfield Tracy Walworth, whom (though Higginson had never heard of him) a newspaper called "a celebrated author" because his novel *Warwick* had sold 75,000 copies, he declares that he does "not think Hawthorne . . . would have accepted these conditions" as characteristic of success. Proceeding to instruct young women about the importance of their answering to internal standards of their own, Higginson cautions "them first to make their own definitions of success, and then act accordingly" and emphatically reminds his readers that "a book may be immediately popular and also immortal, but the chances are the other way. It is more often the case that a great author gradually creates the taste by which he is enjoyed. Wordsworth in England and Emerson in America were striking instances of this" ("Literary Aspirants," *Women* 233–35).

When confronted by Dickinson's verse, however, he seems to have forgotten these dicta. Maintaining that she was somehow flawed, convinced that she "never quite succeeded in grasping the notion of the importance of poetic form" (Sewall, *Life* 573), and thinking Arlo "Bates's criticisms" to be "excellent"—even when he wrote of Dickinson that because this woman "very near . . . to genius . . . never learned her art," one is "impelled to wonder and to pity at the same time" (Bingham, *Ancestors'* 52), Higginson tells a story similar to that of critics who maintain that she was personally maladjusted, neurotic, and agoraphobic. To these late nineteenth-century critics such as Bates, her lyrics are not quite the stuff of great poetry but comprise a portfolio of aberrance and abnormality. Never quite able to bring himself to see that this "wholly new and original poetic genius" was in the process of refashioning tastes so she could be more fully enjoyed, Higginson said, "at first I tried a little—a very little—to lead her in the direction of rules and tradition; but I fear it was only perfunctory, and that she interested me more in her—so to speak—unregenerate condition." Finding that she took great pains to correct the spelling of a word but "was utterly careless of greater irregularities," and that she would not abide by his direction, he "soon abandoned all attempt to guide in the slightest degree this extraordinary nature." To Higginson, Dickinson sometimes pressed obscurity, Coleridge's "compliment" to the reader, a bit "too hard"; and a woman who could never heed his advice "to work as hard to shape the children of her brain as to rear her bodily offspring," and seems to have enjoyed rather than bemoaned the fact of her solitude, "somewhat bewildered" this advocate of women's rights who still maintained the very conventional notion that there is "a greater sensitiveness which runs through all a woman's career, and is the expensive price she pays for the divine destiny of motherhood" (Higginson, "Letters" 448, 451; *Women and the Alphabet* 64).

From her "handwriting so peculiar that it seemed as if the writer might have taken her first lesson by studying the famous fossil birdtracks in the museum of that college town" to her unusual word choice, rhythm, and rhyme, Dickinson surprised him, and he could never bring himself to praise her without qualification. Commenting on "A Route of Evanescence" (Fr1489), he writes, "Nothing in literature, I am sure, so condenses into a few words that gorgeous atom of life and fire of which she here attempts the description. It is, however, needless to conceal that many of her brilliant fragments were less satisfying" ("Letters" 444). Higginson's proclaiming much of Dickinson's poetry "less satisfying" reflects his anxiety over not understanding this woman who was like no other female poet he encountered. He knew she was not merely eccentric, and he admired her yet he felt ambivalent toward one who seemed so aware of conventional expectations but refused to meet them.

Though she is ostensibly the pupil, when Higginson comes for his first visit, Emily Dickinson speaks; he listens. Describing her in a letter to his wife, he compares her to a well-known teacher. Interestingly, he deems her conversation fit for him but not for his wife: "Manner between Angie Tilton & Mr. Alcott— but thoroughly ingenuous & simple which they are not & saying many things which you would have thought foolish & I wise—& some things you wd. hv. lked" (BPL Higg 126, L342a). Higginson not only acknowledges that Dickinson dominated their conversation and that he found her both teacherly and wise, but he also reveals his habit of presuming to know another's tastes. Later, as editor of her poems, he extends this knowing attitude to being certain what will and will not "improve" Dickinson's poetry, making it palatable for public tastes. Though Higginson apparently called her tastes "Tameless" (A807, L353), he recognized that "Tameless" should not be misread as aimless (or shameless): "Yet she wrote verses in great abundance; and though curiously indifferent to all conventional rules, had yet a rigorous literary standard of her own, and often altered a word many times to suit an ear which had its own tenacious fastidiousness" ("Preface," *Poems* iv). In his *Christian Union* essay introducing her to the world, he writes, "Wayward and unconventional in the last degree; defiant of form, measure, rhyme, and even grammar; she yet had an exacting standard of her own, and would wait many days for a word that satisfied" ("Portfolio" 392).

Dickinson perplexes, delights, and continues to fascinate Higginson. He attempts neither to fit her into the canonical tradition nor to discount her altogether. But his writings to her and about her, as well as his editing of her, all reflect his admiring but tired remark that she is "sometimes Exasperating" ("Preface" vi). "Exacting" and "patient enough to wait many days" are hardly synonymous with "'spasmodic'" or "'uncontrolled,'" nor do they seem characteristic of "the seclusion of the portfolio, which rests content with a first stroke and does not over-refine and prune away afterwards." Since he thought her poetry a product of unbridled genius, he considered it worth printing, but not in the unconventional Dickinsonian form he saw as rough and unfeminine: "Her verses are in most cases like poetry plucked up by the roots; we have them with earth, stones, and dew adhering, and must accept them as they are" ("Portfolio" 392).

For a century of literary criticism, Higginson's ambivalence toward Dickinson and his apprehensive yet admiring response to and editing of her poems set the normalizing tone that imbues much criticism of her work. He cannot bring himself to ignore her, but he cannot accept her and her poems just as they are. He cannot imagine a sexual spinster, so he denies those ramifications of "Wild nights – Wild nights" (Fr269); a woman creating the tastes by which she is enjoyed is "foreign" to his thought as "Firmament to Fin" (BPL Higg 52, L265), so he sees Dickinson as gifted but not really intending much of what it appears she might. So even in the twenty-first century, critics still argue over whether her unconventional line breaks and punctuation are purposeful or only a happen (not really intended to be constitutive of her poetry) rather than let her readers decide for themselves. Similarly, though Higginson says her thought takes one's breath away, it is as if he thinks this effect is happenstance, for his commentary acknowledges a wonderful woman, but not a sage.

Thinking, then, that Dickinson strove to be just like one of the women writers he promoted, Higginson set about making corrective suggestions, at least at first. As Monteiro says in his "Introduction" to a collective reprinting of the first three series of Dickinson's poems:

It is ironic that Thomas Wentworth Higginson, whom Emily generously called her "preceptor," never fully understood the young poet cloistered in Amherst, and that he never managed to get beyond a basic, if genuine, appreciation of the daring, creative innovations she was making daily in her poetry—innovations that would in time profoundly affect the course of American poetry. She forged such changes surely but quietly—quietly, of course, because she abandoned at an early stage any hope of publication, any desire for, as she put it, "the auction of the mind." Nor was Higginson the kind of man who could have encouraged her to break with the conventional, marketable poetry of the day. If he knew that her poetry was not in accord with the prevalent taste of his times, it is also clear that he did not suspect that Emily's poetry was in advance of its time. Still, his failure to encourage publication (at times, apparently, he explicitly discouraged it) served the useful purpose, wholly unconscious on his part, of protecting Emily's poetry from the editorial taste of the latter half of the nineteenth century. (ix–x)

Following Higginson's lead, many have, like Johnson's assistant Theodora Ward (Elizabeth Holland's granddaughter), read her initiation of this correspondence as the pleading of a damsel in distress, "urgently asking for help" (Wylder 3).

What has been omitted from discussions of Dickinson's reasons for writing Higginson is that it is likely that the correspondence was started at the urging of Susan Dickinson. That Susan was familiar with the editors of the *Drum Beat* and, of course, the *Republican* is clear. But that it was probably she who encouraged Dickinson to write the esteemed critic has not been made plain. About two months before Dickinson's first letter to him, Samuel Bowles, responding to Susan's requests, wrote: "What a fatality there is in your errands for me! Whittier is out of print, just now ... Higginson has not been done in photograph—so all said—& yet I have a memory of it I think, months ago" (Leyda II, 46). By itself, this indicates little more than the fact that Emily and Susan had mutual interests. But in the context of Dickinson's wanting to make Austin and Susan "Proud – sometime – a great way off" (OMC62, L238; www.emilydickinson. org/safe/zhb74c1.html), her writing to Higginson almost immediately after Susan's asking this favor of Bowles, and Susan's taking an active interest in her sister-in-law's poetry—discussing it with Bowles, reading it aloud in her parlor, and apparently sending it out to be printed—all indicate Susan's intimate involvement with Emily's poetic career. Arguably, Dickinson's initial letter to Higginson is an attempt to launch their "Fleet" (OMC58; Smith, *Emily Dickinson's Correspondences*).

Whosoever idea it was to contact Higginson, the strategy worked. Once Dickinson obtained his attention, she did not, for any significant length of time, lose it. Her correspondence to him is friendly, warm, and often frank; to like him, however, was not to close her eyes to the fact that some of his ways disappointed her. To Higginson, Dickinson writes primarily commentary about the act of writing itself, pithy remarks on living, and, as she does to Susan, Elizabeth Holland, Frances and Louise Norcross, Abiah Root, Samuel Bowles, Henry Emmons, perhaps Otis P. Lord, and others, observations on the value of friendship. As this correspondence makes clear, her letters show a woman who loves people and to whom friends are important. Higginson noticed this: "I never was with any one who drained my nerve power so much. Without touching her, she drew from me. I am glad not to live near her. She often thought me <u>tired</u> & seemed very thoughtful of others" (BPL Higg 126, L342b). When she writes "Whom / my Dog understood could not Elude / Others" (BPL Higg 59, L316, *Emily Dickinson's Correspondences*), she appears to be responding to Higginson's having called her elusive. But in that letter she plainly states that she chooses "not" to "print," and, though she usually cloaks her meaning in metaphor, puts her thoughts "in the Gown" (BPL Higg 51, L261), she comments directly on many aspects of their relationship and answers requests he makes of her.

Their correspondence has hardly commenced when, in her fourth letter to him, Dickinson pictures herself verbally for Higginson and comments on the photographic representation he has asked for:

> Could you believe me
> without? I had no
> portrait, now, but am
> small, like the Wren,
> and my Hair is bold,
> like the Chestnut Bur –
> and my eyes, like the
> Sherry in the Glass, that the Guest leaves –
> Would this do just as
> well?
> It often alarms Father –
> He says Death might
> occur, and he has
> Molds of all the rest –
> but has no Mold of me,

but I noticed
the Quick wore off those
things, in a few days,
and forestall the
dishonor – You will
think no caprice of
me –

(BPL Higg 54, L268)

This letter indicates that Higginson has called her "Dark" (perhaps responding to her suggestion that that is where she is groping) and that he has requested her picture. Her response is to point out, by punning, that, like old bread, portraits are "mold"y. The quick was well worn off the daguerreotype when, three months earlier, the thirty-one-year-old poet wrote the thirty-eight-year-old critic, "Are you / too deeply occupied to / say if my Verse is / alive?" (BPL Higg 50, L260) and enclosed the second version of "Safe in their Alabaster Chambers" (Fr124) which emphasizes the poem's cosmic concerns, "The nearest Dream recedes – unrealized" (Fr304), "We play at Paste" (Fr282), and "I'll tell you how the Sun rose" (Fr204), an assemblage that demonstrates the range of her poetic vision and reveals her as a poet concerned with the universal. The poems subvert her modest, fearful pose and show that she is actually ambitious, not tentative and unsure. This initial self-presentation indicates that, to Higginson, she wanted to represent herself as seer and sayer, as explorer of the "'Undiscovered / Continent'" within each of us (Fr814).

Higginson apparently requested a biographical sketch and perhaps some more poems, for in her second letter, written only ten days later, she describes her literary interests, her family, and her acquaintance with professional men of letters. She encloses "There came a Day at Summer's full" (Fr325), "Of all the Sounds despatched abroad" (Fr334), and "South winds jostle them" (Fr98), poems that show her to be especially sensitive and romantic when she interacts with nature. "There came a Day" hints at the "secret sorrow" often presumed to haunt a woman poet (see Walker). Here it seems she sends lyrics he is more likely to expect from a female poet, yet she also confides her suspicion that he cannot tell her "how to grow" poetically, for, like physical growth, "Melody – or Witchcraft," such processes are "unconveyed." Within two months, Higginson pronounced judgment on the seven poems. On June 7, Dickinson, responding to his criticism, quoted his evaluation: her meter was "spasmodic," allying her with a school of poets many disdained; her fashioning of lyric, "uncontrolled."

Characterizing herself as of "little shape" and promising neither to crowd his desk nor make much noise, she sent him no more poems enclosed on separate sheets or stationery in that letter, but asked:

> If I might bring you
> what I do – not so
> frequent to trouble you –
> and ask you if I told
> it clear – 'twould be
> control, to me –

Then she wove a bit of explanatory verse into her prose:

> The Sailor cannot see
> the North – but knows
> the Needle can –
> The "hand you stretch
> me in the Dark",
> I put mine in, and
> turn away – I have
> no Saxon, now –
> As if I asked a
> Common Alms,
> And in my wondering
> hand
> A Stranger pressed
> a Kingdom
> And I bewildered,
> stand –
> As if I asked the
> Orient
> Had it for me
> a Morn –
> And it should lift
> it's purple Dikes,
> And shatter me
> With Dawn!
>   (BPL 52, L265, Fr14)

Besides showing that she did not consider poetry-making a solipsistic enter-prise, but sought to tell "it clear," the letter voices the power of a poetic sensibil-ity to articulate the simple splendidly, to transform experience, and of a beggar make a king. This is the first letter in which she asks him to be her teacher, though she prefaces her request with this verse that acknowledges there is a spiritual element in aesthetic appreciation that is not formulaic, and implies, therefore, that poetic excellence can never be found by smoothing rhythms and rhymes. Poetry cannot be reduced to rules and regulations and a list of "how tos," which could never capture poetry's nuanced dynamisms. Dickinson knew all of this, and signed her letter assertively, "E. Dickinson." "But," she asks of this champion of regularity, "will you be my / Preceptor," anyway. Though he did not understand what she was doing, Dickinson was enjoying their exchange, and making it seem that she considered him her instructor almost insured its continuation.

Much has been made of her calling herself Higginson's "Scholar" and asking for his instruction, but not nearly enough has been made of the fact that she signs many a letter as she did this one, forcefully with just her surname or with her first initial and surname. Even as she signs with confidence and a sense of power, Dickinson (well aware that she is an unknown woman approaching a frequently published man of letters) maintains a feminine and deferential pose in order to intrigue but never offend him. Hungry for appreciation, she wishes he would not react as others had—conventionally—and tells him so:

> You say "Beyond your
> Knowledge." You would not
> jest with me, because I
> believe you – but Preceptor –
> you cannot mean it?
> All men say "What" to
> me, but I thought it
> a fashion –
> When much in the Woods
> As a little Girl, I was
> told that the Snake
> would bite me, that
> I might pick a poisonous
> flower, or Goblins kidnap
> me, but I went along
> and met no one but
> Angels, who were far
> shyer of me, than I
> could be of them, so I

hav'nt that confidence
in fraud which many
exercise.
I shall observe your precept –
though I dont understand
it, always.

(BPL Higg 55, L271)

Following her assertive remarks with assurance that she is nevertheless obedient, this letter to Higginson evinces her posture as pupil. Time and again she vows she "shall implicitly / follow" his advice (BPL Higg III, L676) and hopes she "in no / way spoke / less reverently / than I felt – / Of a Pleasure / so Priceless" (BPL Higg 100, L546). She always addresses him in a respectful manner and sometimes sounds even reverent. Almost every critic mentions this and many puzzle over this apparent self-doubting, but accounting for the context in which these missives were written explains their tone. In the nineteenth century, how else might an unknown woman approach such a respected man of letters? If she had approached confidently, and argued with him for her spasmodic style, would he have thought her "Ostensible" (BPL Higg 59, L316) and perhaps labeled her abrasive or strident? Certainly an aggressive, vigorous approach traditionally held to be unbecoming for a woman would have been more easily dismissed by Higginson, finally a man of convention (however sympathetic to women and African Americans, he was liberal, not radical), than this beseeching, and very acceptable, feminine approach that asks guidance. Acutely aware of words and their effect, she knew she must certainly select the diction with which she addressed this man; she wanted to capture and hold his attention, and in that she succeeded. In this letter, she subverts her promise of obedience with the punning declaration that she never understands him, and she subverts her deferential proclamation by the poems she encloses. Both are strategies she often used with him.

As Dickinson had in the first letter, often she did not send a letter by itself but published herself to Higginson by enclosing poems that sometimes appear to illuminate a letter's meaning. Dickinson refused to provide a "mold" of herself for Higginson, but pictured herself and her career for him in that more permanent medium—poetry. She not only told him how to read the presentation a photograph provides, but, in poems forwarded to him, told him how to read herself, an odd bird of a poet. For example, when Dickinson reminded him that she "did not print," she enclosed "A Death blow – is a Life blow – to Some" (BPL

Higg 17, L316, Fr966). To versifiers, failure to print in the way preferred (death in the printing world) would probably sound the death of poetic impulse, but as Dickinson declares, after her "Death blow" in the world of print, "Vitality begun." Other important examples of this strategy were enclosed in the "All men say 'What' to me" letter (L271) in which she enclosed not only "Before I got my eye put out" (Fr336) but also "I cannot dance opon my Toes" (Fr381), the second line of which states, "No Man instructed me."

"No Man" instructed her how to publish her writings, but the customs of Dickinson's literary country were such that both original and copied writings were circulated in letters, in parlors, in commonplace books, and in scrapbooks. When Dickinson "published" her poems to Higginson and to every one of her other correspondents, with the exception of Susan Dickinson, she inscribed them on linen, often embossed, usually gilt-edged stationery. Though she sometimes would weave poetry into the prose of her letters to all her correspondents, Dickinson only placed her writings in the container of a scrap, a draft, and on informal stationery to one, Susan Huntington Dickinson (see Smith, *Emily Dickinson's Correspondences*). As the draft pencil copy of "Success is counted sweetest" sent to Susan contrasted with the ink copy of the poem to Higginson, as the verse-letter of "Dear Sue. / Your – Riches – / taught me – poverty!" contrasted with the presentation of the poem "Your Riches, taught / me, poverty – " enclosed in a letter to Higginson, and as the signed verse-letter of "Of all the Sounds / despatched abroad" to Susan contrasted with the unsigned poem "Of all the Sounds / despatched abroad" enclosed in a letter to Higginson show, Emily Dickinson's presentation of her writings to different audiences was not uniform (*Emily Dickinson's Correspondences*). With the exception of her presenting drafts, scraps, and finished poems to Susan on a variety of stationery types, Dickinson presented her poems to her contemporary readers just as she did to Higginson: on formal stationery and finished, just as readers would expect. Her audiences "tooled" her writings in that Dickinson delivered what she knew they would find legible. Of the scores of correspondents, only a single reader proved to be one she perceived as willing to read drafts and receive humorous little ditties on paper torn from shopping bags or other domestic detritus. That is the most obvious story that the containers of her writings, which we are just learning to read, tell. There is a wealth of other tales waiting to be discerned, and the twenty-first-century publishing technologies that offer views of digital surrogates of her manuscripts will, with the software of the highest order—her readers—enable many new, insightful stories of her "letter to the World" (Fr519) to be told.

NOTES

1. Throughout this chapter, "A" refers to documents in Amherst College Special Collections; "BPL" to documents in the Boston Public Library, specifically its Higginson collection; and "H" to documents in the Houghton Library, Harvard University, which readers might encounter if they consult *Emily Dickinson's Correspondences*, rotunda.upress.virginia.edu:8080/edc.

2. The exchange between Susan and Emily Dickinson regarding the writing of this poem can be found in two sources other than *Open Me Carefully* that I have edited: "Emily Dickinson Writing a Poem," *Dickinson Electronic Archives*, www.emilydickinson .org/safe/index.html. Available: 1994 to the present; *Emily Dickinson's Correspondences* (2008). In each of these, the exchange is featured in full. Neither the Johnson nor the Franklin variorum editions of *The Poems of Emily Dickinson* features the exchange *in toto*.

3. This extends my expansion of the term "technology" begun in "Computing: What's American Literary Study Got to Do with IT?" and expanded in subsequent articles.

4. Leyda (II, 127) quotes Higginson's oration-essay "Literature as Art," *Atlantic Monthly* (December 1867). Dickinson read the essay.

5. John W. Burgess, reminiscing about an Amherst College commencement tea in 1867, gives a similarly conventional description of Dickinson: "She did not often appear at the companies given in her father's house, and when she did, she seemed more like an apparition than a reality. At a moment when conversation lagged a little, she would sweep in, clad in immaculate white, pass through the rooms, silently courtseying and saluting right and left, and sweep out again" (Leyda II, 125). Since Burgess did not render this description of Dickinson until 1934, after the myth of "Our Emily" had been well publicized, one wonders whether he is reciting tales. The similarity to Higginson is striking not only in that they relate the same conventionalities, but also because they both acknowledge Dickinson's commanding presence.

WORKS CITED

ABBREVIATIONS

The following letters and letter combinations appear in documentation throughout this book to indicate the most frequently cited sources of quotations from Emily Dickinson. When two or more such indicators appear in parenthetical citation, the first is the text used by the author of the essay. In cases where a letter can be found either in Johnson's edition or Hart and Smith's *Open Me Carefully*, both sources are cited for the convenience of readers who prefer alternative texts. When a poem appears within a letter, the letter number precedes the poem number in Franklin's edition when the author of the essay refers to the letter text.

Fr   *The Poems of Emily Dickinson: Variorum Edition.* Ed. R. W. Franklin. 3 vols. Cambridge: Belknap Press of Harvard University Press, 1998.

J   *The Poems of Emily Dickinson.* Ed. Thomas H. Johnson. 3 vols. Cambridge: Belknap Press of Harvard University Press, 1955.

L   *The Letters of Emily Dickinson.* Ed. Thomas H. Johnson and Theodora Van Wagenen Ward. 3 vols. Cambridge: Belknap Press of Harvard University Press, 1958.

OMC   *Open Me Carefully: Emily Dickinson's Intimate Letters to Susan Huntington Dickinson.* Ed. Ellen Louise Hart and Martha Nell Smith. Ashfield, MA: Paris Press, 1998.

Adams, Percy G. *Graces of Harmony: Alliteration, Assonance, and Consonance in Eighteenth-Century British Poetry.* Athens: University of Georgia Press, 1977.

Addison, Catherine. "Once Upon a Time: A Reader-Response Approach to Prosody." *College English* 56. 6 (1994): 655–78.

Altman, Janet. *Epistolarity: Approaches to a Form.* Columbus: Ohio State University Press, 1982.

Anderson, Charles. *Emily Dickinson's Poetry: Stairway of Surprise.* New York: Holt, Rinehart, and Winston, 1960.

Aresty, Esther B. *The Best Behavior: The Course of Good Manners—From Antiquity to the Present—As Seen Through Courtesy and Etiquette Books.* New York: Simon and Schuster, 1970.

Attridge, Derek. *The Rhythms of English Poetry.* New York: Longman, 1982.

Barber, Jonathan. *The Elocutionist, Consisting of Declamations and Readings in Prose and Poetry, for the Use of Colleges and Schools.* New Haven, CT: Hezekian Howe and A. H. Maltby, 1829.

Barnes, Elizabeth. *States of Sympathy: Seduction and Democracy in the American Novel.* New York: Columbia University Press, 1997.

Barton, Edwin J., and Glenda A. Hudson. *A Contemporary Guide to Literary Terms.* Boston: Houghton Mifflin, 1997.

Baym, Nina. *Women's Fiction: A Guide to Novels by and about Women in America, 1820–1870.* Ithaca: Cornell University Press, 1978.

Beecher, Catharine E. *A Treatise on Domestic Economy: For the Use of Young Ladies at Home & at School.* New York: Harper & Brothers, 1842.

Benfey, Christopher. *A Summer of Hummingbirds: Love, Art, and Scandal in the Intersecting Worlds of Emily Dickinson, Mark Twain, Harriet Beecher Stowe, and Martin Johnson Heade.* New York: Penguin Press, 2008.

Bennett, Paula. "Emily Dickinson and Her American Women Poet Peers." *The Cambridge Companion to Emily Dickinson.* Ed. Wendy Martin: 215–35.

Bianchi, Martha Dickinson. *Emily Dickinson Face to Face: Unpublished Letters with Notes and Reminiscences.* 1932. Rpt. New York: Archon Books, 1970.

———. *The Life and Letters of Emily Dickinson.* 1924. Rpt. New York: Biblo and Tannen, 1971.

Bingham, Millicent Todd. *Ancestors' Brocades: The Literary Debut of Emily Dickinson.* New York: Harper & Brothers, 1945.

———, ed. *Emily Dickinson: A Revelation.* New York: Harper & Brothers, 1954.

———, ed. *Emily Dickinson's Home: Letters of Edward Dickinson and His Family.* New York: Harper & Brothers, 1955.

Bishop, Wendy. *Thirteen Ways of Looking at a Poem: A Guide to Writing Poetry.* New York: Longman, 2000.

Bloom, Harold. *The Best Poems of the English Language.* New York: HarperCollins, 2004.

———. "Emily Dickinson, Blanks, Transports, the Dark." *The Western Canon: The Books and Schools of the Ages.* New York: Harcourt, Brace, 1994: 291–309.

Bourdieu, Pierre. *Outline of a Theory of Practice.* Trans. Richard Nice. New York: Cambridge University Press, 1977.

Braid, Kate, and Sandy Shreve. *In Fine Form: The Canadian Book of Form Poetry.* Vancouver, BC: Raincoast Books, 2005.

Brendel, Otto J. *Etruscan Art.* New Haven: Yale University Press, 1978.

Brown, Daniel. *Hopkins' Idealism: Philosophy, Physics, Poetry.* Oxford: Oxford University Press, 1997.

Browning, Elizabeth Barrett. *Aurora Leigh: A Poem.* 1856. Rpt. Chicago: Academy Chicago Limited, 1979.

Buckingham, Willis J., ed. *Emily Dickinson's Reception in the 1890s: A Documentary History.* Pittsburgh: University of Pittsburgh Press, 1989.

Burke, L. *The Illustrated Language and Poetry of Flowers.* New York: Routledge, n.d.

Cadman, Deborah Ann. "Material Things and Expressive Signs: The Language of Emily Dickinson in Her Social and Physical Context." *Dissertation Abstracts International* 52. 9 (1992): 3279A–80A.

Cameron, Sharon. *Choosing Not Choosing: Dickinson's Fascicles.* Chicago: University of Chicago Press, 1992.

Capps, Jack L. *Emily Dickinson's Reading, 1836–1886.* Cambridge: Harvard University Press, 1966.

Chambers-Schiller, Lee Virginia. *Liberty a Better Husband: Single Women in America, The Generation of 1740–1840.* New Haven: Yale University Press, 1984.

Cheal, David. *The Gift Economy.* New York: Routledge, 1988.

Cikovsky, Nicolai, Jr. "Modern and National." *Winslow Homer.* New Haven, CT: National Gallery of Art and Yale University Press, 1995.

Conway, Hugh. *Called Back.* Chicago: Belford, Clarke, n.d.

Crumbley, Paul. *Inflections of the Pen: Dash and Voice in Emily Dickinson.* Lexington: University Press of Kentucky, 1997.

Dandurand, Karen. "Dickinson and the Public." *Dickinson and Audience.* Ed. Martin Orzeck and Robert Weisbuch. Ann Arbor: University of Michigan Press, 1996. 255–77.

Davinroy, Elise. "Tomb and Womb: Reading Contexture in Emily Dickinson's 'Soft Prison.'" *Legacy: A Journal of American Women Writers* 23. 1 (2006): 1–13.

Decker, William Merrill. *Epistolary Practices: Letter Writing in America before Telecommunications.* Chapel Hill: University of North Carolina Press, 1998.

Derrida, Jacques. *The Post Card: From Socrates to Freud and Beyond.* Trans. Alan Bass. Chicago: University of Chicago Press, 1987.

Dewey, Orville. *On the Duties of Consolation and the Rites and Customs Appropriate to Mourning.* New Bedford, MA: New-Bedford Book and Tract Association, 1825.

Dickinson, Emily. *Dickinson Electronic Archives.* emilydickinson.org. Ed. Ellen Louise Hart, Martha Nell Smith, Lara Vetter, and Marta Werner. Available 1994 to the present.

———. *Emily Dickinson's Herbarium.* Ed. Leslie A. Morris et al. Cambridge: Belknap Press of Harvard University Press, 2006.

———. *Letters of Emily Dickinson.* Ed. Mabel Loomis Todd. 2 vols. Boston: Roberts Brothers, 1894.

———. *The Letters of Emily Dickinson.* Ed. Thomas H. Johnson and Theodora Ward. 3 vols. Cambridge: Belknap Press of Harvard University Press, 1958.

———. *The Manuscript Books of Emily Dickinson.* 2 vols. Ed. R. W. Franklin. Cambridge: Belknap Press of Harvard University Press, 1981.

———. *The Master Letters of Emily Dickinson.* Ed. R. W. Franklin. Amherst, MA: Amherst College Press, 1986.

———. *New Poems of Emily Dickinson.* Ed. William H. Shurr, Anna Dunlap, and Emily Grey Shurr. Chapel Hill: University of North Carolina Press, 1993.

———. *Open Me Carefully: Emily Dickinson's Intimate Letters to Susan Huntington Dickinson.* Ed. Ellen Louise Hart and Martha Nell Smith. Ashfield, MA: Paris Press, 1998.

———. *Poems by Emily Dickinson.* Ed. Mabel Loomis Todd and T. W. Higginson. Boston: Roberts Brothers, 1890.

———. *Poems by Emily Dickinson: Second Series.* Ed. Mabel Loomis Todd and T. W. Higginson. Boston: Roberts Brothers, 1891.

———. *Poems by Emily Dickinson: Third Series.* Ed. Mabel Loomis Todd. Boston: Roberts Brothers, 1896.

———. *Poems (1890–1896) by Emily Dickinson: A Facsimile Reproduction of the Original Volumes Issued in 1890, 1891, and 1896.* Ed. George Monteiro. Gainesville, FL: Scholars' Facsimiles & Reprints, 1967.

———. *The Poems of Emily Dickinson: Reading Edition.* Ed. R. W. Franklin. Cambridge: Harvard University Press, 1999.

———. *The Poems of Emily Dickinson, Variorum Edition.* Ed. R. W. Franklin. 3 vols. Cambridge: Belknap Press of Harvard University Press, 1998.

———. *The Poems of Emily Dickinson.* Ed. Thomas H. Johnson. 3 vols. Cambridge: Belknap Press of Harvard University Press, 1955.

———. Writings, original manuscripts. Cited in text as A and catalog identifiers (Amherst College); BPL and catalog identifiers (Boston Public Library); H and catalog identifiers (Houghton Library, Harvard University).

"Disappearance of Mr. Sweetzer." *New York Times,* January 31, 1874: 2.

Dobson, Joanne. *Strategies of Reticence: The Woman Writer in Nineteenth-Century America.* Bloomington: Indiana University Press, 1989.

Donaghue, Denis. *Emily Dickinson.* St. Paul: University of Minnesota Press, 1969.

Duffey, Mrs. E. B. *The Ladies' and Gentlemen's Etiquette: A Complete Manual of the Manners and Dress of American Society.* Philadelphia: Henry T. Coates, 1877.

Eberwein, Jane Donahue. *Dickinson: Strategies of Limitation.* Amherst: University of Massachusetts Press, 1985.

———. "'Is Immortality True?' Salvaging Faith in an Age of Upheavals." *A Historical Guide to Emily Dickinson.* Ed. Vivian Pollak: 67–103.

———, ed. *An Emily Dickinson Encyclopedia.* Westport, CT: Greenwood Press, 1998.

Edelstein, Tilden G. *Strange Enthusiasm: A Life of Thomas Wentworth Higginson.* New Haven: Yale University Press, 1968.

Emerson, Ralph Waldo. "Gifts." *The Complete Works of Ralph Waldo Emerson.* Vol. 3. New York: Sully and Kleinteich, 1883.

———. "Nature" (1836). *Nature, Addresses, and Lectures.* Ed. Robert E. Spiller. Cambridge: Belknap Press of Harvard University Press, 1971.

———. "New Poetry." *The Dial* (October 1840): 220–32.

———."The Poet." *The Complete Essays and Other Writings of Ralph Waldo Emerson.* Ed. Brooks Atkinson. New York: Modern Library, 1940.

Erkkila, Betsy. *The Wicked Sisters: Women Poets, Literary History & Discord.* New York: Oxford University Press, 1992.

Farr, Judith. "Dickinson and the Visual Arts." *The Emily Dickinson Handbook.* Ed. Gudrun Grabher et al.: 61–92.

———. *I Never Came to You in White. A Novel.* New York: Houghton Mifflin, 1996.

———. *The Passion of Emily Dickinson.* Cambridge: Harvard University Press, 1992.

———, with Louise Carter. *The Gardens of Emily Dickinson.* Cambridge: Harvard University Press, 2004.

Finnerty, Páraic. *Emily Dickinson's Shakespeare.* Amherst: University of Massachusetts Press, 2006.

Fitzmyer, Joseph A. *The Gospel According to Luke (X–XXIV). The Anchor Bible.* New York: Doubleday, 1985.

Franklin, R. W., ed. *The Manuscript Books of Emily Dickinson.* 2 vols. Cambridge: Belknap Press of Harvard University Press, 1981.

———, ed. *The Poems of Emily Dickinson.* 3 vols. Cambridge: Belknap Press of Harvard University Press, 1998.

Frost, S[arah] A[nnie]. *Frost's Laws and By-Laws of American Society: A Condensed but Thorough Treatise on Etiquette and Its Usages in America.* New York: Dick & Fitzgerald, 1869.

Fry, Paul. "Accent." *The Princeton Handbook of Poetic Terms.* Ed. Alex Preminger.

Frye, Northrop. "Charms and Riddles." *Spiritus Mundi.* Bloomington: Indiana University Press, 1976: 123–47.

———. *Fables of Identity: Studies in Poetic Mythology.* New York: Harcourt, Brace, and World, 1963: 193–217.

———. "Verse and Prose." *The Princeton Handbook of Poetic Terms.* Ed. Alex Preminger.

Gardner, Thomas. "Interview with Susan Howe." *A Door Ajar: Contemporary Writers and Emily Dickinson.* Oxford: Oxford University Press, 2006: 138–65.

Gaskell, George Arthur. *Gaskell's Compendium of Forms, Educational, Social, Legal, and Commercial; Embracing a Complete Self-Teaching Course in Penmanship and Bookkeeping, and Aid to English Composition Including Orthography, Capital Letters, Punctuation, Composition, Elocution, Oratory, Rhetoric, Letter Writing, etc.* Chicago: W. M. Farrar, 1881.

Gee, Karen Richardson. "'My George Eliot' and My Emily Dickinson." *Emily Dickinson Journal* 3. 1 (1994): 24–40.

Gelpi, Albert. *Emily Dickinson: The Mind of the Poet.* Cambridge: Harvard University Press, 1965.

Gifford, Carolyn De Swarte, ed. *The American Ideal of the "True Woman" as Reflected in Advice Books to Young Women.* New York: Garland, 1987.

Gilbert, Sandra M. "Emily's Bread." *Emily's Bread: Poems.* New York: W. W. Norton, 1984.

———, and Susan Gubar. *The Madwoman in the Attic: The Woman Writer and the Nineteenth-Century Literary Imagination.* New Haven: Yale University Press, 1979.

Godbout, Jacques T. *The World of the Gift*. Trans. Donald Winkler. Ithaca, NY: McGill-Queen's University Press, 1998.

Godelier, Maurice. *The Enigma of the Gift*. Trans. Nora Scott. Chicago: University of Chicago Press, 1999.

Grabher, Gudrun, Roland Hagenbüchle, and Cristanne Miller, eds. *The Emily Dickinson Handbook*. Amherst: University of Massachusetts Press, 1998.

Guthrie, James. *Emily Dickinson's Vision: Illness and Identity in Her Poetry*. Gainesville: University Press of Florida, 1998.

———. "Exceeding Legal and Linguistic Limits: Dickinson as 'Involuntary Bankrupt.'" *Emily Dickinson Journal* 14. 2 (2005): 89–102.

———. "Law, Property, and Provincialism in Dickinson's Poems and Letters to Judge Otis Phillips Lord." *Emily Dickinson Journal* 5. 1 (1996): 27–44.

———. "Near Rhymes and Reason: Style and Personality in Dickinson's Poetry." *Approaches to Teaching Dickinson's Poetry*. Ed. Robin Riley Fast and Christine Mack Gordon. New York: Modern Language Association of America, 1989: 70–77.

Habegger, Alfred. *My Wars Are Laid Away in Books: The Life of Emily Dickinson*. New York: Random House, 2001.

Halttunen, Karen. *Confidence Men and Painted Women: A Study of Middle-Class Culture in America, 1830–1870*. New Haven: Yale University Press, 1982.

Hart, Ellen Louise, with Sandra Chung. "Hearing the Visual Lines: How Manuscript Study Can Contribute to an Understanding of Dickinson's Prosody." *A Companion to Emily Dickinson*. Ed. Martha Nell Smith and Mary Loeffelholz: 348–67.

———, and Martha Nell Smith, eds. *Open Me Carefully: Emily Dickinson's Intimate Letters to Susan Huntington Dickinson*. Ashfield, MA: Paris Press, 1998.

Hartley, Florence. *The Ladies' Book of Etiquette, and Manual of Politeness*. Boston: Lee and Shepard; New York: Lee, Shepard, and Bellingham, 1875.

Heaney, Seamus. "Old English Language and Poetics: Introduction." *Beowulf, A New Verse Translation*. Ed. Daniel Donoghue. New York: Norton Critical Edition, 2000.

Heginbotham, Eleanor. "Dickinson's 'What if I say I shall not wait!'" *Explicator* 54. 3 (1996): 154–60.

———. "'Paradise fictitious': Dickinson's Milton." *Emily Dickinson Journal* 7. 1 (1998): 55–74.

Herreshoff, David Sprague. *Labor into Art: The Theme of Work in Nineteenth-Century American Literature*. Detroit: Wayne State University Press, 1991.

Hervey, George Winfred. *The Principles of Courtesy: With Hints and Observations on Manners and Habits* (1852). New York: Harper & Brothers, 1856.

Hewitt, Elizabeth. *Correspondence and American Literature, 1770–1865*. New York: Cambridge University Press, 2004.

Higginson, Thomas Wentworth. *Contemporaries*. Boston: Houghton Mifflin, 1899.

———. "Emily Dickinson's Letters." *Atlantic Monthly* 68. 408 (October 1891): 444–56.

———. *The Magnificent Activist: The Writings of Thomas Wentworth Higginson, 1823–1911*. Ed. Howard N. Meyer. Cambridge, MA: Da Capo Press, 2000. 543–64.

———. "An Open Portfolio." *The Christian Union* 42 (September 25, 1890): 392–93.

——. "Preface." *Poems by Emily Dickinson*. Ed. Mabel Loomis Todd and T. W. Higginson. Boston: Roberts Brothers, 1890: iii–vi.

——. "Preface [1890]." *Emily Dickinson: Collected Poems*. Philadelphia: Courage Books, 1991: 13–15.

——. *Women and the Alphabet*. Boston: Houghton Mifflin, 1881 and 1900.

Holland, Jeanne. "Scraps, Stamps, and Cutouts: Emily Dickinson's Domestic Technologies of Publication." *Cultural Artifacts and the Production of Meaning: The Page, the Image, and the Body*. Ed. Margaret J. M. Ezell and Katherine O'Brien O'Keeffe. Ann Arbor: University of Michigan Press, 1994.

Holland, J[osiah] G[ilbert]. *Titcomb's Letters to Young People, Single and Married*. By Timothy Titcomb, esq. 4th ed. New York: Scribner, 1866.

Hollander, John. *Vision and Resonance: Two Senses of Poetic Form*. New York: Oxford University Press, 1975.

Horan, Elizabeth. "To Market: The Dickinson Copyright Wars." *Emily Dickinson Journal* 5. 1 (1996): 88–120.

Hyde, Lewis. *The Gift: Imagination and the Erotic Life of Property*. New York: Random House, 1983.

Irigaray, Luce. *This Sex Which Is Not One*. Ithaca, NY: Cornell University Press, 1985.

Jackson, Virginia. *Dickinson's Misery: A Theory of Lyric Reading*. Princeton: Princeton University Press, 2005.

Jenkins, MacGregor. *Emily Dickinson, Friend and Neighbor*. Boston: Little, Brown, 1930.

Johnson, Thomas H. *Emily Dickinson: An Interpretive Biography*. Cambridge: Harvard University Press, 1955.

——, and Theodora Ward, eds. *The Letters of Emily Dickinson*. 3 vols. Cambridge: Belknap Press of Harvard University Press, 1958.

——, ed. *The Poems of Emily Dickinson*. 3 vols. Cambridge: Belknap Press of Harvard University Press, 1955.

Jones, Howard Mumford. *The Theory of American Literature*. Ithaca, NY: Cornell University Press, 1965.

Juhasz, Suzanne. "Reading Emily Dickinson's Letters." *ESQ: A Journal of the American Renaissance* 30. 3 (1984): 170–93.

——, Cristanne Miller, and Martha Nell Smith. *Comic Power in Emily Dickinson*. Austin: University of Texas Press, 1993.

Kames, Lord (Henry Home). *Elements of Criticism*. London: G. Cowie, 1824.

Kasson, John F. *Rudeness and Civility: Manners in Nineteenth-Century Urban America*. New York: Noonday Press, 1991.

Keane, Patrick J. *Emily Dickinson's Approving God: Divine Design and the Problem of Suffering*. Columbia: University of Missouri Press, 2008.

Kete, Mary Louise. *Sentimental Collaborations: Mourning and Middle-Class Identity in Nineteenth-Century America*. Durham: Duke University Press, 2000.

Kirkby, Joan. "'A crescent still abides': Emily Dickinson and the Work of Mourning." *Wider Than the Sky: Essays and Meditations on the Healing Power of Emily Dickinson*. Ed. Cindy MacKenzie and Barbara Dana: 129–40.

Knight, Charles. "Advertisement." *The Comedies, Histories, Tragedies and Poems of William Shakespeare.* 8 vols. Boston: Little, Brown, 1853.

Lambert, Robert Graham. *A Critical Study of Emily Dickinson's Letters: The Prose of a Poet.* Lewiston, NY: Mellen University Press, 1996.

Lawton, David. "Middle English Alliterative Poetry: An Introduction." *Middle English Alliterative Poetry and Its Literary Background: Seven Essays.* Suffolk: Boydell & Brewer, 1982.

Lease, Benjamin. *Emily Dickinson's Readings of Men and Books: Sacred Soundings.* New York: St. Martin's Press, 1990.

Leslie, E[liza]. *Miss Leslie's Behaviour Book: A Guide and Manual for Ladies* (1859). American Women: Images and Realities Series. New York: Arno Press, 1972.

Leyda, Jay. *The Years and Hours of Emily Dickinson.* 2 vols. New Haven: Yale University Press, 1960.

Lindberg-Seyersted, Brita. *The Voice of the Poet: Aspects of Style in the Poetry of Emily Dickinson.* Cambridge: Harvard University Press, 1968.

Loeffelholz, Mary. "Dickinson's 'Decoration.'" *ELH* 72. 3 (Fall 2005): 663–89.

———. *From School to Salon: Reading Nineteenth-Century Women's Poetry.* Princeton: Princeton University Press, 2004.

Longfellow, Henry Wadsworth. *Kavanagh.* 1849. Rpt. Boston: Houghton Mifflin, 1886 (Vol. 8 of Riverside Edition of Longfellow).

Longsworth, Polly. *Austin and Mabel: The Amherst Affair and Love Letters of Austin Dickinson and Mabel Loomis Todd.* New York: Farrar, Straus and Giroux, 1984.

———. "'The Might of Human love': Emily Dickinson's Letters of Healing." *Wider Than the Sky: Essays and Meditations on the Healing Power of Emily Dickinson.* Ed. Cindy MacKenzie and Barbara Dana: 1–8.

———. *The World of Emily Dickinson.* New York: W. W. Norton, 1990.

Lubbers, Klaus. *Emily Dickinson: A Critical Revolution.* Ann Arbor: University of Michigan Press, 1964.

MacKenzie, Cynthia. *A Concordance to the Letters of Emily Dickinson.* Boulder: University of Colorado Press, 2000.

———, and Barbara Dana, eds. *Wider Than the Sky: Essays and Meditations on the Healing Power of Emily Dickinson.* Kent, OH: Kent State University Press, 2007.

Mamunes, George. *"So has a Daisy vanished": Emily Dickinson and Tuberculosis.* Jefferson, NC: McFarland, 2008.

Martin, Wendy. *An American Triptych: Anne Bradstreet, Emily Dickinson, Adrienne Rich.* Chapel Hill: University of North Carolina Press, 1984.

———, ed. *Cambridge Companion to Emily Dickinson.* Cambridge: Cambridge University Press, 2002.

McCann, Janet. "Marriage." *An Emily Dickinson Encyclopedia.* Ed. Jane Donahue Eberwein: 190-91.

McDowell, Marta. *Emily Dickinson's Gardens.* New York: McGraw-Hill, 2004.

McGann, Jerome. *Radiant Textuality: Literature after the World Wide Web.* New York: Palgrave Macmillan, 2001.

Mellinkoff, David. *The Language of the Law*. Boston: Little, Brown, 1963.

Messmer, Marietta. *A Vice for Voices: Reading Emily Dickinson's Correspondence*. Amherst: University of Massachusetts Press, 2001.

Michael, Ian. *The Teaching of English: From the Sixteenth Century to 1870*. Cambridge: Cambridge University Press, 1987.

Miller, Cristanne. "The Sound of Shifting Paradigms, or Hearing Dickinson in the Twenty-First Century." *A Historical Guide to Emily Dickinson*. Ed. Vivian R. Pollak: 201–34.

"A Missing Merchant." *New York Times*, January 24, 1874: 2.

Mitchell, Domhnall. *Emily Dickinson: Monarch of Perception*. Amherst: University of Massachusetts Press, 2000.

———. *Measures of Possibility: Emily Dickinson's Manuscripts*. Amherst: University of Massachusetts Press, 2005.

(Mitchell, Donald Grant). *Reveries of a Bachelor or A Book of the Heart by Ik Marvel*. New York: Charles Scribner, 1853 (15th ed.).

Monteiro, George, ed. *Poems (1890–1896) by Emily Dickinson: A Facsimile Reproduction of the Original Volumes Issued in 1890, 1891, and 1896*. Gainesville, FL: Scholars' Facsimiles & Reprints, 1967.

Mudge, Jean McClure. *Emily Dickinson and the Image of Home*. Amherst: University of Massachusetts Press, 1975.

Murray, Lindley. *English Grammar*. Bridgeport, CT: Josiah B. Baldwin, 1824 (facsimile reproduction with an introduction by Charlotte Downey. Delmar, NY: Scholars' Facsimiles and Reprints, 1981).

n.a. *The Complete Letter-Writer. Containing Familiar Letters on the Most Common Occasions in Life. Also, a Variety of Elegant Letters for the Direction and Embellishment of Style*. 4th ed. Salem, MA: Thomas C. Cushing, 1797.

———. *The Letter Writer's Own Book; or, The Art of Polite Correspondence, Containing a Variety of Plain and Elegant Letters; on Business, Love, Courtship, Marriage, Relationship, Friendship, &c., with Forms of Complimentary Cards, and Directions for Letter Writing, to Which Are Added Forms of Mortgages, Deeds, Power of Attorney, &c*. Philadelphia: John B. Perry; New York: N. C. Nafis, 1843.

———. *The Young Lady's Own Book: A Manual of Intellectual Improvement and Moral Deportment*. Philadelphia: Thomas, Cowperthwait, 1832.

Nabokov, Vladimir. "Nabokov on *Bleak House*: Excerpts from Lectures on Literature." *Bleak House* by Charles Dickens. New York: Bantam Books, 1992.

Newman, Samuel P. *A Practical System of Rhetoric, or The Principles and Rules of Style, Inferred from Examples of Writing. To Which is Added a Historical Disquisition on English Style* (1834). 60th ed. New York: Ivison, Phinney, 1863.

Newton, Sarah E. *Learning to Behave: A Guide to American Conduct Books before 1900*. Westport, CT: Greenwood, 1994.

Oakes, Elizabeth. "Welcome and Beware: The Reader and Emily Dickinson's Figurative Language." *ESQ* 34. 3 (1988): 181–206.

Olsen, Tillie. "A Biographical Interpretation." Rebecca Harding Davis, *Life in the Iron*

Mills and Other Stories. New York: Feminist Press at the City University of New York, 1984.

Orzeck, Martin, and Robert Weisbuch, eds. *Dickinson and Audience*. Ann Arbor: University of Michigan Press, 1996.

Payson, J. W., S. Dunton, and W. M. Scribner. *Payson, Dunton, & Scribner Manual of Penmanship*. New York: Potter, Ainsworth, 1873.

Petrino, Elizabeth A. *Emily Dickinson and Her Contemporaries: Women's Verse in America, 1820–1885*. Hanover, NH: University Press of New England, 1998.

Phillips, Elizabeth. *Emily Dickinson: Personae and Performance*. University Park: Pennsylvania State University Press, 1988 and 1997.

Poe, Edgar Allan. "The Philosophy of Composition." *Selected Writings of Edgar Allan Poe*. Ed. Edward H. Davidson. Boston: Houghton Mifflin, 1956.

Polak, Sara. "Emily Dickinson's Epistolary Immortality." *Emily Dickinson International Society Bulletin* 18. 2 (November–December 2006): 4–7, 19.

Pollak, Vivian R. "American Women Poets Reading Dickinson: The Example of Helen Hunt Jackson." *The Emily Dickinson Handbook*. Ed. Gudrun Grabher et al.: 323–41.

———. ed. *A Historical Guide to Emily Dickinson*. Oxford: Oxford University Press, 2004.

———, ed. *A Poet's Parents: The Courtship Letters of Emily Norcross and Edward Dickinson*. Chapel Hill: University of North Carolina Press, 1988.

———, and Marianne Noble. "Emily Dickinson 1830–1886: A Brief Biography." *A Historical Guide to Emily Dickinson*. Ed. Vivian Pollak: 13–63.

Pollitt, Katha. "Poetry Makes Nothing Happen? Ask Laura Bush." *The Nation* (February 24, 2003). Online. www.thenation.com/doc.mhtml?i=pollitt. 10/07/2003.

Porter, Ebenezer. *The Rhetorical Reader, Consisting of Instructions for Regulating the Voice*. New York: Mark H. Newman, 1835.

Powell, Claire. *The Meaning of Flowers: A Garland of Plant Lore and Symbolism from Popular Custom and Literature*. Boulder, CO: Shambhala, 1977.

Preminger, Alex, ed. *The Princeton Handbook of Poetic Terms*. Princeton: Princeton University Press, 1986.

Pugh, Christina. "Ghosts of Meter: Dickinson, After Long Silence." *Emily Dickinson Journal* 16. 2 (2007): 1–24.

Rabuzzi, Kathryn Allen. *The Sacred and the Feminine: Toward a Theology of Housework*. New York: Seabury Press, 1982.

Radner, Joan N., and Susan S. Lanser. "Strategies of Coding in Women's Cultures." *Feminist Messages: Coding in Women's Folk Culture*. Ed. Joan Newlon Radner. Urbana: University of Illinois Press, 1993.

Rathje, Annette. *The Etruscans: 700 Years of History and Culture*. Rome: Editzione DAGA, 1987.

"The Rev. Dr. Adams Dead." *New York Times*, September 1, 1880: 8.

Reynolds, David S. "Emily Dickinson and Popular Culture." *Cambridge Companion to Emily Dickinson*. Ed. Wendy Martin: 167–90.

Rich, Adrienne. "Natural Resources." *The Dream of a Common Language: Poems 1974– 1977*. New York: Norton, 1993.

Robinson, Nugent, ed. *Collier's Cyclopedia of Commercial and Social Information and Treasury of Useful and Entertaining Knowledge on Art, Science, Pastimes, Belles-Lettres, and Many Other Subjects of Interest in the American Home Circle*. New York: Peter Fenelon Collier, 1882.

Rugoff, Milton. *The Beechers: An American Family in the Nineteenth Century*. New York: Harper & Row, 1981.

Rukeyser, Muriel. *The Life of Poetry*. Ashfield, MA: Paris Press, 1996.

St. Armand, Barton Levi. *Emily Dickinson and Her Culture: The Soul's Society*. Cambridge: Cambridge University Press, 1984.

———. "Keeper of the Keys: Mary Hampson, the Evergreens, and the Art Within." *The Dickinsons of Amherst: Photographs by Jerome Liebling*, with Christopher Benfey and Polly Longsworth. Hanover, NH: University Press of New England, 2001. 107– 67.

Saintsbury, George. *A History of English Prose Rhythm*. London: Macmillan, 1912.

Salska, Agnieszka. "Dickinson's Letters." *The Emily Dickinson Handbook*. Ed. Gudrun Grabher et al.: 163–80.

———. "Emily Dickinson's Letters: The Making of a Poetics." *Crossing Borders: American Literature and Other Artistic Media*. Ed. Jadwiga Maszevska. Warsaw: PWW, 1992: 4–19.

Sanborn, Geoffrey. "Keeping Her Distance: Cisneros, Dickinson, and the Politics of Private Enjoyment." *PMLA* 116. 5 (October 2001): 1334–48.

Scharnhorst, Gary. "A Glimpse of Dickinson at Work." *American Literature* 57. 3 (1985): 483–85.

Schlesinger, Arthur M. *Learning How to Behave: A Historical Study of American Etiquette Books*. New York: Macmillan, 1947.

Sedgwick, Catharine Maria. *Means and Ends; or Self-Training*. 4th ed. Boston: Marsh, Capen, Lyon, and Webb, 1840.

Sewall, Richard B. "Emily Dickinson's Perfect Audience: Helen Hunt Jackson." *Dickinson and Audience*. Ed. Martin Orzeck and Robert Weisbuch: 201–13.

———. *The Life of Emily Dickinson*. 2 vols., 1974. Reprint, 1 vol., New York: Farrar, Straus and Giroux, 1980.

———, ed. *The Lyman Letters: New Light on Emily Dickinson and Her Family*. Amherst: University of Massachusetts Press, 1965.

Shaw, Robert B. *Blank Verse: A Guide to Its History and Use*. Athens: Ohio University Press, 2007.

Sheridan, Thomas. *Course of Lectures on Elocution*. New York: O. Penniman, 1803.

Sherwood, Mrs. John [Mary Elizabeth Wilson]. *Manners and Social Usages* (1884). New and Enlarged Edition. New York: Harper & Brothers, 1887.

Shoptaw, John. "Listening to Dickinson." *Representations* 86 (Spring 2004): 20–52.

Sigourney, Lydia. *Letters to Young Ladies*. New York: Harper, 1838.

Small, Judy Jo. *Positive as Sound: Emily Dickinson's Rhyme*. Athens: University of Georgia Press, 1990.

Smith, Martha Nell. "Computing: What's American Literary Study Got to Do with IT?" *American Literature* 74. 4 (2002): 833–57.

———. "The Poet as Cartoonist." *Comic Power in Emily Dickinson*. Suzanne Juhasz et al: 63–102.

———. *Rowing in Eden: Rereading Emily Dickinson*. Austin: University of Texas Press, 1992.

———. "Suppressing the Books of Susan in Emily Dickinson." *Epistolary Histories: Letters, Fiction, Culture*. Ed. Amanda Gilroy and Wil Verhoeven. Charlottesville: University Press of Virginia, 2000: 101–25.

———. "Susan and Emily Dickinson: Their Lives, in Letters." *The Cambridge Companion to Emily Dickinson*. Ed. Wendy Martin: 51–73.

———, and Mary Loeffelholz, eds. *A Companion to Emily Dickinson*. Malden, MA: Blackwell, 2008.

———, and Ellen Louise Hart, Lara Vetter, and Marta Werner, eds. *Dickinson Electronic Archives*. emilydickinson.org. Available: 1994 to the present.

———, and Lara Vetter, eds. *Emily Dickinson's Correspondence: A Born-Digital Textual Inquiry*. Consulting editor, Ellen Louise Hart. Charlottesville: Rotunda New Digital Scholarship of the University of Virginia Press, 2008.

Sprague, William Buell. *Letters on Practical Subjects to a Daughter*. 7th American ed., revised and enlarged. Albany, NY: E. H. Pease, 1849.

Steele, Jeffrey. "Keys to 'the labyrinth of my own being': Margaret Fuller's Epistolary Invention of the Self." Conference paper presented to the American Literature Association, April 2007.

Stewart, Susan. *Poetry and the Fate of the Senses*. Chicago: University of Chicago Press, 2002.

Stoddard, Elizabeth. *The Morgesons and Other Writings, Published and Unpublished, by Elizabeth Stoddard*. Ed. Lawrence Buell and Sandra A. Zagarell. Philadelphia: University of Pennsylvania Press, 1985.

Stonum, Gary Lee. "Dickinson's Literary Background." *The Emily Dickinson Handbook*. Ed. Gudrun Grabher et al.: 44–60.

———. *The Dickinson Sublime*. Madison: University of Wisconsin Press, 1990.

Stowe, Harriet Beecher. *The Minister's Wooing*. New York: Penguin Books, 1999.

Strickland, Georgiana. "In Praise of 'Ramona': Emily Dickinson and Helen Hunt Jackson's Indian Novel." *Emily Dickinson Journal* 9. 2 (2000): 120–33.

Sweetser, Catherine. "Letter to Edward Dickinson, May 12, 1835." Houghton Library, Harvard University.

Sweetser Family Papers. Amherst College Library.

Taggard, Genevieve. *The Life and Mind of Emily Dickinson*. New York: Alfred A. Knopf, 1930.

Taplin, Gardner R. "Introduction" to Elizabeth Barrett Browning's *Aurora Leigh*: ix–xxiii.

Taylor, Timothy Alden. *The Solace; or, Afflictions Lightened*. Boston: Congregational Board of Publication, 1849.

Todd, Mabel Loomis, ed. *Letters of Emily Dickinson. New and Enlarged*. New York: Harper and Brothers, 1931.

[Tomes, Robert]. *The Bazar Book of Decorum*. New York: Harper & Brothers, 1873.

Torelli, Mario. *The Etruscans*. London: Thames and Hudson, 2001.

Turco, Lewis. *The New Book of Forms: A Handbook of Poetics*. Hanover, NH: University Press of New England, 1986.

Vendler, Helen. "The Unsociable Soul." *New Republic* 207. 6 (August 8, 1992).

Wald, Jane. "'Pretty Much All Real Life': The Material World of the Dickinson Family." *A Companion to Emily Dickinson*. Ed. Martha Nell Smith and Mary Loeffelholz: 70–103.

Walker, Cheryl. *The Nightingale's Burden: Women Poets and American Culture before 1900*. Bloomington: Indiana University Press, 1982.

Walker, John. *Critical Pronouncing Dictionary, and Expositor of the English Language*. Bellows Falls, VT: Blake, Cutler, 1824.

———. *Elements of Elocution*. Boston: D. Mallory, 1810.

Ward, Theodora Van Wagenen. *The Capsule of the Mind: Chapters in the Life of Emily Dickinson*. Cambridge: Belknap Press of Harvard University Press, 1961.

———, ed. *Emily Dickinson's Letters to Dr. and Mrs. Josiah Gilbert Holland*. Cambridge: Harvard University Press, 1951.

Wardrop, Daneen. *Emily Dickinson's Gothic: Goblin with a Gauge*. Iowa City: University of Iowa Press, 1996.

Watson, Thomas. "Sermon Against Popery." In *A Compleat Collection of Farewel Sermons*. (Sermons by Calamy, Manton, et al.) London, 1663. Original in Folger Shakespeare Library; online version, Early English Books Online series.

Watts, Emily. *The Poetry of American Women from 1631 to 1945*. Austin: University of Texas Press, 1977.

Webster, Noah. *An American Dictionary of the English Language*. New York: White and Sheffield, 1843.

Weiss, Harry B. *American Letter-Writers 1698–1943*. New York: New York Public Library, 1945.

Wells, Anna Mary. *Dear Preceptor: The Life and Times of Thomas Wentworth Higginson*. Boston: Houghton Mifflin, 1963.

———. "The Soul's Society: Emily Dickinson and Colonel Higginson." *Nineteenth-Century Women Writers of the English-Speaking World*. Ed. Rhoda Nathan. New York: Greenwood Press, 1986: 220–29.

Welter, Barbara. *Dimity Convictions: The American Woman in the Nineteenth Century*. Athens: Ohio University Press, 1976.

Werner, Marta L. *Emily Dickinson's Open Folios: Scenes of Reading, Surfaces of Writing*. Ann Arbor: University of Michigan Press, 1995.

Whicher, George Frisbie. *This Was a Poet: Emily Dickinson*. New York: Charles Scribner's Sons, 1938.

Wineapple, Brenda. *White Heat: The Friendship of Emily Dickinson and Thomas Went-worth Higginson*. New York: Alfred Knopf, 2008.

Wolff, Cynthia Griffin. *Emily Dickinson*. New York: Alfred A. Knopf, 1986.

Wolosky, Shira. "Emily Dickinson: being in the body." *The Columbia Companion to Emily Dickinson*. Ed. Wendy Martin: 129–41.

Woolson, Constance Fenimore. *Women Artists, Women Exiles: "Miss Grief" and Other Stories*. Ed. Joan Myers Weimer. New Brunswick: Rutgers University Press, 1988.

Wylder, Edith. *The Last Face: Emily Dickinson's Manuscripts*. Albuquerque: University of New Mexico Press, 1971.

Notes on Contributors

PAUL CRUMBLEY is Professor of English and American Studies at Utah State University and President of the Emily Dickinson International Society. He is the author of *Inflections of the Pen: Dash and Voice in Emily Dickinson*, co-editor of *The Search for a Common Language: Environmental Writing and Education*, and contributing editor for *Body My House: May Swenson's Work and Life*. His second book on Dickinson, *Winds of Will: Emily Dickinson and the Sovereignty of Democratic Thought*, will be published in 2010 by the University of Alabama Press.

KAREN DANDURAND is Professor of English at Indiana University of Pennsylvania. She is the editor of *Dickinson Scholarship: An Annotated Bibliography, 1969–1985*, and author of groundbreaking articles on Dickinson poems published during the Civil War years. She was a founding editor of *Legacy* and a founding vice-president of the Society for the Study of American Women Writers.

JANE DONAHUE EBERWEIN is author of *Dickinson: Strategies of Limitation* and editor of *An Emily Dickinson Encyclopedia* and *Early American Poetry: Selections from Anne Bradstreet, Edward Taylor, Timothy Dwight, Philip Freneau, and William Cullen Bryant*. A founding board member of the Emily Dickinson International Society, Eberwein is Distinguished Professor Emerita at Oakland University. She takes particular interest in New England Puritanism and Emily Dickinson's relationship to the religious culture of the nineteenth-century Connecticut Valley.

JUDITH FARR is the author of *The Passion of Emily Dickinson* and *The Gardens of Emily Dickinson*. Also a novelist, Farr published *I Never Came to You in White* and is currently working on a novel about the women in Robert E. Lee's family. She is Professor of English Emerita at Georgetown University.

JAMES R. GUTHRIE is Professor of English at Wright State University. He is the author of *Emily Dickinson's Vision: Illness and Identity in Her Poetry* (University Press of Florida, 1998), and of several articles published in *The Emily Dickinson Journal.*

ELLEN LOUISE HART, manuscript scholar and textual editor, is currently studying the prosody of Dickinson's letters and poems in relation to the visual features and acoustic strategies of Dickinson's manuscript writings. She is co-author of *Open Me Carefully: Emily Dickinson's Intimate Letters to Susan Huntington Dickinson* (1998), and contributing editor to the *Dickinson Electronic Archives* and to a digital edition of a selection of poems and letters, forthcoming from the University of Virginia Press. She has published articles on editing Dickinson's letters, on manuscript prosody, and on the healing power of Dickinson's poetry in a struggling and damaged American democracy. She taught for 22 years at the University of California at Santa Cruz and now teaches at Portland State University in Portland, Oregon. Since 1995, Hart has served on the board of the Emily Dickinson International Society.

ELEANOR HEGINBOTHAM, Professor Emerita, Concordia University, Saint Paul, and Lecturer, English Department, University of Maryland, is the author of *Reading the Fascicles of Emily Dickinson* as well as of chapters and articles on Dickinson.

She is an active member and past board member of the Emily Dickinson International Society and has participated in Dickinson events around the world including during a Fulbright Scholar year in Hong Kong.

CINDY MACKENZIE is the author of *A Concordance to the Letters of Emily Dickinson* and contributing co-editor, with Barbara Dana, of *Wider Than the Sky: Essays and Meditations on the Healing Power of Emily Dickinson* in the Literature and Medicine Series, Kent State University Press. An active member and past board member of the Emily Dickinson International Society, MacKenzie has presented papers at conferences in the United States, Europe, and Japan. She teaches English at the University of Regina in Regina, Saskatchewan, Canada.

MARIETTA MESSMER is Senior Lecturer in American Studies at the University of Groningen (The Netherlands). Her current teaching and research interests focus on the cultural and political situation of ethnic minorities within the United States (in particular Chicanos/as and Native Americans); theoretical debates on multiculturalism, assimilation, integration, and identity politics; and the United States in international and hemispheric contexts. She is the author of *A Vice for Voices: Reading Emily Dickinson's Correspondence* (Amherst: University of Massachusetts Press, 2001), has edited several critical volumes on America's interliterary and intercultural relations as well as its (trans)national identity constructions, and is managing editor of the series *Interamericana: Inter-American Literary History and Culture*, published by Peter Lang Verlag.

MARTHA NELL SMITH has produced several books on Dickinson after her first, *Rowing in Eden: Rereading Emily Dickinson* (1992). For Blackwell, she edited the *Companion to Emily Dickinson* (2008) with Mary Loeffelholz, and has also written *Emily Dickinson: A User's Guide* (2009). With Ellen Louise Hart, she co-authored *Open Me Carefully: Emily Dickinson's Intimate Letters to Susan Dickinson* (1998) and with Cristanne Miller and Suzanne Juhasz, *Comic Power in Emily Dickinson* (1993). Coordinator and executive editor of the *Dickinson Electronic Archives* projects (emilydickinson.org) with Lara Vetter, Smith is general editor of *Emily Dickinson's Correspondence: A Born-Digital Inquiry*, forthcoming 2010 from Rotunda New Digital Scholarship, University of Virginia Press.

STEPHANIE A. TINGLEY is Professor of English and Coordinator of the American Studies Program at Youngstown State University. Her work on Dickinson has centered on the poet's correspondence with Josiah and Elizabeth Holland, including, most recently, editing the Dickinson-Holland correspondence for the Dickinson Electronic Archive. Her current research project is on teaching Dickinson.

Index of Letters

Index of Poems

General Index